ECONOMIC DEVELOPMENT AND SOCIAL CHANGE IN SOUTH INDIA

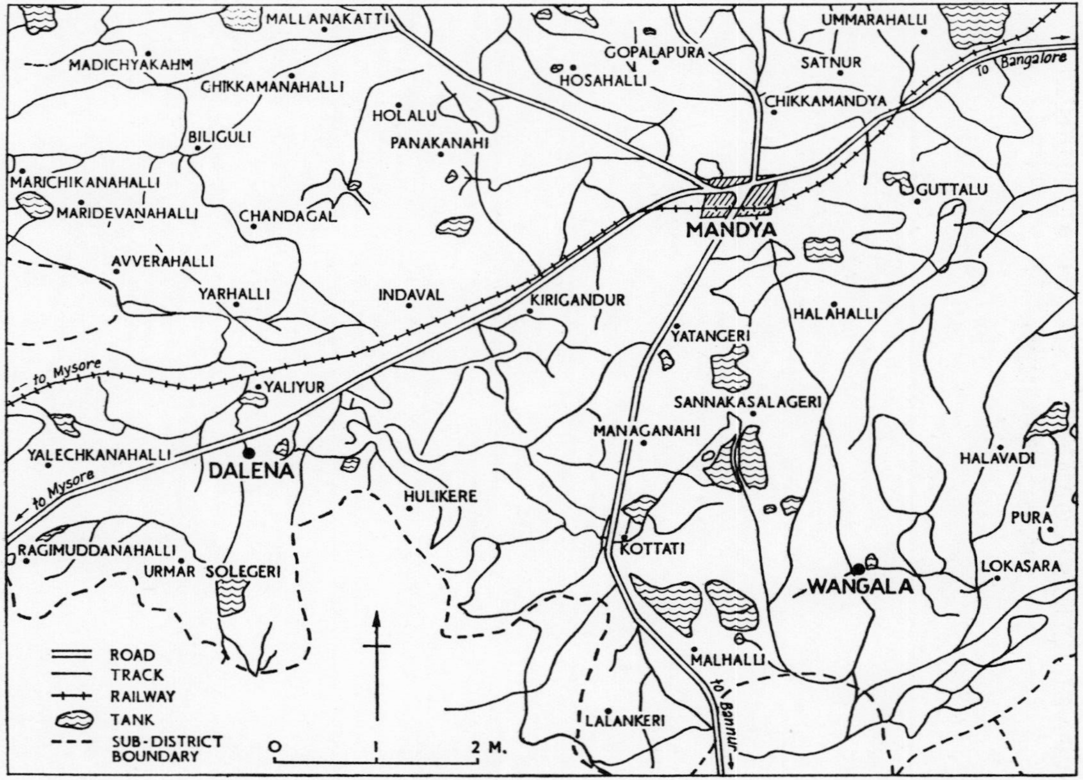

Frontispiece

ECONOMIC DEVELOPMENT AND SOCIAL CHANGE IN SOUTH INDIA

by

T. S. EPSTEIN

MANCHESTER UNIVERSITY PRESS

Published by the University of Manchester at
THE UNIVERSITY PRESS
316–324 Oxford Road, Manchester, 13

First published 1962
Reprinted 1964, 1967

GB SBN 7190 0253 2

Distributed in the U.S.A. by
The Humanities Press Inc.
303 Park Avenue South,
New York, N.Y. 10010

Printed in Great Britain by Butler & Tanner Ltd, Frome and London

To

Siegfried and Rosa Gruenwald

FOREWORD

by W. Arthur Lewis

Principal of the University College of the West Indies, sometime Stanley Jevons Professor of Political Economy in the University of Manchester

Mrs. Epstein studied at the University of Manchester, first in the Department of Economics, and then in the Department of Anthropology. By the time she went to India, to live in and observe the two villages which she describes in this book, she was thoroughly qualified to practise either profession, and exceptionally well qualified to bring the two disciplines together. The result is a distinguished contribution to the small literature of economic anthropology.

Economics is concerned with the phenomena of production and of distribution. Market and non-market economies have the same purposes to serve, but economists have concentrated on studying the market economy, and have left the study of the non-market economy to the anthropologist. Moreover, in studying the market economy, economists have tended to take institutions for granted, and have tended to neglect inter-actions and conflicts between the market and other social institutions. This has left a gap into which some anthropologists are now sliding. They slip into factories, and study how workers set or react to production norms; they watch directors at work in the board-room; or they study the effects of prestige on occupations. It is clear that the anthropologist's technique of observation, and his understanding of the inter-relations of social institutions, have an important contribution to make to the study of even the most advanced market economies.

Economists have no equally clear contribution to make to the study of non-market economies. They have taught the anthropologists what the problems are, and what to look for; they have also insisted on more precise statistical methods, and on greater respect for the measurement of economic phenomena. But whereas the anthropologist retains his technique when he studies the market economy (he mingles with a small group and observes inter-relations between people), the economist who studies the non-market economy has to abandon most of what he has learnt, and adopts the techniques of the anthropologist.

The most fruitful area for the hybrid trained in both anthropology and economics is the study of societies which are changing over from the non-market to the market economy. Here the interplay of institutions is important, and calls for anthropological treatment. But the market forces are also important, and this is the economist's field. Since two-thirds of the world's population live in societies where this transition is now occurring rapidly, the scope for studies of this kind is almost unlimited. The work to be done is both descriptive and theoretical. We need many accounts of societies in which the transition is occurring, so that we may generalise both about the effect of changing economic opportunities upon social institutions, and also about the effect of different kinds of social institutions in inhibiting or assisting response to changing opportunities.

Mrs. Epstein's first task has been to describe what is happening in her villages. As a good economist she has collected innumerable statistics of income, expenditure, costs, capital, distribution, the balance of payments, and other quantitative expressions, which give an unusually full account of the results of economic activity. And as a good anthropologist she has also all the usual data on social institutions, on kinship, caste, class, religion, political allegiance, and the rest. What makes the book especially valuable is the purpose to which she puts the data, which is to show how the institutions have responded to changing opportunities.

The method is to take two villages which are close together, and which up to 25 years ago had very similar social institutions. Then 25 years ago their economic opportunities changed, as a result of the arrival of canal irrigation in their district. The lands of one village could be watered from the canal; for topographical reasons the lands of the other could not. Hence one village had the new opportunity to use water; the other had the opportunity to exploit the prosperity which other towns and villages nearby derived from water. In the first village, social institutions were little affected, as agriculture was confirmed as the basis of wealth; but in the second village the new economic opportunities were inconsistent with some established social rules, which were in consequence eroded. This is the bare story, which the book works out in fascinating detail.

Mrs. Epstein's emphasis is on the effect of economic opportunities on social institutions. In order to study the effect of social institutions on economic response, one would have to turn the method round, and study two villages where the economic opportunities were the same, and the social institutions were to begin with different. We know something about this problem, because we know how rapidly the market economy has spread around the globe, and how effectively it is forcing different social institutions everywhere to accommodate themselves to its requirements. Wherever we study the effect of economic change on institutions, the basic answer seems always to be the same, namely, that the love of money is a powerful institutional solvent.

This is a reason both for sadness and for rejoicing. We rejoice because we favour economic progress, and are glad that incompatible social institutions will not stand in its way. Poverty is a curse upon the human race, from which it is our duty to escape. We have often been told that some societies are poor mainly because their peoples do not have the right attitudes (for example, to work, to money, or to thrift), or because their institutions (for example caste, or the extended family) inhibit economic effort. This book lends no support to this approach to the theory of economic development. Many countries have indeed attitudes and institutions which inhibit growth, but they will rid themselves of these attitudes and institutions as soon as their people discover that they stand in the way of economic opportunities.

However, there is also room for apprehension. The Bible tells us that the love of money is the root of all evil. Accordingly, we do what we can to hedge it in, so that it may not damage society inordinately. The young are taught to value other things beyond money, and new laws are made every day restricting the means by which money may lawfully be acquired. The non-market economies have inherited very strict rules of behaviour, through the centuries, which are designed to keep the acquisitive instincts in check. The great danger to these societies is that, as they make the transition to the market economy, and rid themselves of ancient institutions, they may also rid themselves of the checks which every society needs for social health.

Mrs. Epstein does not philosophise about such matters, but light is thrown on them by her comparisons. What we need to know is just how powerful a solvent the love of money is. The answer seems to be that it dissolves what stands in its way, but nothing more. In one of the villages, where the new opportunities did not conflict with existing institutions, there was virtually no institutional change; in the other village, changes were widespread, but only such changes occurred as were directly linked with new economic opportunities. This accords with experience in Japan where, broadly speaking, the market economy spread with relatively small effect on other social habits, at any rate for the first fifty years. Presumably a society as it changes seeks to establish a new equilibrium between the economic and the non-economic values which its institutions embody. How much is changed depends partly on how much is incompatible, and partly on how closely interrelated the various institutions are. We do not know enough about these processes. Our main hope of learning more rests upon the accumulation of studies of the kind which Mrs. Epstein has pioneered with such distinction.

CONTENTS

LIST OF MAPS

LIST OF PLATES

LIST OF TABLES

TABLES 22–50

COMPARATIVE FIGURES FOR THE TWO VILLAGES

Appendix I, pp. 336–46

ACKNOWLEDGEMENTS

THIS book is based on field-work which I carried out in Mysore, South India, in 1954–6. My thanks are due to the Trustees of the Rockefeller Research Foundation, New York, through whom alone the study was made possible.

I wish to express my great debt to my teachers, Professor Arthur Lewis, who gave me my first training in economics and who took time off from his many duties to write the Foreword; to Professor Max Gluckman, who introduced me to the study of anthropology and always provided me with stimulus and encouragement; to Professor Ely Devons, whose penetrating criticism at seminars has made me reconsider many of my first rash statements; and to Professor M. N. Srinivas, who first introduced me to Indian society and whose friendship guided me throughout my stay in India.

I also want to thank Professors R. Firth, H. Johnston, J. A. Barnes, T. Swan, H. Arndt as well as Drs. K. Martin and F. G. Bailey, and Mr. E. K. Fisk, all of whom have worked patiently through the manuscript and offered constructive criticism. I am heavily indebted too to my colleagues in the Departments of Economics and Anthropology at Manchester University for their stimulus and help in preparing this book.

My thanks are also due to my two assistants Mr. A. P. Suryanarayana and Mr. M. S. Sharma without whose keenness and concentration much of the data would never have been collected, and to Mr. Balraj, Deputy Commissioner, Mandya District, Mr. Swaminathan and Mr. B. G. Dasegowda, Chairman and General Manager respectively of the Mandya sugar factory, Mr. H. P. Narasimha Murthy, Project Evaluation Officer, Mandya, through whose kind assistance I was able to collect much information relevant to this study.

My stay in the villages was greatly eased by the comforts and hospitality offered to me by many friends throughout India of whom I can mention only a few: A. P. Srinivasa Murthy, M. N. Parthasarathy, Evelyn and Kamela Wood, Sachin Chaudhuri, Maurice and Taya Zinkin, George Rosen and John D. Van Ingen.

Above all my gratitude goes out to those many friends and informants in the Mandya area who so patiently answered my questions and helped me over the difficulties of learning their language.

Last but by no means least I want to thank my husband who has been a great help at each stage of the preparation of the manuscript, who has cheerfully borne my spasms of depression when the difficulties in handling my material seemed insurmountable and who has always encouraged me in my work.

CHAPTER I

INTRODUCTION

The Problem

Since the last war, the development of 'underdeveloped areas' has increasingly attracted the attention of political scientists, economists, social anthropologists and others. Most of these areas lie in tropical or sub-tropical regions where the large mass of the population is still settled in small scattered villages and ekes out a subsistence living on poor soil. Widespread poverty, low levels of education and technology and limited capital resources present the major obstacles to the initiation of economic growth in 'underdeveloped countries'. Given the availability of funds, the problem of developing these 'backward' economies has three main aspects:

(1) There is the assessment of economic resources and the way they are to be employed. In most 'backward' countries there exists a dearth of even the most basic statistics, the collection of which in itself presents a major task.

(2) There is the question of how to initiate economic growth in largely stagnant economies. This involves a decision on the priorities to be allocated to the various sectors of the economy: whether industry or agriculture should receive primary attention; whether industries are to be centralised or dispersed; whether some areas should be selected for agricultural development or limited funds be spread thinly over the whole country, and so on.

(3) Finally, there remains the question how far an initial impetus to change will lead to further, self-perpetuating development. In approaching this aspect of the problem, the economist can only assume a certain set of reactions to certain economic incentives. To investigate more closely the reactions of a people to new economic opportunities falls within

the sphere of other disciplines in the social sciences, such as psychology, political science and social anthropology.

Each of the disciplines within the social sciences specialises in the study of particular aspects of social relations and has developed techniques for handling its own range of problems. These different aspects, however, are not independent: they are interrelated, so that some problems cannot be adequately analysed within the framework of a particular discipline. But the inter-disciplinary approach to such problems often raises considerable difficulties simply because of the different techniques involved. For example, the economist tries to confine his field of interest to measurable phenomena. By using sampling methods he can study a larger universe and make broader generalisations. The social anthropologist, on the other hand, tends to select a small universe (usually a village or tribe) which he studies intensively for a lengthy period in order to analyse its intricate system of social relations. His universe is rarely selected on the basis of scientific sampling, and indeed this would be difficult because of the complexity of social life and the cultural variations that exist even within a small region. Therefore the social anthropologist cannot generalise easily beyond the boundaries of his universe. His major contribution has been in the field of qualitative rather than quantitative analysis, though in recent years anthropologists have made more and more efforts to devise techniques whereby phenomena previously regarded as unmeasurable may now be measured. While the anthropologist has taken over some of the statistical techniques of the economist, the latter, particularly in the field of economic development, has also found it necessary to take into account non-measurable factors of the kind studied by other social disciplines. For instance, Professor Lewis devotes the first part of his book on *The Theory of Economic Growth* to an analysis of the part played by social factors such as family, kinship structure and religion in economic development.

Few anthropological studies deal specifically with economic phenomena. Many modern anthropological reports do include a great deal of economic data, but these are generally only a by-product of the study of social relations of which economic relations form an important part. In this connection Professor Firth's works constitute a pioneering effort in the field of economic anthropology; they show the interaction between economic and other variables within a social system. These and other similar studies bring out clearly the problem of applying to a subsistence or barter economy many of the concepts developed from a cash economy; and they also point out how some western economic concepts may have to be modified to suit the conditions of subsistence economies.

The present book is an attempt to follow up these studies by the joint application of economic and anthropological techniques to the problems of economic and social change. I shall discuss the impact of irrigation on the economic and social organisation of two villages within a regional economy. *Dalena*, a dry, and *Wangala*,[1] a wet village are situated close to each other within the same culture area in Mysore State, in South India. I chose these particular villages because of their multicaste composition, and because they lay outside the sphere of the Community Development Project. Both Wangala and Dalena were of course also subject to direct government influence and control. Thus the Public Works Department provided canal irrigation, the Agricultural Department had been teaching the Japanese method of paddy cultivation, while the Electricity Department provided power, and so on. These services were supplied without any direct pressure being exerted upon the villagers to accept them. However, in villages within the Project it is the task of the Village Level Worker to induce villagers to change over to improved methods of farming, better housing and the like. Thus while the Mysore State Government makes a conscious effort to improve the lot of all villagers, for the purpose of the present study I have treated the external administrative structure as given, and do not discuss its workings in any detail. At the end of my field-work I toured villages in a Pilot Project situated about 30 miles north-east of Wangala in order to draw comparisons between those

[1] I have changed the names of the two villages slightly in order to conceal the identity of my informants. All names given in the text are fictitious.

villages falling within the project and those without. I hope to discuss this in a later publication.

Cultivated land in India falls into two major categories, dry and wet. Dry lands are those which depend solely on rainfall for their cultivation, whereas wet lands receive a supplementary water supply from rivers, canals, tanks or wells. In zones with low annual rainfall, irrigation can yield substantial benefits to the farming population; the artificial supply of water to the fields may increase considerably the productivity per acre; large areas of complete waste may be brought within the margin of cultivation once they are irrigated. By making the farmer largely independent of natural rainfall, irrigation reduces the risk in agricultural production and increases the earning potential. The importance of irrigation as a means of stimulating economic growth was emphasised in India's First Five Year Plan. The Plan concentrated on increasing agricultural output: 54% of the expenditure for agricultural development was devoted to irrigation schemes.

Irrigation is by no means a recent innovation; it has been known for many centuries in India. Mysore State, with an area of 29,489 square miles, has more than 30,000 tanks. These tanks or artificial reservoirs, known as *keres*, vary in size from small ponds to extensive lakes. Referring to these tanks, Sir Charles Elliott, the first Census Commissioner for India, remarked in 1870 that 'the ingenious method in which each valley was made to contain a chain of irrigation tanks, and each river to feed a series of irrigation channels, left the British Officers who administered the Province little to do but to put the old works in thorough repair'.[1] Mysore State thus had many sources of irrigation well before the establishment of *Pax Britannica* in 1799; but all these were dispersed and only very few were sufficiently large to facilitate the development of exchange economies. The extent of irrigated lands in the different villages was small, and therefore wet crops, like dry crops, were largely cultivated for subsistence. Sugarcane, a major wet crop, was even then a cash crop. But it requires processing, and this must be done immediately after harvest to avoid deterioration of its sugar content. The extent of cane cultivation

[1] *Census of India*, 1951, Vol. XIV, Mysore, Part I, p. 6.

was not only limited by the small area under irrigation, but also by the general lack of cane-crushers. There used to be a number of cane-crushers, operated by bullock-power, where cane was crushed and processed into brown sugar, but in the main the wide dispersal of wet lands and the lack of transport facilities made production of sugar on a larger scale uneconomical. Major Wilks, the first of the British Administrators to survey economic resources in Mysore, wrote in 1805:

Besides rice, sugar is the only crop depending on artificial irrigation which deserves particular notice; although an exhausting, it is a very profitable crop; and it is cultivated and manufactured in Mysore, of good quality and to an extent exceeding the internal consumption. Sugar candy has lately been made equal to that which is imported for common use from China, and this manufacture may be enlarged to the extent of supplying the internal consumption; but without irrigation and water carriage, it cannot meet the produce of China in other markets.[1]

Authorities in Mysore were thus already in the eighteenth century aware of the limits to the benefits from irrigation set by the existing system of dispersed tanks and communications. During the nineteenth century tanks were repaired, irrigation channels extended, and roads and railways built. For many years the Government of Mysore considered a project for a dam across the Cauvery river to extend irrigation in the State. In 1911 construction was finally begun on a big dam at Caniambadi, 12 miles from Mysore City. The dam was later named 'Krishnarajasagar' after the ruling Raja of that time. It was planned to irrigate 125,000 acres through a widespread canal system in an area limited by the configuration of the countryside. Irrigation from this dam began to flow through the canals and channels in 1931, but the full scheme was not completed by 1956; only about 100,000 acres had been irrigated by that time. The newly irrigated land facilitated the cultivation of cash crops and led to the establishment of a sugar refinery at Mandya, right in the centre of the area and suitably situated on the major highway and railway

[1] Major M. Wilks, *Report on the Interior Administration, Resources and Expenditure of the Government of Mysore* (1805), p. 39.

connecting Bangalore and Mysore, the two largest cities in Mysore State. The refinery is able to produce a white sugar which is of superior quality to the coarse brown sugar produced by the village crushers and which is easily stored and exported.

In 1931 Mandya was no more than a small market town with a population of about 6,000. The establishment of a sugar factory in 1933 started a big expansion of Mandya. In the first place, the building of the factory, offices and quarters for staff and workers attracted labourers and entrepreneurs from a wide area, including the neighbouring State of Madras. The population of Mandya increased rapidly; it had grown to 11,000 by 1941 and to 21,000 by 1951. In 1936 Mandya District was carved out of Mysore District, and the town became the seat of the new District Administration. The presence of the Administration added a further expansionary element to the growth of Mandya; new offices were built; clerks and orderlies were recruited; lawyers set up practices to act at the newly established magistrate's courts, and so on. Mandya's resident population, together with the constant stream of farmers delivering cane to the factory, converted the town into a large shopping centre for the whole region. Mandya's weekly fair now fetches crowds from within a radius of about 25 miles. As the town grew it developed the amenities of urban centres—a picture house, coffee shops, bazaars, etc.—which provide added attractions for the farming population of the region.

All these changes, which stem from modern canal irrigation, are quite different in kind from those which followed the introduction of irrigation under the ancient tank system. In contrast to the tank system, the modern river scheme irrigates many thousand of acres concentrated in a limited area. While tank irrigation increased agricultural output only slightly, the great increase in agricultural output through river irrigation has resulted in the establishment of agricultural processing industries and thus in cumulative economic changes. In this way, villages which previously were largely economically independent have now come to form an economically integrated region.

Since the extent of irrigation is determined by topographical factors, some villages have been more fortunate than others in the extent to which their village lands have come under irrigation. In the irrigated villages small owner-occupiers or *ryots*—and most land is held by such *ryots*—took to the cultivation of sugar-cane. This demanded considerably more labour and capital than the dry crops to which the farmers had been accustomed. Certain new services were also required, such as transporting the cane to the factory, the repair of carts and iron ploughs, and so on. At the same time, villages on the fringe of the irrigation belt—where lands remained partly or wholly dry—were also able to join in the economic expansion of the region by providing secondary and tertiary services for neighbouring irrigated villages and for the growing town of Mandya. Thus the less fortunate farmers of dry land did not have to emigrate in search of employment, but were able to share in the growing regional prosperity, while the farmers of newly irrigated land could concentrate on cultivation of their more remunerative wet lands without worrying about the supply of the new services they now required. Such specialisation developed particularly at the fringe of the irrigated area and is least pronounced at the centre where there is a network of irrigated villages. Thus the development of villages can be adequately understood only in terms of their role in the regional economy.

Wangala and Dalena, the two villages to be discussed in this book, represent two types of village in the Mandya region. Wangala is a wet village right in the centre of the irrigated area and Dalena a dry village on the fringe of it. Before the advent of irrigation in the Mandya region the two villages were almost identical in all aspects of their economic and social life. Apart from irrigation, both villages have come under the impact of the same external stimuli, but the basic economic difference of wet and dry land has been responsible for the two villages assuming distinct roles in the regional economy. It might be suggested that the differential location, rather than irrigation, is responsible for the two villages starting on different paths of development. Though Dalena is certainly more favourably situated for incorporation into the wider economy—it lies just off a major highway, near a railway station and near the main electric lines—the mere fact that both villages regard the advent of irrigation as the turning point in their recent history points to the importance of irrigation rather than location. The establishment of flour mills is probably the only economic activity that was induced by Dalena's more favourable situation. During the last war lorries full of black market paddy used to run along the major road and stop outside the village to enquire after the nearest mill. This gave two Dalena men the idea of starting flour mills. The availability of electricity and the proximity of a railway station further facilitated their enterprise. As regards electricity, Wangala is nowadays not much less favourably situated than Dalena. Electricity is available at the next village at about one and a quarter mile distance, so that the cost of installing it into Wangala would not be much higher than it was in Dalena. But Wangala men concentrate their interests upon farming and therefore are not keen on branching out into industrial enterprise such as Dalena men have done. Thus while in Dalena one man paid a large part of the installation cost, in Wangala not a single man was prepared to do that, nor was the village as a group willing to carry this extra financial burden.

Dalena's greater participation in the wider economy cannot be explained simply in terms of its more favourable location. Living on a main road offers little advantage to villagers, for they usually walk or cycle into town and only rarely take a bus. Though prior to 1936 when a road was built near Wangala, villagers could more easily get to town from Dalena than from Wangala, Dalena villagers had little occasion to go to Mandya then. Firstly, their economic and social life was concentrated in their own village before the advent of irrigation in the area; and secondly, Mandya was then only a very small market town which did not offer many attractions to surrounding villages. Thus the greater ease with which Dalena men could get to Mandya prior to irrigation cannot account for their closer links now with the wider economy. To-day, Wangala is even more favourably situated in relation to Mandya than Dalena; Wangala is two miles nearer the town and lies on a good secondary road, which is more suitable for bullock carts, the major means of transport employed by villagers, than the asphalted main road near Dalena.

Yet Wangala has retained its wholly farming economy, whereas Dalena's economy has become diversified and more subjected to urban influences. The construction of roads and canals near Wangala between 1936 to 1942 offered employment opportunities to villagers, but they accepted these only temporarily. They looked upon work as contractors or labourers as stop-gap measures only and returned to farming as soon as their lands had become irrigated. This behaviour contrasts with Dalena villagers' continued service in the Public Works Department. Dalena's response is due not to its more favourable location, but rather to the drive of its men to participate in the expanding regional economy. Thus we can see that the different economic development that Dalena and Wangala have undergone during the past 20 years can hardly be accounted for by their differential location, but rather may be attributed to the different roles occupied by wet and dry land villages in the wider economy.

My own studies do not enable me to regard the development of the two villages as necessarily representative of the region. However, short field trips to a number of villages in the locality lead me to believe that similar changes have taken place in villages of these two types throughout the whole of this area.

Irrigation of Wangala lands brought what I may term unilinear changes in the sense that the new opportunities were in line with the former mode of economic organisation. The interests of Wangala's population continued to be vested in agriculture. There have of course been considerable changes in Wangala's economic life: for instance, irrigation has resulted in greater investment in agricultural capital, i.e. implements and working animals, and a higher labour input. But because these economic changes were unilinear, they brought about only minor changes in the traditional social system. By contrast Dalena's social system has changed considerably in the same period. Irrigation in the region brought multifarious economic opportunities to Dalena villagers: their economic activities and their interests diversified as they accepted the challenge of the new opportunities and provided secondary and tertiary services for neighbouring irrigated villages and the growing town of Mandya. These multifarious opportunities were responsible for a radical change in Dalena's former farming economy.

In my comparison of economic and social change in Wangala and Dalena I shall show that Wangala's social system has changed only slightly because irrigation strengthened the traditional farming economy. I shall also argue that Dalena's social system changed radically, because the diversification of its economy changed economic roles and relations within the village. Wangala's persisting social system has incorporated many of the cultural changes now characteristic of the wider society; similarly, Dalena's changed system still shows the effects of traditional relations and values. The study of the two villages throws into relief the interplay of old and new values in the process of social change.

The Area

Dalena and Wangala are situated in the plains of Mysore State. The State lies on the Deccan plateau in South India. It borders Madras and Bombay State. Though Mysore State is situated in a tropical zone, its climate is equable as the elevation of the major portion of the State is over 2,200 feet and no part of it is far distant from the sea. Temperatures range from a minimum of 50 degrees in winter to a maximum of about 100 degrees in summer in the shade.

The year comprises three different seasons—the monsoon season, winter and summer. The south-west monsoon starts about the beginning of June and lasts usually four months. It is followed by the north-east monsoon which rarely extends to December. Winter lasts from December to January and summer from February till May.

The Hindu calendar, which begins roughly in April, is divided into 27 periods, each of about a fortnight's duration; each of these periods is further subdivided into four quarters called *padas*. The various agricultural operations in their sequence are fixed in relation to these fortnightly periods and their *padas*, and the weather conditions during these periods also enable the farmer to forecast roughly the conditions of the weather and its likely effects on the crops of the succeeding period.

Mysore State is naturally divided into two distinct parts: the hilly part called *Malnad* which lies in the west, and the plains called *Maidan* which lie in the east. The *Malnad*, with its hills reaching up to 6,000 feet, towers over the plains which have an elevation of about 2,200 feet. The western fringe of the *Malnad* has an extremely high annual rainfall of about 300 inches. This contrasts with the low annual rainfall in the *Maidan* of about 25 inches. Torrential rains, perennial streams, and fertile black soil create an abundance of verdant vegetation in the *Malnad*. But the high seasonal concentration of rains and the topography of the *Malnad* make the cultivation of subsistence crops very difficult and have thus hampered the growth of villages. Large parts of the *Malnad* remained virgin soil until European enterprise cleared great parts of the jungle for coffee and tea estates, for which the area is ideally suited and which attract labour from a wide region. Apart from the 'coolie' lines on the estates, settlement in the *Malnad* is still highly dispersed; villages of even a dozen houses are rare.

The transition from the *Malnad* to the *Maidan* is in some places very marked. Dense forests give way to wide-spreading plains, the solitary farm to village clusters and populous towns. The undulating countryside of the plains offers larger stretches of cultivable land, though soils in most areas are dry and of poor quality. The greater extent of cultivable area facilitated the settlement and growth of villages. The *Maidan* has a much denser population than the *Malnad*, although the soil fertility is much higher in the *Malnad*. The prevailing type of soil in the *Maidan* is a red loam. 'Poor in nitrogen and phosphoric acid, moderately well supplied in potash, the predominant type, i.e. red loam, is rich in iron and deficient in lime.' [1] The soils in the Cauvery River Valley, especially in Mysore and Mandya Districts, are highly gravelly and of particularly poor quality. These gravelly soils and the low annual rainfall created the necessity for widespread irrigation in the *Maidan* and are thus responsible for the many tanks in Mysore State. The red soils are the typical ragi-bearing (*eleusine corocana*) soils of the State which supply the majority of the population with its staple diet.

[1] Hayavadana Rao C., *Mysore Gazetteer*, 1927, Vol. III, p. 18.

The population of Mysore amounts to about nine million, 24% of whom live in towns and the remainder in villages. The crude density of population for the State as a whole is 308, but the density of population per cultivable square mile is as much as 617.[1] For a country like Mysore, which is mainly rural and has large stretches of uncultivable soils, the Cultivable Area Density is a better index of the density of population. Mysore's population has practically trebled in the last hundred years. Part of this increase is due to an excess of immigrants over emigrants. In the years between 1931 and 1951, during which period the population has increased by about 40%, about 12% of the increase was due to immigration.[2]

In 1901, 92% of the population were recorded as Hindus; in 1951 the figure was 90%. The proportion of Hindus in the total population has thus remained stable. Mysore's Hindus are stratified into many castes, of which the Peasants[3] are the most numerous. Due to the Government's stated policy of ignoring caste differentiation, no data on caste were included in the 1951 census; the 1941 census showed the Peasants formed about 20% of the total population and that the Adikarnataka Untouchables[4] constitute the second largest community, forming about 15% of the population.

The distinctive language of Mysore is Kannada. It is spoken by 66% of Mysore's inhabitants. Kannada belongs to the group of South Indian languages known as Dravidian. Its written characters are derived from the Brahmi, the parent of all the modern alphabets of India. The Dravidian languages of South India are quite distinct from the Aryan group of languages of the North. But modern Kannada does include very many words from

[1] These population figures refer to Mysore State before its re-organisation in November 1956.

[2] *Census of India*, 1951, Vol. XIV, Part I, p. 220.

[3] The names of castes are given in English and printed with a capital initial. For instance, a Peasant is a person belonging to that caste, a peasant is a farmer. Similarly, a Blacksmith is a man of that caste, whereas in his occupation he is referred to as blacksmith. All the servicing castes are called by the collective name of Functionary castes. The vernacular names of castes are indicated in an English-Kannada glossary in Appendix II.

[4] I use the abbreviation A.K. Untouchables for Adikarnatakas.

Hindi, the major language of the North, as well as a number of Persian terms. The use of a large number of Hindi, Sanscrit and Persian words in the Kannada vernacular reflects the great cultural influence of the North on South India. For instance, it is significant that the Hindi word 'Jati' meaning 'caste' is used in most of the vernaculars throughout the whole of India, there being apparently no local term for this institution.

The penetration of the Northern Aryan culture into South India took place many centuries ago. By about the ninth century B.C. South India had undoubtedly already come under the impact of the empires flourishing in the North. The actual introduction of Brahminical Hinduism into Mysore is assigned to the second century A.D.[1] In the same century the indigenous Ganga dynasty appears to have been established in Mysore; this dynasty lasted for about eight centuries.

The natural frontiers of the Indian sub-continent formed by mountain ranges in the north-east and oceans in the west, south and east, made the country vulnerable to invasion only from the north-west, until seafaring powers sent military expeditions by sea to South India. The waves of overland invaders from Persia affected directly only the North of India, but indirectly also the South. The Deccan plateau on which Mysore lies has always formed the great middle rampart of India and the powers of the North were not able at any time to establish their authority over it on a secure footing.

The history of Mysore is largely one of wars between feudatory princes who contested for sovereignty over wide areas. In the tenth century the Chola invasion from the east of the plateau overthrew the Ganga power. Chola dominance was in turn overthrown by the Hoysalas in the twelfth century, whose overlordship lasted until the fourteenth century when the Wodeyar prince, an ancestor of the present Rajpramuk[2] of Mysore, became paramount throughout the South.

It was not until the sixteenth century that a northern power

[1] Hayavadana Rao C., op. cit., Vol. I, p. 281.

[2] Since Mysore joined the Dominion of India in 1947 its Maharajah was given the title of Rajpramuk, hereditary governor.

managed to subject part of the Deccan plateau. Then the Moghul ruler Akbar, having conquered the Gangetic valley power, successfully campaigned against princedoms in South India, and brought some of them under his rule. Akbar and his successors struggled with the South for over a century, but could never establish a firm empire there. Thirty-two years after the death of Aurangazab, the grandson of Akbar, geographical conditions became once more the determining factor in the political organisation and the Deccan plateau regained its independence from northern rule. The Moghul conquest in the middle ages and the Mysor Muslim rulers in the eighteenth century, who insisted on conversion to Islam by force if necessary, left Mysore with a distinct cultural heritage.

In a war during the eighteenth century against the Marathas, one of Mysore's neighbouring powers, Nanja Raja Wodeyar appointed Hyder Ali, a descendant of a Muslim immigrant from the Punjab, to the position of Chief Commander of the forces. The war coincided in time with the wars waged by the East India Co. against a number of Rajas in the south. This enabled Hyder Ali, a most capable commander and diplomat, to exploit his dominant position as military leader to gain influence also in the political sphere. By clever manœuvring he managed to usurp the powers of the young Raja and to place himself at the head of Mysore government. Through his capable administration he organised the country's resources to support his many military ventures. Hyder Ali created a strong empire and considerably enlarged the Mysore territories. His son Tippu, who succeeded him on his death, did not possess Hyder's qualities of leadership nor his fortune in warfare. Tippu's military expeditions drained the country's resources and weakened the empire his father had built. Tippu was a despotic ruler who propagated his religion at the edge of the sword. To support his war ventures he extorted exorbitant dues and services from the inhabitants of Mysore by cruel force. He combined with the French against the British and managed to repel a number of British attacks, but in 1799 he was finally defeated by British forces and was himself killed in the last battle at Seringapatam.

The East India Co. restored the Mysore Wodeyar dynasty to power, maintained a resident at the court of the Raja, and appointed Purnaya, a Brahmin who had been Tippu's finance minister, to be chief minister. Purnaya's administration proved eminently successful in pacifying the country and repairing the ravages of a century of intense warfare. Purnaya favoured members of his own caste with jobs in the administration and with land grants. It is possible that the seed of present-day persecution of the Brahmins in Mysore was sown during the period of Purnaya's administration. In 1812 the newly installed Raja deposed his chief minister and took charge of the government himself. His abilities as administrator did not equal those of Purnaya and the State's funds dwindled; consequently the dues to the East India Co. could not be paid. A rebellion in 1832 was taken by the East India Co. as the occasion to take decisive steps to protect its interests in Mysore. The Company used a clause in its original treaty with the Wodeyar dynasty to justify the deposition of the Raja and the appointment of a British Commission. The Commission ruled for fifty years, during which a great number of economic and administrative reforms were initiated. In 1881 the Wodeyar dynasty was once more returned to power and Mysore State passed again under Hindu rule.

The effects of *Pax Britannica* resulted in considerable economic improvement during the nineteenth century. Villages which had suffered greatly during the many years of war and turmoil, developed settled economies with regular cultivation. Lands were surveyed and rights in land and taxes were fixed. Irrigation tanks were repaired and roads and railways were built; electricity schemes were started. Though there was some industrial and commercial development in Bangalore, the biggest city in Mysore State, where the British had set up a Cantonment, Mysore's major economic reforms applied mainly to rural areas. Efforts were made to improve Mysore silk, the only cash product derived from dry land; successful experiments were also made to improve the quality of sugarcane grown in Mysore.

The nineteenth century was largely a period of consolidation. The ravages of the war years were repaired and the basis laid for future and more far-reaching economic changes. At the beginning of the present century the Government of Mysore invested in major irrigation and hydro-electric schemes. These schemes presented new economic opportunities to the rural population, though some areas were more fortunate than others. Some 16,000 Mysore villages were affected by these new economic opportunities, although, as we shall see from our study of Wangala and Dalena, the response was not everywhere uniform.

Mysore remained a 'protected' State under the rule of its Maharaja until 1947 when it joined the newly established Dominion of India under part 'B' of the first schedule. Since then Mysore is known as one of the part 'B' States of the Union of India and its Maharaja has become Rajpramuk, which means that the position of hereditary head of State will cease with the death of its present occupant.

Until the recent re-organisation of Mysore, Peasants were the most numerous caste in the State, and occupied most strategic political positions; they dominated the legislature and the civil service. In many villages the hereditary headmanship is vested in a Peasant family. Wangala and Dalena are typical in this respect. They have a Peasant headman and Peasants constitute the majority of the population. The majority of Peasants in Mysore belong to the Gangadikar sub-caste.

'The Gangadikar and Nonaba Vokaligas (Peasants) are doubtless the representatives of indigenous tribes who formed the subjects of the Gangavadi and Nonambavadi provinces which occupied the greater part of Mysore up to the twelfth century.' [1] The Gangadikar Peasants claim that they are descendants of the Ganga dynasty which was the predominant power in Mysore from the second to the tenth century A.D. The 1891 census reports 'the Gangadikar seem to claim the topmost rank of their caste gradation [i.e. Peasants], although each subordinate division is not backward in asserting its own pre-eminence'.[2]

As yet it is impossible to say how the State's re-organisation will affect the political dominance of Peasants in rural areas.

[1] Lewis Rice, *Mysore and Coorg Gazetteer*, 1878, Vol. I, p. 339.

[2] *Census of India*, 1891, Vol. XXV, Part I, p. 225.

Certainly, the position of Peasants in the State Administration has changed radically since the State has been enlarged and its population almost doubled. In the re-organised State, Lingayats, worshippers of the god Siva, are the most numerous caste and Peasants have been relegated to second place. A Lingayat has replaced a Peasant as the Chief Minister of Mysore State. These overall political changes will no doubt have important implications for social change in future. My own field studies, however, were already completed before the re-organisation of Mysore State, which took place on November 6th, 1956. Therefore my analysis of social change in the two Mysore villages is based on the political structure as it existed prior to re-organisation.

PART ONE

WANGALA, A WET VILLAGE

CHAPTER II

ECONOMIC ORGANISATION AND CHANGE

WANGALA is situated in the *Maidan*, the plains of Mysore State, about four miles from Mandya, the nearest town. Its position on a secondary road makes Wangala easily accessible by bullock cart and bus. This road itself is one of the many innovations in the area since the coming of irrigation. Prior to 1939 only a cart track linked Wangala with its neighbouring villages and informants say that during the monsoon season they often had to wade knee-deep through large pools of water on their way to Mandya. The whole of Mandya region is now traversed by a network of roads and canals; almost every major canal-arm is bordered by a road running alongside it. The road from Mandya to Wangala winds its way through undulating countryside and crosses several canals by way of Irish bridges. On its four-mile stretch from Mandya the road runs through two villages; the spacing of these villages is typical of the Mysore plains and indicates the high density of villages.

The picture of the countryside varies with the season. In the summer months long stretches of bare red soil show paddy and ragi fields under the plough; some summer crops and sugarcane of varying height are interspersed between acres of waste and ploughed soil. During the monsoon season the bright green paddy and ragi crops seen against the background of the red soil and intermingled with the blue blossoms of the sugarcane present a colourful picture. In the winter the yellowing crops herald the harvest season.

Wangala itself lies on top of a knoll. Its 958 inhabitants[1] make it one of the largest villages in the area. The Mandya road touches only the fringe of Wangala; the village streets run at right angles to the east of it. This strategic economic position by the roadside has encouraged small entrepreneurs to start coffee and grocery

[1] Population figures are according to my census taken in 1954.

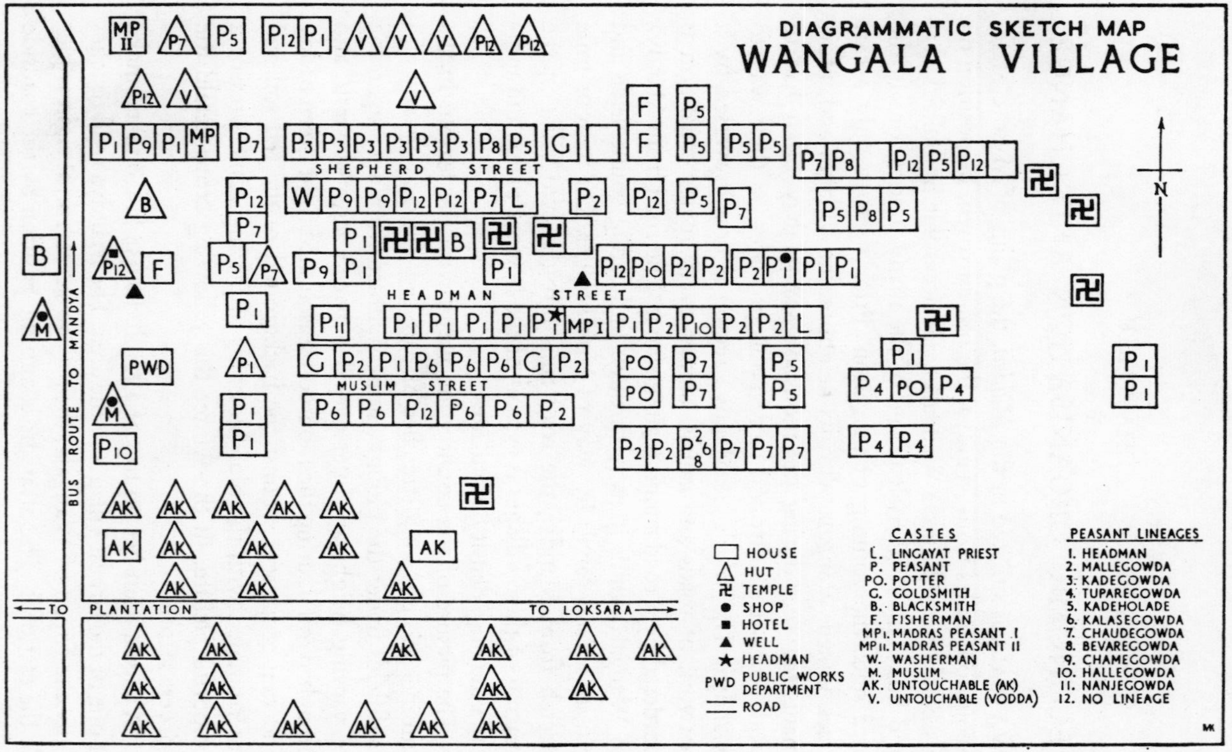

DIAGRAMMATIC SKETCH MAP
WANGALA VILLAGE

BUS ROUTE TO MANDYA

TO PLANTATION

TO LOKSARA

SHEPHERD STREET

HEADMAN STREET

MUSLIM STREET

N

▭	HOUSE
△	HUT
卍	TEMPLE
●	SHOP
■	HOTEL
▲	WELL
★	HEADMAN
PWD	PUBLIC WORKS DEPARTMENT
═	ROAD

CASTES

L.	LINGAYAT PRIEST
P.	PEASANT
PO.	POTTER
G.	GOLDSMITH
B.	BLACKSMITH
F.	FISHERMAN
MP I.	MADRAS PEASANT I
MP II.	MADRAS PEASANT II
W.	WASHERMAN
M.	MUSLIM
AK.	UNTOUCHABLE (AK)
V.	UNTOUCHABLE (VODDA)

PEASANT LINEAGES

1. HEADMAN
2. MALLEGOWDA
3. KADEGOWDA
4. TUPAREGOWDA
5. KADEHOLADE
6. KALASEGOWDA
7. CHAUDEGOWDA
8. BEVAREGOWDA
9. CHAMEGOWDA
10. HALLEGOWDA
11. NANJEGOWDA
12. NO LINEAGE

MK

MAP 2

shops by the roadside. These shops are only small mud huts with thatched roofs, but they do quite good business, particularly on market days. Four buses are scheduled to run daily on this route: they are always overcrowded, and usually stop at Wangala to let their passengers have a rest from the bumpy journey. In the little coffee shop (called 'hotelu' in the vernacular) the travellers and passing lorry drivers squat on the floor and drink coffee or tea out of glasses or take some sweet relish. These stops also provide an occasion to exchange gossip with people from other villages. All this has made sites along the road more attractive to Wangala men and there is a noticeable trend in recent years for the village to expand along the roadside and to the west of it.

The first house by the roadside, and the only brick structure in the village (apart from the temples), is a Public Works Department bungalow which was built about 1939 to house an engineer engaged on the construction of roads and canals in the vicinity. The bungalow had been empty for the past six years until I occupied it. In front of it is a large open space, in the middle of which is a well and a small servant quarter, constructed at the time of the bungalow. The well was originally solely for the use of the Public Works Department staff; however, since the bungalow has become vacant the well is used free of charge by all caste households in the village, but is not for use by Untouchables. The servant quarters are still occupied by the village water-overseer, the *saude*, an employee of the Public Works Department whose job it is to see that village lands are irrigated according to the official regulation; however, he has nothing to do with the distribution of water among Wangala village lands.

Wangala villagers were pleased to get the use of the Public Works Department well. It is fully finished and equipped with a pulley, but like the only other well in the village, it is not sufficiently deep and therefore runs dry during the summer. In the summer months the well has water only during the early hours of the morning and the shortage of water leads to continuous quarrels amongst village women. The other well is opposite the headman's house; as it is not even equipped with a pulley the drawing of water is most difficult. Shortage of drinking water is acute in Wangala and all villagers are agreed that they need at least one or two more wells; what they disagree about is their location.

Wangala's population is composed of members of several castes, which include a majority of Peasants and a number of Functionary or so-called village servant castes, such as the Potter and Blacksmith, and two Untouchable communities (see Table 1). The caste households are set along four streets. The streets are

TABLE 1

Wangala population and landholding by caste

Caste	*Households*		*Landholding (Wangala and elsewhere)*	
	No.	*%*	*Acres*	*%*
Lingayat Priest (Saivite)	3	1·70	9·00	1·40
Peasant	128	66·50	562·00	88·90
Potter	4	2·10	5·50	1·20
Goldsmith	5	2·70	4·00	0·50
Blacksmith	4	2·10	3·75	0·50
Fisherman	4	2·10	1·00	0·20
Madras Peasant I	3	1·70	—	—
Madras Peasant II	2	1·00	—	—
Washerman	2	1·00	1·50	0·20
Muslim	2	1·00	2·00	0·40
Untouchable (A.K.)	28	14·60	42·75	6·70
Untouchable (Vodda)	7	3·50	—	—
Total	192	100·00	631·50	100·00

crooked and bumpy and the headman's street is the only one that has drains running alongside to collect the refuse water from the houses. However, due to the shortage of wells in the village, households use as little water as possible and therefore not enough water runs through the drains and they become containers of stagnant water providing breeding ground for mosquitoes. Most of the houses in the caste streets are square in shape with walls made of red mud and roofs of hand-made tiles. Only a few of the caste households live in huts with thatched roofs. Most of the houses have verandahs and their front walls are neatly whitewashed. Colourful paintings on the walls of scenes from the great Hindu epics indicate that a wedding has taken place in the house in the last year or two. During the hot months villagers sleep out on their verandahs, which also provide convenient shelter for groups of chatting men or women. During the cooler months villagers sleep inside their houses. Usually, one half of the house is used as living space for the inhabitants and the other half acts as stable space for the farm animals. Most of the houses are terraced so that they have no space for their carts except to park them outside in the street; carts are too big to be placed inside the house. Usually householders try to claim the space in front of their house as belonging to them; chillies and other crops are spread out in the street for drying in the sun. Thus parts of the village street are often completely blocked and quarrels arise when bullocks or carts have to pass through.

All the streets in Wangala lead to the village square, which is surrounded by temples on three sides. (See map 2). All villages in the area have a temple to Maramma, the goddess of cholera and plague. The Marichoudi temple dedicated to Maramma is a brick structure with an open front containing at shrine with the image of the goddess. This temple is the centre of village social life; it is the village hall where men gather as night and where the village council meetings take place; it provides shelter for visiting officials and sleeping space for pilgrim passing through the village; it also houses the school. By its side is another large brick-built temple standing in an enclosure dedicated to the All-India deity Hanuman, the monkey-god. Next to it are two smaller temples, one dedicated to Basava, the sacred bull, the other to Boraya, the deity of the knoll. The largest of Wangala's temples stands outside the village, about half a mile away to the north-east in the middle of fields, and is dedicated to Siva, another All-India deity—it is around this temple that the village myth of origin revolves.[1]

About 200 yards south of the village square lies the village pond from which caste women can fetch water. Near the pond passes an arm of the canal where caste women clean their brass vessels

[1] See below, pp. 171–2.

with the gravel of the canal bed and wash their dirty clothes by beating piece after piece against a large stone.

Wangala's Untouchables are not allowed to fetch water from the village well or pond or from any part of the canal where caste women do their cleaning. Untouchables have to fetch water for their households from an insanitary little pond about 200 yards west of the village and they use the same pond for cleaning their vessels.[1]

The Untouchable quarter is set apart from the village caste houses, from which it is separated by a dumping ground for collecting manure and for defecation. Untouchable habitations are mostly small mud huts with thatched roofs. These huts are scattered on both sides of a road which crosses the Mandya road and connects two large sugarcane farms situated in the vicinity of Wangala. The Untouchable settlement has its own small temple dedicated to the local deity Huchamma. The small huts, hardly big enough to house a family, and the small starved-looking bullocks tied up outside these huts, show the Untouchable settlement to be the poorest quarter in Wangala.

The immediate surroundings of Wangala's village site are dry fields on which are grown ragi and jowar, the two major dry crops. In accordance with a Government regulation designed to cut down the danger of malaria the fields nearest to the village are not irrigated. Thus the first belt surrounding Wangala is made up of dry fields; but the next wide belt is formed by irrigated fields on which are grown paddy and sugarcane. Some fields benefit directly from the canal water, others only indirectly by drawing water from neighbouring irrigated fields. The position of fields in relation to the canal is of vital importance to the cultivation of wet crops and competing interests for a limited supply of water to the fields is the most frequent cause of quarrels in Wangala. An analysis of the impact of irrigation on Wangala's economic organisation and political and social institutions provides the theme of the succeeding chapters.

[1] Before I left the village, construction was started on a well for the Untouchables; Wangala's A.K. Untouchables supplied labour free of charge and the Government paid a contractor to finish the well.

NEW ECONOMIC OPPORTUNITIES

Prior to 1939 Wangala's cultivable acreage was mainly dry land: only one-eighth of the cultivable area was irrigated from

TABLE 2

Wangala ownership and use of village lands

Ownership

Land	*Villagers*		*Factory Plantation*		*Other Outsiders*		*Government*		*Total*	
	Acres	%	*Acres*	%	*Acres*	%	*Acres*	%	*Acres*	%
Irrigated	352	68	119	23	46	9	—	—	517	100
Dry	249	60	12	3	154	37	—	—	415	100
Waste for grazing	—	—	—	—	—	—	542	100	542	100
House sites, roads and paths	42	65	—	—	—	—	23	35	65	100
Tanks and ponds	—	—	—	—	—	—	118	100	118	100
Total	643	39	131	8	200	12	683	41	1,657	100

TABLE 3

Wangala type and location of land owned and cultivated by villagers

Type of land

Location of land	*Irrigated*		*Dry*		*Total*	
	Acres	%	*Acres*	%	*Acres*	%
Wangala	352·00	58	249·00	42	601·00	100
Other villages	30·50	100	—	—	30·50	100
Total	382·50	61	249·00	39	631·50	100

a village tank, and many a year the tank failed to provide sufficient water to irrigate even this limited area. Paddy was the major crop grown on tank-irrigated lands. Sugarcane was rare and grown only for making jaggery, which is handled in the form of big cubes of brown sugar. Ragi (*eleusine corocana*) and jowar (*sorghum vulgare*) were the staple crops grown on Wangala's dry lands. Wangala's economy was then largely a subsistence economy: the village as a whole produced most of the food required for its own consumption; farmers cultivated ragi and jowar, which provided their staple diet; they also produced a number of pulses and cultivated their own spices, vegetables and fruit in small gardens. Though villagers in Wangala are not vegetarian by religion, except for a few Lingayat Priestly households, they used to eat meat very rarely; their meagre meat ration was made up of snakes and field rats, for only on festive occasions did they slaughter one of their goats or sheep. Some of the Untouchables used to be weavers who exchanged their produce of cloth for grain with farmers in the village. Sericulture provided the only major source of cash income, but was not widely practised, because it required considerable skill, working capital and trading experience: silk worms have to be fed with mulberry leaves grown in bushes on dry lands, and the silk cocoons have to be delivered and sold to filatures at a distance of over 80 miles. When silk prices dropped during the world depression in the early 1930s even those few farmers in Wangala who had practised sericulture now found it uneconomic and changed back to food crops. To this day sericulture has not been taken up again by any of the farmers in or around Wangala, although silk prices have risen considerably during the last 10 years.

Fortunately for Wangala, canals began to be built in the area just when villagers could no longer derive a cash income from sericulture. The construction of canals and roads immediately offered a number of employment opportunities to Wangala men. It was the policy of the Public Works Department to place some of the labouring jobs out on contract. Contracting out means that the contractor undertakes to have a certain job finished by a specified date at a price fixed in advance and it is the contractor's part of the bargain to employ, supervise and pay labour for the performance of the given task. Thus while contractors were paid, for instance, per cubic foot of digging, they themselves had to pay labourers per time unit worked. Contractors could therefore make a profit or loss according to their ability to keep wages down, employ able labourers and supervise them efficiently. In most cases contractors did make a profit, though part of it had to be surrendered as bribes to the Public Works Department engineer and clerk who claimed their dues for handing out the work. In Wangala I found five men who had accepted the challenge of the new opportunities and come forward to act as contractors. They all found contracting a profitable though most tiresome enterprise; they complained that it had taken them away from their accustomed activities as farmers. When their lands became irrigated they all gave it up. Quite a number of Wangala men had worked as daily labourers for contractors or directly for the Public Works Department, but they too returned to farming soon after the irrigation of village lands. Thus it seems that for Wangala villagers employment as contractors or unskilled labourers was no more than a stop-gap measure. As soon as water from the newly built canals reached Wangala lands these men returned to cultivating fields either as farmers or as agricultural labourers.

The advent of irrigation in Wangala in 1939 coincided with the beginning of the second World War. During the war, food shortages led to rationing of such staple foods as rice and ragi. As a concomitant of rationing, a black market developed. Their newly irrigated lands enabled Wangala farmers to grow paddy on a larger scale and thus they could easily have become black marketeers. Yet none of the Wangala farmers was ever known to have had black market dealings to any large extent. Black market selling presupposes a knowledge of the market mechanism and prices as well as a technique to circumvent the law. Wangala farmers are small landowners, *ryots*, whose first interest lies in their land provided it can yield a 'reasonable' living to their families. Irrigation made their lands more productive and also more remunerative and therefore Wangala farmers showed little interest or aptitude in exploiting the black market. The rich men of Wangala are always referred to as 'sugarcane-made-rich' and never as black market profiteers, as are, for example, their counterparts in Dalena.[1]

Sugarcane became the major crop on wet lands in the Mandya

[1] See below, p. 202.

region. At first villagers in the region were reluctant to experiment with what was to them a new plant. The staple dry crops of ragi and jowar and even paddy, a wet crop, are all half-yearly crops, whereas sugarcane takes 12 to 14 months to mature. The difference in the crop period and the considerably higher investment and working capital required for sugarcane deterred Wangala farmers from starting sugarcane cultivation. Only those few farmers who had some ready cash and the necessary enterprise ventured into sugarcane cultivation immediately after their lands were irrigated. These men are to-day the richest in Wangala.

In the early years of its operation the management of Mandya's sugar factory faced the difficult task of convincing farmers in the region that the cultivation of sugarcane would bring them prosperity. The factory introduced several measures to overcome the farmers' resistance to cane-growing: it offered to buy the full cane crop grown on an area under contract at a price per ton fixed in advance; it allowed the farmers credit facilities for the purchase of fertiliser and gave cutting advances, all at 6% interest p.a. instead of 12% p.a., the ruling rate in the area; it employed fieldmen who advised farmers on cultivation problems and notified the factory when the cane was ready to be cut; it also started an experimental farm where farmers could get advice on the problems involved in cultivating sugarcane.

These various measures helped to make sugarcane the staple cash crop in the Mandya region. In 1955 the factory entered into contracts with the *ryots* in the region for about 8,000 acres of wet land per year. It also operated its own plantations, though the factory has found that its own produce is more costly than the cane bought from *ryots* and a number of its plantations have been closed down in the last three years. *Ryots* find cane the most profitable crop, though it is also the most exhausting one to work. In the beginning, when the sugar factory still had difficulty in contracting for sufficient acres to secure a flow of cane to its refinery, each farmer could get a contract for as many acres as he was prepared to put under cane cultivation. Nowadays so many want to cultivate cane that they compete for contracts and the sugar factory has had to introduce a policy whereby each farmer can get a contract for no more than two acres, so that contracts may be spread over as many farmers as possible.

The opening of the sugar factory and the subsequent development of Mandya created a considerable number of new employment opportunities. In the first instance, labourers were required for the new buildings that began to spring up in the town. Mandya now houses the headquarters of the District Administration; it has a secondary school and an intermediate college, which cater for the whole region. The factory has its own staff and labourers' quarters for its 1,200 employees. Some of the employees originate from the Mandya region, but a large number come from further afield; quite a considerable proportion of the unskilled labourers originate from the neighbouring State of Madras.

Except for the Muslims, to whom I shall refer below, Wangala men have not sought after the jobs that became available with the expansion of Mandya. At the time of my study there was only one man from Wangala who worked in Mandya and he was a newcomer to the village. He was a Muslim postman, who owned a bicycle and cycled daily to work in Mandya. Prior to irrigation a number of Wangala men had migrated even as far as the *Malnad*, the hilly area in Mysore, where they worked as plantation labourers on the European-managed coffee and tea estates. Once land had become irrigated, most of the migrants returned to Wangala to claim their share of the ancestral estates. The increased labour requirements of sugarcane cultivation was a further inducement to return to Wangala. At present there is only one of Wangala's Peasant families living outside the village. The family lives in Mysore city.

The sugar factory has a cane plantation on Wangala lands and this constitutes the only alternative employment that Wangala men have accepted on a more permanent basis. Twelve Wangala men (about 5% of men of working age) are employed as agricultural labourers on the factory plantation. They all belong to castes: most of them are Peasants and have small farms of their own. The plantation workers form indirect links with Mandya and the wider economy; they receive regular fixed monthly wages and a cost of living bonus according to an agreement between the management and the trade union; they receive holidays with pay; they work six eight-hour days per week; they are members of the factory's co-operative society and some of them even have savings in the co-operative savings bank. But they remain primarily farmers. They try to fit in their working hours at the plantation so as to suit the cultivation requirements of their own estates. Their interests remain vested in agriculture, and their economic and social relations with the villagers remain almost undisturbed.

Wangala's Functionaries were also affected by the changes due to irrigation. They are now all part- or full-time cultivators. The Potter cultivates cane, and makes pots only occasionally; the Washermen are also farmers and plantation workers; the Goldsmiths have experienced an increased demand for their services, for irrigation has put more money into farmers' pockets which is spent lavishly on jewellery; Wangala's only native Blacksmith has been similarly affected, for cultivation of sugarcane requires iron ploughs which need more complicated maintenance than the wooden ploughs used on dry land.

The increased income of Wangala men and the village's strategic position on the roadside have created new commercial opportunities. I have already referred to the 'hotelu' (coffee shop) and grocery shops set up by the roadside. When I re-visited Wangala in February 1956, three months after I had left the village, another 'hotelu' and another shop as well as a bicycle repair shop had been opened. All the enterprises started along the roadside are owned and run by immigrants to Wangala. The two 'hotelus' were started by Peasants coming from other villages while the shops and the bicycle repair shop are run by Muslims. One of the four village caste streets is still called the 'Muslim' street although neither of the two Muslim households now lives in it. There used to be about 15 Muslim households in Wangala who all lived in the one street, which still bears their name. As Mandya began to expand these Muslims were attracted to the town where they opened bazaars and cycle shops. The two families now in Wangala had returned from Mandya to open stores

A Muslim roadside shop

PLATE I. WANGALA

in the village. One of these, although an illiterate man, continues to work as postman in Mandya while his wife looks after the shop.

Muslims have never participated in any of the village feasts; they never have had a representative in Wangala's village council. They are allowed to draw water from the caste well but none of the caste or Untouchable households will eat cooked food from a Muslim kitchen. Moreover, since they remain largely outside the network of social relations in Wangala, they find difficulty in securing labour during the busy times in the agricultural year. Significantly, they have to bring relatives from other villages to help and rely on the immigrant Vodda Untouchables to work as casual labourers. It is difficult to analyse the position of Muslims in Wangala's social organisation now that there are only two families, and these returned only seven years ago. But it is possible to speculate that the fact that Muslims seem to have remained on the fringe of the society has made them more enterprising and more versatile. Their greater enterprise cannot be explained by a lack of interest in the land, for they, like the Wangala Peasants, are small landowners. Many of my Peasant informants regarded a shop as a gold mine. When I enquired why they themselves did not open shops, they stated emphatically that it would never do for a Peasant to squat on the floor of his shop and offer goods to passers-by, who might be of lower caste or even Untouchables. 'A Muslim can do this, but not a Peasant.' They also claimed that if a Peasant opened a shop (and there are in fact two caste shops in the village), he could never really make money like a Muslim shopkeeper, because a Peasant was expected to be charitable and therefore obliged to sell goods on credit; a Muslim need not do this. This was quite true. One of the Muslim shops in Wangala sells against cash only, the other gives credit but only to men employed on the factory plantation. On pay day at the plantation the wife of the Muslim shopkeeper usually turns up at the plantation and after many curses collects the money from her debtors. Social pressure does not have the same effect on Wangala's Muslims as it has on Wangala's Peasants and Untouchables.

The new commercial opportunities affected mostly Muslims in Wangala, whereas the additional labour requirements for wet crops affected other sections of the village population in a differential manner. During the busy seasons in the agricultural year there is usually a shortage of labour in Wangala. For instance, when paddy has to be transplanted round about the middle of August, farmers require groups of about ten women per acre to transplant paddy from the nursery to the fields. Most of the women who transplant, weed or harvest, are Untouchables. Those Peasant women who do work are usually widows, for it is regarded as a lowering of social status if a woman works as daily labourer. Since irrigation has brought increased incomes to Wangala farmers they consider it as lowering their prestige if their womenfolk work at all in the field. Thus while the demand for female labour has increased since the introduction of wet crops, the supply has actually decreased, while the population has increased only slightly. The bigger Peasant farmers expect their womenfolk only to take food to the fields for the agricultural labourers, but not to work in the fields themselves. Consequently there is now a greater demand for Untouchable labour. This in turn has largely deterred Wangala's Untouchables from seeking employment outside the village, for the increased earning opportunities coupled with the general social security, which is a concomitant of traditional relations between Peasants and Untouchables, outweigh the attractions of insecure employment elsewhere.

The advent of irrigation forms the turning point in Wangala's recent history. Events are dated and referred to according to whether they happened 'before' or 'after' irrigation. Before irrigation villagers cultivated ragi and jowar, crops which need little work compared with paddy and sugarcane; before irrigation villagers ate mainly ragi and only very rarely rice; then they had more leisure but very little cash; men smoked neither beedies (tobacco wrapped in leaf) nor cigarettes but used cheap snuff; they wore no more than a loin cloth and turban. Before irrigation there were no roads but only cart tracks; villagers ventured to Mandya only very rarely, and only few as far as Mysore, the nearest city about 30 miles away.

Irrigation changed Wangala's ecology: with it came new economic opportunities to Wangala men which changed their pattern of living. Wangala's economy changed from a largely subsistence to a largely cash economy. Wangala men now wear shirts and a number also wear dhotis; their wives wear colourful saris bought with money and they all spend lavishly on weddings; Wangala men pay frequent visits to Mandya where they visit coffee shops and toddy shops; rice has replaced ragi as their staple diet.

All these changes have occurred since irrigation but not all are due to irrigation. There were other external economic stimuli operative simultaneously, such as food shortages and a black market, alternative employment opportunities, the impact of the growing town of Mandya, and the improved system of communications. All these stimuli acted simultaneously upon Wangala's economy, and brought about change inside the village, but this change was 'unilinear' in so far as it was in line with Wangala's traditional organisation. Of the various external economic stimuli affecting Wangala, irrigation was dominant; it made land more remunerative, centred the farmers' attention on cultivation, and therefore strengthened the rural economy.

Economic Activities

All economic activities in Wangala centre on agriculture; the large bulk of the village population are *ryots*, small owner-occupiers, who cultivate their own estates. The smaller *ryots* supplement the income from their own estates by working as labourers for the larger *ryots* in the village. Only 20% of the total 192 households in Wangala at the time of my census were landless. Of the landless households no more than one-third were natives of Wangala; the remainder were immigrants who had settled in the village during the last 10 years. These immigrants represent a marginal addition to the available labour force in Wangala; they came after irrigation had brought about a rapid expansion of the village economy. About half of them had settled in Wangala simply because they had been transferred from other plantations owned and run by the management of the Mandya sugar factory. They are a highly mobile part of Wangala's population, for there is a continual shifting of labour between factory plantations to meet the varying demand for labour, and consequently they remain on the fringe of Wangala's social system. Similarly, the Vodda Untouchable immigrants are a marginal section in Wangala's population. They speak Tamil, and originate from the neighbouring State of Madras whence they emigrated in search of work and food. They are by far the poorest section in Wangala: they are dressed scantily in rags, their household property consists of a couple of mud pots, and they live in grass huts, which are cheaply and quickly constructed. They migrate through Mysore State and a large number of them have been attracted to the Mandya region by the new employment opportunities. A considerable number have found work in Mandya's sugar factory, while others have settled, at least temporarily, in surrounding villages where the cultivation of newly irrigated lands demanded more labour. Four of Wangala's seven Vodda Untouchable households have been living in the village for about five years and are likely to stay provided they continue to find work. They work as labourers on the land, particularly for Muslim families who have difficulty in securing labour during the busy seasons of the agricultural year. Muslims strengthen this employment relationship with the Voddas by giving them groceries from their own shops during the slack seasons when Vodda men cannot earn enough to feed their families. Vodda Untouchables also work as farm labourers for the local Functionaries.

Village Functionaries cater either for the household needs of farmers or they make and repair agricultural equipment. The Potter makes mud pots for use in the kitchen and tiles for house roofs. The Goldsmith makes jewellery out of pieces of gold or silver handed him by the villagers; he repairs and remodels jewellery and he also acts as pawnbroker. The Washerman washes some of the caste households' clothes and all the menstrual cloths. The Barber lives in the next village and comes once or twice weekly to Wangala to shave and cut the hair and trim the moustaches of Wangala men. The Blacksmith is trained to make and repair wooden ploughs and has branched out into making and repairing iron ploughs, carts and houses.

All the native Functionaries in Wangala own some land, though none of them is a big landowner. Apart from the Potter and Goldsmith, all Functionaries have a hereditary relationship with Wangala Peasants: they are paid annually in kind for doing certain defined jobs throughout the year; for any extra work they are paid in cash. The quantity of grain and hay that constitutes their annual reward has not varied at all during the last 25 years, though prices and the work performed have changed considerably in the same period. Their reward, translated into money terms, depends therefore on the price of grain, and not on the work performed. For instance, the Blacksmith must sharpen all agricultural equipment of the households with which he has a hereditary relationship; in years of drought when farmers have little need for his services and when due to the shortage of grain prices are high, the Blacksmith's annual reward is high expressed in money terms, though the quantity he receives remains on the whole unchanged. But in years of bumper crops farmers need a lot of repairs to their agricultural equipment. Good harvests however also bring down the price of grain and consequently in money terms reduce the Blacksmith's annual customary income. The traditional relationship between Functionaries and Peasants thus eliminates risk in the Functionaries' activities for they are paid the same quantity of grain and fodder whether harvests are good or bad. At the same time it puts a damper on incentive in an expanding economy. It is a relationship basically consistent with a static economy.

Wangala's indigenous Blacksmith was eager to meet the challenge of the new opportunities that resulted from irrigation. He wanted to exploit the increased demand for his services and in turn was prepared to accept the risk of years of depression, as long as he had the security of his own lands. This led him to put his case to the village council. He submitted that he wished to sever all his traditional obligations and instead to establish economic relations on a purely cash basis. It is essential for Wangala farmers to have an artisan in their village who can repair a broken plough on the spot or sharpen its iron tip. Only very few of Wangala's farmers have learnt to repair ploughs themselves and it would be most inconvenient and a waste of time if they had to take their repairs to some other village or even as far as the nearest town. Therefore village elders objected to the Blacksmith's proposal and demanded that he must first find a substitute if he himself chose to cut the traditional bonds; they threatened that unless he did so he would find his life in the village very uncomfortable. Had he not also been a landowner in Wangala, Veerachari, the indigenous Blacksmith, might simply have walked out of Wangala and settled in some other village. But the ownership of land confers prestige and also provides an ultimate security. He himself explained to me that he might earn more out of his craft in good years, but when there are droughts—and these used to occur periodically before irrigation and still threaten to some extent—nobody demands his services; nobody wants new ploughs or new houses when the harvest is poor. In such years he might have no income at all if he had not his land to fall back on.

Social pressure forced the Blacksmith to find a substitute. Veerachari himself was an only son, But he had a cousin who, because he was the youngest of five sons, was redundant in his own village, and was only too glad to undertake his traditional craft in Wangala under the customary conditions of pay.

Veerachari was an enterprising man: he owned land which he had inherited and his house was the first one in Wangala to be built to the West of Mandya road; he learned to make the type of iron plough necessary for the cultivation of cane; he repaired carts; and he became a housing contractor. Altogether he performs all those tasks of a blacksmith which do not fall within the sphere of traditional Blacksmith work and he is paid for this work in cash, whilst his cousin accepted Veerachari's customary obligations of work for Wangala's Peasants against customary pay. This transfer of economic obligations was facilitated by the fact that the Blacksmith has no function in Peasant life-cycle rituals. A severance of his economic relationship with individual Peasant households did not entail a change in ritual relationship. By contrast, Washermen and Barbers do perform important functions in Peasant household rituals. The ritual content of the hereditary relationship helps to perpetuate economic relations of Washermen and Barbers with their Peasant customers. Peasants still continue to pay annual rewards to the Barber and Washerman, though their requirements of these Functionaries has steadily decreased over the last years. Since the introduction of soap many women now wash their own saris and even their men's clothes; some of the younger men take their dirty shirts to town where they get them not only washed but also ironed. Younger men also prefer to have their hair cut in one of Mandya's hairdressing saloons where they can get a Western style haircut rather than the local tonsure. For all these reasons Peasants have less use for the regular services of the indigenous Washerman and Barber. But they do need the Washerman to wash menstrual cloths, while both the Washerman and the Barber have ritual roles they are required to perform at Peasant weddings and funerals. The continued, though weak demand for the services of the Washerman and Barber and the strength of the ritual ties between Peasants and these Functionaries deter the former from breaking their hereditary economic obligation to the latter.

All of Wangala's native Functionaries are also small farmers on land most of which they inherited. The cultivation of a small estate of dry land requires little labour and yields only a small return. Functionaries who own small estates of dry land need to spend only a very small percentage of their working days on the cultivation of their estates and devote the major part of their working time to performing services for the Peasants from whom they derive the major part of their income. In the past they regarded their farming activities as secondary and subordinate to their own hereditary tasks. The irrigation of their lands, however, radically changed the relative emphasis put on farming and hereditary tasks. The cultivation of wet crops requires more labour than dry crops but it also yields bigger returns. Consequently to most of the Functionaries farming became a major if not a wholetime activity and their hereditary occupation assumed secondary importance. Irrigation strengthened the agricultural aspect of Wangala's economy. Functionaries and Peasants alike concentrated their attention on the cultivation of crops upon the more remunerative wet lands.

Dry and Wet Crop Cultivation

As elsewhere in India, with the village of Wangala is associated a demarcated tract of land. Wangala's total acreage amounts to 1,657 acres, of which according to village records 54% are uncultivable comprising tanks, ponds, roads, paths, house-sites and complete waste. Official village records have not yet taken into account the fact that some of the land became irrigated as early as 1932. Land Revenue Authorities were planning a new survey in the Mandya area, but until 1956 their land accounts were still based on the last survey taken in 1926, a few years before irrigation reached the area. In fact, some of the land classified in the records as complete waste has come under cultivation since irrigation; some of it forms part of the factory plantation; and some of it, as we shall see, is being cultivated unofficially by villagers. According to my own census of landholding in Wangala 56% of the village lands are under cultivation (see Table 2). The system of canals and channels passing through the area irrigated 55·5% of Wangala's cultivable land. The factory plantation owns 23% and other outsiders own 9% of the irrigated cultivable land; the remainder is owned by inhabitants of Wangala. 61% of the land owned and cultivated by Wangala villagers is wet land and the rest is still dry. Irrigation has not yet reached the limits on Wangala lands; more of the land classified as uncultivable may yet become irrigated through the building of channels and some of the dry land may also get water in this way. But some of the land will always remain dry in accordance with the Government regulation that each village site must be surrounded by a belt of dry land so as to reduce the danger of malaria.

Prior to 1935 only about 12·5% of the lands cultivated by Wangala farmers were wet lands and these were irrigated from a tank—not a very reliable method. The major crops grown on dry lands were ragi and jowar. Ragi and jowar also formed the staple diet of villagers, ragi being the more favoured of the two crops. These grains are ground and eaten boiled in the form of balls dipped into curry. Since irrigation these grains have given way to rice as the staple diet. Wangala men are now ashamed to admit that they still eat ragi or jowar for some of their meals, although they readily agree that ragi is the more nourishing diet. Rice-eating is associated with high social status in South India, where rice is the staple diet of the Brahmin, the highest caste. Ragi is graded as the poor men's food and anyone who wants to illustrate his own extreme poverty complains that he has to eat ragi and cannot afford rice.

Ragi and jowar are 2–4 months crops, while rice is a 5–6 months crop. Provided the soil is sufficiently fertile two crops can be sown per year. Crops sown at the beginning of July with the start of the heavy south-west monsoon showers are called *hain* crops and those sown in January are called *kar* crops. The *hain* crops are by far the more important variety in Wangala, *kar* crops having a lower yield and being of poorer quality. Wangala farmers are good judges of the fertility of their soil. They carefully examine the soil for its gravel content and they also judge it by its shade and colour. Experience has taught them that two crops per year grown on one acre reduce the yield of each crop by so much that in most cases it is more economical to grow a *hain* crop only and to leave the land fallow to restore itself during the rest of the year. Of the 631 acres cultivated by Wangala men only 15% bore two crops in the year of my survey. Whenever two crops are grown, farmers rotate ragi and jowar on dry land and rice and ragi on wet land. Otherwise on dry land it is usual for a farmer to plant ragi year after year in the same field. There is also the practice of growing a mixed or subsidiary crop of pulses side by side with ragi or jowar. Farmers reckon that this interposition of a leguminous crop neutralises in some degree the evil effects which would follow a succession of the same crops on the same soil. The crop of pulses is also a welcome addition to the household's consumption.

Knowledge of soil fertility and cultivation techniques have been handed down from father to son through generations of farmers in Wangala. Although there is a certain uniformity in the cultivation methods of farmers in Wangala, farming techniques, costs and yields differ greatly between holdings, according to the efficiency of the particular farmer, his financial resources, the size and fragmentation of his holding and the quality of his land. These many different yet interdependent variables, which account for the profit or loss of an estate, make it difficult to illuminate Wangala's farming economy by reference to an 'average' acre or an 'average' estate. For instance, in order to measure the profitability of applying fertiliser to an acre of ragi, we would have to compare the net product of one acre having received fertiliser with one that had not, while in all other respects the two acres are alike: having the same soil composition and being cultivated by farmers of the same efficiency with the same methods. Such comparison was beyond the limits of my competence, for it would have involved among other things a chemical analysis of the soils of Wangala. Though I am aware of the severe limitations in using averages as an exposition of cultivation costs, techniques and profits, I feel that my statistical data nevertheless throw some light on the operation of Wangala's farming economy and the set of values by which it functions.

(*a*) *Collection of Data*

My statistics are based on a stratified random sample, which I arrived at in the following way. First, I took a full census of population and landholding of all households in the village. Thus my first enquiry is based on a complete sample of my universe. Secondly, I gave each household a point value according to the size of wet and dry land holding. As the price relationship of wet and dry land is three to one, I allocated 12 points for one acre of wet land and four points for one acre of dry. Thirdly, I tried to eliminate the impact of the different size and age composition of households, for I might have one household with a point allocation of 100, which in fact consisted of three nuclear families all living jointly. Therefore I utilised the concept of the consumption unit. I accepted Lusk's coefficient[1] for the allocation of consumption units. Then I divided the number of allocated points per household by the number of consumption units each contained.

[1] Ministry of Labour. *Report on an Enquiry into the Conditions of Agricultural Workers in the Village Archikarahalli, Mysore State*, Government of India Press, New Delhi, 1951, p. 15. (See foot of page opposite.)

Thus I arrived at a point allocation per consumption unit per household.[1] I then proceeded to list these point values into several categories at a group interval of five, which gave five categories for Wangala. I subsequently combined these five into three economic categories by joining the first two and the second two into one category each. About 40% of the total households belong to the poorest section, 57% belong to the 'middle-farmers' and 3% to the 'magnates'. The five richest households fall into the category of 'magnates' because they hold the highest acreage of wet land. Equally, it is true to say that they hold the highest acreage of wet land because they were the richest already before irrigation reached Wangala. Irrigation re-emphasised their economic predominance.

On the basis of households grouped according to their economic status I selected a third in each category completely at random. Thus my sample is at random in so far as the actual households selected in the sample were selected at random, but it is stratified inasmuch as households had been previously put into economic categories on the basis of landholding and the size and age composition of the household.

All the 64 sample households in Wangala were subjected to most intensive enquiry. I collected from each one of them details of the production of the four major crops, and of their income and expenditure and property.

For each crop I prepared schedules which include all the operations involved in its cultivation. These schedules have separate columns for each operation to show who performed the work, i.e. whether it was the farmer or his own household labour, or exchange or hired labour; then there are columns to

Lusk's coefficient

Age	*Consumption unit*
Men above 14 years	1·00
Women above 14 years	0·83
Either 10 years but below 14 years	0·83
Either 6 years but below 10 years	0·70
Either 1 year but below 6 years	0·50
Either below 1 year	Nil

[1] The total number of consumption units in Wangala is 738.

indicate the daily rate for hired labour and how many men or women had been employed for how many days. The data on labour time were collected in units of labour days or fractions thereof. Wangala farmers usually reckon half a day to be the smallest labour unit, but in my own calculations I included as one quarter day the two hours men usually work after dinner in the evening to check irrigation to their cane fields.

The schedules also show the number of bullock-, plough-, or cart-days each operation requires and indicate whether these capital items were the farmers' own or whether they were hired; if they were hired the rate is indicated. Furthermore, the schedules asked for information on the quantity and price of seeds, manure and fertiliser. I also collected details of all tools and equipment the farmer employs in the cultivation of each crop, by noting the price of each item of equipment, how old it was and its annual maintenance charge. As regards output, I enquired the yield of the major crop as well as all subsidiary crops, such as pulses on ragi fields, and the yield of hay.

Each informant was asked to give details of his cost of production of each crop for an area he actually cultivated: thus if a farmer cultivated half an acre of paddy, he would give details for that half acre, if he cultivated two acres he would give details for two acres. Therefore crop details on the schedules showed data for different sizes of area cultivated. For purposes of comparison I converted all schedules into a common denominator of one acre. Thus if a farmer had given details for half an acre I doubled all his figures to show his details for one acre. This conversion assumes constant costs, which is a reasonable assumption judging from the data I collected. In most cases I found that one acre requires about twice the amount of labour input that half an acre does. For sugarcane the conversion problem hardly arose, because most farmers did cultivate cane in units of one acre.

After I had converted all schedules into one acre figures in real terms, I faced the problem of evaluating subsistence labour. I decided to evaluate it at the ruling daily wage rate in the village. All money figures throughout the book are expressed in rupees.[1]

[1] One rupee equals about 1*s.* 6*d.* in sterling.

But although I decided to evaluate subsistence labour at the ruling wage rate in the village, I always calculated farmers' wages and profits together, which is the important item each farmer most wants to know. He never thinks of evaluating his unpaid labour in money terms. Many of my informants were very keen to supply input and output data correctly, for they themselves wished to find out how much it cost them to cultivate the various crops. They gave very detailed answers to all my questions as to how many days they themselves worked on their lands and how many days they had to hire labour. For output figures, too, the information seemed fairly accurate. I managed to check a number of output details myself by observation and in each case the details almost tallied with those supplied by the farmer. Measurement of food crops is in *pallas*, a measure of volume about equal to one bag of paddy or ragi or jowar. One *palla* of paddy weighs about 194 lb., of ragi 208 lb. and of jowar 215 lb. Barter transactions in these crops are carried out in units of *seers*; one seer is one hundreth part of a *palla*. Sugarcane is measured in tons and I usually managed to get from the farmer the factory weighing tickets, showing the exact weight of cane supplied by him to the factory. Although some farmers supply cane from non-contracted fields to the factory along with cane grown under contract, so that the yield per acre may be slightly exaggerated, by living with the villagers I knew pretty well everybody who supplied 'black' cane to the factory and could make allowances for the yield of the acre for which I was given details by the farmer. Because of my close knowledge of the farmers and local conditions I assume that there is only a small error in my basic material.

In my calculation of agricultural capital I did not include landed property, nor did I include an interest charge on investment in land among my items of overhead expenditure. I omitted these items, because, since land is sold only rarely these days, it is very difficult to estimate the price of any particular piece of land. Therefore inclusion of landed property among items of agricultural capital and overhead expenditure would have meant a large increase in the possible error of my basic data. The items included under the heading of agricultural capital are as follows: draught animals, ploughs, carts and all other tools and equipment used for farming. In order to calculate overhead expenditure I collected details on maintenance, depreciation and interest. Maintenance included the upkeep of draught animals, repairs of tools and equipment, part of which was met by subsistence production. I calculated depreciation at 7% because 15 years is roughly the lifetime of a pair of bullocks, a cart and ploughs, and interest at 12%, the ruling rate in the village.

Another problem I encountered in the preparation of crop statistics was deciding on the allocation of subsistence and cash overhead expenditure of the estates among the acres under the various crops. Farmers had supplied me with details of their estates' overhead expenditure, but, of course, they could not give me any idea of how to allocate this expenditure to the different crop acres. On considering this problem I realised that draught animals, ploughs and carts are the major items of agricultural capital. Since I had collected data on their use for the various crops, I could calculate the average relationship between the utilisation of these major items of agricultural capital on the four major crops. I found this relationship to be 60% for cane, 20% for paddy, 10% each for dry or wet ragi and jowar. If a farmer cultivated one acre each of the four major crops and his total cash or subsistence overhead expenditure was Rs. 100, Rs. 60 would be allocated to his acre of cane, Rs. 20 to his acre of paddy and Rs. 10 each to his one acre of wet or dry ragi and jowar. Thus the weights given to the acreage under the various crops were 60 for cane, 20 for paddy, and 10 each for wet or dry ragi and jowar.

Thus I compiled information on the four major crops per acre, as well as data on the whole farm. They indicate details of all items of input and output. Output totals of food crops were evaluated at the average price for the year of my survey. Prices of food crops vary throughout the year; there is about Rs. 5 variation per *palla* of paddy between the harvest season when paddy prices are at their lowest and the autumn when paddy prices are at their highest.

(*b*) *Dry Crops*

My analysis of average input and output per acre of the four major crops in Wangala clearly singles out jowar as the least remunerative and also the least costly crop to cultivate. We may therefore ask why farmers grow jowar at all instead of ragi, when both crops can be grown on the same soil and ragi is by far more remunerative. There appear to be three main considerations.

TABLE 4

Wangala cost, output and income per acre

Estimated average

	Cane		*Paddy*		*Wet ragi*		*Dry ragi*		*Jowar*	
	Rs.	%	*Rs.*	%	*Rs.*	%	*Rs.*	%	*Rs.*	%
Cost:										
a. Subsistence Labour	116	13	73	24	47	24	25	18	15	20
b. Hired Labour	126	13	66	22	16	8	32	24	5	7
c. Subsistence: Seeds and Fertiliser	112	12	54	18	68	36	45	32	18	23
d. Cash: Seeds and Fertiliser	373	40	30	10	8	4	5	3	1	1
e. Hired Equipment	40	4	12	4	12	6	4	3	1	1
f. Subsistence: Overhead Expenses	94	10	33	11	20	10	16	11	20	27
g. Cash: Overhead Expenses	64	7	23	7	11	6	10	8	14	19
h. Tax	14	1	14	4	14	6	1	1	1	2
i. Total Cost	939	100	305	100	196	100	138	100	75	100
j. Subsistence Cost ($a+c+f$)	322	35	160	52	135	68	86	62	53	71
k. Cash Cost ($b+d+e+g+h$)	617	65	145	48	61	32	52	38	22	29
l. Output	1,597	100	281	100	415	100	188	100	92	100
k. Cash Cost ($b+d+e+g+h$)	617	39	145	52	61	15	52	28	22	24
m. Income: Farm wages and profits ($l-k$)	980	61	136	48	354	85	136	72	70	76

Firstly jowar is used as a means of rotating crops; secondly, some of the soil is so poor and rocky that farmers do not want to risk the greater expenditure involved in growing ragi; and thirdly, some farmers are too busy with their wet land cultivation to spend time and money on cultivating ragi. Only 25% of the sample households cultivated jowar at all, while 30% cultivated ragi on dry land. The average output per acre of jowar amounts only to Rs. 92 and average farm wages and profits to Rs. 70 (see Table 4). 56% of the farmers cultivating jowar recorded farm wages and profits of less than Rs. 60 (see Table 25). Cash input constitutes 24% of total output and the remaining 76% accrue to the farmer as his wages and profits. Jowar requires very little labour: 12 male and 12 female labour days suffice for a one-acre crop per year. Therefore farmers who cultivate jowar can usually manage with the labour of their own household and rarely need to hire labour. Very few farmers apply any fertiliser at all to jowar crops and my data show no correlation between the application of fertiliser and the yield per acre. While direct costs—that is to say, cost of labour and seeds and fertiliser—are low, indirect costs are relatively high. Even the poorest soil must be ploughed and even the smallest crop of grain must be threshed, operations for which certain tools and a pair of draught animals are absolutely essential. Draught animals and ploughs can be hired, but for several reasons they are hired rarely. Firstly, since the demand is concentrated into certain periods in the year, they are difficult to hire just when needed; secondly, ownership of draught animals and ploughs affects prestige. No farmer is regarded as fully established unless he owns a pair of draught animals and a plough. Thus the smaller the holding the heavier is the burden of overhead cost per acre, even if the total capital involved is small. Indirect cost constitutes as much as 46% of the total input per average acre of jowar. This large percentage of overhead costs also reflects the poverty of farmers who grow jowar. Of the average cultivation costs per acre of dry land ragi only 19% is accounted for by overhead expenditure as compared with the 46% in the case of jowar. This marked difference in the proportion of indirect costs between the two major dry crops does not reflect a greater capital requirement in the case of jowar, but shows rather that those farmers who cultivate ragi have more economical holdings than those who cultivate jowar.

Ragi crops are of two kinds: those grown on wet land and those cultivated on dry lands. Both ragi crops require considerably more labour than jowar. The average labour input is 23 male and 30 female labour days per acre of dry land ragi and 28 male and 30 female labour days per acre of wet land ragi. In terms of wages paid and also roughly in terms of work performed one male labour day equals 2 female labour days. Thus ragi needs more than double the labour required for jowar cultivation. If we bear in mind that labour requirements are highly concentrated into a few days on four occasions throughout the crop period, namely ploughing, sowing, weeding and harvesting, and that a farmer may have two or three acres of ragi, it becomes obvious that farmers have to enrol labour from outside their own household during these crucial periods in the agricultural year. 58% of the labour per acre of dry land ragi is hired and paid in cash. This high percentage of hired labour in a village of owner-occupiers indicates a widespread network of economic relations, in which most farmers also work for wages.[1]

Prior to irrigation, farmers used to apply only a little manure to ragi crops, but since they have learned to cultivate cash crops they have become aware of the benefits that can be derived from the application of manure and artificial fertiliser. Even before irrigation some farmers did appreciate the importance of fertiliser, but they could hardly afford to buy it. The growing of cash crops both induced and enabled Wangala farmers to apply fertiliser and also to acquire stronger draught animals. They are now able to apply more manure because their strong bullocks yield more dung than the weak cows they owned before irrigation. The greater awareness of the importance of manure and fertiliser and the ability to purchase them have led to an increase in the yield on dry land as well as on wet land. Seeds, manure and fertiliser now account for 46% of the total input per average acre of wet land ragi and for 35% of dry land ragi. High correlation between the application of manure and fertiliser and the yield per acre of ragi (the correlation coefficient of the sample is 0·60) justifies the

[1] Only 46% of the sample households derived no income from agricultural wages.

farmers' assumption that a greater yield will result from the application of more fertiliser, though of course this may not hold true in every case, depending on the quality of the soil.

The average output per acre of wet ragi amounts to as much as Rs. 415, of which 85% accrue to the farmer in wages and profits. This relatively high yield per acre is largely a result of the high fodder yield: about 40% of the total yield is in the form of fodder and only about 60% is in the form of ragi and subsidiary crops of pulses for human consumption. Wet ragi grows to much greater height than dry and provides more fodder. The average yield per acre of dry ragi amounts to no more than Rs. 188, but only about 20% of this is in the form of fodder. Therefore, whereas the average yield of one acre of dry ragi amounts to only 45% of the wet ragi yield, the average human food output per acre of dry ragi amounts to as much as 60% of wet ragi. Average farm wages and profits per acre of dry ragi are Rs. 136, which represent only 38% of those of wet ragi. Thus the difference in the profitability between ragi grown on wet and dry land is considerable. In fact ragi is an even far more remunerative crop on wet land than paddy. The average wages and profits per acre of wet ragi amount to as much as Rs. 354 and those per acre of paddy only to Rs. 136, which is just as much as average wages and profits per acre of dry land ragi. Yet relatively few farmers grow ragi on wet land: only 14% of the sample farmers grew wet ragi. This apparently uneconomic choice may be explained by three factors:

(*a*) Most food production is for subsistence, and farmers prefer rice to ragi. Besides, they can grow sufficient ragi for their own consumption on their dry lands.

(*b*) There is prestige attached to growing paddy as well as eating rice. Each farmer is proud if he is able to produce sufficient paddy to meet his own household's demand.

(*c*) There is no ready market for ragi, because ragi is the staple dry crop in the region. No lorries tour the area to purchase ragi, whereas plenty of wholesalers pass Wangala and enquire whether any farmer has surplus paddy for sale.

Therefore, whilst it would be profitable for farmers to grow ragi on their wet lands, sell the produce and purchase rice for their own consumption, the absence of a ready market for ragi acts as a deterrent to grow ragi on their wet lands.

At the time of my survey in 1954/5, Wangala farmers grew 228 acres of paddy, 237 acres of ragi, 116 acres of jowar, and 129 acres of sugarcane. Sugarcane, a one-year crop, accounted for 20% of all the cultivated acreage. 66% of the crops grown were half-yearly crops grown on acres left fallow for the remainder of the year and only 15% of the cultivated acreage yielded two crops per year. Apart from the two major dry crops of ragi and jowar, Wangala farmers produce a variety of subsidiary crops on small plots: They grow chillies for their own consumption and a number of green vegetables. Most of these plots occupy no more than 5 square yards and require little labour, usually female. Of the total 631 acres cultivated by Wangala farmers only 2% was under these various vegetable crops. Therefore I almost ignored these different crops and concentrated my analysis on the economic activities connected with the four major crops, which together account for the cultivation of 98% of all crops grown by Wangala farmers.

Before irrigation a considerably higher proportion of the total cultivated area was devoted to vegetable crops; farmers produced sufficient pulses, vegetables and spices to meet their household needs. Nowadays Wangala men and women walk to the weekly fair in Mandya where they purchase these items, and in their farming activities they concentrate on the production of the staple subsistence and cash crops. The change from a subsistence to a predominantly cash economy is the concomitant of Wangala's specialisation. Irrigation and specialisation have increased the farmer's income. He could probably buy with the net cash profit from one acre of sugarcane about twelve times the quantity of pulses or vegetables he might have produced on that one acre in the same period before it was irrigated. However, while sugarcane is certainly a much more profitable crop than ragi, pulses or other dry crops, it also requires much more labour and capital. Dry crop cultivation requires little working capital and investment: a pair of cows[1] worth about Rs. 150, a wooden plough and a few other implements altogether worth about Rs. 10 suffice. Dry soil requires surface ploughing only, for which a pair of decrepit cows and a wooden plough are adequate; dry land also needs fewer ploughings than wet land. The upkeep of a pair of small cows and the maintenance of wooden ploughs and the few other implements required cost very little, so that the farmer can cultivate dry crops even with the meagrest of resources. In Wangala, the lack of capital made it difficult for the poorest farmers to benefit immediately from the irrigation of their lands. Wet crop cultivation, particularly that of sugarcane, necessitates considerably more capital assets: wet soil needs several deep ploughings before the sowing or planting of seedlings, and this requires a pair of bullocks worth about Rs. 400, iron ploughs and other implements worth at least Rs. 50. Sugarcane must be delivered to the factory in Mandya and fertiliser and manure taken to the fields, so the farmer also needs a cart. A new cart costs about Rs. 350. In addition these various items involve considerable expenditure on maintenance and repairs. Then again wet land has to be levelled for cane cultivation and terraced for paddy cultivation.

Altogether wet crops require about four times as much capital investment as dry crops. According to the sample surveyed, the average farmer in Wangala has agricultural capital worth Rs. 660 apart from land. (See Table 27.) The distribution of agricultural capital in the sample ranged from nil to Rs. 1,650: 36% had less than Rs. 400 agricultural capital, 56% less than Rs. 800, and 80% had less than Rs. 1,000. (See Table 28.) The amount of agricultural capital owned per estate is directly related to the size of wet land holding (the coefficient of correlation is 0·75). Although these figures were collected a long time after the introduction of irrigation, they still indicate three things: firstly, how much more capital is required for wet than for dry crop cultivation;[2] secondly, how difficult it must have been for the smaller and middle-farmers in Wangala without financial resources to accumulate

[1] Mysore Peasants have no religious objection to the use of cows for ploughing.

[2] For further discussion see below, pp. 231–2.

funds for the purchase of the more costly equipment; thirdly, that most Wangala farmers did manage to surmount the initial difficulty of shortage of funds for investment.

By creating the need for larger investment in agricultural capital before the benefits from irrigation could be fully enjoyed, irrigation re-emphasised the economic predominance of the richest farmers. The five richest families to-day were also the richest before irrigation. These five magnate households had been traders as well as farmers: they had been familiar with the working of a money economy and they had cash available for investment and working capital. These were the dominant factors in their continued success after irrigation.

(c) Sugarcane Farming

Sugarcane was a new crop to Wangala farmers. Its cultivation was not just a matter of changing from one crop to another. Apart from greater investment it also involved far-reaching adjustments in the organisation and practice of agricultural production. Through time and experience, Wangala farmers had developed a rhythm of dry crop production in which each participant had a certain task to perform, and each operation had its proper date and time. Unless the production techniques of a newly introduced crop harmonise with those of the customary crops, the new crop must affect the customary productive rhythm. Sugarcane takes 12 to 14 months to mature and requires attention throughout this period. By contrast, dry land *hain* crops require little labour and this is concentrated in a few months of the year. After the harvest in January until the ploughing in May or June, farmers are practically free of cultivation. Immediately after the harvest season a series of large cattle fairs takes place in Mysore State which is attended by villagers from a wide area. At the same time negotiations for marriages begin and the marriage season lasts throughout April and May. After the marriage season ploughing marks the beginning of the new crop season. Such is the accustomed rhythm of economic and social activities of dry-land farmers. Sugarcane cultivation completely upsets this accustomed rhythm. The most common season for planting cane is

February and March or October, but throughout the year some cane is planted. This ensures a steady flow of supplies to the sugar factory, but it demands a radical readjustment of the farmers' productive organisation and social life. Whereas, after the January harvest of his dry crops, he was free in former times to visit cattle fairs, go on pilgrimages, or negotiate his children's marriages, he is now often tied during this period: he may have just then to level and plough his wet land ready for the planting of cane seedlings or to perform some other operation necessary to the cultivation of cane. Sugarcane can be grown in the Mandya area only under the most assured sources of irrigation which bring water to the crop throughout the whole year; particularly during the first six months of its growth, sugarcane needs constant irrigation and attention. If the young crop is left without water for a few days it will deteriorate very quickly and may be ruined altogether. This constant need for irrigation of cane crops induces many a farmer to walk to his fields at night so as to ascertain that the channel carrying water to his land has not been blocked by some ambitious and selfish neighbour. Many a careful farmer even sleeps for weeks near his cane crop to make certain of the water supply to his lands. Altogether cane cultivation requires a great deal more labour than the dry crops. The average labour requirements per acre of cane amount to 178 male and 30 female labour days. Farmers can usually meet this heavy labour load only by hiring labour and by working overtime themselves.

The normal working day starts at about 7.30 a.m. and finishes at about 5.30 p.m. There is a break for lunch from about noon to 2 p.m., so that the working day lasts eight hours. In the case of cane cultivation, farmers usually work overtime. Some employ labourers, but during the peak periods most farmers go themselves to their fields for about another two or three hours' work after their evening meal, when there is a moon. The average farmer meets 50% of the total labour requirements per acre of cane from his own household or by 'inviting' unpaid friends to come and help. The rest he has to hire. The average gross product per acre of cane amounts to as much as Rs. 1,597 of which 61% accrue to the farmer in wages and profits (see Table 4). The bulk

(*a*) Planting of sugarcane seedlings

(*b*) Bundling of sugarcane at harvest

PLATE II. WANGALA

of his production cost has to be met in cash: as much as 65% of the total cost involves expenditure in cash, the remaining 35% being made up of unpaid labour, fodder, manure and seedlings produced for which no cash expenditure is required.

The large quantity of labour and working capital required for sugarcane cultivation has re-emphasised the economic interdependence of Wangala villagers; for each farmer cultivating cane has to hire local labour and most farmers have to borrow to cope with a whole year's working and household expenditure before they can draw cash from the sale of cane. As already noted, Mandya's sugar factory helps to ease the financial burden by offering cultivation and cutting advances at 6% rate of interest, which is half the rate ruling in Wangala. According to the factory's records, the average credit offered to cane growers in Wangala in 1953 amounted to 40% of the gross amount due to farmers. Such credit suffices to pay for the manure and fertiliser, but leaves little for other working expenses and is no help at all in meeting household expenses. Farmers therefore have to rely on loans, usually from men in their own village, to help them over the long waiting period before they reap the reward for the effort and cash put into cane cultivation. In this respect it makes it easier for them that cane is not a strictly season-bound crop and that its period of maturation varies from 11 to 14 months. For this means that throughout the year there are always some farmers who are delivering cane and drawing cash from the factory. Whenever a farmer receives his payments, his creditors are always anxious to be repaid, because they in turn may be short of cash—and there are always debtors waiting to borrow more. Cash is always particularly short in supply during the wedding season when the struggle for status tempts Peasants to spend lavishly on marriage feasts. Anyone receiving his cane payments about that time finds himself swamped by demands for loans. However, most of the debtor-creditor relationships are of long standing and the debt is never quite settled, so that each creditor has a quasi-hereditary relationship with a number of debtors. Similarly, the relationship between the farmer and his hired labour does not dissolve when a particular job is done and paid for, but persists over generations: the same households supply labour to certain farmers, unless sickness or a quarrel upsets the arrangement.

Sugarcane is a risky crop to grow. It cannot be consumed in the household if there is no market for it, nor can it be stored, for it requires processing. Cane may be processed either in crushers and made into jaggery or refined at the factory and made into white sugar. In either case processing should follow immediately after the cane has been cut. Otherwise its sugar content deteriorates rapidly. Prior to the establishment of a sugar refinery at Mandya, all cane grown in the area was processed into jaggery at village cane-crushers. Indeed, most of Mysore's sugar consumption was then in the form of jaggery. In the town, households have mostly changed over to consumption of refined sugar, although for certain relishes jaggery is still preferred. Villagers still use jaggery for sweetening more often than sugar, although jaggery contains a number of impurities and usually no more than 60% sugar, whereas fine sugar has a 100% sugar content. But sugar is certainly replacing jaggery, for since more sugar has come on to the market, the demand for jaggery has been declining.

The price of jaggery shows a downward trend since 1953. There will always be some demand for jaggery, because some of the Indian dishes of sweet relish can be made only with jaggery. But it seems clear that sugar will drive jaggery off the market as the supply of sugar becomes more plentiful. The price of jaggery is inversely related to the supply of sugar. When in 1953 wholesalers hoarded white sugar for speculative reasons, the price of jaggery soared temporarily. The high price of jaggery induced cane farmers to have as much of their cane as possible made into jaggery and consequently supplies of cane to the factory declined, which in turn aggravated the shortage of sugar. When steps taken by the Government forced wholesalers to release their hoards of sugar, jaggery prices began to fall again and farmers are now eager to sell even non-contracted cane to the factory. At the same time, demand for jaggery is declining, so that the reduced supply of jaggery does not push its price up again.

At the prices of cane and jaggery ruling in May 1956, for every ton of cane produced the farmer could get Rs. 39.75 by selling to

(*a*) A bullock cart delivering cane to Mandya

(*b*) Ploughing of wet paddy lands

PLATE III. WANGALA

the factory and only Rs. 35 by processing the cane into jaggery and selling it as such. For 10 tons of cane delivered to the factory the farmer received Rs. 397.50. These 10 tons yield about one ton of sugar with a 100% sugar content, which is sold at Rs. 800 wholesale. The same 10 tons of cane may be processed into jaggery to produce about 3,500 cubes, which also weigh one ton, but this ton of jaggery has only 60% pure sugar content. To produce 1,000 cubes in a power cane-crusher costs Rs. 20. Therefore 3,500 cubes cost Rs. 70 to produce and in May 1956 the price of jaggery paid by wholesalers in the Mandya area to farmers was Rs. 120 per 1,000. Thus while the farmer could get Rs. 397.50 for 10 tons of cane delivered to the factory, he could get only Rs. 350 for them if he went to all the trouble of having them processed into jaggery and sold to wholesalers, and he forgoes the advantage of cheap credit from the factory. At this relationship between the factory cane price and the producer's jaggery price obviously all farmers are anxious to sell their cane to the factory.

Cane delivered to the factory is grown under contract: the factory enters into contracts with farmers in the Mandya area to buy the output of a specified acreage. Farmers are always keen to grow cane under contract to the factory, since this reduces their risk. The terms of the contract between the farmer and the factory allow the farmer room for manipulation; the factory undertakes to purchase at a price fixed in advance all the cane produced on a contracted acre and does not specify the tonnage it will buy. This enables the farmer to vary the quantity he delivers to the factory to suit his own interest. If it is more profitable to have cane made into jaggery, farmers reduce the quantity of cane they deliver to the factory and have the balance of their crop processed into jaggery. If the price of jaggery falls, as it has done in the last few years, farmers try to deliver to the factory some of the cane grown on non-contracted acres. In fact there is a sort of black market in cane; farmers who have grown sugarcane without contract to the factory offer their crop to farmers who have a contract and who are prepared to buy this cane well below the price fixed by the factory, so that they can make a profit by re-selling it to the factory at the agreed price, together with the crop from their own contracted acreage. The sugar factory tries to protect itself against such deceit by employing fieldmen whose main job is to advise farmers on cultivation problems, but who are also there to see that the actual crop produced on an acre of contracted land will be delivered to the factory.

The factory fieldman is only a minor official and has a low status in the factory, but in the villages he occupies a very important position. He recommends which of the farmers should have their contracts renewed and he reports when cane is ready for cutting. After about a year of hard work cane cultivators are always eagerly waiting to receive a cutting permit from the factory so that they may harvest the cane, deliver it and finally get their payment. Presents to the fieldmen or open bribery win favours from him and speed up cutting permits. The factory tries to avoid this by frequent transfers of fieldmen between different areas, so that their relations with villagers are of limited duration. During my stay in Wangala the fieldman who had been responsible for the village was to be transferred. Significantly, I was asked to forward a petition signed by four of the magnates and a number of the richer middle-farmers to request the factory to leave the fieldman in the area with which he was already familiar. Those who organised and signed the petition were obviously the ones most affected by his transfer, for it always takes time and more money before favours can be obtained from a new man. The system of bribery of small officials brings them within the orbit of village politics and reduces the rigidity of the rules which they are there to enforce. Once an official has accepted bribery he becomes partly dependent on his donors. Though the fieldman's strict duty is to make sure that only contracted cane is delivered to the factory, bribery induces him to allow some farmers a margin.

As I have already pointed out, Wangala farmers are all anxious to secure contracts, but the capacity of the sugar factory limits the contracts it can enter into. The factory management pursues a policy of dispersing contracts over as many farmers as possible and each farmer's contract is usually for no more than two acres of wet land. This policy has encouraged Wangala farmers to partition their estates, so as to secure contracts for a greater acreage. Whereas previously a father only reluctantly yielded to his son's demand that he partition the estate, the policy of dispersing cane contracts has made fathers more amenable to the idea of partitioning, since it is in the interest of all in a family to secure a contract for as many acres as possible. Though the break-up of the extended family had begun well before the factory introduced its policy, the policy has certainly hastened the decline of the extended family unit. Previously, actual partitioning long preceded the corresponding alteration of official village land records. Nowadays the change of title to land often precedes the actual partitioning of property. For instance, Wangala's headman lives jointly with his three sons, of whom only the oldest is married though still childless. But the headman has already transferred part of his lands into the names of his two elder sons. The official transfer of title enabled him to secure contracts for four acres of wet land, instead of the two he would otherwise have been able to secure. Though in most cases the transfer of title is looked upon by the father as mere formality in the interest of expediency, it does affect the relationship between father and sons: the latter show more independence, which usually first expresses itself in greater demands for spending money and soon leads to many quarrels, so that the mere formality of transfer of title finally results in an actual partitioning of the households. The headman's eldest son, whose wife was just then expecting her first child, had many quarrels with his father in his attempt to assert his independence and he made no secret that, as soon as his wife had given birth and was ready to look after a household, he wanted to start his own ménage and cultivate independently of his father the lands already officially registered in his name.

The formal transfer of title may be the first step towards partition, and in most cases it is an economic necessity that the actual partitioning of the estate comes after the official transfer of title. It requires a considerable initial investment to undertake wet crop cultivation, particularly to bring wet land under cane cultivation, which a son starting independent cultivation might not be able to afford, even though he might be able to secure a contract from the factory. The case of Lingegowda, one of the poorer middle-farmers, illustrates this. Lingegowda has two sons of whom the elder, Kempegowda, is already married but not yet living with his wife. Lingegowda has already transferred the title to one acre of wet land and one acre of dry land to Kempegowda, though they still live and work jointly. The acre of wet land had only recently come under irrigation by means of an extension of channels through neighbouring fields. It is poor soil and Lingegowda used to grow jowar on it. Since it has become irrigated and he could secure a contract for ¾ acre by asserting that it belonged to his son, he put it under cane cultivation. He had to invest much labour in levelling the land for cane and restoring it with fertiliser. But in spite of all his efforts, the total cane yield of the ¾ acre amounted to no more than 17 tons for which he received a gross amount of Rs. 676. From this Rs. 11 was deducted for interest on the Rs. 516 of fertiliser given him on credit and another Rs. 76 for overdue tax and irrigation contribution,[1] so that the net amount he received from the factory was only Rs. 73. In fact he had actually hired labour for Rs. 102, quite apart from his own and his son's labour that went into the cultivation of the ¾ acre. Lingegowda was prepared to make this investment in the expectation that in future years it would pay dividends when he hoped the cost of cultivating the ¾ acre would be lower and its yield higher. Lingegowda could finance this investment with the income derived from the remainder of his holding, but Kempegowda, his son, could not possibly have made the investment had he actually begun to farm independently when his father transferred to his name the title to the two acres of land. The period between the formal transfer of title to land and the actual partitioning of the estate allows the embryo estate to develop, sheltered and cushioned by the resources of the larger estate. As part of the larger estate the embryo holding receives an investment of labour and fertiliser, which in subsequent years,

[1] According to an agreement between the Revenue Authorities and the factory administration, the latter is given a statement of tax arrears of each cane grower and deducts these overdue amounts from the payments to the cane grower concerned.

when it becomes an independent cultivation unit, may help to make it an economic proposition. Up to a limit, and this limit does not yet seem to have been reached in Wangala, there is a high correlation between the input of labour and fertiliser and the total yield per acre of cane (the sample shows a coefficient of correlation between labour and output of 0·89 and between fertiliser and output of 0·71). Therefore it is more economical in a period of agricultural expansion for new estates to be allowed to develop under the shelter of the parent estate.

The contracted cane acreage in Wangala has fluctuated greatly during the past ten years. Fluctuation depends on a number of variables: on the factory's policy, which in turn is influenced by its own capacity and by the availability of irrigation water in the canals, on the price offered by the factory for cane and the price of jaggery. The prices of cane fixed by the factory have also fluctuated considerably during the last ten years; these prices are tied to All-India prices, and are therefore outside the scope of the present analysis.

The dominant variable in the determination of the total acreage of Wangala lands contracted to the sugar factory is the availability of sufficient irrigation water. Sugarcane requires irrigation almost throughout the whole of its twelve months maturation period. Mandya derives its irrigation water from the Cauvery river which rises in Coorg. If the monsoon fails there, Mandya cane crops are adversely affected.

> To the greatest surprise and disappointment of all, the Krishnarajasagara Reservoir which has been feeding the area through the Visvesvaraya Canal went dry for the first time in 1949 after 20 years, due to drought conditions that prevailed at the time for want of rains. That came as a terrible blow and the loss sustained by the Company as well as the sugarcane growing *ryots* in the area was of no small magnitude.[1]

In 1949 of the total 103 acres of Wangala lands contracted with the factory only 12 acres bore a crop at all, and that was very poor. For the 1949 cane crop Wangala farmers received Rs. 5,404 as

[1] B. G. Dase Gowda, *Mysore Sakkere*, October 1955, p. 7.

gross amount for cane delivered whereas the factory advanced as much as Rs. 12,294. The factory, in which the Government holds the major share, decided to write off the deficit as a bad debt. In 1956 irrigation once more threatened to fail and the factory then advised *ryots* in the area to stop planting cane on contracted land. The management of the factory took great pains to make it clear that no compensation could be given to any *ryot* affected by the drought. This meant that any credit advanced by the factory to farmers on the basis of contracted land would have to be repaid whether or not the crop for which it was advanced materialised. The threat of a failure in the supply of irrigation water induces farmers to plant paddy or ragi rather than cane on their wet lands. In 1954, which was a normal year as regards irrigation, 33% of Wangala's wet lands were under cane cultivation, 60% under paddy and 7% under ragi crops. Thus for every acre of cane Wangala farmers cultivated about two acres of paddy in that year.

(*d*) *Rice farming*

Paddy is a much less remunerative crop than sugarcane, but it is a food crop, most of which may be used for subsistence consumption; it can be stored; and surplus can be sold without any need for processing. Paddy is a half-yearly crop which fits into the accustomed rhythm of production, and it requires considerably less labour and working capital than sugarcane. Paddy requires on an average 97 male and 28 female labour days per acre, which is just over half the labour requirement for one acre of sugarcane. The average wages and profits per acre of paddy are however far less than those on the average acre of cane. Average wages and profits per acre of paddy crop amount to Rs. 136 and per acre of cane crop to Rs. 980. So while the relationship of labour input between an acre of paddy and an acre of cane is about 1 : 2, the relationship between wages and profits per acre of paddy and cane is about 1 : 7·2. Of the sample farmers cultivating paddy 4% made a loss, 48% earned less than Rs. 120, 73% earned less than Rs. 160; the modal wages and profits amounted to Rs. 150 (see Table 23). Wangala farmers complain that the yield of paddy is very low; it is much lower than that of ragi grown on wet land. Yet, as might be expected, the yield of paddy is considerably higher than that of dry ragi: the output of one acre of dry ragi amounts to only about 66% of an acre of paddy. But the much higher cash costs involved in paddy cultivation are responsible for equalising farm wages and profits of the two crops. Cash costs constitute as much as 52% of paddy output and only 28% of dry ragi yield. However, since both crops are for subsistence the higher total output of paddy is of more importance to the farmer than his wages and profits.

The Mysore State Agricultural Department, which has an office in Mandya, advocates the Japanese method of paddy cultivation to increase the yield of paddy. This method differs from the indigenous method of paddy cultivation in four aspects: firstly, it carefully selects seeds planted in the nursery and sows them in rows instead of haphazardly, using only a quarter of the seeds used in the indigenous method; secondly, it applies a lot more manure and fertiliser to the nursery; thirdly, it transplants the seedlings at equal intervals into the fields; and fourthly, it applies more manure and fertiliser per acre of paddy.

It is claimed for the Japanese method that it can increase the yield of paddy as much as fourfold. However, the success of the method depends largely on the quality of the soil, for not all soils respond favourably to it. On all soils it offers certain advantages: by intensive cultivation of the nursery and fewer plants, the seedlings are more fertile; by transplanting these seedlings equally spaced in rows, each seedling has more room to grow and a better chance to derive benefits from the application of fertiliser.

Fieldmen of the Agricultural Department tour the area to advise farmers on the Japanese method. At first Wangala farmers did not believe that fewer paddy plants could give a greater yield, but they finally managed to understand this. Yet not a single farmer has attempted to use the Japanese method, in spite of the fact that the Agricultural Department offers credit facilities to the first few farmers in a village who are prepared to experiment with it. A number of farmers have learnt to select paddy seeds more carefully, but none of them has tried to space the plants. Such spacing would upset the transplanting techniques to which female labour—and paddy, we must remember, is always transplanted by women—is accustomed. Ten or twelve women form a group, called *gumpu* in the vernacular, who work as a team for transplanting, weeding and harvesting. Each team has a leader whose job it is to collect her colleagues for work whenever a farmer requires their labour. Usually the team is paid a rate for a job, that is to say, so much per acre transplanted or weeded, and the leader receives the pay from the farmer and divides it among her fellows, keeping for herself a slightly larger share. These teams are accustomed to the traditional method of transplanting and their members are reluctant to change over to the more tedious way of transplanting according to the Japanese method. The new method would also take much longer and since teams are paid a rate per acre, rather than a daily rate, they are obviously reluctant to experiment with a new technique without the assurance of an increase in pay. Farmers on the other hand, as we shall see, are bound by the customary rates of pay in the village and therefore cannot offer higher pay even if they are prepared to do so. Altogether it is difficult for the enterprising farmer in Wangala to exert any pressure on these female labour teams to experiment with the Japanese method of transplanting, for just when he needs the team there is usually great demand for it and if he started being difficult he would find himself waiting until the team had more time.

The lack of enterprise as regards the Japanese method of paddy cultivation contrasts with the considerable enterprise Wangala farmers have shown in their cultivation of cane. Cane was a new crop which required new techniques and a productive rhythm different from that of the customary crops. Paddy cultivation by the Japanese method also meant changes in cultivation techniques, but farmers were less enterprising about it. Three factors are probably responsible for this difference. Firstly, it appears to be easier to learn all about the cultivation of a new crop than to adopt new methods in the cultivation of a customary crop. In this respect Wangala farmers behave according to the pattern familiar in

(*a*) A *gumpu* transplanting paddy

(*b*) A *gumpu* weeding paddy

PLATE IV. WANGALA

industry, where it has been found that it is more efficient to train a new worker in new techniques, than to make an experienced worker change his techniques. Secondly, a fixed rate per job impedes the introduction of new techniques. Again, this is a fact with which we are familiar in industry. Thirdly, Wangala farmers experienced far less difficulties in adopting new techniques where these affected the farmer's own labour, than where these affected hired labour, in particular that of women. No single household in Wangala includes a sufficiently large number of women of working age to form a working team, nor do farmers want their own womenfolk to work on the land. Thus as long as transplanting is done in teams and the rate for the job is fixed, farmers will find difficulty in experimenting with the Japanese method however enterprising they may be in other spheres of economic activity.

Animal Husbandry

Before irrigation, Wangala farmers used mainly cows for ploughing and they did quite an extensive trade in farm animals. The trade involved trips through the countryside in search for sellers and buyers, which took up a lot of time and which were usually fitted in during the period between the January harvest and the first ploughing in May. Irrigation and the cultivation requirements of sugarcane have upset the farmer's plan of activities throughout the year. Few of the richer farmers can now afford the time to trade in farm animals and the poorer men, who might have the necessary time, lack the necessary capital. In addition, trading in animals requires a certain skill, which is not so easily acquired. Wangala still has its bullock-agents (*dalalis*) who act as middlemen whenever a sale of bullocks takes place in the village: they do not trade on their own account, but act only as intermediaries at sales.

Wangala has nine bullock agents: five of them inherited the office, the others gaining it through their personal aptitude and experience of sales transactions. The agent's fees are very small, only about Rs. 2 per transaction irrespective of the value of the sale. The low reward received by the agent makes it surprising that farmers are at all interested to act in this capacity; but though their monetary reward is small, agents are marked off as keymen in the village. They also hear all the gossip from other villages, for whenever other villagers come to Wangala in search of buyers or sellers of bullocks, one of the agents is contacted. It is his job to bring together buyers and sellers. Agents also act as intermediaries at all the sales between inhabitants of Wangala. An agent's function is to narrow the gap between the price asked by the seller and that offered by the buyer. One such sales transaction may take a day or more with both buyer and seller haggling over every fraction of a rupee and the agent cushioning the argument between the two parties. He represents the buyer to the seller and the seller to the buyer. Men usually settle down on the verandah of a big house or in an open space to transact a sale, each party supported by his own followers. Whenever one states a new price, the agent consults the other and tries to make him accept the price. Since his reward is not related to the value of the sale, his main interest is to clinch the sale. His mediating activities enable the two parties to a sale to continue social relations after they have faced each other as bitter opponents in the process of bargaining.

Most of the farmers who own wet land possess a pair of bullocks but only a few have more than one pair. One pair is sufficient to cultivate 4–5 acres of wet land or 10 acres of dry land or an equivalent combination of wet and dry land. Stronger bullocks might be sufficient for 6 acres of wet land, but certainly no more than that. The indivisibility of bullocks sets certain limits to the extension of a farmer's estate. It is uneconomical to buy an extra acre of land if this necessitates the purchase of an extra pair of bullocks which would be under-employed. In Wangala, where landholding is highly dispersed and 77% of all households own less than 6 acres of land, very few households need in fact consider the profitability of purchasing more land, though for the few richer farmers it is an important consideration. Kempegowda, one of the middle-farmers with a holding of 3 acres of wet land and 3 acres of dry land, turned down the chance of buying another half acre of wet land from his Untouchable client, because his own pair of bullocks was just able to cope with the cultivation of his present estate. The extra half acre would have involved him in laying out, on top of the money for the land, money for another pair of bullocks and for their upkeep. As land sales have become very infrequent in recent years, he had little hope of being able to buy a sufficiently large acreage to make the purchase of an additional pair of bullocks an economic proposition.

Farmers, even with the smallest estates, need draught animals, although in fact the majority have an idle bullock capacity. The purchase of a pair of draught animals is the first step of a newly established farmer. A farmer without a pair of draught animals cannot function as a full farmer. It is the constant complaint of the poorest Untouchable farmers that although it is now the Government's policy to enable them to buy land well below the market rate, they still cannot become farmers without the necessary money to invest in a pair of bullocks and a plough. The capacity of an iron plough roughly equals that of a pair of bullocks. So in fact the economic size of a holding is largely governed by the capacity of bullocks and ploughs. Increasing population in Wangala, where each son has an equal right to a share in his father's estate and where the extended family has largely disappeared, makes the size of holdings more and more uneconomic. If all holdings were of a size sufficient to use bullock capacity to the full, probably one-third of all bullocks in Wangala could be dispensed with. But Wangala farmers prefer to be independent however uneconomic the size of their holding may be. Joint ownership of bullocks outside the joint family is non-existent and there are only a few joint families in Wangala.

A bullock's maximum life is about 14 years. The young bulls are castrated at the age of about three and they can then be put to work. Farmers usually keep their bullocks for a few years only, when they sell them to a poorer farmer and buy a better pair. The poorer the farmer, the older his bullocks or cows. Untouchables in Wangala usually own the most decrepit animals, which they eventually sell to Muslims who slaughter them. Bullocks are sacred animals to the Hindu and Peasants do not plough on Monday, the day of Siva, whose vehicle was a bull, but this religious rule does not stop them from utilising their bullocks to take their carts to Mandya on a Monday, or from allowing bullocks to be sold for slaughter. If a bullock or cow dies while owned by a Peasant, his Untouchable client has to bury the carcass in the Peasant's field.

The following statistics on animal husbandry are based on a full coverage of the whole village, for I was able to collect details from each household in the village. My calculation of the value

TABLE 5

Wangala value and incidence of livestock ownership

Type of livestock	*Holding households*		*Average value per holding household*	*Non-holding households*		*Average value per household (all households)*	
	No.	%	*Rs.*	*No.*	%	*Rs.*	%
Bullocks (pair)	102	53	382	90	47	203	59
Cows (pair)	58	30	144	134	70	43	12
Buffaloes	72	37	265	120	63	77	22
Sheep	29	15	143	163	85	20	6
Goats	19	10	26	173	90	3	1
Total						346	100

of livestock per household is based on each informant's estimate of the sales value of his animals, crosschecked by his neighbours' evaluation, which usually tallied. I did not include chickens in my enumeration of animals per household, because the number of chickens owned varied from week to week and chickens are relatively cheap; one chicken costs about Rs. 2 to 3. Quite a number of Peasant and Untouchable households do keep chickens and sell eggs, though usually chickens are kept for home consumption. Thus my census figures of livestock ownership include only the more important animals kept by households in the village. But the census covers all village households and average figures are therefore true averages and not sample averages.

53% of Wangala's households own bullocks for agricultural work and 30% own cows. Most of the cows are kept for dairy or breeding purposes, only some for draught. The average price of a pair of bullocks in Wangala is Rs. 382 and the average price of a pair of cows is Rs. 144 (see Table 5). A pair of cows is usually given no more than Rs. 0.25 worth of fodder per day: for the rest it is grazed on the village waste lands and on harvested fields. A pair of bullocks usually receives fodder worth Rs. 1 per day. Bullocks are fed with paddy or ragi hay, sugarcane leaves, horse-gram and cotton seeds. The annual maintenance charge of a pair of cows amounts to no more than Rs. 90. Most of what they eat is produced on the farm itself and does not involve a cash purchase. The annual maintenance charge of bullocks amounts to Rs. 360 per pair of which about 20% involves cash purchase. Cows are obviously much cheaper than bullocks, but they are not sufficiently strong to plough wet land. Whenever a farmer can afford it he buys therefore a pair of bullocks rather than a pair of cows.

Buffalo cows are kept for dairy farming. 37% of all Wangala households own buffaloes; each household owns only one or two buffaloes and there is not a single buffalo bull among them. Buffalo milk has a higher fat content than cow's milk, and therefore may be more easily watered down. The average price of buffalo cows in Wangala is Rs. 265. Buffaloes are never given fodder but are always taken grazing; they subsist on very little. The average buffalo cow may bear four calves and yield milk for about 8 years: the average milk yield per day is about one seer[1] of milk at a price of Rs. 0.50. Buffalo calves are usually sold for between Rs. 70 to Rs. 100, the buffalo heifer fetching the higher price. Thus the initial investment in a four-year-old buffalo cow yields an average gross income of about Rs. 230 per year over eight years, at the end of which it can be sold for about Rs. 20 to a Muslim for slaughter. Buffaloes are a relatively profitable investment and it may therefore seem surprising that so few households keep them. The explanation seems to be that dairy farming is the domain of women. While the initial investment is made by the farmer, the yield is usually pocketed by the woman, who spends it on extras for herself and her children, but never

[1] One seer of milk equals two pints.

saves for the replacement of the buffalo. The purchase of a buffalo means in fact an expensive present of a farmer to his wife or daughter, which few farmers are keen to make.

Sheep and goats are the concern of the farmer himself, though they are tended by young boys. They are reared mainly for meat production, though sheep are sheared by visiting Shepherds (*Kurubas*) from neighbouring villages who trade one blanket for the wool of ten sheep. Most of the meat consumed in the village is derived from sheep or goats slaughtered in Wangala itself. The average price of a sheep or goat is Rs. 20. Usually a number of households combine to purchase the meat of a sheep or goat.

Sheep and goat farming is not very profitable, and is undertaken only by the wealthier households; 15% of all households own sheep, and only 10% own goats. Animal husbandry in Wangala is subordinated to the needs of agricultural production. The shortage of good grazing land and fodder in general make animal husbandry as a separate line of farming an uneconomic proposition.

Farm Labour

All Wangala men and about 40% of the women of working age, i.e. between the ages of 15 to 55, are engaged part-time or full-time in farming activities. Even boys and girls from the age of five onwards take part in farming activities. Small children are allowed to play together until they reach the age of five, when the training begins, which marks off the separate path of boys and girls. Boys are trained to become farmers or farmhands: their first tasks usually are to take the bullocks grazing, lay out their fodder, and take them to the canals to drink. This initial training provides the basis for the farmer's attachment to his farm animals. Small boys also act as shepherds, and they are apprentices in the cultivation of crops. Little girls are trained in household duties. They are also taught to look after buffaloes, to milk the buffalo cow, and eventually to make butter out of buffalo milk; they also learn to tend chickens.

The production of milk, butter and eggs is the sphere of

Wangala's farming which is regarded as the domain of women, and the sale of this dairy produce provides women with a small but independent income. Thus it is very important for the young girl to learn dairying. Young Peasant girls used to be taught to transplant, weed and harvest, but this is now disappearing. Wangala men regard it as a matter of prestige that their womenfolk do not work on the land; Peasants are reluctant to admit that their women help in the cultivation of the family estate, and it is thought to be very degrading for a Peasant woman to work as hired labourer. The only work on the land that a 'respectable' Peasant woman is expected to do is to look after the vegetable crops. The magnates and richer middle-farmers brag that their womenfolk do not even know how to weed or to transplant. Conversely, to say that a man's wife works as 'coolie' is to point out his low social status. Among the richer families, the cultivation skill of women is dying out. Bochamma, the mother of one of Wangala's magnates, is a widow of about 65 years. She used to complain bitterly that though she found her son a wife who could help him on the land, her daughter-in-law had become lazy, and that her granddaughters and the wives of her grandsons did not even know how to work the land. Her son, whom she had helped a lot in the accumulation of the family's wealth, regarded her complaints as the whims of an old woman. Bochamma still insisted on turning up to weed their fields, though she now walks with great difficulty. None of her granddaughters ever do so and they laugh at the old woman's eccentricity.

Though the richer farmers do not expect their daughters to be trained any longer to work on the land, neither do they send them to school. Wangala's primary school has 72 pupils on its register, of whom only 5 are girls. Of the 72, only 23 attend the school with any regularity and they do not include any girls at all. In fact, there is not a single literate girl below the age of 15 in Wangala. Of the boys below 15 years 22% are literate. Boys get their initial school training between the ages of 5 to 10, then until they are about 15 or 16 years old most of them work at least a few weeks in the year as boy farmhands on a daily hire rate. At the time of my survey the daily wage of a boy farmhand was

Rs. 0.50, which was the same as the daily wage for adult female labour. Adult male labour was paid Rs. 1.25 per day. All boy farm-hands and adult female as well as male labourers working a whole day received on top of their wages one main meal, valued at Rs. 0.25; half-day work did not warrant a meal. Some operations on food crops are still paid in kind: for instance, the pay for a day's harvest is eight seers of paddy or ragi.[1]

Most of Wangala's farmers have to call on labour from outside their own household to help during the rush periods in the agricultural year. The very nature of agricultural production, which concentrates the large bulk of labour requirements into a few rush periods in the year, forces an extensive system of labour relations on Wangala *ryots*. The majority of Wangala men work at some time or other during the year on land that is not their own. In other words most farmers are both employers and employees. This accounts for their readiness to keep to a wage rate agreed by the village council at a meeting attended by all Caste householders. There is no council record of this meeting. According to informants the present rate has remained stable since it was agreed about 1948. The wage rates paid in Wangala are the same as those paid in many villages in the Mandya area, though they are higher in some villages, as I shall show in my discussion of Dalena, the dry village.

Farm labour in Wangala falls into six categories:

(1) *Unpaid labour of members of the farm household:* As I have outlined above, the labour contribution of the household's womenfolk to farming is declining among the richer farmers. There is a straight inverse correlation between the social status to which the farmer aspires and the amount of agricultural work performed by the women of his household. For the farmer himself there is no such correlation: the proportion of agricultural work performed by the farmer himself of all the labour that goes into farming his lands is in no way related to his social and economic status. All the magnates are keen farmers who personally work their lands and supervise their farmhands: none of

[1] A seer is a measure of volume. One seer of paddy or ragi weighs about 2 lb. and costs about Rs. 0.20.

them has an estate big enough to warrant his becoming a non-cultivating manager. The farmer's sons work the land with him jointly until they partition their joint holding.

(2) *Exchange labour:* Exchange labour, for which I shall use the Kannada word '*muyee*', is of two different kinds, though in the vernacular the same term is used for both. Firstly *muyee* refers to a straightforward exchange of labour between farmers. About six men may decide to form a mutual aid group for certain operations, such as ploughing or harvesting. This means that the members of the group perform jointly certain operations in turn on the land of each of them. Membership of *muyee* groups is restricted to Peasants, but it cuts across lineages. *Muyee* groups are usually composed of a number of friends of about the same age. *Muyee* labour is practised only among men; women never work on an exchange basis.

The second kind of *muyee* labour is that performed by men for their creditors. Such *muyee* labour is not taken into account as a payment of interest or debt, but is done simply to 'keep in' with one's creditors. This kind of *muyee* labour cuts across caste and includes Untouchable labour. The magnates, who are also the chief moneylenders in the village, command the highest amount of this *muyee* labour in Wangala.

(3) *Untouchable client labour:* The hereditary patron-client relationship between Peasant and Untouchable households, which will be dealt with in greater detail in chapter IV, puts the client under an obligation to provide labour for his patron whenever the latter requires it. This may mean that the Untouchable client himself works for the patron or he may have to bring other Untouchable men along with him to make up a ploughing or harvesting team, or it may mean again that the women of the Untouchable client household have to organise a *gumpu*, i.e. a group of ten women to work the patron's land; the kind of labour required depends on the type of operation that has to be performed on the patron's land and the size of his estate.

The Untouchable client suffers no economic disadvantage through his obligation to work for his patron since he is paid at the general rate for hired labour in the village. In an economy where wages are fixed the hereditary relationship between Peasant farmers and Untouchable clients merely helps to organise labour in a more orderly fashion at the rush periods in the agricultural year when labour is in great demand. If wages were allowed to vary labour would be drawn to the highest bidder, so that the richest farmer with sufficient working capital, who could afford to pay higher wages, would have the first claim on the available 'coolie' labour in the village at times of labour shortage. However, even without wage competition the richest farmers still command sufficient labour to meet their requirements under the customary system of client labour.

Temporary labour shortages arise in Wangala because cultivation is very much conditioned by the weather; for instance, to reap the fullest benefit from the north-east monsoon showers, dry land should be ploughed no later than a few hours after the rain ceases. Consequently, after every monsoon shower each farmer wants to plough his dry lands. This demand mobilises temporarily most of Wangala's male labour force, although during slack periods throughout the year there is considerable under-employment in Wangala. However, the temporary shortage of labour in the village is never so acute as to make it impossible for a farmer to cope with the cultivation of his lands; merely some farmers' lands are worked before those of others. The client-labour system, which helps to allocate labour in times of labour shortage and which ensures a fair distribution of employment when labour is plentiful, is preferred by Wangala Peasants and Untouchables to straightforward competition. The system also marks off the Peasants as an economic in-group: outsiders without traditional ties in the village find it more difficult to secure labour during busy periods.

(4) *Contract labour:* Wangala's 'magnates' and a number of middle-farmers have contract servants who have an annual income of about Rs. 80, and receive food and two sets of clothing per year. At the time of my survey 13 Peasant households and one Potter household in Wangala had such contract servants. Seven of the fourteen servants were landless Peasants who had immigrated from other villages, and the rest were Untouchables from Wangala. No Wangala Peasant seemed prepared to work as a

contract servant in his own or any other village, though many of the poorest Peasants were always complaining about being unable to get sufficient work in the village. Contract service is accorded very low prestige, firstly, because only a landless man would become a contract servant and land is the most important index of status among Peasants, and secondly, because contract service has grown out of '*jeeta*' or serf labour. '*Jeeta*' was expressed in an idiom of indebtedness: the poorest Peasants borrowed money from the wealthier and if they were unable to pay even the interest on the debt, they had to work off their debt by service to the creditor. There was no fixed salary for '*jeeta*' servants, which made them cumulatively more and more indebted to their patrons so that generations of '*jeeta*' servants were forced to continue the service. To-day there are no '*jeeta*' servants in Wangala,[1] though there is still the practice of working off one's debt, but nowadays servants are paid a fixed wage. Thus three of the Untouchable contract servants in Wangala are in service to pay overdue interest; they are the young sons of Untouchables, and their contract wages help to pay off the family's debt. The contract can be terminated by either party at about 3 months' notice, but if either party defaults the matter is brought before the village council.

Three Peasant farmers in Wangala are still recognised to be sons of '*jeeta*' servants; their fathers were released from '*jeeta*' bondage by marriage into the master's household or by inheriting some land from their master. That they are the sons of '*jeeta*' servants is still whispered behind their backs, and they still find it difficult to achieve high status in the society. For instance, Timma, who is among the richest of the middle-farmers, is the son of a '*jeeta*' servant whose master had no sons and only one daughter. The master arranged a marriage between his daughter and his '*jeeta*' servant, which finally freed the latter from '*jeeta*' bondage. Later the servant became an independent farmer on the land he inherited from his father-in-law. Timma is now struggling to acquire status in the village. He does all the things and acquires all the articles that yield prestige: he owns a bicycle; he wears a

[1] *Jeeta* service was outlawed by an Act of 1915.

dhoti; he smokes beedies and an occasional cigarette; he visits Mandya frequently and sends his son to middle-school in Mandya; he gave a big feast for all the village on the occasion of his daughter's wedding. To establish a following in the village he began to lend money, which he in turn had to borrow from friends and relatives in other villages. Yet, the stigma of his father's '*jeeta*' service is still attached to him; though he holds land, he has no established lineage in the village and therefore no voice in the traditional village council. The stigma attached to '*jeeta*' and its association with contract service prevent Wangala's landless Peasants from taking up service, though the earnings would probably be a most welcome addition to their income.

(5) *Gumpu labour:* All the operations that involve female labour in the cultivation of crops usually require team labour: transplanting, weeding and harvesting are operations best performed by a group. Such groups are known in Wangala as *gumpu*. Each *gumpu* has a leader for a stable nucleus of about eight women and a marginal fringe of about four women. Caste and Untouchable women never work together in one *gumpu*: there are separate Peasant and Untouchable *gumpus*. The leader of the *gumpu* is responsible for the performance of the team, and if the team is paid per acre worked and not by time, the leader is paid by the farmer and she shares out the money among all the members of the *gumpu*. Her own share is slightly larger than that of the other members.

Most of the Peasant women belonging to a *gumpu* are widows or wives of landless Peasants. Peasant women are always obviously conscious that working as labourers denotes their low social status. Even the meanest and greediest of sons does not like to see his widowed mother doing paid work on the land of another farmer. One old widow in Wangala always had to threaten her son that she would go and work with a *gumpu* before he was prepared to let her have some pocket money. Untouchable women do not have the same complex about working for wages on the land of others. They are therefore much happier than caste women when they go to work, and they joke and sing while they work together.

(6) *Daily labour:* The pool from which daily labour is drawn is made up of Untouchables and caste men, mostly Peasants. At least two-thirds of all Peasants of working age work as hired labour at some time or other in the year. Wages have been fixed by the village council and are the same for Untouchable client labour and daily labour. However, Untouchable client labour has a greater obligation to work for its patrons, but it also has some non-monetary advantages which are not shared by ordinary daily labour.

Farmers use a few relatively simple tools but they do not adopt modern labour-saving devices. This is not surprising if we remember that most Peasant farmers have a traditional relationship with Untouchable households, which obliges them to provide at least a minimum of subsistence to their Untouchable clients. If the Peasant farmer employed fewer of his clients, he would still have to give them in charity almost as much as he might save in wages. Therefore even a weeding hook, which is a small, cheap and easily employed implement that saves a considerable amount of labour, is rejected by Wangala farmers. They are not irrational or conservative in this matter. On the contrary, they know full well what it is like when their clients squat outside the house begging for food, broadcasting their meanness to the whole village.

Under-employment in Wangala is extensive in spite of the temporary labour shortages that occur at rush periods, and as population increases it will no doubt get worse unless more land is brought under cultivation or alternative employment opportunities are created. Malaria, which spread with irrigation, retarded the growth of Wangala's population. Malaria affects adversely human fertility and it was commonly said in the area that as soon as irrigation water reached a village one could no longer see a pregnant woman. There was so much malaria in the area that the authorities decided to set up a Malaria Control Centre in Mandya in 1949. Since then D.D.T. spraying has greatly reduced the number of malaria-carrying mosquitoes and consequently the birth rate in Wangala is rising.

In 1954 Wangala's population included 276 men and 251 women of working age. Of these 276 men, 12 work as labourers on the factory plantation. For a calculation of the degree of underemployment in Wangala they are deducted from the available labour force leaving a total of 264 men. To this must be added the 48 boys between the ages of 10 to 15, whose labour is counted as half of that of an adult male—in other words a total male labour force of 288 was found in Wangala. The total labour input of the four major crops amounted to 51,921 man days and 20,106 female days during the agricultural year 1954/5. If this labour were equally distributed among Wangala's population of working age, each man would work 180 days per year and each woman 80 days per year on the cultivation of the four major crops. This calculation of Wangala's labour requirements with the present techniques and implements is based on an eight-hour labour day, that is to say the two hours' overtime worked by farmers after dinner are counted as an extra quarter day labour required. This exaggerates the number of labour days required for the cultivation of the four major crops. But the calculation does not include labour spent on any of the vegetable crops, or on animal husbandry, house repairs and household tasks in general. It is difficult to calculate the amount of labour spent on these various subsidiary activities, for a lot of them are drawn out simply because the farmer has spare time on his hands. For instance, some farmers hand-feed cane leaves to their bullocks. This is more a labour of love, a leisure activity, than an economic activity. Probably the average farmer does not spend more than 30 labour days per year on his various subsidiary economic activities.

Therefore we may say that all labour performed by Wangala men of working age would keep each man busy for about 210 days out of every year, if each were to work the same number of days. In fact the richer farmers work a lot more days per year than the poorest farmers and landless, whose labour output depends on the number of days for which they are hired by the richer farmers.

Wangala's 288 men of working age work a total of about 60,561 days per year. 201 men could cope with this total number of days by each working 300 days per year. In other words, at least 30% of Wangala's men could be placed into other activities

A farmer hand feeding his bullocks with sugarcane leaves

PLATE V. WANGALA

without reducing the volume of output in Wangala, even with the present tools and techniques, provided extra labour could be called upon at rush periods. Improved cultivation techniques and labour-saving tools could bring about an even greater redundancy, but until there are other income-earning opportunities available to the poorest section of Wangala inhabitants it is unlikely that farmers will take any steps to reduce their labour requirements in farming. The availability of more income opportunities would no doubt lead to a greater specialisation, and farmers would produce less of the subsistence and subsidiary crops and articles themselves, if they could buy them more cheaply on the market in Mandya. Since irrigation, specialisation has already proceeded to a certain extent; farmers grew a greater variety of vegetables and pulses when their land was dry; sugarcane has brought them a cash income, part of which they now utilise to purchase cheaply vegetables, pulses and fruit from market gardeners at Mandya's weekly fair.

Factory Plantation Workers

Under-employment of men in Wangala induces them to look for additional work that can fit in with their own farming activities. The establishment of a large cane plantation by Mandya's sugar factory on Wangala lands provided such employment. The plantation regularly employs about seventy farm-hands with an additional number hired at rush periods. The labour force is drawn from many villages in the area and from migrant labour. The factory farmhands work an eight-hour day for six days per week: they receive a monthly wage of about Rs. 40 plus a bonus; and they get a fortnight's holiday with pay and generally benefit from regulations laid down for factory workers. Though most of the young men in Wangala, even the richer middle-farmers, would like to work on the farm, few have managed to secure such employment.

In fact only twelve out of Wangala's male labour force of 276 work on the Wangala factory plantation and only one Untouchable widow works on another factory plantation. All of the twelve men belong to a caste: 7 are Peasants, 2 are indigenous Washermen, 2 are immigrant Madras Peasants, and one is an immigrant Blacksmith. Though the 7 Wangala Peasants working on the factory plantation fall to a certain extent into the category of wage-earners, they are still largely farmers. They always try to fit in their working time on the plantation so as to be able to cultivate their own holdings. For instance, Bora always works nightshift fetching manure or fertiliser for the plantation from Mandya whenever he has to work his lands. But even if he is working days on the plantation, after he returns from his daily work there, he walks to his lands to check the irrigation channel; or he sows and ploughs in the early mornings. The work performance of the few Peasants who work on the factory plantation exemplifies how much more Wangala men could and would work if they were given the opportunity.

Young plantation workers have a regular cash income which they utilise to build up their farm resources and their prestige in the village. Bora, a young man of twenty-four, lives with his widowed mother and her mother in a small thatched hut. He inherited two acres of wet land and one acre of dry land from his father, but no draught animals. Bora has been working on the factory plantation for four years. He cultivates his own land, plants one acre of cane, one acre of paddy and one acre of ragi. He has to hire bullocks for ploughing, which he admits very reluctantly. With the first savings from his wages he got himself married. A pair of bullocks is scheduled to be his next big expenditure. After that he will start saving to build a mud house. In the meantime he clothes himself in good shirts which he gets washed and ironed in Mandya; he wears a dhoti on festive occasions; he smokes beedies and an occasional cigarette; and he gives a lot in wedding presents. In order to gain prestige he emphasises his relationship to one of the magnates, who is the husband of Bora's mother's mother's sister's daughter, a type of relationship not usually remembered among Peasants. When this magnate's son married, Bora gave a wedding present worth Rs. 20 though the usual amount even for nearer relatives is no more than one or two rupees. He explained his generosity by pointing out his kinship tie with the magnate. The pattern of Bora's expenditure exemplifies his attempt to establish himself as a farmer with prestige in his village, and his behaviour is representative of the other young Wangala Peasants who work as plantation farmhands.

Village Functionaries

Wangala's population includes a number of Functionary caste households: four Blacksmiths, five Goldsmiths, four Potters, four Fishermen and two Washermen. But for most of them farming has become the major occupation and source of income. Of the four Blacksmith households three are recent immigrants. The indigenous Blacksmith owns two acres of dry land and one acre of wet land. As I have already mentioned,[1] he is an enterprising man and has branched out into manufacturing a new type of plough, building houses and so on, but he still regards his lands as his ultimate security. His cousin, who has taken over the customary obligations of the indigenous Blacksmith, has no land; neither have the other two immigrant Blacksmith households, one of which has come to work on the factory plantation and the other to repair tools for Wangala farmers for cash.

Only one of the four Potter households still makes pots, and this Potter only works as such at certain times in the year. All four are farmers. The Potter who still practises his craft derives about 70% of his annual income from farming and the remainder from the sale of pots. There are several reasons for the decline of the Potter's craft in Wangala: firstly, since irrigation has made their lands more productive, Potters find it more profitable to devote their labour to farming; secondly, to cultivate wet lands at all they must devote more labour than to dry lands; thirdly, since irrigation there is not sufficient suitable clay for pottery work to be found in the vicinity of Wangala; fourthly, Wangala villagers regularly visit the fair at Mandya and therefore Wangala Potters have greater competition; fifthly, brass, aluminium and stainless steel vessels are more durable and have a higher prestige value than mud pots, which reduces their demand. In another generation

[1] See above, p. 37.

the art of making mud pots will probably have died out completely in Wangala.

The five Goldsmith families in Wangala all own a little land; they also practise their craft and work as daily labourers on the land of the richer farmers. They derive about 70% of their income from the exercise of their craft, 10% from working their own land, and the remainder from working as daily labourers. The demand for the services of the Goldsmith has actually increased since irrigation, but even so cannot occupy fully all the five Goldsmith brothers in Wangala. Two of them move temporarily to other villages during the wedding season in order to earn more money, but their ownership of land in Wangala stops them from migrating permanently. The landed wealth of a Wangala man depends largely on the economic status of his father and the number of his brothers. The Goldsmiths were unfortunate that their father had many sons but very little land. The law of inheritance, which gives each son a right to an equal share in the ancestral property, raises a great obstacle to mobility. Ownership of even the smallest plot prevents a craftsman from trying his fortune elsewhere. It is quite likely that Wangala's Goldsmiths might have been better off had some of them settled in Mandya where the influx of people from the region has created a big demand for goldsmith work. Alas, the ownership of even a fraction of an acre deterred them from moving out of Wangala.

None of the Fisherman households practise their caste occupation. The Fishermen's occupation in Wangala is connected with the supervision of irrigation. Before canal irrigation reached Wangala, irrigation from the village tank was the only supply of water to the fields, apart from the rains. A Fisherman then held the hereditary office of *neerugante*, or water overseer, which carried a Government grant of irrigated land. In the pre-canal system of irrigation the *neerugante* held an important office; he controlled irrigation to particular fields and he received bribes to give favours. With the advent of canal irrigation the tank was allowed to dry up and the *neerugante's* office disappeared, though the Government-granted land attached to the office was not withdrawn. The *neerugante's* importance has greatly declined and he now spends most of his time in a neighbouring village where there is a majority of Fishermen. Another Fisherman, the head of an immigrant household, is a *saude*, an official of the Water Department. The *saude* is not responsible for the irrigation of individual fields, but only for the canal irrigation near Wangala as a whole. As a government official he is always likely to be transferred and in fact he received his transfer orders shortly after I left Wangala.

The heads of the two Washerman households are first cousins; each has a hereditary obligation to about half of Wangala's Peasant households and each owns a small estate. Linga, the head of one of the Washermen's households, and Kempa, the younger brother of the head of the other, are both employed on the factory cane plantation. Linga's wife does most of the obligatory washing, but Linga himself performs the ritual part of the Washermen's obligations to the Peasants. He asserts that there is now so little washing to do that his wife can well cope with it all. His wages form about 60% of his income, his reward for washing forms about 30%, and the yield from his land about 10% of his income. In the other Washermen's household, where Kempa works on the factory plantation, the household head himself performs all the economic and ritual aspects of the Washermen's obligations to the Peasants. He also cultivates a joint small holding. Kempa wants no part of the Washermen's hereditary duties and rights; his aim is to accumulate funds to purchase land and become a whole-time farmer.

The process of Wangala consumers' integration into the regional economy confronted Functionaries with intense competition: villagers now weigh up the price charged by village craftsmen and the quality of their performance against the goods offered in Mandya. In the face of this competition, Wangala's Functionaries have either branched out into new activities, like the Blacksmith, or turned to farming as independent farmers or plantation labourers, like the Potters and Washermen. However, the decline in demand for the services of some of the village Functionaries did not affect the general social relations between Peasants and these Functionaries because Functionaries are so few and don't emigrate; the Washerman and Barber still perform their ritual functions for the Peasant households and still receive the customary annual reward. The ritual aspect of the customary relationship perpetuates the hereditary ties even though the economic content of the relationship is declining.

Land in the New Cash Economy

Land is the basis of Wangala's economy: most inhabitants derive at least the major part of their income from the cultivation of land; landholding is the key to economic, political and social status. Every Wangala man wants to be a farmer and most conversation centres on farming problems. Wangala's cash income is derived from the sale of cash crops. Prior to irrigation of Wangala lands the village economy was predominantly subsistence: households produced most of their own needs. Functionaries were paid in kind, and the little cash required to purchase a few pieces of cloth for the family per year was earned by the sale of some garden produce in the town. Some cloth was also produced by Untouchables in the village, who bartered it to the Peasants for quantities of ragi. With the introduction of a cash crop, the whole nature of Wangala's economy changed: villagers no longer produced the major part of the goods they consumed but began to specialise in cash crops. With the cash earned from these specialised crops, in particular from sugarcane, they now buy the major part of their household requirements, though most of the staple diet is still subsistance produce. The cultivation of cash crops brought Wangala's economy into the regional market. Farmers deliver sugarcane to the factory in Mandya and there they purchase their groceries, vegetables, fruit, clothes and household articles. The sugar factory provides the major source of Wangala's cash income. However, the contract between the factory and cane farmers makes it unnecessary for the farmer to become involved in bargaining or trading; the cane price is fixed in advance and can in no way be affected by the bargaining skill of the individual farmer or by the quantity of cane he sells. Thus the cane farmer earns a cash income without being drawn into the commercial or industrial activities of the regional economy; his interests remain centred in the cultivation of his lands. He has no need to establish stable economic relations with traders in Mandya, for the sugar factory is the sole buyer of cane—except for the occasional sale of jaggery to wholesalers touring the area—and therefore is able to lay down terms over which the farmer has no influence at all. Correspondingly, he buys from a number of small sellers with whom he has only casual economic links. His stable economic relations are confined to his own village where he has to rely on exchange or daily labour to help him in the cultivation of his crops. Though Wangala has to a certain extent become integrated into the regional economy through the production of a cash crop, as a producing economy it is still largely closed; the sale of cane provides the only important channel through which cash enters Wangala and this cash originates from one source, namely the factory. In the years when canal irrigation failed to supply sufficient water for the cultivation of cane, Wangala largely reverted to a subsistence economy.

Irrigation changed Wangala's economy from subsistence to cash, but the economy remained wholly rural. By making land more productive, irrigation in fact emphasised the agricultural nature of the economy. Landholding in Wangala is highly dispersed. 20% of the households are landless and another 20% own less than two acres of land. Prior to irrigation, the price of an acre of dry land was fairly uniform over all Wangala village lands, though there were slight variations according to the degree of fertility and convenience of situation. The village land records show that the average price of an acre of dry land in the five years preceding the advent of canal irrigation was about Rs. 150. As irrigation spread to Wangala lands, land prices began to rise rapidly. The frequency of land sales increased immediately after irrigation, though the total acreage sold always remained only a small percentage of the total village lands. The demand for land in Wangala came from three sources: firstly, from the richer farmers in the village; secondly, from richer farmers in neighbouring villages that had not yet received irrigation or were not likely to receive it; and thirdly, from the *nouveaux riches* in the nearby towns. Immediately after irrigation, the two groups of outsiders (villagers and townsmen) were the chief buyers of land in Wangala. Wangala *ryots* were induced to sell land for a variety of reasons. Firstly, the small *ryot* was attracted by the increased land prices to sell part of his holding. He was pleased with what appeared to him as a windfall profit. An acre worth Rs. 150 as dry land could be sold for double the price after it was irrigated. Some farmers sold their land because they feared that prices might drop back to pre-irrigation level. They sadly remember their mistake and complain bitterly that they had to pay many times the money they got when they bought back their land years after irrigation. Secondly, some farmers sold land because they needed cash urgently to meet some contingency. Thirdly, the smaller farmers were forced to sell part of their holding to raise sufficient money to finance wet-crop cultivation on the remainder of their estate.

Most of the outsiders buying land in Wangala were townsmen who sought a stake in the rural prosperity. But they found it very difficult to get their Wangala wet lands cultivated. Tenancy arrangements are rare and unsatisfactory for both landlord and tenant in this area of small owner-occupiers. The sugar factory refuses to enter into a contract with a tenant cultivator, because it is not sure who is entitled to the payment for the cane. The tenant therefore could only grow paddy or ragi on the wet land. Wet land requires considerable initial investment in the preparation of fields and application of fertiliser, and tenants were not prepared to make such investment on lands held only on lease. Only six Wangala farmers entered into tenancy agreements with absentee landlords and grew paddy.

There are two types of tenancy agreement common in the Mandya region: *guttige* and *vara*. *Guttige* is a straightforward rent per acre paid in units of crop or in the equivalent cash; *vara* means crop-sharing, half of the produce being due to the landlord and the other half being the cultivator's share. Under both types the tenant has to meet all cultivation costs. Immediately after irrigation the fixed rent of *guttige* was about three *pallas* of paddy per acre per year; it has since risen to five *pallas*. The average price per *palla* of paddy was Rs. 22 in 1955. This meant that the rent per acre amounted to Rs. 110, which is slightly less than the average farm wages and profits per acre of paddy. The high rent deters farmers from entering into such tenancy agreements. The Wangala farmers who entered into tenancy agreements with outsiders all had estates of their own and the cultivation of the land held on lease was secondary to the cultivation of their own lands. Therefore the yield on land cultivated by tenants was considerably lower than that on the *ryots*' own land. Absentee landlords attributed the low yields to cheating on the part of the tenant and quarrels always arose when the landlord came to collect his dues.

The case of Shrinkantaya illustrates well the difficulties of an absentee landlord. Shrinkantaya belongs to the Merchant caste and lives in Bangalore about eighty miles from Wangala, where he is a contractor. His father is a merchant in Bangalore and he himself started his career as a clerk in the Public Works Department. When he realised how profitable contracting could be, he branched out on his own. In 1941 a landbroker, who was one of his friends, told him that land was to be got cheaply in Wangala because mortgages had not been paid off. He was offered nine acres of wet land for Rs. 3,500, which seemed a great bargain. The newly irrigated land held out great promise. Shrinkantaya thought he would be able to grow sugarcane and make an annual net profit of about Rs. 500 per acre. When I discussed the matter with him once, he kept emphasising that though contracting might be more profitable 'agriculture is the only way to make an honest, worthwhile living', and he planned to retire in the country. However, his hopes were sadly disappointed. He could not get a tenant to cultivate the land, nor sufficient labourers to work under his supervision. So for three years the land lay completely idle. He then brought five Vodda Untouchables to cultivate paddy on his lands for a wage: three of them ran away and the other two embezzled money he had given them for working expenses. Shrinkantaya then approached Wangala's headman to recommend a tenant or some agent in the village who would cultivate the land. The headman recommended Chickegowda, a recent Peasant immigrant to Wangala, and Chickegowda agreed to act as agent cultivator, and to be paid for his work. Shrinkantaya bought a pair of bullocks, ploughs and other equipment and put them at the disposal of Chickegowda; later he complained that Chickegowda sold the bullocks and replaced them with a much cheaper pair. He spoke bitterly of the headman's refusal to take responsibility for the action of Chickegowda whom the former had recommended. Finally, Shrinkantaya got so irritated with all the difficulties that beset the cultivation of his land in Wangala that he offered it for sale to the headman. All the time Shrinkantaya held the land he had to pay Rs. 25 per year per acre in tax and water rate and contribution to the Government, expenses which were scarcely met by the yield of the land. In 1955 the headman's younger brother finally bought Shrinkantaya's land for Rs. 9,000 on behalf of three villagers who had owned seven of the nine acres before irrigation. Shrinkantaya had held on to his lands in Wangala for thirteen years in spite of all the difficulty he encountered in trying to cultivate the holding. Other landlords were less patient and sold their lands sooner. There was a steady increase of sales of Wangala wet lands from absentee landlords to Wangala residents beginning in 1940 and reaching a peak in 1948.

Farmers of neighbouring villages were a little more fortunate in cultivating their wet lands in Wangala. Provided they lived sufficiently near they could personally supervise the cultivation of cane or paddy, but even they found it difficult to secure the water supply to their fields. Water supply to cane and paddy fields gives rise to many quarrels, in which outsiders, even if they are Peasants, are at a disadvantage. In order to strengthen his foothold in Wangala, the outsider owning land in the village calls on caste and kin loyalties. Forgotten kinship ties are revived and caste councils revitalised. Thus, Puttegowda is a rich Peasant from a neighbouring village who cultivates two acres of wet land in Wangala; his only kinship tie with Wangala is through his wife whose sister is married to the headman's younger brother. Economic expediency induced Puttegowda to cultivate the relationship; whenever he goes to his lands in Wangala he calls at the house of his sister-in-law and often brings some small present.

Whenever any trouble arises over water supplies to his lands his wife's sister's husband represents his interests in Wangala. In addition, Puttegowda is a member of the inter-village Peasant caste council, on which there are also some elders from Wangala. Through these various links he thus tries to overcome the difficulties of an outsider cultivating wet land in Wangala. Land sales to Peasants of neighbouring villages knitted Wangala tighter into the pattern of inter-village relations within the area and boosted Peasant caste and kin ties between villages.

The landholding pattern reflects the difficulties outsiders encountered in cultivating Wangala wet lands. Only 9% of the village wet lands is still owned by farmers residing in neighbouring villages. A few years after irrigation outsiders did own nearly 20% of Wangala's wet lands, but subsequently villagers repurchased some of the wet lands they had sold. By contrast outsiders still own 37% of Wangala's dry land (see Table 2). About half of these dry lands had been owned by outsiders for several generations, usually as a result of inter-village kin ties, but the other half were speculative purchases made round about the time when irrigation reached Wangala; some farmers from neighbouring villages bought Wangala dry land expecting it to be irrigated, but have so far been disappointed.

When irrigation first reached the village, those Wangala farmers who sold land usually sold only part of their estates, so as to raise funds for the cultivation of the remainder of their holdings. Indirectly, the purchasers of the land helped Wangala farmers to meet the temporary need for working capital. But as we have seen, the difficulties of cultivating land, which confronted absentee landlords in Wangala, led them to resell after some years. This enabled many farmers who had sold some of their holdings to repurchase. For example: Kareya sold two acres of wet land to an official at the Sub-district Office in Mandya during 1940 for Rs. 650 and repurchased the same two acres in 1952 for Rs. 2,800. Kempegowda sold one acre to a clerk in the District Administration in Mandya for Rs. 400 in 1940 and repurchased it in 1946 for Rs. 900. Dodkaregowda sold two and a quarter acres of dry land in the year before irrigation reached Wangala to a man from

Bangalore for Rs. 250; he migrated to Mysore to work in a textile mill. The lands he had sold were irrigated and bought back by another villager in 1948 for Rs. 2,800.

The difference in the price of Wangala lands between 1940 and 1955 reflects both a general inflationary tendency and the way land prices have soared since irrigation. The wholesale price index for all India might give some indication of the extent of the overall inflation. With the basic year being 1939, the wholesale price index had risen to 350 by September 1955. Thus the wholesale price relationship between 1939 and 1955 is 1 : 3·5, whereas the relationship between Wangala land prices for the same period is about 1 : 10. In 1955 the price of an acre of wet land amounted to about Rs. 1,500, whereas dry land commanded only Rs. 500 per acre. Thus while the increase in the price of an acre of dry land from Rs. 150 to Rs. 500 between 1939 and 1955 was about in line with the general inflationary tendency, the price rise from Rs. 150 to Rs. 1,500 reflects the impact of irrigation on land prices. Land prices in Wangala have been fairly steady during the last few years, and the frequency of land sales has greatly declined. In fact the supply of land has become highly inelastic. Land is still the most desired object of investment, but few farmers will sell land nowadays. The few land sales that do take place usually follow the partitioning of an estate. Thus the richer farmers have little chance of accumulating larger landholdings for themselves. Some try to get over this difficulty by conniving with the Accountant and the Revenue Inspector, whom they have to bribe year by year to acquiesce in their cultivating land to which they have no legal title. For instance, there are still parcels of land entered in the village land records as waste available for grazing, but which were in fact irrigated in 1939 and so are now well worth cultivating. Kempegowda applied to purchase one which bordered his own land but the Accountant, through whom such application must be forwarded, explained that only Untouchables are now entitled to purchase land from the Government. But Kempegowda soon got over this difficulty. He now cultivates the land and gives every year Rs. 20 to the Accountant and another Rs. 20 to the Revenue Inspector. In the short run this arrangement is quite satisfactory to the Peasants who cultivate land illegally, but the insecurity of their tenure makes it in the long run a risky enterprise; their investment in the land may be lost to them if at any time the matter should become known to a higher Government official.

Another way in which a rich farmer can increase the size of his holding is by accepting pledged land from any of his debtors in settlement of a loan. Usually such pledges are given by Untouchables to Peasant farmers, for most of the Untouchables hold Government-granted land in their capacity as town-criers, drummers and so on. This land may be inherited and partitioned, but it must not be sold or mortgaged. This restriction was initially intended for the protection of Untouchables, but in practice it compels them to mortgage and lease their land well below the market rate. For example, Sidamma, an Untouchable widow, wanted to arrange the marriage of her son for which she urgently required Rs. 100. She approached Eeregowda, her Peasant patron, and he agreed to advance the money provided she pledged some land to him. Because of the legal restrictions attaching to Government-granted land, no legal document could be drafted to cover the transaction. Eeregowda simply made out a document which stated that Sidamma was to pay Rs. 12 interest per year on the Rs. 100 he was lending her. In fact the arrangement involved Sidamma pledging half an acre of her Government-granted land to Eeregowda for four years in order to cover the payment of the debt and interest. This meant that Eeregowda rented the half-acre for about Rs. 37 per year, whereas the market rate is Rs. 55. Had Sidamma been allowed to mortgage her Government-granted land she could have got more favourable terms. A considerable proportion of the Government-granted land held by Wangala Untouchables is pledged in this way to their Peasant patrons. Thus the practice by which the poorest farmers pledge their small plots to raise ready cash for contingencies acts as a mechanism to increase the size of the cultivation unit, by redistributing land in favour of the richer Peasants.

But in the main, given the present margin of cultivation, the possibilities of richer farmers increasing their holdings remain few, because land sales have become so rare in Wangala. Their investment opportunities are therefore severely restricted. Landholding has remained dispersed and no single Peasant household owns more than 15 acres, in spite of the fact that irrigation gave the richer farmer a better chance to benefit from the growing of cane and therefore emphasised economic differentiation. Irrigation might have led to a higher concentration of landholding if certain forces had not intervened; inheritance laws, the disappearance of the joint family, the practice of adoption and an increasing population set up obstacles to the accumulation of wealth over the generations. If for successive generations an estate has a single heir it will remain undivided and therefore gain in relative economic status as compared with the division of even the largest estates among several sons over the same period. Since estates cannot be tied-up and landholding is the index of wealth, economic status is much more fluid and more easily acquired and lost than political and general social status.

Property, Income and Expenditure Pattern

The relative economic status of households in Wangala changes periodically. The fortunes of a man depend basically on the size of his father's estate and the number of heirs with whom he will have to share his inheritance. Accident of birth favoured the present magnates: four of them are only sons and the other had one brother, who died as a young man. However, each of the present magnates has several sons, so that their wealth will in the next generation be dispersed over a number of households. The same inheritance laws that apply to land also apply to personal, household and house property. Thus, for example, one house may be inherited by four sons; each will form a separate household with his family and cattle and occupy one corner of the house. If one brother accumulates sufficient funds to build a house of his own he will sell his share of the common house to one of his brothers. Kitchen utensils and jewellery are also inherited and are shared among the sons when they partition, or on the death of either parent, though daughters are also usually given a share of their mother's jewellery.

The collection of data on property, which also covers non-productive property, was relatively easy: all I had to do was to compile a list of all the possible items that a villager might possess, and then enquire how many he owned, how long he had owned them, and at what price he had purchased them and, if he knew, at what price he could purchase them to-day. I enquired also how he had acquired all the items he possessed. Thus I got a complete picture of a household's property; but the difficulty arose when it came to evaluating the items of property, for I had to allow some rate of depreciation on old items, or appreciation in the case of jewellery. What I did in fact was to find out the market rate of old items, so as to check the accuracy of my informants' estimates of to-day's value of their old possessions; in most cases I found that they had been correct. In Mandya's bazaars I could relatively easily ascertain prices of old jewellery and old safes and I verified my informants' estimates there. To-day's market price of old houses was more difficult to verify. But although there are only few sales of old houses, a number of householders who had built new houses and sold their portion of their common house to their brothers, could act as guides in the determination of the market price of houses in Wangala. Here again I found that informants' estimates largely coincided with the actual prices paid for similar houses, or portions thereof. Thus I decided to accept as the value of the property the price stated by the informant as being to-day's market price for each of the items he listed.

Since I had decided to take the household as my unit of enquiry, I had to collect property details for each of my sample households[1] and therefore included households of different size, age and sex composition. For purposes of comparison I again utilised the concept of the consumption unit and divided the total property of each household by the number of its consumption units. Thus the figures I show for non-productive property are all based on property per consumption unit.

Most of my informants were most keen to find out the value of their property and, apart from those few who were eager to brag of their riches or to impress their poverty on me, they were

[1] See pp. 42–4.

on the whole honest about the number of items they possessed. But in each case I tried to cross-check informants' data with observation as well as by enquiry from their spouses, relatives and neighbours. The interest of my informants to get an idea of the total value of their non-productive property, and my extensive cross-checking of the data they supplied, lead me to believe that the error in my basic data is only small: but this is merely an impression and I have no means of substantiating it.

I have divided these capital possessions into three categories, namely, personal property, household chattels and house property. As shown in Table 6 the value of average non-productive

TABLE 6

Wangala average value of non-productive property per consumption unit

Type of property	*Rs.*	%
Personal property	79	17
House	341	74
Household chattels	42	9
Total	462	100

capital per consumption unit amounts to Rs. 462, of which 17% is personal property, 9% is household chattels and 74% is house property. The sample showed a wide range in the value of non-productive property from Rs. 10 to Rs. 1,650 per consumption unit, with the value of the modal property being as low as Rs. 300. Of the sample households 25% owned less than Rs. 200 in non-productive property per consumption unit (see Table 34). The major part of non-productive property was inherited and not acquired. Of the average value of non-productive property per consumption unit only 32% was bought with cash by the present owners; 64% was received in the form of gifts, which includes inheritance; only very little was acquired through barter and 4% was home-produced (see Table 7).

Most non-productive property acquired with money is personal property. This is reflected in a slight correlation between personal non-productive property and the economic category to which a

TABLE 7

Wangala sources of average non-productive property per consumption unit

Source of property	*Rs.*	%
Home-produced	20	4
Barter	2	—
Gift	295	64
Cash purchase	145	32
Total	462	100

household belongs, the coefficient of correlation being 0·47. Personal property is more perishable than the other types of non-productive property as it includes clothes, and therefore each individual household has to acquire items of personal property with cash. The richer the household, the more it seems to spend on personal property. There is no such correlation between household chattels and a household's economic category. This may be explained by the greater durability of articles making up household property and by their being inherited rather than bought with cash by individual households: brass pitchers, silver lamps and similar items are passed on from generation to generation. However, the lack of correlation here compared with the high correlation between economic category and agricultural capital per household—the coefficient is 0·75—throws into relief another important fact, namely, that as they become richer, farmers spend more on agricultural investment than they spend on non-productive property.

Of the three categories of non-productive property, personal property is the one that most clearly indicates the use of cash as a criterion of prestige. Personal property per consumption unit of the sample households ranged from Rs. 10 to Rs. 310; nearly one-third of all the sample households owned less than Rs. 40 in personal property per consumption unit and only 8% owned more than Rs. 160, the modal personal property per consumption unit being as low as Rs. 20 (see Table 35). Household chattels per consumption unit ranged from Rs. 10 to Rs. 190 among the sample households with 56% of them owning less than Rs. 40 and only 3% owning more than Rs. 100 (see Table 37). As I have pointed out already, most of the household chattels are inherited, received as gifts or home-produced. The only items of household chattels which are acquired with cash and which do reflect the attempt to express economic differentiation are pictures and images of All-India deities and brass or stainless steel kitchen utensils. As the household gets richer, it displays more pictures and images of All-India deities; and most of these pictures and images are recent acquisitions. These pictures and images are manufactured *en masse* in factories and are on sale at Mandya. This emphasis on All-India deities over and above the lineage and village deities reflects the greater integration of present Wangala villagers into All-India Hinduism, following their economic integration as consumers into the wider economy now that they are able to grow a cash crop.

New housing has higher priority among Wangala villagers than more and better household equipment. Wangala's richest magnate lives in the best house in the village. His is the only one that has cement flooring throughout and a Mangalore-tiled roof, though otherwise it is built in the same style as all other houses in Wangala. Between 1948 and 1954 one or two new houses were built in Wangala every year. Some of these are still uninhabited, although they have been ready for some time. For instance, Puttegowda's house has been ready for over a year, and its walls are whitewashed and colourfully decorated with paintings of scenes from the *Mahabharata*, but his family still lives in their old house which they share with Puttegowda's three brothers. Puttegowda's wife is reluctant to change her kitchen to the new house. She explained that it is all right for a young woman to move into a new kitchen but not for an old one like herself. The new house was first used for Puttegowda's son's wedding and will probably not be inhabited until Puttegowda's son sets up his independent household. Yet whether or not the house is in use, everyone in the village knows that it belongs to Puttegowda and that he has spent Rs. 3,500 to build it complete with Mangalore tiles and a cemented verandah. Puttegowda built the house above all to gain prestige, rather than to house himself—or even his son

Colourful decorations on the exterior of Puttegowda's house

PLATE VI. WANGALA

—more comfortably. In line with the recent tendency in Wangala, Puttegowda's house is built by the roadside. Shortly after I left the village two of the magnates acquired sites and started building houses along the Mandya road. It is probable that this part will develop into an *élite* quarter.

The value of house property per consumption unit varies with the size, quality and age of the house as well as with the number who occupy it. Among the sample households, house property ranged from nil to Rs. 1,450 per consumption unit; 47% owned less than Rs. 200 and only 7% owned more than Rs. 800 (see Table 36). Most of the houses in Wangala are old, in a poor state of repair and occupied by a number of families. 151 families live in 102 houses, 37 other families live singly in huts, and two huts are occupied by two families each. The price of a new mud-walled hut with a thatched roof varies from Rs. 50 to Rs. 300 according to its size. The price of a new house roofed with tiles ranges from Rs. 1,500 to Rs. 5,000, according to the size and quality of finish. The design of houses has remained unchanged and cementing of floors in the part occupied by the family is the only innovation in the richest house. Whitewashing and decorations of exterior walls of houses present the only way in which houses are used as a means of expressing the struggle for status.

Everyone in Wangala is very conscious of prices. The first reaction of a villager when shown any article is to ask its price. The higher the price of the article the greater the prestige it holds in his eyes. Villagers often brag about and 'inflate' the price they actually paid for an article when they display it in the village, but their audience is always suspicious. When Wangala villagers go to Mandya for the weekly fair they often make a point of checking the price of articles which had been so proudly displayed in the village. All presents are also immediately priced by the recipients. Those anxious to avoid this kind of scrutiny, such as the parents of a groom before the wedding, will venture to the bigger cities to do their shopping, where it is more difficult for their fellow villagers to establish the prices they actually paid.

The explanation of this extreme 'awareness' of money among villagers may be found in the recent conversion from a subsistence to a cash economy. Before irrigation cash was scarcely used in Wangala's economic life. A cash purchase was a special event, and elders relate the excitement they felt in their youth when a trader came to the village and actual cash transactions took place. They complain how blasé the modern youth are about all the things that are bought for them.

Availability of cash introduced a new element into the system of according prestige without displacing the factors yielding prestige in the traditional system; political and ritual offices which are filled on the basis of the hereditary principle are still the ultimate determinants of prestige, but cash expenditure is now used as a stepping-stone to achieving status in the traditional system. For instance, one of the magnates has managed to become a village council member, though council membership is in theory limited to lineage elders who succeed on a hereditary basis: through certain flexibilities in the traditional system[1] this magnate was able to translate his economic status into equivalent political status. His position as moneylender and his general cash expenditure helped to establish his economic status in the village, and this in turn helped him to achieve political status.

Given the superimposition of a cash economy on a subsistence economy, cash expenditure becomes an important element in prestige rating. Thus the price a villager pays for an article, rather than the article itself, becomes important. Everyone is eager to express his property in money terms, though most of it was acquired without the use of cash. Cash prices quoted for old articles are related to the appropriate prices charged in Mandya's second-hand goods bazaars. For instance, in the course of collecting property details I came across an old iron safe which the present owner had inherited from his grandfather; the owner did not know how the safe had been acquired originally, but he readily stated a price for it. He claimed that this was the price he would have to pay for a similar safe if he were to purchase one in the bazaars to-day. I checked on this and found that the price stated by the villager for his old safe tallied with the ones quoted in Mandya for similar safes. Part of the villagers' pleasure in a visit

[1] For a detailed discussion of this case see below, pp. 127–8.

to Mandya is to value their own property in terms of prices ruling in the town bazaars. This 'awareness' of money plays an important part in integrating Wangala's economy into the regional economy and it no doubt facilitated the collection of property details in an economy that still has a large subsistence sector.

In the compilation of household budgets I encountered much greater difficulties than in the collection of property details, for here villagers were torn between two conflicting interests: they wanted to impress me with their great expenditure but they also wanted to show their extreme poverty by underestimating their incomes. So in the first instance most budgets showed a deficit. But I collected three monthly budgets to cover seasonal variations throughout the year, and therefore managed to get nearer the truth. Usually husband and wife acted jointly as informants on their household's expenditure: for all items of regular consumption, such as food and firewood for instance, I noted how much they used of each item during the unit of time the villager himself indicated; thus, for example, for rice it would be so much per meal, for vegetables and other items they buy at the Mandya fair, it would be so much per week, while for other items it might be so much per month or so much per year. For items of irregular consumption such as clothes I enquired the total bought in the particular month of my enquiry. On the basis of this information I calculated monthly totals of expenditure for the sample households. I do not claim, however, that I covered fully all consumption per household interviewed, for such items as water-snakes or field rats, which are also eaten, but which the villager does not like to confess that he consumes, are not included since they have no market value. But I do believe that I have covered most marketable items of expenditure in my schedules. I tried to check informants' data on expenditure by personal observation and by enquiry from relatives or neighbours, but the many different items of expenditure and the different length of period during which each item was supposed to be consumed made an accurate check very difficult. However, the three budgets collected from each of the sample households during my one-year stay in the village exposed the worst of the inaccuracies. Prices were taken as those ruling at the time of the collection of the budgets. Thus the three monthly budgets should even out the seasonal price fluctuations throughout the year. The three monthly budgets per household were finally averaged and the monthly total per household calculated. Again in order to bring the household totals on to a basis for comparison I calculated expenditure per consumption unit.

The collection of income details was even more difficult than that of expenditure. I could not very well ask a farmer his monthly income, when his subsistence and cash income is derived from his crop harvests once or twice a year. I could get details of the household's subsistence income by enquiring for each item of consumption whether it was self-produced, bartered, received as gift or bought with cash. But to arrive at the household's cash income I had to fall back on my crop input-output details collected for each of the sample households. Also I was able to check the records of the sugar factory with regard to Wangala's income from cane cultivation. By these means I was able to work out fairly accurately the major source of cash income of sample households. It was much more difficult to collect details on minor sources of cash income, such as the occasional sale of paddy, and it was most difficult to collect details about the income of women from the sale of milk and butter. But by checking the income of each sample household three times during one year I think I have fairly well covered all sources of income and items of expenditure, and if I failed to collect all the details correctly, I suspect the error can only be small. In order to balance income with expenditure I had to calculate income per consumption unit per household. Therefore all the averages of income and expenditure referred to below are monthly averages per consumption unit of all the sample households.

As Table 8 shows, current average income per consumption unit amounts to Rs. 33, of which 68% is cash income and only 29% is subsistence income. Of the cash income 65% is derived from crop sales and 17% from agricultural labour; only 4% is derived from trading profits, and 4% from rent and interest (see Table 38). From these figures it emerges that the major sources

TABLE 8

Wangala average monthly budget per consumption unit

Income from:	*Rs.*	%	*Expenditure on:*	*Rs.*	%
Subsistence	9·00	29	Food	15·00	45
Barter	0·50	2	Clothes	3·50	10
Gifts	0·50	1	Sundries	3·00	10
Cash:			Ritual expenditure	0·50	1
Manufacturing and trading profits	1·00	3	Household overheads	3·00	10
Interest	1·00	3	Gifts	1·00	3
Crop sales	14·50	44	Interest	1·50	4
Animal products	1·00	2	Miscellaneous	0·50	1
Crafts	0·50	1	Savings	5·00	16
Wages (agricultural)	4·00	12			
Wages (non-agricultural)	—	—			
Miscellaneous	1·00	3			
Total income	33·00	100	Total expenditure	33·00	100

of income in Wangala are crop sales, subsistence production and agricultural labour. 27% of the sample households sold no cash crops at all, 58% sold crops worth less than Rs. 15 per consumption unit, and only 19% sold crops worth more than Rs. 25 per consumption unit (see Table 45). The cash income derived from crop sales is dispersed within Wangala through payment of labour among those who have no cash crops to sell.

The bulk of the average household's income is spent on food, namely 45%. Expenditure on food varies greatly according to the total income. Among the sample households it ranged from Rs. 5 to Rs. 30 per consumption unit per month (see Table 41). Variation in the amount of food expenditure represents not so much a variation in the quantity of food consumed, as in the type of food consumed. Rice, meat, vegetables and fruit are the food of the richer people, ragi or jowar balls with curried sauce, the diet of the poorer.

Expenditure on sundries, such as tobacco, betel leaves and nuts, visits to coffee shops and so on constitutes 10% of the total expenditure per average consumption unit, as much as expenditure on clothes. The comparatively low current expenditure on clothes is in line with the villagers' practice of wearing the same clothes on ordinary days, irrespective of the economic status of the individual. Thus current replacement costs of clothes are the same throughout most households. However, I must point out here that total expenditure on clothes is partly concealed by the fact that I do not include in the present budgets the sometimes heavy expenditure incurred for special occasions such as weddings. The average monthly expenditure per consumption unit on sundries amounts to Rs. 3, but the range among the sample households varied from nil to Rs. 8, with 72% spending less than Rs. 4, and only 5% spending more than Rs. 6 per consumption unit per month on sundries (see Table 42). The younger men, particularly plantation workers, like to display their economic status by smoking cigarettes as well as beedies and drinking coffee in the village 'hotelu' or the Mandya bazaar coffee shops.

The clearest expression of economic differentiation since irrigation can be seen in the rituals and expense of weddings in Wangala. Weddings used to last for one day only. Nowadays most weddings take three days and involve elaborate rituals and feasts. Weddings of course are rare occasions and therefore I could hardly expect to throw much light on wedding expenditure from the data of income and expenditure of my sample households surveyed for one year. Therefore I did not include wedding expenditure in the budgets of the sample households. Instead I was able to collect wedding expenditure for the fourteen marriages which took place during my stay in Wangala. These marriages were of two magnates, nine middle-farmers and three of the poorest households. Among Peasants the groom's parents have to carry most of the wedding expenditure, while the bride's parents spend but little. Therefore I collected wedding budgets only from the groom's parents and ignored the expenditure of the bride's household. I am utilising four 'typical' wedding budgets to illustrate how economic differentiation appeared in weddings (see Table 9): one budget represents the magnate households, two represent the complete range of middle-farmers, and one the wedding practice of the poorest.

The poorest is represented by an A.K. Untouchable household.

TABLE 9

Wangala wedding expenses for four selected households

Item of Expenditure:	*Magnate*		*Middle-farmer (rich)*		*Middle-farmer (poor)*		*Poorest*	
	Rs.	%	*Rs.*	%	*Rs.*	%	*Rs.*	%
Food	874	31	663	32	543	45	97	36
Clothing	367	13	890	42	205	17	61	22
Ornaments	1,139	40	274	13	303	25	68	25
Functionaries	103	3	43	2	5	—	—	—
Miscellaneous	383	13	240	11	162	13	46	17
Total	2,866	100	2,110	100	1,218	100	272	100

The wedding lasted only one day and was performed by an Untouchable priest from another village. The actual ceremony, which is usually conducted in the house of the bridegroom, took place outside the village Siva temple under a canopy erected specially for the occasion. Thus no decoration of the wedding house was involved. One meal of rice and curry was given to all Wangala A.K. Untouchables. The bridegroom's father bore the cost of the wedding, which amounted to Rs. 272. Compared with Peasant weddings the Untouchable one was strikingly austere, although the procession from the Untouchable quarter to the temple was heralded by a band hired for the day at a cost of Rs. 20.

The wedding expenses of one of the poorer middle-farmers compared with those of the Untouchable household throw into relief the wide gulf between the poorest and the middle-farmers. The poorer middle-farmer spent Rs. 1,218 on the wedding of his son, more than four times the amount spent by the Untouchable. All the middle-farmers' and magnates' weddings lasted for three days. The richer the household, the more elaborate the feast it offered to the village and the greater the expense on clothing and ornaments. Middle-farmers compete among themselves for novel ways of displaying their wealth, and the magnates have to keep pace. One of the magnates purchased an expensive woollen

Western-style jacket and a pair of shoes for his son to wear during the wedding. The son proudly and bravely sweated in his heavy jacket and limped his way between his house and the temple on aching feet unused to footwear. The richer middle-farmer hired an old car to come 30 miles to the village to drive the bridal pair in procession through the three bumpy village streets. Another magnate hired an expensive jeep, which was decorated with a canopy of coloured lights worked from the car battery; as they drove through the village, the bridal pair looked like a couple of images in a procession. Each wedding has a band, and the richer the household the bigger the band hired; the band accompanies every single one of the numerous rituals throughout the three days and nights of the wedding ceremony.

The total expenditure of the richer middle-farmer amounted to Rs. 2,109 and that of the magnate to Rs. 2,866. The difference between the wedding expenses of the middle-farmer and the magnate is much smaller than that between the wedding expenses of the poorest and the middle-farmer. This is in line with the general economic stratification in Wangala; since irrigation the gulf has widened between the poorest and the middle-farmers. The poorest, who are either landless or at least own very little land, gained least from the irrigation of village lands.

Another point emerges from the comparison of the four wedding budgets: the amount and percentage devoted to Functionaries increases with the economic status of the household. The Untouchable wedding household gave nothing to Functionaries, because none of the village Functionaries serve Untouchables. However, all the village Functionaries receive presents on the occasion of a Peasant wedding, whether or not they perform their customary economic and ritual functions for the Peasants. The richest inhabitants in Wangala perpetuate traditional practices even when some no longer involve economic services by Functionaries for Peasants. For instance, on the occasion of his son's wedding the magnate donated some money even to the *neerugante*, the Fisherman village water-overseer whose function had altogether ceased with the coming of canal irrigation. The Untouchable client always helps in the preparations for a wedding in his Peasant patron's household: he weaves a canopy out of strips of banana leaves and puts it up in front of his patron's house; he helps to chop firewood for the cooking of the wedding feast. These services are part of the obligations by the Untouchable client for his Peasant patron and are therefore not paid. Though weddings in Wangala have become more expensive and elaborate since irrigation and now include many novel items which represent the impact of the wider economy and culture, each wedding at the same time revitalises the traditional system and stresses the interdependence of Peasants and their Functionaries and Untouchable clients.

Every wedding involves the wedding household in expenditure which is excessive in relation to its income. Even the magnates had to borrow to meet their wedding expenses, although in theory they could of course have recalled some of the money owed to them by other villagers. They were reluctant to do this because they usually lend on a long-term basis. The magnate could meet 70% of his wedding expenses out of his available funds and borrowed the remainder from a relative in another village. The richer middle-farmer paid 50% of his wedding expenses out of his accumulated savings and borrowed the remainder from three men in Wangala and one in a neighbouring village. The poorer middle-farmer had to borrow 60% of his total wedding expenses from four Wangala Peasants, and the Untouchable borrowed 75% of the Rs. 272 he spent on his son's wedding, half of which he borrowed from his Peasant patron and the remainder from another Peasant. About one-third of Wangala's households are both creditors and debtors at the same time, and most credits and debts are limited to the village.

The structure of indebtedness relations illustrates clearly the patron-client system operating throughout Wangala's society: each of the five magnates heads a pyramidal structure of debtor-creditor relations, and the poorest form the base of it. If the magnates borrow, they usually borrow from sources outside the village. Their financial resources make it quite easy for them to borrow from institutions or unofficial moneylenders outside Wangala. They are the chief moneylenders in the village; each of them lends to a number of middle-farmers who in turn lend to the poorer farmers and the landless, although each magnate also lends directly to his Untouchable client family.

The pyramidal structure of indebtedness spreads the risk in lending among many creditors, it facilitates the turnover of money throughout the economy, and it strengthens the network of master-servant relations throughout the village. These pyramidal structures of indebtedness are linked at each level of the hierarchy with neighbouring villages through loans among kin and friends in different villages. None of the small borrowers have sufficient securities to borrow from Rural Credit Institutions which lend at 6% rate of interest. Only the richest Wangala farmers qualify for such loans. Thus the richest can borrow at 6% rate of interest and lend in the village at 12% interest. Only one man in Wangala had actually received an agricultural improvement loan, but during my stay two others were negotiating for such loans and each was a village moneylender himself. The smaller debtors prefer to borrow in their own village, rather than from individuals in other villages, because disputes over repayment of the debt or interest are usually settled within the village, whereas indebtedness to outsiders frequently results in costly and frightening court cases. Only one case of a dispute between a creditor and a debtor who were both inhabitants of Wangala has been taken to court during the past five years; all other cases are settled privately by the debtor pledging labour or land in lieu of interest payment, or they come before the village council whose members are well familiar with the financial position of the debtor and therefore usually give a judgment possible of fulfilment. In this they differ from the courts, which merely rule that a man must pay his debt, without considering whether he is able to repay it or not.

Moneylending is the major profit-yielding investment for which savings can be utilised in Wangala: it pays 12% per annum in interest and is accompanied by a number of non-monetary advantages, such as social status and availability of client and *muyee* labour during rush periods in the agricultural year. 62% of the sample households saved part of their current monthly income and 38% had a deficit in their budgets. Part of the savings on current income is eventually spent on weddings, which in the economic sense represents delayed consumption expenditure, or on building new houses. Only 18% of the households have a saving of more than Rs. 12 per consumption unit per month, but savings ranged from nil to Rs. 53 per consumption unit per month among sample households (see Table 50). Deficits ranged from nil to Rs. 11 with only 12% having a deficit of more than Rs. 4 per consumption unit per month (see Table 49). The average budget showed a saving of 16% out of current monthly income. Most of this is saved for contingencies such as weddings, but a large part of it is also invested in moneylending, or in building new houses. The average monthly income per consumption unit from interest amounts to Rs. 1 only, while the average monthly expenditure per consumption unit on interest amounts to Rs. 1.50. According to this calculation there is only a very small difference between the income from and expenditure on interest; but the average calculation hides the true picture of a few rich households deriving a larger income from interest and many poorer households paying smaller amounts in interest.

The distribution of income from and expenditure on interest among the sample households provides a better picture of indebtedness in Wangala. Income from interest varied from nil to Rs. 15 per consumption unit per month; 67% of the sample households derived no income at all from interest, another 25% derived less than Rs. 5 per consumption unit per month and only 2% derived more than Rs. 10 (see Table 47). Whereas monthly interest payments per consumption unit ranged from nil to Rs. 10, only 6% of the sample households do not pay any interest at all, another 91% pay between Rs. 0.10 and Rs. 4 per consumption unit per month and only 3% pay more than Rs. 4. The distribution of income and expenditure on interest indicates the existence of a few large-scale lenders, a middle layer of medium lenders and borrowers and many small debtors. These figures bear out the picture I present of Wangala's pyramidal structure of indebtedness relations.

Though unfortunately there are no figures available on pre-irrigation budgets in Wangala, qualitative information enables me to make the following summary points on the changing pattern of income and expenditure of Wangala households.

(1) The large cash sector represents the major change in the pattern of income and expenditure;
(2) Expenditure on food has increased considerably, which indicates a change in the diet from ragi to rice rather than an increase in the quantity of food consumed.
(3) Expenditure on sundries is a new item of outlay for most villagers who used to be satisfied with chewing betel leaves grown in their own gardens and spiced with chalk scratched from the whitewash of walls.
(4) The increase in expenditure has been considerable since irrigation, but it has not outstripped the increase in income; the average household still makes a saving on current income.
(5) Most of the savings are spent on weddings when economic differentiation displays itself in lavish feasts.
(6) Some of the savings are invested in moneylending. Indebtedness has increased since irrigation, which seems the logical consequence of more villagers becoming creditworthy.

These few points throw into relief the greater prosperity produced by irrigation of Wangala lands and its impact on the pattern of income and expenditure of village households.

Wangala's Trading Position

Irrigation has brought Wangala within the sphere of the regional economy: Wangala villagers now sell most of their produce and some of their labour for cash to buyers from outside their own village and in turn they utilise this cash to purchase the major part of their current requirements in the town. Yet, Wangala is to some extent still an 'isolated' economy, because its links with the wider economy are few. The sugar factory is the sole buyer of Wangala's cane crop and the sole employer of Wangala labour outside the village. Sale of Wangala produce to any other buyer but the refinery in Mandya is rare; there are only the occasional sales of paddy or jaggery to wholesalers who tour the region. Thus the sugar factory provides practically the sole channel through which cash reaches Wangala. Furthermore, the nature of the contract between the refinery and the individual farmer is such that he has no need or possibility to bargain; he knows in advance the price he will receive and he is free to concentrate his efforts on producing a good crop. Consequently he remains first and foremost a farmer, and does not need to bother about the market mechanism, prices and economic links with buyers outside the village. Even the nine native Wangala men who work as farm-hands on the factory cane plantation near the village are still mainly farmers. The only one in Wangala who receives a regular income from a source outside agriculture is the Muslim postman who works in Mandya.

In order to illustrate Wangala's links with the wider economy I have tried to show its trading position by compiling a balance of payments for the village as a whole. I have utilised details from input and output of crops, as well as details of income and expenditure emerging from my sample enquiry, to arrive at a village balance of payments. Thus for cash spent on food and other items of current expenditure I utilised the average monthly figures per consumption unit from which I deducted subsistence consumption. The resulting totals were then multiplied first by twelve to arrive at annual amounts and secondly by the total number of consumption units in the village so as to arrive at amounts valid for the whole of Wangala. For expenditure on weddings I took my data of wedding expenses and calculated the cash spent for all weddings held in the one year I stayed in the village. The total for new houses and house repairs I calculated from my general knowledge of what was going on in the village; I knew who was buying tiles from another village and for what amount. Cultivation expenditure was calculated on the basis of crop details I had collected; for instance expenditure on fertiliser is based on the average input of cash fertiliser per crop acre, multiplied by the number of acres under each crop.

For receipts I utilised the details I had calculated of the average output of cane per acre and checked those with the records from the sugar factory. I also computed the total of wages received by Wangala men who were working on the factory plantation. Furthermore, I made a very rough allowance of about Rs. 0.50 for manufacturing and trading profits, of about Rs. 0.50 for wages and of about Rs. 0.25 for miscellaneous income per consumption unit per month; the amount of this allowance is not based on any detailed calculation, but is in accord with general observations of sales of paddy, butter and milk and of labour working for farmers in neighbouring villages. Thus the totals of Wangala's balance of payments are not as accurate as those of my other statistics and I suppose the error may be as much as 10%. Nevertheless the figures do throw into relief the significant features of Wangala's economic organisation. 91% of the village cash income stems from sale of cane to the sugar factory (see Table 10). A further 4%

TABLE 10

Wangala estimated balance of payments for 1955

Cash Receipts			*Cash Expenditure*		
	Rs.	%		*Rs.*	%
1. Manufacturing and trading profits[1]	4,960	2	1. Food[1]	38,983	17
2. Cane sales[2]	206,010	91	2. Clothes[1]	30,123	14
3. Plantation labour[3]	8,640	4	3. Sundries[1]	28,351	13
4. Wages (agricultural)[1]	4,960	2	4. Household articles[1]	13,289	6
5. Miscellaneous[1]	2,430	1	5. Weddings:[4]		
			Food	1,500	5
			Clothes	5,010	
			Ornaments	4,780	
			6. New houses and repairs[5]	3,000	1
			7. Farming:[2]		
			Fertiliser	56,327	25
			Miscellaneous	18,930	8
			8. Tax and water rate[2]	5,530	2
			9. Balance	21,177	9
Total	227,000	100	Total	227,000	100

[1] Based on sample budgets.
[2] Based on sample input and output details.
[3] Based on calculation of wages earned by plantation farmhands.
[4] Based on calculation of wedding expenses during 1955.
[5] Token estimate.

also originates from the same source in the form of wages for factory plantation workers. Thus only 5% of Wangala's cash receipts from outside the village come from sources other than the sugar factory. On the other hand, cash expenditure by Wangala's residents outside their own village is distributed over many items at many occasions and to many different suppliers. Current food consumption is usually purchased weekly by the householder or his wife during a visit to Mandya's fair; clothes are mostly bought at the three festive occasions in the year in the town bazaars; sundries are bought at many different little stalls in the town bazaars and in a number of town coffee shops. To purchase food, clothes and ornaments for weddings Wangala's residents often venture to more distant towns such as Bannur (about 16 miles) and Mysore (about 34 miles). Expenditure in connection with houses and estates often links Wangala farmers with neighbouring villages rather than with the town; to build new houses, two villagers have purchased bricks in a nearby village; many farmers also buy farm animals and even manure or seeds and seedlings from other villages. Thus cash expenditure links Wangala residents with many different places in the region: with neighbouring villages, with Mandya and other towns as well as with Mysore, the nearest city. But all these many economic links are fluid and in no way permanent or formalised.

Wangala's balance of payments indicates that almost as much of cash income is spent on current food and clothes consumption as on improving cultivation, i.e. fertiliser, improved stock and so on. The bulk of the expenditure for the improvement of cultivation is devoted to the fertilisation of cane lands and is spent by purchasing fertiliser on credit from the sugar factory. Thus although most of the food consumed is subsistence-produce, the total cash devoted to it is almost as much as to fertiliser which is mainly purchased with cash. Another striking feature of Wangala's cash expenditure is the high percentage spent on sundries, exactly half as much being spent on sundries as on fertiliser. Expenditure outside Wangala in connection with the 14 weddings held in 1955 constituted as much as 5% of the village cash income and according to my calculations only a small margin, viz. 9%, was left as trade surplus. Although from the point of view of the Wangala community as a whole the trade surplus means money hoarded, from the point of view of the individual it may represent money saved for future investment.[1] Probably the margin is even smaller than my figures indicate, for while my data on income are fairly accurate because income is derived from only a few sources, data on expenditure may be less reliable since expenditure is dispersed over time and place. However, even if the margin is smaller than 9% it does not seem likely that the error in the basic data is so large as to hide a deficit in the village balance of payments. Wangala does pay its way in the regional economy, but from the pattern of expenditure it would appear that current expenses take up almost the whole of the village cash income and leave little for accumulation of funds. Unfortunately, no data are available on the pattern of expenditure prior to irrigation and therefore I cannot compare Wangala's balance of payments past and present. However, case histories of Wangala farmers indicate that immediately after irrigation, their consumption remained fairly much the same as in previous years, while they devoted most of their newly acquired cash to consolidating the resources of their estates to cope with wet crop cultivation. Subsequently, consumption seems to have grown at a greater rate than income and less remains for agricultural investment. Thus to-day Wangala still has a considerable area of village land, at present classified as uncultivable, which might be brought within the margin of cultivation, if it could be levelled or drained, as in the case of tank land. But apart from the Government's lack of initiative in extending the area under cultivation, even if the richest Wangala farmers were given the chance to purchase some of the tank land, they would find difficulty in raising sufficient additional cash to bring it under the plough. Consumption takes up so much of village income that little remains for further agricultural improvement. It might have proved to be in the interest of the farmers in the region, if the factory had adopted the function of a marketing board and accumulated funds for the further development of land in the region out of cane payments to farmers. The refinery does fulfil

[1] See also p. 273.

this function to some extent, for it is responsible for the construction and maintenance of a road network in the Mandya area. But it is not concerned with sponsoring the extension of cultivation or more intensive cultivation.

In this chapter I have tried to show the great impact of irrigation on the productivity of Wangala lands. Irrigation greatly increased the labour requirements for farming, but although there is still under-employment in the village, none of Wangala's residents, apart from the Muslim postman, is at present employed in the town. Stable economic relations have remained limited to the village, even after irrigation. I have argued that irrigation has helped to perpetuate the traditional pattern of economic relations in Wangala by putting more emphasis on farming.

CHAPTER III

POLITICAL ORGANISATION AND CHANGE

WANGALA has been subjected to the impact of external forces of change during the past twenty years. Irrigation was no doubt the major external economic force operative in this period, but other economic forces were affecting Wangala simultaneously with the advent of irrigation. Proximity of a growing town with a big market and alternative opportunities for employment, development of communications and the spread of electricity throughout rural areas, and war shortages accompanied by a black market, all played their part in producing the changes in the village economy described in the previous chapter.

Simultaneously, Wangala was also affected by external political and social forces: education, westernisation and the impact of the city formed the major external social forces. Political forces affecting Wangala were of more recent origin. India's newly-gained independence aroused a new wave of nationalism in the cities which was accompanied by a re-orientation towards India's cultural heritage in the villages. Accordingly, the educated city Indian now tended to turn to 'village culture' and make 'pilgrimages' to villages where previously he might have been keen to forget his rural origins. State legislation introduced revolutionary measures into political institutions: for the first time in Indian history the vote was given to all adult citizens, and villagers were drawn into State politics;[1] henceforth political party agitation and wooing of the electorate included villagers.

[1] Mysore State has had a Representative Assembly since 1887. The privilege of voting was conceded to those paying higher land revenue (Rs. 100 to 300). In 1923 this property qualification was greatly reduced and entitled persons paying land revenue of no less than Rs. 25 p.a. to vote. In terms of land tax paid by Wangala farmers, i.e. Rs. 1.50 per acre, this would mean that only a villager owning more than 17 acres had the vote. Since no single estate in Wangala has more than 15 acres, no Wangala farmer was entitled to vote in the State Assembly elections prior to the recent introduction of universal adult franchise.

The enfranchisement of Wangala villagers widened their political horizon. But since they were unused to problems of State politics, Wangala's electorate could be wooed only on the basis of caste allegiance. Although the new legislation condemns all caste differentiation, the need to woo an illiterate and politically innocent electorate reaffirmed the very system that the legislators sought to eliminate. On the one hand the Government tries to do away with caste, on the other hand by making special provisions for 'Scheduled Castes' it perpetuates caste distinction. This contradiction runs right through the whole political structure of India. The Constitution of India outlaws Untouchability[1] and at the same time makes provisions for reserved seats for 'Scheduled Castes and Tribes'.[2] The special treatment of 'Scheduled Castes and Tribes' is laid down for each level of political Administration ranging from village to All-India political representation.

Wangala Peasants now know they voted for a Peasant to represent them, though they do not know where he actually is supposed to act on their behalf; they know that the leading men in Mandya are also Peasants, and are particularly proud that the general manager of the sugar refinery is himself a Peasant. But apart from this new awareness of belonging to a powerful community spread over a wide area, Wangala Peasants are not at all concerned with State politics. Political party agents who had made frequent visits to Wangala before the election and promised many improvements in the village never came back and their promises remained unfulfilled, once the election was over. Nobody in Wangala ever looks at a newspaper although newspapers are cheap and readily available at Mandya, and State politics have no place at all in the villagers' discussion. To the villager, the State Administration appears to be completely beyond his sphere of influence: in his eyes the State is omnipotent and can allow or deny the villagers' requests, but cannot be directly influenced by them. Wangala men were completely oblivious of the impending re-organisation of Mysore State in spite of all the political meetings and demonstrations organised in Mandya by leaders of the Peasant

[1] *The Constitution of India*, as amended up to date, 1955, p. 6.
[2] Ibid., p. 104.

community to protest against the proposed scheme. One day some Wangala villagers went to Mandya and found all the shops closed. When they enquired the reason they were told that it was a protest against the suggested State re-organisation and the displacement of the Maharaja of Mysore. When they related this to villagers in Wangala no one was concerned about the political implications of State re-organisation, they were only concerned and upset about the possibility of their Maharaja being deposed. However, a few days later even this news item was completely forgotten and no one made any attempt to follow it up.

Recent State legislation in Mysore introduced universal adult franchise and elected authority into village political institutions. The latter, and legislation favouring the 'Scheduled' castes, affect Wangala's political life more directly than their enfranchisement for State elections. In compliance with the new law, election officials have to arrange and attend elections to village councils and make certain that each village council is composed of the appropriate number of members representing the various castes and Untouchables in the village.[1] Direct interference of external authorities in Wangala's political organisation is a very recent development. It operates simultaneously with those external economic forces already described. Their impact on the political organisation of Wangala forms the topic of the present chapter.

Traditional Caste and Village Council

In Wangala, Peasants are the dominant caste in terms of numbers, wealth, political power and ritual performance. Peasants form 66·50% of the total number of households, and they own 88·90% of the total lands owned by Wangala inhabitants. All the members of the traditional village *panchayat*, or village council, are Peasants; and Peasants play a dominant part in all village rituals. All intra-village disputes used to be settled by the village or caste *panchayat*, depending on the nature of the case. Offences against

[1] The appropriate number of representatives of the various castes is determined by the size of each of the castes in relation to the total village population. Seats are reserved for 'Scheduled' castes, which in Wangala involves the Untouchables.

morality or the Peasant caste code of behaviour are tried by the caste *panchayat*; other cases are deliberated by the village *panchayat*. Although the village *panchayat* in Wangala consists of Peasants only, there exists a clear distinction between village and caste *panchayat*.

The Peasant caste *panchayat* consists of elders from a group of five villages, and all cases concerning a breach of the Peasant caste code in any of the five villages must be heard by the caste *panchayat*. The wider judicial platform of elders from five villages stresses caste unity as opposed to village unity and ensures that caste offences do not become the subject of intra-village political intrigue, or faction fights; and it secures the preservation and greater uniformity of caste rules. The case of Chaudegowda *v.* Chaudamma, which took place some years ago, shows clearly the function of the caste *panchayat* as opposed to a village *panchayat* in preserving the caste's code of morals. Chaudamma and Chaudegowda were both young unmarried Peasants whose marriage was possible according to Peasant marriage rules. Chaudamma was an orphan who lived with her widowed sister. Chaudegowda was an elder son living with his widowed mother and younger brother and sister. When Chaudamma had an affair with Chaudegowda and became pregnant, the elder of her lineage, himself a member of the village *panchayat*, put the case before Wangala's village *panchayat* to induce Chaudegowda to marry the girl. The case immediately became a platform for faction fights among Peasants: indeed Wangala villagers nowadays always cite the case as the source of present factional strife or what they call 'too much party'. Chaudegowda refused to marry Chaudamma. In an open quarrel the girl threw a sandal in her lover's face. This was the worst possible insult for, his face having been touched with leather, Chaudegowda required ritual purification. He left the village and went to his uterine kin where his marriage with a girl of that village was arranged. The village was about 10 miles from Wangala and therefore outside the sphere of influence of Wangala's caste *panchayat*. In the meantime his mistress gave birth to a baby daughter and settled with her child in the house of her widowed sister. She belongs to a ritually dominant but economically declining lineage which forms the core of one major faction in Wangala. As soon as her lineage elder took up her case with the village *panchayat* the leader of the opposing faction rallied to the support of Chaudegowda. The girl's lineage elder then took the case to the caste *panchayat*. The young man's household was declared polluted by his offence against the caste moral code and he was ordered to pay Rs. 150 to his mistress and Rs. 100 to the *panchayat* fund before the caste *panchayat* elders would agree to recognise his return to caste by attending a purification rite in his household. The young man returned to his home, bringing his new wife with him, but refused to pay the penalty. He held a purification rite in his household which was attended by the elders of the lineages forming one faction, but this was insufficient to bring him back into the ranks of the Peasant caste. He was debarred from worshipping in any of the village temples and his sister's wedding was not allowed to take place in Wangala. The weight of the caste *panchayat*, composed of elders of several villages, overruled the factional support that he received in his own village. Finally, he paid his fine and the subsequent purification meal was attended by all caste *panchayat* elders: his household was once more accorded full caste recognition.

Functionary castes and Untouchables in Wangala each claim that they too have their own caste *panchayat*, but I was not able to trace a single case in which a Functionary or Untouchable caste *panchayat* actually met.[1] Untouchables do have their *panchayat* in their own settlement in Wangala, but it does not include members from other villages. It consists of the Untouchable headman and two elders. The Untouchable community in Wangala consists of only twenty-eight households so that all householders can easily gather to discuss a case when an offence against the Untouchable code of ethics has been committed, but the decision remains with the *panchayat*. Other disputes between Untouchables are usually deliberated by Peasant elders, in particular by the Peasant patrons concerned.

[1] There is evidence of a Washermen Caste *panchayat* meeting given by M. N. Srinivas in 'A Caste Dispute among Washermen of Mysore', *Eastern Anthropologist*, 1954, Vol. VII, Nos. 3 and 4, p. 149.

The role of the Untouchable *panchayat* in Wangala is seen in the case of Lingaya. Amongst Wangala Untouchables, the father must provide a feast for all members of the Untouchable community in the village on the occasion of his child's wedding. In the present instance, Lingaya had arranged a marriage between his daughter and his wife's brother's son, whom he had brought up himself. Lingaya hoped that since both bride and groom were marrying from the same household, one feast would suffice to fulfil his obligations to the community. As soon as Lingaya's plans became known, a meeting of all Untouchable householders was called which demanded that he comply with the custom, and provide two feasts, one for the bride and one for the groom. If Lingaya had ignored the *panchayat* he would have been excommunicated, the wedding of his daughter boycotted and his life in the community made impossible. In the end custom was re-affirmed, Lingaya gave two feasts but cut down the quantity served at each.

Cases which do not directly concern caste rules come within the jurisdiction of Wangala's village *panchayat*. The *panchayat* is the judicial authority in the village dealing with disputes between Peasants, between Peasants and Functionaries and even with disputes among Functionaries or among Untouchables. It is also the legislative and executive organ of the village.

Membership of the *panchayat* is made up of elders of the 'major' *votharas*, lineages. The village headman and accountant, both hereditary offices, form the link between the village *panchayat* and the State. In the Mandya area, village headmen are usually Peasants, and accountants are always Brahmins. The origin of the Brahmin's hereditary accountantship probably dates back to the period immediately after the fall of Tippu Sultan at the beginning of the nineteenth century when the East India Company made the Brahmin Purnaya Chief Minister of Mysore State. Purnaya had been Finance Minister under Tippu and resisted conversion to Islam. Under the East India Company he used his political office to favour members of his own caste. Brahmins, who of course are a literate group, became village accountants with a vested interest in the collection of taxes. The office became hereditary and even to-day the village accountant gets commission on the tax he collects. A land grant is also attached to the office, so that all accountants also hold land in the village for which they officiate.

In former days, when tax was still paid in kind and based on an assessment of the yield, accountants wielded great power in the villages. Lewis Rice wrote in 1877: 'In consequence of the capricious and intricate system of assessment, all real power had passed into the hands of the hereditary village accountant, the recognised custodian of the records relating to the measurement and assessment of land; and as no permanent boundary marks had ever been erected, it rests with them to regulate at will every *ryot's* payments.' [1] With the establishment of survey and settlement records, and the fixing of tax to be paid in cash, the power of the accountants declined and they became mere tax collectors. They still have certain unofficial discretionary powers: for instance, they sanction the unofficial cultivation of land for which they now demand a bribe, but they are no more the arbitrators in land disputes nor the assessors of tax.

The village headman assists the accountant in the collection of taxes and together they represent the village to the State Authorities: all petitions from villagers to Regional or District Authorities must be signed by the headman; he must always be literate. Conversely, he represents the State to the village. It is his responsibility to ensure that State legislation affecting village administration, such as rules about drainage and sanitation, are implemented in the village. He has also to induce *panchayat* members to carry out certain State regulations regarding local government duties and powers.

Ad hoc and Formal Village *Panchayats*

The village *panchayat* has no written constitution but operates on the basis of accepted social convention. It does not meet regularly but only for special purposes, such as to try a case or to discuss the arrangements for a village feast. Villagers distinguish between formal and *ad hoc panchayat* meetings. *Ad hoc panchayat*

[1] Lewis Rice, *Mysore and Coorg Gazetteer*, 1878, Vol. I, p. 592.

meetings involve a meeting of a few of the members to settle some minor dispute on the spot. *Ad hoc panchayat* meetings settle day-to-day disputes; they are efficient and quick. For instance, if a quarrel arises over the blocking of a village street through the parking of carts or the drying of vegetables, a few elders gather and usually manage to settle the quarrel there and then by ordering the offender to make way for the cart that wants to pass through. These *ad hoc panchayats* can also impose small cash fines. On one occasion, for example, a Peasant farmer had pulled a woman by her ear-ring and torn her lobe when he surprised her in the act of diverting water from his fields to her own. She ran screaming back to the village and her husband, a crippled Peasant, gathered a crowd to tell them that his wife had been attacked in the fields, and he pointed at the trickle of blood running down her neck. He prepared his cart, made his wife sit on it and threatened that he would take her to the police in Mandya. His wife never touched the trickle of blood now slowly drying up in the sun, so as not to remove the evidence. Four *panchayat* members arrived and settled down to discuss the case before an audience of about fifteen men including the plaintiff and defendant. The *panchayat* members made it clear that they did not approve of violence, but they took into consideration that the defendant had been provoked by the woman's prior wrong in diverting water from his fields. They unanimously decided to ask the defendant to pay compensation of Rs. 15 to the wronged woman's husband. The defendant argued that he could not afford to pay so much and pleaded that he had been provoked into attacking the woman. Finally, the *ad hoc panchayat* agreed to reduce the amount to Rs. 5 and they induced the plaintiff to accept this. The latter unyoked his bullocks, got his wife down from the cart and sent her back to work in the field. The whole quarrel had been settled within a couple of hours from its starting. The existence of an external political authority to which cases may be taken for arbitration puts a pressure on *panchayat* members, who wish to keep disputes within the village and away from Mandya courts or police, to find a solution acceptable to both parties to a dispute. Thus possibility of access to external political authority re-affirmed rather than weakened Wangala's indigenous political system; it induced *panchayat* elders to solve a dispute quickly to the satisfaction of both parties, to prevent the quarrel being taken to Mandya police or courts.

Though villagers do not specify the quorum of *ad hoc panchayat* meetings, I have never seen less than three *panchayat* members constitute an *ad hoc panchayat.* If there are only two *panchayat* elders available on the spot they try to collect another member before they start hearing evidence in a case. Thus in practice three is the quorum of an *ad hoc panchayat* in Wangala. *Ad hoc panchayats* take place so frequently that villagers jokingly refer to any group of a few men sitting together discussing something or other, as a '*panchayat*'.

Formal *panchayat* meetings are rare, and require the presence of most *panchayat* members; six members appear to form the quorum. Whereas *ad hoc panchayat* meetings are held on the spot wherever a dispute arises, formal meetings must be announced by the Untouchable village town crier and are attended by most Peasant householders; they are held in the *Marichoudi*, the village temple. Though all Wangala caste householders are entitled and invited to attend, it is only rarely that they all do so. Caste men squat on the verandah of the village deity temple or in front of it. There is no formal seating arrangement for *panchayat* members who sit intermingled with the crowd; Untouchables are not allowed to enter the temple and if any of them do come to listen they stand discreetly at the fringe of the village square.

Every caste member is entitled to express his opinion at a meeting, but the decision must be unanimous among the *panchayat* members. This need for unanimity may cause one meeting to continue many hours over several evenings. Factional differences make the proceedings of a formal *panchayat* more difficult and probably account for the many *ad hoc panchayats* to settle day-to-day disputes quickly.

During my year's stay in Wangala, nine formal *panchayat* meetings were convened. Four meetings were held to discuss the arrangements for village festivals. One meeting was called when an epidemic among buffaloes killed twelve beasts in one day and villagers had to take steps to prevent further deaths. Another was called to discuss the electrification of the village and the repair of the village deity temple. Two others were convened to arbitrate disputes, of which one was a dispute between a Muslim householder and his Muslim farmhand, and the other a dispute between two Peasants. Finally, one meeting was held to discuss the steps to be taken against an act of disobedience by Untouchables. Of the nine meetings, seven were held to reach decisions on matters in which all caste householders were equally interested, but only in the emergency of the buffalo epidemic and in the measures against Untouchable disobedience did the *panchayat* actually come to any clearcut decision; the discussion of the arrangements for village festivals in three out of four cases ended in a deadlock over the question how much food and firewood each household was to contribute and who was to prepare the food. The discussion of electrification and repairs of the temple also ended in a deadlock: no agreement could be reached on the contribution each household would have to make towards the cost of the proposed schemes.

The dispute between the two Muslims was settled at a *panchayat* meeting. A Muslim householder had employed a farmhand at a fixed sum per month, but so far had neglected to make payment; he was ordered to make good his default. It is interesting to note that the dispute was not taken to a Muslim council but rather to the village *panchayat*; the farmhand simply appealed to some *panchayat* members who convened a meeting to discuss the case. Although the Muslims in Wangala live on the fringe of the village social structure, they nevertheless respect the village *panchayat* as the body qualified to settle disputes among themselves. The Muslim employer adhered to the judgment given by the *panchayat*. He is a shopkeeper, and though he has no hereditary economic or ritual links with Peasants, disregard for the *panchayat's* decision would have been bad for his business.

The dispute over land between the two Peasants that was heard by the *panchayat* had in fact been going on for the last five years, vacillating all the time between the *panchayat* and the State courts. While one party, Kempa, had strong support among the members of the *panchayat*, the other, Timma, had successfully contested a number of appeals right up to the Court of the District Commissioner. Having won his case, Timma was entitled to police protection if anyone interfered with his cultivation of the disputed plot. On one occasion Timma's wife was planting seedlings there when Kempa and his brothers appeared and tried to stop her. Timma at once rushed off to Mandya on his bicycle to fetch the police. The police warned Kempa that he must not interfere with Timma's cultivation of the plot which the courts had ruled belonged to Timma. But in spite of police backing, Timma did not dare to touch the disputed land and shortly afterwards the case was once more discussed at a formal *panchayat*, when a compromise was suggested to divide the quarter-acre of disputed land between the two men, both of whom had already spent in legal fees at least twice the plot's market price. But the compromise was not accepted by either Kempa or Timma; both men hoped to be able to substantiate their claim to the whole of the disputed plot. Both men are middle-farmers, but whereas Kempa belongs to the lineage of the headman, Timma is the descendant of a *jeeta* servant[1] and therefore has no elder representing his lineage in the *panchayat*. His only hope of gaining support within Wangala's indigenous political system is to ally himself to the faction in opposition to the one to which Kempa belongs. This he has tried to do, but with little success; his *jeeta* ancestry deters the faction leaders from expressing their support to him. When I left the village the case was still unsettled and the disputed land remained fallow. As long as Wangala's traditional political organisation continues to function, the case will probably remain unsettled, unless Timma can be bullied into accepting a *panchayat* judgment in Kempa's favour. This case well illustrates two points: firstly, it shows that Wangala Peasants who cannot raise support within the village's political system turn to the external political authority; secondly, it throws into relief the strength of the village's indigenous as opposed to the wider political system.

Each of the nine formal *panchayat* meetings lasted for at least one or two whole evenings. These meetings are much more un-

[1] For a discussion of *jeeta* service see above, p. 75.

wieldy and less effective than the *ad hoc panchayats*. They provide a platform for the display of the political strength and support of the two opposing factions in the village, unless the meeting is convened to discuss some matter concerning the Peasants as a group opposed to some other group, as in the case of the Untouchables' disobedience,[1] or to discuss an emergency affecting all villagers, as in the case of the buffalo epidemic. If the formal *panchayat* discusses intra-Peasant caste matters, such as the arrangement of a feast, faction differences come into play, and the meetings end in a deadlock with each faction blaming the other for its unjustified obstinacy. Yet providing the arena for the display of strength by the two opposing factions is probably one of the most important functions of the traditional *panchayat*.

Flexibilities in the Customary Political System

Wangala's traditional village *panchayat* consists of nine members: the headman and his younger brother represent their lineage and seven other elders each represent a 'major' lineage (*dod vothara*). The office of lineage elder (*yajman*) and *panchayat* member is hereditary and passes in the patrilineal line of descent. If an elder dies before his son reaches adult age, the nearest agnatically related adult male takes over active authority until the deceased elder's son reaches maturity and can assume the functions of an elder. Lineage elder is both a political and a ritual office: the elder arbitrates minor disputes among members of his own lineage, he represents the lineage in the village *panchayat*, and he has certain ritual functions in ceremonies symbolising the unity of the lineage.

In theory, positions in Wangala's political structure are always filled on the basis of a rigid hereditary principle. This is the picture Wangala Peasants still paint of their own political organisation. In practice, political organisation in Wangala has considerable flexibility. This is essential in a system in which office is inherited but individual successors may not have the qualities to fill a position of political importance. It is also necessary to enable mobility

[1] For a detailed discussion see below, pp. 183–9.

in the economic sphere to find expression in the political sphere. The hereditary system still operating in Wangala accommodates accident of personality and leadership and economic mobility in two different ways: first, a temporary division of political authority may be made to resolve the problem of personal deficiency of a particular office holder; under this arrangement the office holder retains nominal authority, while actual authority vests in the nearest capable agnatic kinsman, whose heir of course has no right to inherit the political office temporarily held by his father; secondly, new political positions may be created within the traditional system and in turn become hereditary.

The character of the present headman in Wangala compelled such a division of political authority. Wangala's headman is weak and incapable of exercising the authority expected of a headman. His younger brother, on the other hand, possesses most of the qualities usually associated with the office. Consequently, the headman's younger brother has become acting headman. He is generally referred to in the village as 'chairman', for the villagers use the English word in their vernacular. The 'chairman' heads discussions in the *panchayat*: he is the one *panchayat* member most frequently called on to arbitrate in *ad hoc panchayat* meetings and he is regarded as the expert in deciding the amount of fine to be imposed on an offender. Yet all the time the 'chairman' is conscious of the fact that the hereditary authority of headman rests with his elder brother. The headman is still the one who helps the accountant collect taxes and gets the commission. The transfer of active authority from the headman to his younger brother does not bring any financial advantage to the latter and the headman is glad not to be bothered with all the quarrels and complaints in the village. Nevertheless, all villagers, including the 'chairman' and his sons, know and agree that the eldest son of the headman should be the future headman and he is already referred to as 'small headman' (*chick patel*). There is no question of the 'chairman's' son aspiring to take on the headmanship. It is too early to say what will happen to the position of the 'chairman' when the present headman dies. Evidence of similar occurrences in Wangala's past suggests that the position will disappear as the need for the delegation of the headman's authority also disappears. In the past, according to the recollection of my informants, temporary executants of otherwise hereditary offices have not created precedents for the establishment of new offices or a change in the line of inheritance to the existing office, nor has there been a decay of political offices.

New political offices within the traditional political system are created only when they are warranted by relative changes in economic status among Wangala Peasants, and they then become hereditary. The concept of the 'major' lineages (*dod votharas*) composing the *panchayat* provides flexibility in the otherwise rigid hereditary principle. The loose formulation of what qualifies a lineage to rank as 'major' allows minor lineages to claim majority status, provided their economic power warrants it. Wangala at present has eleven Peasant lineages of which eight are recognised as major: the other three are called miscellaneous lineages (*childre votharas*). All lineages are thought of as being unrelated. Every lineage has its hereditary office of elder, who, save in the case of the miscellaneous lineages, represents it on the village *panchayat*. Thirteen of Wangala's 128 Peasant households (10%) are said to belong to 'no lineage'. Most of them are recent immigrants from other parts whose lineages are simply not known in Wangala. A few of the 'no lineage' households are descendants of *jeeta* servants. Genealogies indicate that it takes at least three generations for 'no lineage' households either to be grafted on to indigenous lineages or to be recognised as a small lineage in their own right.

The number of households does not necessarily decide the status of a lineage. Two of the miscellaneous lineages have each the same number of households as two of the 'major' lineages. Since irrigation, one of the lineages previously classified as miscellaneous has raised its status to that of 'major' lineage. It is the lineage of one of the magnates, whose grandfather immigrated to Wangala. The magnate's father had acquired wealth before irrigation by acting as sales agent in sericulture, but his father was not a *panchayat* member, because the lineage branch of which he was elder was not recognised as an independent 'major' lineage in Wangala. The present magnate inherited his father's wealth undivided, because his only brother had died before his father's death, and he further increased his wealth after irrigation. Through his dominant economic position in the village, he began to exert pressure in the political sphere; his intelligence and strong character made it easier for him to establish a firm political following on the basis of his economic status. He made his voice heard at *panchayat* meetings, and since a number of the *panchayat* members were his debtors they could hardly help but listen to him. Gradually he became an integral part of *panchayat* meetings. His membership of the village *panchayat* was rationalised in terms of his lineage having become a 'major' lineage in the village. There was no special *panchayat* decision nor any special ceremony to incorporate this extra lineage into the group of 'major' lineages. His opponents in the village still talk of the days when the magnate's household was still classified as a 'no lineage' household, and they note quickly that the magnate's lineage has no part in any of the village rituals. Nevertheless, this magnate has become one of the most important *panchayat* members, next in importance only to the 'chairman'. His eldest son is expected to succeed his father in the *panchayat*. Thus to incorporate one of Wangala's magnates into the village *panchayat*, his lineage was raised to the status of 'major' lineage, while the new political position he occupies in turn is likely to become hereditary. These flexibilities operating within the restrictions of the hereditary system make it possible to accommodate the political mobility of a lineage within Wangala's Peasant caste structure; they also provide a means whereby an individual can express his higher economic status in political terms, provided he has a lineage through which he can manipulate his economic mobility in the political sphere. Thus we find that in Wangala economic and political mobility are based on two different principles: economic mobility is based on the individual and political mobility on a group. The different units involved are responsible for the time lag between economic and political mobility and cause friction in Wangala's social system, which is expressed in village factions.

Village Factions

Within the limits of Wangala's traditional political system, informal and loosely organised groups in mutual opposition form the active political units. I shall refer to these political units as factions, though the villagers themselves refer to them in their vernacular as 'parties,' using the English word. In every situation that involves the display of prestige and influence, factions become active; they are most obvious therefore during weddings, village rituals and *panchayat* meetings. In Wangala, where Peasants are the dominant caste, factions operate only within the Peasant caste. Functionaries are only rarely allied to intra-Peasant caste factions, since they are too few in number and economically not important. In opposition to the Untouchables, Peasants present a united front.[1] In everyday social life, factions play little part; except for the few leading members of the two opposing factions, who never speak to each other, members of the two opposing factions mix freely; they work for each other and they sit together at night and chat. Factions in Wangala are therefore not rigidly opposed groups, but groups which come into play only in certain social situations. I shall examine the membership and the social situations which activate factions to throw some light on their nature and functions.

Membership of factions is on the basis of kinship; the units involved are lineages. A whole lineage jointly supports one or other of the factions, or it remains neutral. In the whole of Wangala, Tupa is the only Peasant who has associated himself with a faction to which his lineage does not ally itself. He broke away from his lineage over a dispute with his father when his joint family property was partitioned. As the eldest of five brothers Tupa's share of the ancestral property was so small that he was not able to start cultivating independently. He asked therefore to be given in addition part of the property which his father had acquired by purchase. Such land does not form part of the ancestral property, so that the father is entitled to refuse the demands of his son to partition. When this happened in Tupa's

[1] For further discussion see below, pp. 183–9.

case, he turned for support to one of the leading men in the faction to which his lineage is in opposition. He struck up a strong friendship with one of the faction leaders, from whom he received financial support. His own lineage excommunicated him. At his cousin's wedding it would have been his ritual duty to fetch sanctified water from the pond to the bridegroom's household; Tupa was not even asked to attend the wedding and his place in the ritual was taken by his younger brother. Though he has attached himself closely to one faction, he has no kinship ties with it; and, since in Wangala social, ritual and political status is largely based on kinship or at least expressed through kinship, his dereliction prevents him from achieving the prestige that he sought.

Tupa originally ventured to partition from his father's household in order to gain prestige as an independent farmer. In the process he was driven into opposition to his family and so made it impossible to achieve the prestige he wanted. Even members of the faction with which he is associated decry his disagreement and breach with his own lineage. The general condemnation of a man who breaks away from his lineage throws into relief the value Wangala Peasants attach to lineage unity and shows the importance of agnation in the political system. The organisation of factions on the basis of lineage emphasises the political aspect of kinship ties in Wangala's social system.

Most of Wangala's lineages are attached to one of the two opposing factions, but there are some uncommitted lineages which vacillate between them. The hard core of one faction, which I call the 'conservative' faction, is made up of the two ritually most important, though economically less successful lineages. The other, which I call the 'progressive' faction, is made up of two of the structurally younger, but now economically dominant lineages. If I talk of economically dominant or declining lineages, I do not wish to imply that internally lineages have uniform economic status; in fact lineages are economically highly differentiated. Nevertheless, for an economically successful Peasant to achieve social status in Wangala he must act through the medium of his lineage. Thus the ambitious Peasant must necessarily redistribute some of his own savings among his lineage in the form of feasts, gifts, or loans so as to stress his own importance through the status of his lineage as a whole. Accordingly, lineages which include a magnate are to a certain extent economically dominant as a whole, though they are themselves differentiated internally.

In almost every society without a centralised authority and without a revolutionary movement, but with a number of leading men of roughly equal social status, we can expect to find factions. If there is a lack of congruence between the different criteria of social status among leading men, then the fight for such congruence will form the core of factional activities.

The main cleavage between the two opposing factions in Wangala is caused by the imbalance between economic, political and ritual status. Economic differentiation and political and ritual differentiation are based upon different principles. In Wangala economic status depends upon landholding. The size of an estate depends much upon the ability and initiative of the individual; but equally, if not more, important factors are the size of the ancestral estate and the number of heirs amongst whom it had to be shared. Consequently, through the accident of birth and death, changes in economic status must always have been part of Wangala's social system. On the other hand, political and ritual status depends on the comparatively rigid principle of hereditary succession. There must always have been therefore some imbalance between economic, political and ritual status, which found expression in the social system through the institution of factions. In times of economic expansion, such as the present, economic mobility increases, and even greater emphasis comes to be laid on factional differences. Thus Wangala villagers themselves complain that factions to-day are much more active than they were in the past. This may be partly the expression of an idyllic view of the past, but it is certainly based on some facts. To take an example: a number of village ceremonies which mark stages in the annual agricultural cycle used to be performed by all Peasants as a group, but during the last fifteen years their joint performance has become rarer and rarer. Factional differences have become so acute that during the year I stayed in the village only one ceremony, namely that devoted to Maramma, the village deity, was held jointly by all Peasants, and even this was not celebrated in the customary fashion by a joint feast outside the temple.

As I have already explained, the 'progressive' faction is composed of two of the economically dominant lineages and includes three of the five magnates. But since these lineages are comparatively recent arrivals to Wangala they do not hold any office in traditional village rituals. We find here an imbalance between economic, political and ritual status in the village and since ritual status is regarded as the ultimate criterion of social status, the 'progressive' faction is led continuously to bring its ritual status into line with its economic dominance. It utilises its political influence, which was gained through high economic status, to achieve this end. Thus whenever *panchayat* meetings are held to discuss a forthcoming village ceremony, the leading 'progressives' attempt to find some place for their own lineage in the rituals. Such attempts are resisted by the ritually dominant lineages, which form the 'conservative' faction. Because their own economic and political status has declined, they react all the more sharply to what they see as an encroachment on their traditional ritual privileges. There are also a number of uncommitted lineages which do not enter into factional alignments in the village. Two of these tend to side with the 'conservative' faction on ritual issues, but vacillate on political issues according to expediency. These lineages are economically dominant—they include the two remaining magnates—and by tradition they have an important role to play in the performance of village rituals. Thus secure in their dominant status in the village, they can afford to stand outside the system of factional opposition and judge political issues on their merits.

The process of factional opposition and alignment is well illustrated in the following incident over the Kalamma feast. Kalamma is one of the local deities, whom Wangala Peasants honour with a festival in February or March after the major harvest is over and before the wedding season begins. The feast symbolises the interdependence of Peasants, Functionaries and Untouchables, and through a ritual redistribution of food stresses the obligation of Peasants to share their harvest with the Functionaries and Untouchables. The feast also provides occasion for the display of wealth before the opening of the wedding season: individual households bring goats and sheep for sacrificial slaughter; the carcasses are skinned on the spot and the hides sold to a Muslim who comes to the village specially for this purpose; meat is shared among kin and friends. At the end of the two-day ceremony Peasants used to hold a joint feast for all villagers. In February 1955 Peasants in Wangala began to discuss arrangements for the Kalamma feast. A formal *panchayat* meeting was called but after many hours of discussion, in which the leaders of the two factions featured most prominently, they still could not agree who should perform which part of the rituals and how much each household should contribute towards the joint feast. In the end it was unanimously decided to hold the ceremony without a joint meal.

On the first day of the ceremony the Washerman prepared in customary fashion an image of the deity out of clay. He decorated it with silver plates, which he stores on behalf of the village, and placed it in a leaf-covered structure specially erected for the occasion in the middle of the temple square. According to custom, each Peasant household sent a young girl (or young woman if there was no unmarried girl in the house) to carry the '*puja*' plate, containing articles of worship, to the deity. A hereditary ritual executant officiated in front of the deity by splitting the coconuts of the '*puja*' plates brought by the young girls, who then returned to their homes with the sanctified articles. The hereditary ritual specialist on the occasion I observed was a Peasant belonging to one of the lineages forming the 'conservative' faction. He began to officiate for households of both factions fetching their *puja* plates, until a member of the 'progressive' faction made his way to the image of the deity and began to perform the rite for a household belonging to his own faction. The hereditary specialist objected and appealed to elders to stop the intruder. The latter refused to give way and invited anyone who wished to stop him, to do so by force. After a lot of harsh words and abuse, all in front of the sacred image of the deity, the leaders of both factions agreed to stop the performance of the ceremony. An *ad hoc panchayat* meeting was arranged on the spot, but neither faction was prepared to compromise. The 'conservative' faction insisted that the hereditary specialist was the only one who could officiate at this particular stage of the ritual, and the 'progressive' faction insisted that, since there were now many more households in the village, it would take too long for one man to officiate for all Peasant households, so each lineage should have its own specialist on this occasion. The meeting ended in a deadlock and each faction decided to hold the Kalamma ceremony independently. The 'conservative' faction proceeded to carry out the ceremony the following day and it was attended by all except the hard core of the 'progressive' faction. All the uncommitted lineages sided with the 'conservative' faction on this issue. Each faction secured the participation of the Functionaries and Untouchables who were only too happy to be given two feasts instead of one. The two factions vied with one another over the performance of the rituals and the number of animals sacrificed: the 'conservative' faction sacrificed only 35 goats and sheep, whereas the 'progressive' faction sacrificed as many as 45 goats and sheep, in spite of the fact that its ceremony was attended by far fewer people.

The tension between the two factions has led to a duplication of village ceremonies. The following year the *panchayat* made no further attempt to hold the feast jointly and each faction arranged its own ceremony. The same Peasants officiated again at the ceremony of the 'progressive' faction, as had done the previous year, and presumably they will now become specialists and their offices hereditary. The duplication of ceremonies thus creates a number of new ritual offices which enable the 'progressive' faction to acquire ritual status although they do not hold any ritual office by hereditary right. However, this ritual status is not yet recognised by members of the 'conservative' faction, nor by the neutral lineages. Nevertheless, the economic dominance of the 'progressive' faction adds weight to its claim to ritual status.

The 'progressive' faction insists on performing ceremonies to honour Kalamma, the deity worshipped in the traditional village rituals, instead of choosing another from among the great number of regional and All-India deities, thus signifying that it does not wish to break away from customary Peasant rituals or from Peasant unity, but rather wishes to compete for office within the traditional ritual structure of the village. During the one year I stayed in Wangala I witnessed three ceremonies celebrated separately by the two factions. In each case the neutral lineages, which include two of the economically dominant lineages, attended the feast held by the 'conservative' faction and stayed away from that held by the 'progressive' faction. Support for the 'conservative' faction from economically dominant neutral lineages adds strength to the former's resistance against the attack on their ritual privileges by the 'progressive' faction. Without such support the 'conservative' faction would no doubt have difficulty in raising sufficient finances to celebrate ceremonies in the customary manner and this might induce them to compromise with the 'progressive' faction over some of its privileges in the performance of rituals. Thus the economic support of some of the neutral, but ritually and economically dominant, lineages for the 'conservative' faction's ceremonies perpetuates factional opposition.

Support of magnate lineages for the 'conservative' faction in opposition to the 'progressives' possibly suggests that the factional differences are in fact a struggle between the magnates only, but this is ruled out by the combination of neutrals and 'progressives' in certain political situations, such as in disputes brought before the *panchayat*. Moreover, the 'progressive' and neutral lineages continue to have friendly formal relations; marriages are arranged between them, while during the last ten years not a single marriage has taken place between the two opposing factions. Weddings, like village ceremonies, are occasions when village unity is stressed by feasts for all, when villagers display their best clothes and valuable jewellery, and when prestige rating is expressed in the priority of distribution of betel leaves and nuts to wedding guests. Weddings that take place in one faction are not attended by members of the other, but weddings in the neutral lineages are attended by 'progressives' and 'conservatives'. This sometimes gives rise to difficulty. Thus the members of the 'conservative' faction faced a dilemma on the occasion of the wedding between the brother of a leader of the 'progressive' faction and the daughter of a richer Peasant of one of the neutral lineages. The 'conservative' faction is uncompromisingly committed to boycott ceremonies that take place in households of the 'progressive faction'; but they are also committed to support the neutral lineages which help them in the celebration of customary village rituals. They had to resort to a compromise: they attended the actual marriage ritual, but they refused to attend the wedding meal. The wedding household had gone to a lot of trouble and expense to prepare special sweet relish and the children of the 'conservative' faction kept swarming around, eager to pick up some of the relish, but their elders insisted that they stay away and impressed on them the deep enmity that existed between the factions.

At any one time, members of the opposing factions do not see their mutual hostility as a conflict of long standing, but each successive incident which expresses the conflict is blamed for its perpetuation. I have already mentioned that at the present time villagers regarded the case of Chaudegowda *v*. Chaudamma as the source of all factional differences. Similarly, villagers look upon the dispute over the performance of *dasayas*, or acolytes, as the cause of factional opposition. The 'conservative' faction complains bitterly that the 'progressives' refuse to act as *dasayas* in their households. *Dasaya* is a hereditary ritual office that carries low prestige among Peasants, in spite of the fact that the acolyte performs a necessary part of domestic and wedding ritual. This may possibly be because the office is a heritage of tribal custom, now being replaced by All-India Hinduism.[1] There are no acolytes among the 'conservative' faction, but there are some among the 'progressives' and some among the neutral lineages. In fact one of the leaders of the 'progressive' faction should have inherited the office from his father, but as he had also inherited land from his father's brother, he gave his younger brother a sum of Rs. 100 to become an acolyte in his stead. Because of his high economic status

[1] The totemic content of some of the rituals performed by the acolytes leads me to suggest that the office may have a tribal origin, but I have no data to support this speculation. Thurston in his *Castes and Tribes of Southern India* describes these acolytes as an occupational division within certain Sudra castes. 'Among certain castes (including Peasants) the custom of taking a vow to become a Dasari prevails. In fulfilment of that vow the person becomes a Dasari, and his eldest son is bound to follow suit, the others taking to other walks of life' (Vol. II, p. 115).

he refused to be associated with the office of acolyte; on the other hand, he is one of the men who have come to officiate at village rituals performed by the 'progressive' faction, because the latter confers high ritual status within Wangala's Peasant society. The refusal of 'progressive' acolytes to serve 'conservative' households dates about 15 years back, when a young boy of the latter faction insulted one of the 'progressive' acolytes. Compensation was offered but the 'progressive' acolyte refused to accept it and was unwilling to perform his duties for 'conservative' households. The other 'progressive' acolytes expressed their solidarity by supporting his decision. The refusal of acolytes belonging to the 'progressive' faction to officiate in the domestic ritual of households belonging to the 'conservative' faction has forced the latter to invite acolytes from neighbouring villages. Thus the faction differences have resulted incidentally in an extension of ritual relations of Wangala Peasants outside their own village.

Factions in Wangala are referred to by the villagers as 'parties', and they will complain, for example, that there are 'too many party fights'. That villagers employ an English word to denote an indigenous group signifies some relationship between the wider economic and political system and the existence of factions within Wangala. Presumably there have always been informal and loosely organised groups in opposition to one another throughout the history of Wangala, but in times of relative economic and political stability these oppositions were only of a temporary nature and did not reflect a major conflict within the traditional system. Through the impact of the wider economic and political system Wangala has undergone considerable economic changes in recent years. They have been accompanied by economic differentiation and mobility, but the traditional political and ritual system has not changed in consonance with economic change. Thus in the last fifteen years some Peasant farmers managed to get richer, but their economic status in itself was insufficient to give them political and ritual status of the same order. Inversely, some Peasant farmers became relatively poorer in the same period because they were too cautious immediately after the advent of irrigation or because they had to share their ancestral estate with a number of brothers, but their economic decline did not immediately affect their hereditary political and ritual privileges.

Thus economic expansion caused an imbalance between the economic, political and ritual status of individual households in Wangala, which created, I suggest, the cleavage between what I call the 'progressive' and 'conservative' factions. The villagers refer to these factions by the names of their leaders, which implies what is in fact happening, namely that factions are manœuvred and manipulated by a few leaders. These leaders secure the support of their lineages through kinship ties which are strengthened by political and economic relations. For instance, if a man is involved in a dispute he has to rely on the political support of his lineage elder when the case is discussed at an *ad hoc* or formal *panchayat* meeting; similarly, if a Peasant is in economic difficulties his first appeal for help is to dominant men of his own lineage.

The fact that factions are organised on the basis of kinship indicates the strength of the traditional political system, which is based on kinship. Yet, while factions are organised on the basis of kinship, they are also political groups and provide a mechanism whereby economic mobility may be translated into political and general social mobility. Oscar Lewis, in his study of 'Group Dynamics' in Rampur, underestimates the political function of factions when he says: 'It is important to note that, they [factions] are not political groupings or temporary alliances of individuals to fight court cases, although some of them take on political functions and become involved in power politics. Rather they are primarily kinship groupings which carry on important social, economic and ceremonial functions in addition to their factual struggle against one another.' [1] Lewis does not state explicitly the economic, political and ritual status of the leaders of the various factions and attributes the sharp increase in the number of factions since 1939 to 'the gradual weakening of the joint family, increased vertical mobility, with some families going up and others going down'.[2] He also relates that 'All factions operate as more or less cohesive units on ceremonial occasions, particularly birth, be-

[1] Oscar Lewis, *Group Dynamics in a North Indian Village*, Government of India, 1954, p. 30. [2] Ibid., p. 31.

trothal and marriages; in court litigations; in the operation of the traditional caste *panchayats*, and in recent years district board, state and national elections.'[1] From these statements it would appear that factions in Rampur perform largely the same function as in Wangala, i.e. they provide a mechanism by which the traditional village political system based on kinship and the hereditary principle is adapted to accommodate the impact of external economic changes.

The study of 'Leadership and Groups in a South Indian Village'[2] provides an even better basis for comparison with factions in Wangala than does the Rampur study in North India. Haripura is situated in the Mandya region; as in Wangala, Peasants form the dominant caste and its lands were irrigated through the extension of canals in 1942. The study discusses changes in the relative economic status of families which it correlates with an increased number of factions and faction fights. Both the study of Rampur in North India and the study of Haripura in South India stress the division of one caste into several factions. Both studies seem to regard the division of kin groups and temporary alliances between them as producing the same sort of groups as I described as 'factions', i.e. informal pressure groups. However, from my own study it would appear that it is not the number of factions that is important, but rather the way hostilities between the opposing factions are expressed. In any one dispute there can only be two opposing factions and a neutral one. Therefore, in my own analysis I have concentrated on the expression of mutual hostilities between the opposing factions, rather than on the number of different factional divisions or alliances.

In Haripura, as in Wangala, the conflict between factions finds expression in competition for political and ritual status: 'Some of the persons who are not from families with inherited claims for *yajmanship* (lineage elder) have attained leadership status by virtue of their wealth . . . It may however be noted that many *yajmans* continue to play the role of leaders and are invited to attend

[1] Ibid., p. 15.

[2] Planning Commission, *Leadership and Groups in a South Indian Village*, Government of India, June 1955.

panchayat meetings even after becoming poor, although their importance as leaders decreases considerably.'[1] The struggle for ritual status by Peasants in Haripura was expressed at a harvest festival when one faction ignored the ritual precedence of another kin group by driving its own animals through the fire-line at the same time. This led to a fight and subsequent court litigation which resulted in a ban on all ceremonies in the village for three years. In Haripura, as in Wangala, the cleavage between the factions stems from recent economic expansion and was expressed in the performance of village rituals. But whereas all ceremonies in Haripura were stopped through the intervention of the external administration, in Wangala the ceremonies became duplicated, with each faction performing the same ceremony independently.

In Haripura, as in Wangala, factions are not self-contained and mutually opposed groups in everyday life. It is true in both villages that there is more intensive social interaction between members of the same faction than between members of different factions, simply because faction alignment is based on kinship; members of one faction live in clusters of houses because they are also close kin. Yet apart from the faction leaders themselves, members of opposing factions mix quite freely except on ceremonial occasions. And even the leaders of the two opposing factions form a united front in opposition to other castes, to the external administration and frequently even to Peasants of other villages. Here again the picture is similar to that found in Wangala: factions are political groups within the Peasant caste structure and are therefore active only within the field of intra-Peasant caste relations; if the field of social relations widens, factional differences become subordinated to the importance of a common front in opposition to other social units.

Village and Government

Until very recently Government made little attempt to interfere in intra-village matters: the Administration was mainly interested in exacting taxes from farmers and concerned itself with intra-

[1] *Leadership and Groups in a South Indian Village*, p. 120.

village matters only in cases of a complaint or appeal from a villager. Even in the past there was legislation affecting village political institutions, but much of it was purely declaratory, confirming and validating what was already existing practice. Thus, the Village *Panchayat* Act of 1926 merely gave recognition to traditional practice when it provided that each village must have a *panchayat* and that members should be nominated by the headman and accountant in conjunction with the Revenue Inspector.

M. N. Srinivas in his paper on 'The Social Structure of a Mysore Village' emphasises the relative independence and isolation of villages in India: 'The overall political authority does not seem to have been much more than a tax-collecting body in its relations with these villages. As long as a village paid its taxes and no great crime was committed, it was allowed to go its own way.'[1] Srinivas goes on to quote Sir Charles Metcalfe, who wrote in 1832: 'The village communities are little republics, having nearly everything they want within themselves, and almost independent of any foreign relations.'[2]

Wangala has two hereditary Government officials: the village headman and the accountant. As described in the earlier discussion,[3] they represent the village to the Government and vice-versa. The headman still belongs completely to the village system; he is first and foremost a member of the village and his responsibilities to the Administration are secondary. Wangala's accountant is no longer part of the village's internal social system, because he now lives in Mandya, where he acts as writer of petitions and other documents for illiterate villagers, from which he derives an additional income. Like many other accountants in the area he had been attracted to Mandya by the demand for clerks in the growing administration of the town and the region. When he comes to collect taxes, he is looked upon more as a Government official than as a member of the village.

Politically, Wangala is still largely an independent unit: the sight of a policeman in Wangala is very rare. In fact, during my year's stay only once did a Police Inspector visit the village, and

[1] M. N. Srinivas, 'The Social Structure of a Mysore Village' in *India's Villages*, E.B.G.P., Calcutta (1955), p. 21. [2] Ibid., p. 21. [3] See above, p. 119.

then he was called by one of the Peasant farmers in the course of a dispute over a small plot of land.[1] The Revenue Inspector is the only representative of Government with whom villagers have regular contact. He is a civil servant at the lowest level of Administration. His duties embrace mainly the collection of taxes from village accountants in a ward of about 20 villages. In the eyes of the villagers, the Revenue Inspector represents Government, because the collection of taxes has for so long been the main link between villages and the Administration. But in addition the Revenue Inspector is also obliged to supervise the working of village political institutions.

The Revenue Inspector is a city man, wears city clothes and has a certain level of education. He is a civil servant, and yet he is sufficiently involved in intra-village intrigues to come within the sphere of manipulation by villagers. It is in his power to offer them certain favours: he can support petitions to the Authorities; he can turn a blind eye to farmers cultivating village waste land; he can be lax about collecting overdue taxes or entering illegal land transactions in village records. On the other hand, he also needs the willing co-operation of the villagers: his future promotion largely depends on his ability to cajole villagers into such preparations for the periodic visits of higher grade Administrators, that their village will convey, at least superficially, the impression of a keen, efficient and, in recent years, also a progressive administration. To achieve this is not always easy: weeks before the visit of a Deputy Commissioner, the Revenue Inspector has to pay frequent and regular visits in order to persuade the villagers to make the necessary preparations, for they themselves show little concern about official visits, or the need to sweep the village streets and erect an arch of welcome.

Visits of higher officials always highlight the dependence of the Revenue Inspector on the co-operation of the villagers. Immediately before such visits, villagers are able to, and do in fact, exert pressure on the Revenue Inspector, for now he is most amenable to their requests. All this emerged very clearly on the occasion of the announced visit of the Deputy Commissioner in

[1] For a detailed discussion of this case see above, p. 123.

connection with the Bhoodan campaign[1] launched by the Government of Mysore. The Revenue Inspector was hard pressed to achieve the target set by his superiors in regard to the amount of land he had to collect from each village. He paid frequent visits to Wangala and had talks with leading Peasants, almost begging them to donate some of their lands. But Wangala farmers could see no reason why they should donate any land at all when each was keen only to acquire more land for himself. However, when they realised how important this matter was to the Revenue Inspector, the larger farmers began negotiations. One of the magnates, for example, owned two acres of very poor dry land which he hardly bothered to cultivate. He had his eyes on an acre of village waste land, which could be irrigated by extension of channels from neighbouring fields and which would be a real bargain if he could purchase it from the Government. He had discussed the matter already on several occasions with the Revenue Inspector, but the latter always refused to forward the petition to purchase because recent legislation provides that Scheduled Castes should have priority in the acquisition of Government land. Now, however, the Revenue Inspector was so hard pressed for donations of land that he agreed to sponsor the magnate's petition in return for a gift of the two acres of poor land to the Bhoodan campaign. From the point of view of the Revenue Inspector, there were no Untouchables in Wangala who could be expected to donate any land, so he saw no reason why he should respect their privilege to purchase Government land, though in doing this he was of course acting against the law.

In this fashion, the Revenue Inspector had to strike a hard bargain with the richer farmers before he managed to collect a total of eleven acres of dry land. Wangala villagers do not appreciate the State's function in the redistribution of property or income: their village political system is still largely independent of the wider Administration and Government to them is a tax-collecting authority only.

In opposition to the Government, Wangala village offers a united front. This was demonstrated once when one of the poorest

[1] The Bhoodan campaign aims to solicit land gifts for redistribution.

Peasant farmers was unable to pay his overdue taxes and contribution for the irrigation of his lands. Beva belongs to one of the lineages which form the hard core of the 'progressive' faction: he is an elderly man who has experienced a good deal of personal misfortune. He had married twice, but each wife had died without bearing him any issue. He married again, but the third wife went blind after bearing him a son. Not physically strong himself, he finds it difficult to cope successfully with the cultivation requirements of his land and his other household duties and he has therefore fallen increasingly into debt.

Beva had not paid his taxes for years and at last the Revenue Inspector decided to auction an acre of his land so as to raise the amount overdue to the Government. Villagers are always interested in the possibility of buying more land, especially now that so little land in Wangala comes on to the market. They settled down in small groups to discuss the matter. When the leader of the 'conservative' faction learnt what was afoot, he declared immediately that no one would attend the auction. He argued that to bid at such an auction would be supporting the Government against a man of one's own village. Quite a number of villagers toyed with the idea of getting an acre of wet land cheaply and some tried to persuade me to bid, so as to get a real bargain. But an *ad hoc panchayat* which was attended by the leaders of both factions unanimously decided that no one should attend the auction. When the Revenue Inspector turned up he was informed of the *panchayat's* decision and the auction was cancelled. At the same time, individual Peasant farmers began to negotiate with Beva for the purchase of the acre in question; in the end he managed to borrow to meet part of his debt to the Government by pledging it for two years to a magnate of his own lineage.

The case of Beva demonstrates village unity in matters affecting the relationship between village and Government: although Beva belongs to the 'progressive' faction, the 'conservative' faction did not exploit his plight to its own advantage. Factional differences were subordinated to the need to display a united front against the Government. The case also illustrates the economic differentiation among the 'progressive' faction and the ultimate economic interdependence of richer and poorer men within a lineage.

Srinivas, writing of Rampura, describes a similar demonstration of village unity in the face of a Government order. When the Government decided to auction the fishing rights in a tank near the village, the villagers refused to attend the auction and the visiting Government official had to return without having accomplished his task. Rampura villagers regarded the Government's interference in fishing rights as 'encroaching on something that belonged to them'. What is probably more important in this case, the Government's action meant an interference with the rights of particular elders to organise ceremonial fishing expeditions. Neither intra-village factions nor caste differentiation prevented the villagers of Rampura from combining to reject a Government order which might have provided an opportunity for some villagers to score over others by acquiring fishing rights.[1]

The behaviour of Rampura over an auction of fishing rights was identical with the behaviour of Wangala over the auction of land: in both cases villagers refused to let the Government set them to competing with each other; their feeling of unity as against the Government outweighed the economic interests of individual villagers. The context of a social situation determines the unit to which a Peasant in Wangala feels and expresses his allegiance: stated simply, in his everyday economic activities he regards himself as a farmer or farmhand; on ceremonial occasions he acts as a member of a kinship unit; on political occasions he acts as a member of a faction; in his relations with other castes and Untouchables in Wangala he acts as a member of the Peasant caste; and in his relations with the Adminstration he acts as a Peasant of Wangala.

The State machinery lies outside the political system of which Wangala Peasants regard themselves as part: their political relations, either intra-village or inter-village, are based on kinship, and they consider their caste and village *panchayats* to be the ultimate judicial authority in all matters, except disputes over land. Villagers realise that the ultimate ownership of land is vested in the

[1] M. N. Srinivas, op. cit., p. 23.

State. They know full well that the State has the power to exact taxes and to withdraw the freehold from any *ryot* who fails to pay his taxes. Also the *ryot* is liable to be affected by any legislation passed by the Government concerning land: for instance, when the Government undertook the large irrigation scheme at Krishnarajasagar, legislation was passed which made *ryots* liable to pay a certain amount in contribution towards the cost of the scheme. All this makes Wangala villagers realise that their own *panchayat* has little power over tax and landholding, and that the State holds ultimate jurisdiction in these matters. This induces them to take their disputes over land to the State's courts, although as we have seen in the case quoted earlier,[1] political and social pressures within Wangala are still important forces in the settlement of a land dispute, even if a court judgment has been sought.

In matters connected with land Wangala villagers recognise the power of the State, but in all other political matters the *panchayat* is their ultimate political authority. In fact, the power of the village *panchayat* indicates a closing of the ranks against the encroaching Government. This makes it difficult for innovative legislation to be implanted in Wangala; villagers do not appreciate the State's legislative and executive powers in such spheres as public health or village economic or political organisation.

The Revenue Inspector is the authority through whom land, as well as innovative legislation, reaches the villagers. As we have seen, the Revenue Inspector is in an intermediary position: he is on the one hand part of the local Government system and a civil servant who represents Government to the villagers; on the other hand, his promotion in the hierarchy of the civil service depends largely on his ability to secure the villagers' co-operation in displaying a keen administration to his superiors. His dependence on the villagers involves him in the village political system: in his office therefore, the system of State Government and village government overlap. In this way, the intermediary position of the Revenue Inspector at once reflects the friction between the two systems, and also serves to reduce it.

[1] See above, p. 124.

The Impact of Democratic Legislation

Recent legislation demonstrates the Government's attempt to embrace village political institutions in the State machinery. The *Mysore Village Panchayat and District Board Act 1952* revolutionised, at least in the legal sense, the composition, constitution, rights and duties of village *panchayats*. It introduced universal adult franchise and substituted elected for hereditary authority; it made every member of a *panchayat* or District Board, and every officer and servant maintained by or employed under a *panchayat* or District Board, a public servant. It separated village administration from Land Revenue and Survey Authorities by incorporating it into a system of Local Government bodies ultimately controlled by a Commissioner for Local Self-Government appointed by the Government. *Panchayat* members are to be elected by all adult residents in a village, unless specially disqualified, and *panchayat* members elect delegates to the District Board. The *panchayats* and District Boards are given obligatory and discretionary duties which are mostly in the sphere of innovative legislation, and concerned with sanitation and public health, roads and buildings, schools and the like. The transactions of *panchayats* are formalised through the introduction of *panchayat* secretaries appointed by the Commissioner for Local Self-Government, whose duties are to ensure the operation of village *panchayats* in accordance with regulations of the Act.

The Act provides for a quorum for *panchayat* meetings and the deciding power of the majority vote. These regulations contravene the customary practice of *ad hoc panchayats* and the rule of unanimity in decision. The Act further stipulates the number of *panchayat* members in relation to the total village population and reserves a certain number of seats for Scheduled Castes. Within the framework of elected authority the Act retains the hereditary offices of headman and accountant, but they no longer have a claim to membership of the *panchayat* by virtue of their office, and must also be elected. While retaining these hereditary offices, the Act creates a new elected office in the form of the village *panchayat* chairman who is elected by *panchayat* members and whose duties and powers include many of those previously held by the headman.

The Mysore Village Panchayat Election Rules 1954 provide that villages with a population of less than a thousand should vote by show of hands, others by secret ballot. In the case of election to the village *panchayat*, the 'Election Authority' in any sub-district is the Amildar, the highest official at that level of Administration in the Land Revenue and Survey Department. In a ward the Revenue Inspector is the 'Election Officer'. Thus the Government utilises as election authorities officials of the Land Revenue and Survey Department, who hitherto had been in charge of all matters affecting village administration. In the previous section I discussed the relationship between village and Government in the traditional system and described the Revenue Inspector's intermediary position in this situation. His intermediary authority is also evident in his role of 'Election Officer', and plays an important part in introducing the provisions of the recent democratic legislation into village political institutions.

The first election in Wangala since the passage of the new Act took place in the spring of 1955, and I was fortunate enough to observe the process of its preparations and actual conduct. In Wangala the Revenue Inspector faced a difficult task, for villagers showed no interest in the suggestion that they should hold a *panchayat* election. He paid several visits and discussed the matter with the headman, 'chairman', and other elders. On no occasion did he visit the Untouchable quarters to inform them of the forthcoming elections and their right to seats in the legally constituted village *panchayat*. Though not himself a Peasant, the Revenue Inspector is a caste Hindu, he belongs to the Shepherd caste, and visits Untouchable quarters only when he deems it absolutely necessary. (During my stay in Wangala I never saw him enter the Untouchable quarter.) Except for the Peasant elders, no one in Wangala even knew of the forthcoming political event. Though the rules lay down that elections must be publicised in the village by affixing a notice in the village temple hall, from which in practice Scheduled Castes are debarred, and by beating a drum in the village fifteen days before the election, no notification was given at all in Wangala. Whenever I tried to discuss the forthcoming election with any of the villagers, either they disclaimed all knowledge of it, or they regarded it as another whim of Government. They saw no reason at all to bother about the composition of their *panchayat* when it had been constituted without elections for as long as anyone in the village could remember.

The Revenue Inspector came to see the headman the day before the election to make final preparations and to instruct him to announce through the towncrier that the election was to be held the next day at 10 a.m. in the village temple hall. Every time the Revenue Inspector visited Wangala in connection with the election, the intermediary nature of his authority became apparent: as Election Officer he had to ensure that the election would take place so as to present his superior officers with a list of elected *panchayats* as evidence of his ability to implement the new legislation in the villages under his control. But villagers did not share his interest, which they exploited by demanding favours; every time he broached the subject of the election he had to listen to all the demands of the powerful elders on their own behalf or on behalf of the village: 'Could one buy some Government land at the fixed rate?' or 'Could the village get another well if the election took place as the Revenue Inspector wanted it?' These were just two of the many requests put to him and to some he had to yield in order to ensure an election at all.

On the eve of the election the headman suddenly remembered that he had not complied with the Revenue Inspector's request to announce the elections in the village. He quickly called the towncrier and at about 10.30 p.m., when most villagers were already asleep, the towncrier went round the village making the announcement. It was completely unintelligible to most villagers, so, the following morning, when the Revenue Inspector and Accountant arrived from Mandya, most villagers had already gone off on their daily duties and only a few elders sat around waiting to hold the election. The Revenue Inspector instructed the towncrier to go round every single house and hut in the village and inform villagers, men and women, of the election and also to make a tour of fields near the village to call people back from their work. After another hour a group of about 60 men, comprising no more than about a fifth of the total adult male population, gathered at the village temple hall; not a single woman had appeared to vote, but a group of five Untouchables stood at the fringe of the village square. The Revenue Inspector began to explain the meaning of the new Act to the gathering and invited nominations to *panchayat* membership. Since Wangala has a population of less than a thousand, voting was to be by show of hands. The mode of election to the *panchayat* was completely alien to Wangala men. One of the elders asked: 'What good is a seat in this new *panchayat*? You cannot take it with you when you die, nor do your children inherit it.' And, in fact, the headman and a few other elders who were nominated by other Peasants declined to take office in the new *panchayat*. During the discussion over nomination, the notion began to take shape among those present that membership of the new *panchayat* would involve no honour or status, but simply a lot of unpleasant duties connected with sanitation and public health in the village. Thus names of the least respected villagers came up as nominations. Then faction opposition also came into play. Peasants discussed and fought over who should be elected, not because they regarded this in itself as important, but simply because it was one more occasion for the display of political power and influence. The nominations thus included a queer mixture of the most and least respected men in the village. One Peasant nominated the indigenous Blacksmith and later explained to me that he thought that since the Blacksmith acted as housing contractor, he ought to be responsible also for cleanliness in the village; this would induce him to build houses with proper outlets for refuse water. Another Peasant nominated Timma, the descendant of a *jeeta* servant, who is a party to the long-standing dispute over a small piece of land; it was thought that if Timma could be kept busy making sure that streets were swept up, this would keep him out of mischief and of the courts of Mandya. Others nominated elders because they seriously thought that elders are the ones who should be responsible for order in the village. Thus, the Revenue Inspector was overwhelmed with nominations and the refusal of nominees to accept office even if they were elected.

After seven hours of discussion he finally accepted that it was impossible to conduct the election according to the Act. Being familiar with the traditional political system based on kinship, he encouraged Peasants to nominate elders to represent each of the lineages. Then, to terminate the election quickly, he declared that he would accept the first ten nominations, and indeed he made a list of the names as they were mentioned and closed it as soon as he had collected ten names. The nominations included some of the traditional village elders, and some new names: in line with the whole discussion of nomination, the final choice of nominees showed little consistency. The Revenue Inspector refused to listen to nominees who wanted to avoid becoming members of the 'legally' constituted *panchayat*. He completed the election returns and got every nominee to sign or put his thumb imprint on the document to verify his acceptance of office. During the whole long discussion over nominations the question of Untouchable membership never arose. When the Revenue Inspector had completed the 'election' of caste members to the *panchayat*, he suddenly remembered that according to the regulations Wangala's *panchayat* must include two representatives from the Untouchable community. He asked the small group of Untouchables who had watched the election to come nearer and decide among themselves who their representative should be. But they just shrugged their shoulders and remained silent. Finally, the two towncriers, whose job it was to be on hand when the Revenue Inspector needed messengers, were literally forced by some Peasants to put their thumb mark on the election form so as to signify their consent to becoming members of the newly 'elected' village *panchayat* in Wangala.

The concept of elected authority is foreign to Wangala's indigenous political system and therefore had little meaning for its people; no internal changes have taken place to change the village political system, which is still organised around the hereditary principle. That the Revenue Inspector was able to compile a list in hand of elected *panchayat* members was simply due to the fact that he was familiar with the traditional political system and understood the attitudes and manœuvres of the Peasants. Had the Election Officer been a complete stranger to the village, whose promotion was independent of his success in organising the election, there would no doubt have been a greater clash between the externally stressed democratic and the internally practised hereditary principles. The Revenue Inspector realised that the names he was submitting were somewhat different from the active members of the traditional *panchayat*, and in his subsequent relations with the village he continued to regard the traditional *panchayat* as the political power in the village.

When it came to the election of the office of '*panchayat* chairman', a few of the 'legally' elected *panchayat* met, namely those men who are members of both the 'legal' as well as the traditional *panchayat*, and automatically nominated the village 'chairman', whose name had fortunately been mentioned among the first ten that the Revenue Inspector accepted when he closed the election proceedings. The chairman, however, does not function under the provision of the new Act, but remains chairman in the customary sense, i.e. he acts as headman since his elder brother does not possess the necessary qualities for leadership. The statutory *panchayat* never met as a body after the election, nor had a *panchayat* secretary been appointed when I left the area. None of the Untouchables ever attended the village *panchayat* meetings, except as silent observers sitting well apart from the caste men. The traditional *panchayat*, composed of the elders of the 'major' lineages, continues to function and the statutory *panchayat* is no more than a *de jure* authority. The only time villagers have to remember whose names were put forward at the election is when the village, as a corporate body, wishes to petition the authorities: the petition must then be signed by all 'legally' recognised *panchayat* members. In practice this means that the *panchayat* draws up the petition, which is signed by all members of the traditional *panchayat*, and when they hand it to the Revenue Inspector he reminds them that a few signatures must be added: an elder then simply sends a messenger to the persons concerned to come and append their thumb-mark. Thus the existence of two bodies, the statutory and traditional *panchayats*, makes little difference to Wangala's inhabitants; the traditional political system continues to function unimpaired by the new democratic legislation.

The conduct of the election of Wangala's *panchayat* was hardly that envisaged by the Act. The difficulty arose from the attempt of the State to revolutionise village political institutions in situations where there had been no revolutionary change in the indigenous economic or political organisation of the village. Such changes as had taken place in Wangala since irrigation are in consonance with the traditional system and could therefore be absorbed in it: irrigation raised with one stroke the productivity of land to a much higher level, but the change left economic roles and relations basically unaffected. The new distribution of wealth remained largely consistent with the traditional political and ritual ranking of castes and lineages within the Peasant caste; it therefore involved very little structural change. Changes in economic status take place within the framework of the traditional system, for they are associated with the accident of birth and death, and other factors of chance; although they have become intensified as a result of irrigation, they are still accommodated within the traditional system, largely through the mechanism of factions. Wangala has remained a rural economy which has most of its lasting economic relations within the boundary of the village. Thus Wangala is still to a large extent a discrete economy and, consequently, a discrete polity in which economic and political relations are organised on the customary pattern. The intermediary position of the Revenue Inspector helps considerably to mitigate the friction between the external Administration and the traditional political system of the village. It remains to be seen how the conflict will be resolved once the functioning of the village *panchayat* is taken out of his hands and transferred to an appointed secretary.

CHAPTER IV

SOCIAL ORGANISATION AND CHANGE

In previous chapters I have outlined traditional economic and social relations in Wangala and discussed how they have changed as a result of the impact of external forces. In the course of the discussion I have shown how economic and political relations are interconnected with what I may call general social relations, such as caste, kinship and ritual relations. For instance, in my analysis of Wangala's labour force I had to take into consideration the hereditary relations between Peasant and Untouchable households; or again, in my discussion of village political institutions and factions I had to refer to kinship and ritual relations. Thus we have seen that economic, political and general social relations are interconnected in Wangala's social system. Yet each sphere of social relations has an autonomy of its own and to this extent may be discussed independently. In this chapter I confine myself to an analysis of how general social relations, such as caste, kinship and ritual relations, have affected and been affected by change in the economic and social sphere.

Irrigation, as I have shown, has been the dominant factor affecting changes in Wangala during the past fifteen years: it led to the conversion of the village economy from subsistence to cash; it increased income and agricultural capital; it increased the labour requirements for the cultivation of Wangala lands; it also increased economic mobility and intensified differentiation. However, all these changes have been in line with the practices of the customary rural economy.

Since irrigation, the membership of the three economic categories, the magnates, middle-farmers and poorest, has hardly changed. Economic differentiation has intensified between those who own land and can grow sugarcane, and those who own only a little dry land or are landless. Thus irrigation has widened the gap between the middle-farmers and the poorest. Increased mobility has affected mainly the middle-farmers, amongst whom the process of economic and status differentiation is most marked. Since the economic categories largely coincide with caste affiliations, economic changes have not radically affected inter-caste relations, though they have affected relationships within the Peasant caste. The fact that Peasants are the dominant caste in Wangala, in the sense that they are numerically, economically, politically and ritually the most important single social group, and that economic changes since irrigation affected mainly intra-Peasant caste relations, explain and justify my pre-occupation with intra-caste rather than inter-caste relations. The only other numerically important social group in Wangala are the Untouchables. Irrigation again has had more impact on relations among Untouchables, than between Peasants and Untouchables. It is within the Untouchable community that we can find traces of differentiation, for irrigation has strengthened the economic dominance of Peasants in Wangala and therefore made it more difficult for Untouchables to challenge the status of Peasants, even in the economic sphere. I have argued that State democratic legislation, which sets out to favour the Scheduled Castes, has been altogether ineffective in altering Wangala's political institutions, and that the legally reserved seats for Untouchables in the village *panchayat* are nothing but a fiction in Wangala. Political power and economic success remain the prerogative of Peasants in Wangala.

Differentiation between Castes and Untouchables in village ritual reflects the persisting economic and political differentiation between the two groups. Functionaries are numerically not important, nor have any managed to achieve very high economic status in the village. It is difficult to say how far the relative stability in the relationship between Peasants, Functionaries and Untouchables is due to a fairly constant size of population. For instance, in some Punjab villages, population has grown so much that Peasants have no need for the labour of Untouchables and consequently the hereditary relationship between Peasants and these Untouchables has been severed.[1] It is quite possible that a rapid growth in

[1] Ram Lall Bhalla, *Economic Survey of Bairampur, Hoshiapuor District, Board of Economic Enquiry, Punjab, Lahore*, 1922, p. 142.

Wangala's Peasant population would also make Peasant farmers self-sufficient in their labour requirements and lead to a severance of Peasant-Untouchable relations. For the purpose of the present discussion it is sufficient to note that there is no evidence that Wangala's population has in fact increased greatly over the past few decades.[1] In any case, in discussing economic, political and general social changes in Wangala I have confined myself to changes that resulted from the impact of external forces such as irrigation and State legislation and have only dealt superficially with changes which are part of the system itself, such as population growth, factors of personality, and so on. I have treated Wangala as one social unit exposed to the impact of external forces and attempt in this chapter to show how these external forces affected kinship, caste and ritual relations.

Caste Composition

In Hindu society caste differentiation is normally reflected in the commensal pattern: from whom a caste eats what kind of food reflects its rank in the caste hierarchy. Various items of diet are associated with certain positions in the caste structure: meat eaters rank lower than vegetarians; eating pork or beef is more degrading than eating goat or mutton. But there are exceptions to the general rule, as I shall point out below. If two castes freely interdine, they demonstrate that they regard one another as having equal status; if two castes have a mutual ban on interdining, this reflects that each of them questions the superiority of the other caste; if the dining arrangements are not mutual, the caste which accepts cooked food from another indicates that it also accepts its own status as inferior.

According to Hindu ideology, the relationship of one caste *vis-à-vis* all other castes is strictly defined. But social reality differs from Hindu ideology. In Wangala, for instance, different criteria are employed in different situations to determine the place of any

[1] According to the Census of Mysore, Wangala's population amounted to 689 inhabitants in 1941 and to 761 by 1951 (1951 *Census Hand Book*, Mandya District, p. 128); but unfortunately these figures cannot be regarded as reliable.

one caste in the village caste hierarchy. In all political situations Peasants have highest caste rank, because they are dominant in the economic sphere and are numerically also the most important single caste. In village ceremonies, too, Peasants have most ritual privileges. Yet, according to the interdining pattern, Peasants accept the ritual superiority of the Lingayat priestly caste. However, even the interdining pattern cannot be taken as a clear reflection of caste rankings. For instance, the Wangala Blacksmiths are vegetarians, yet not even an Untouchable will take cooked food from a Blacksmith kitchen. This may be explained in terms of Right and Left Hand divisions among castes in South India. Hutton includes the Blacksmiths in the Left Hand division and the Untouchables (Holeya) in the Right Hand division:

> Between these two divisions there is a very strong sentiment of factious rivalry, leading to frequent clashes, often with riot and violence, generally occasioned by some real or supposed encroachment by castes of the Left Hand on privileges claimed as belonging exclusively to the Right.[1]

Buchanan relates an incident when

> thirty of the Weavers (belonging to the Left Hand side) joined themselves to the Teliga Banijigaru (belonging to the Right), and were encouraged by them to use all the honorary distinctions claimed by the Right Hand side. This gave great offence to the Panchum Banjigaru (a subcaste of the Banjigaru Right Hand caste) and the Whalliaru or Holeya [whom I call Untouchables] were let loose to plunder.[2]

As early as the beginning of the nineteenth century we have evidence of Untouchables of the Right Hand division supported by castes of the same division expressing their claim to superiority over castes of the Left Hand division in open fights. Thus the refusal of Wangala's Untouchables to eat from the vegetarian Blacksmith is in line with traditional practice and indicates that caste associations and differentiation is based on a number of principles,

[1] J. H. Hutton, *Caste in India*, 1946, p. 59.

[2] Francis Buchanan, *A Journey from Madras through the countries of Mysore, Canara and Malabar*, 1807, Vol. I, p. 80.

with different principles assuming importance in different situations. Sometimes all castes join in opposition to Untouchables, on other occasions castes of the Right Hand division join with Untouchables of the same division against castes of the Left Hand division or, as we have seen in the case described by Buchanan, a Right Hand caste in opposition to another Right Hand caste may support a Left Hand caste.

Cross-cutting ties between castes and Untouchables are partly responsible for the lack of a clearly defined caste structure in Wangala. Another difficulty in this connection arises out of the mobility of castes. Although in theory the status of each caste is clearly defined in relation to all other castes, in practice it is never clearly defined nor is it static. The literature shows numerous examples of castes or sub-castes in any one area, having achieved higher economic status, trying to establish itself at a higher level in the caste structure. Srinivas calls the process whereby a caste tries to raise its status in the ritual sphere 'Sanskritisation'. He writes: 'A low caste was able, in a generation or two, to rise to a higher position in the hierarchy by adopting vegetarianism and teetotalism, and by Sanskritising its pantheon.'[1] On the other hand, it should be remembered that Sanskritisation in itself, without appropriate economic and political status, does not result in a rise in status. Furthermore, Bailey has shown that the caste barrier provides an insurmountable obstacle for Untouchables to raise their status in the village caste structure. Neither improved economic status nor Sanskritisation will help Untouchables to cross the caste barrier.[2]

In Wangala, where Peasants are in the great majority and the only other numerous community are Untouchables, caste mobility and Sanskritisation are less important than in multi-caste societies such as those described by Bailey and Srinivas. Nevertheless, there is some evidence of Sanskritisation in Wangala. Thus, for instance, Peasants who have become richer and visit the nearby town more frequently are Sanskritising their pantheon. They decorate their houses with pictures of All-India deities and have scenes from the great Hindu epics painted on the exterior walls of

[1] M. N. Srinivas, *Religion and Society among the Coorgs of South India*, 1952, p. 30.
[2] F. G. Bailey, *Caste and the Economic Frontier*, 1957, p. 227.

their houses. Whenever they worship a local deity, nowadays they go on to worship one or other of the All-India deities. The one Peasant magnate who has managed to become a member of the hereditary *panchayat* and to have his lineage accepted as one of the 'major' lineages declares that he is a vegetarian. There is plenty of evidence that his household does consume meat, but he still maintains the fiction of being vegetarian and villagers respect him for it. Whether or not villagers believe that a Peasant is actually vegetarian depends very much on his political and economic influence. A few of the poorer Peasants who declare that they are vegetarian are only ridiculed: villagers remark jokingly that anyone who does not have enough money to buy meat is necessarily a vegetarian.

A.K. Untouchables deny that they eat beef or pork, and they have also begun to Sanskritise their pantheon, though local deities are still of greater importance in their household and communal rituals. Through the process of Sanskritisation A.K. Untouchables try to differentiate themselves from the Vodda Untouchables. A.K. Untouchables call Vodda Untouchables dirty and will not allow them to settle near their houses, nor let them fetch water from their own pond. In the same way castes in Wangala describe A.K. Untouchables as 'dirty', i.e. ritually unclean, and will not allow them to fetch water from the village well.

Wangala Untouchables do not rebel against the caste system, but only against their low position in it. They themselves operate the caste system against the Vodda Untouchables. They object to the big gap between Castes and Untouchables in Wangala's caste structure, but not to the caste structure as such; they want to change caste differentiation in degree but not in character. Their biggest complaint is that the caste barrier operates in the economic as well as in the social sphere. If I mentioned to them the benefits from irrigation, they simply shrugged their shoulders and pointed out that Peasants have grown so much richer in the last decade while Untouchables have remained poor. Nanja, the headman of the A.K. Untouchables, explained that prior to irrigation Peasants did not need much Untouchable labour and therefore there were fewer occasions on which Untouchable clients met their Peasant masters or worked for them. The link between them was then much more ritual than economic in nature. Since irrigation, the economic aspect has become more important. But even before irrigation the relationship had an economic content.

The Untouchables of Wangala describe themselves as *Holeya*; a *holeya* means a man of a dry field. The name indicates their close attachment to the soil. Thurston describes them as the 'backbone of cultivation in the country'.[1] He further notes 'some interesting facts denoting the measure of material well-being achieved by, and the religious recognition accorded to the outcastes at certain first-class shrines in Mysore'; and he brings out the important place Holeyas occupied in villages.

> In the pre-survey period, the Holeya or *Madig Kulvadi*, in the *maidan* or Eastern division, was so closely identified with the soil that his oath, accompanied by certain formalities and awe-inspiring solemnities, was considered to give the *coup de grâce* to long existing and vexatious boundary disputes. He had a potential voice in the internal economy of the village, and was the *fidus achates* of the patel [village headman].[2]

Thurston's account of the Holeyas shows that they have long been an integral part of villages. He relates the myth which he was given as an explanation of the Holeyas' right to enter the temple at Melcote, a place of pilgrimage about thirty miles from Wangala: it shows that even the Untouchables claim close links with Brahmins. The story goes that when the Brahmin Saint Ramanujacharva went to Melcote and found that the image of god Krishna had been taken away by the King of Delhi, he demanded the assistance of Brahmins and other castes to recapture the image but they refused, and only the Holeyas agreed to help. For this they were rewarded by admission to the temple. 'The service also won the Outcastes the envied title of Tiru-kulam or the sacred race.'[3] Thus long before Gandhi came to name Untouchables 'Harijans', or 'Children of God', they had already gained a similar name in Mysore, though it is now rarely used.

[1] E. Thurston, *Castes and Tribes of Southern India*, 1909, Vol. II, p. 332.
[2] Ibid., Vol. II, p. 335.
[3] Ibid., Vol. II, p. 332.

Even though Untouchables occupy the lowest status in the ritual hierarchy, they have always had an important role in the social system of the village, which is expressed in village and life-cycle rituals. No important ritual can take place without their co-operation. Most rituals take place to the accompaniment of drums, which can be beaten on such occasions only by Untouchables. Therefore, ritual links between Peasants and Untouchables in Wangala are still strong. Whilst economic change since irrigation has emphasised economic differentiation between Caste members and Untouchables, it has at the same time stressed the importance of Untouchable labour in Wangala's village economy. Thus while the gulf between Castes and Untouchables has widened, their interdependence has increased.

Peasants and A.K. Untouchables constitute together 81% of Wangala's population. The rest is made up of eight different castes, two Muslim households, and one immigrant Untouchable community. Two of the castes, namely the two Madras Peasant castes and the Vodda Untouchables, are recent immigrants: they are landless and, though they were attracted to Wangala by the new opportunities since irrigation, they have established few permanent ties with the village. Since they are landless they are mobile and might easily emigrate if better opportunities were offered elsewhere. It is also important to note that these marginal communities occupy a lower caste status in Wangala than they do in the areas whence they migrated. In Madras the two Peasant castes occupy positions equal to that of Peasants in the Mandya area; and even Voddas are not graded as Untouchables, for their caste occupation is stone cutting. In Madras villages Voddas do not live in a section apart as do the Untouchables. They are described as 'the navvies of the country, quarrying stone, sinking wells, constructing tank bunds and executing other kinds of earth work more rapidly than any other class, so that they have got almost a monopoly of the trade'.[1] But their migration in search of work has led them to performing tasks which degraded them to Untouchables. 'In Mysore numbers of Oddes [Voddas] are now permanently settled in the outskirts of large towns, where both

[1] E. Thurston, op. cit., Vol. V, p. 422.

sexes find employment as sweepers, etc. in connection with sanitation and conservancy.'[1] Thus occupation, ownership of land and length of residence are also important criteria in the determination of caste rank in any one area.

The Blacksmith and Goldsmith belong to the Panchala Group of castes which consist of the five Artisan castes: Carpenters, Masons, Goldsmiths, Coppersmiths and Blacksmiths. All the Panchala Castes belong to the Left Hand division, and some of them are Lingayats, worshippers of god Siva, but otherwise they have little in common. Thus, for example, while the Wangala Blacksmiths are vegetarian, the Goldsmiths are not. They also follow different sets of customs and worship different local deities. Srinivas notes the discrimination against the Smiths throughout peninsular India, and suggests that it may be the result of their attempts in the past 'to rise high in the caste hierarchy by means of thorough Sanskritisation of their customs'.[2] To understand the position of the Panchala castes in the village social structure we would need more data on the relationship between Lingayats and Hindu castes, which to my knowledge are not available. There is, however, plenty of evidence to show that Left Hand Lingayat castes have made many attempts in the past to achieve acceptance as castes equal to Brahmins. 'The Goldsmiths have long been fighting both in and out of season, and now and then in the translucent garb of legal actions against individuals for the establishment of their right to be recognised as Visvakarma Brahmins.'[3] However, this attempt to achieve higher status by claiming to belong to a section of Brahmins is obviously not just peculiar to the Panchala castes.

The Bedars [a cultivator caste] set themselves up as Valmiki Brahmins, claiming direct descent from the celebrated author of the Ramayana, the Potters described themselves as Gundu or round Brahmins and piling on the agony, the Madigas or chucklers [Untouchables] as Matanga Brahmins, whipping out for the occasion a certain so-called Purana as their charter. Indeed, it is a significant

[1] E. Thurston, op. cit., Vol. V, p. 424.

[2] M. N. Srinivas, 'The Social System of a Mysore Village', *Village India*, p. 24.

[3] *Census of India*, 1891, Vol. XXV, Part I, Mysore, p. 239.

feature of the upheaval and ferment just now going on among the Hindus that while every fragmentary body is anxious to level down the caste heights above, it is most repugnant to the obliteration of inequality below.[1]

The relationship between a caste and its inferiors on the one hand, and its superiors on the other, is still a characteristic of caste differentiation. Therefore, there is always a difference between the status which a caste ascribes to itself and the status which others accord it. Nor is there general consensus about the status of any one caste in the caste hierarchy, except for recognising Brahmins as the highest and Untouchables as the lowest caste.

Relativity of caste status is an important factor in the mobility of castes. For instance, Potters in Wangala used to regard themselves as equals to Peasants, and refused to dine in Peasant houses. Peasants, on the other hand, regarded Potters as inferior and refused to eat from Potters' houses, while the lower castes, such as the Washermen and Barbers, thought that Potters were only slightly below Peasants. In recent years Potters have established themselves as farmers and Peasants have come to regard them more as their equals. Men of the two castes now interdine, though their womenfolk still refrain from interdining. A leading Peasant, belonging to one of the ritually dominant lineages of the 'conservative' faction, has an extra-marital alliance with a Potter widow: it is an open secret that he walks the length of one of the village streets every night to visit his Potter mistress and takes his food with her. He cultivates her lands, since her children are still small and there is no adult male to help her. The affair has now lasted for several years. Caste endogamy prevents the Peasant from taking her as his second wife, but the Peasants of Wangala acquiesce in this inter-caste liaison. Their acceptance of the situation reflects Peasant recognition of Potters as a caste similar in status to their own, and indicates a narrowing of the structural distance between Potters and Peasants, seen from the latter's point of view.

The Washerman caste and Fisherman caste each regards itself as of higher status than the other, and mutually refuses to interdine.

[1] Ibid., p. 240.

None of the other castes, not even the Untouchables, take food from a Washerman or Fisherman kitchen. The Fisherman caste was important as long as the office of tank irrigation overseer rested with one of the village Fishermen; since irrigation this office has lost importance and Fishermen in Wangala have tended to strengthen their kin ties with Fishermen in nearby villages where they are in the majority. They seek economic advantages and higher prestige through their relations with their own caste men in villages where they are economically and politically important, if not dominant, and do not struggle for higher status within Wangala's caste structure.

Washermen still perform certain hereditary functions in Peasant rituals: when a Peasant girl reaches puberty after her betrothal, it is the Washerman's duty to carry the news to the husband's parents together with offerings from the girl's parents. At weddings, the Washerman has to lay down saris on which the people walk in the procession. He also carries the *devaru pettige*, or god's box, containing certain sacred objects. Furthermore, he has to prepare the clothes for dressing a body before burial. While Wangala Washermen still perform their hereditary functions in Peasant and village rituals, their economic functions have lost importance. Many Peasant women now wash their family's clothes and a number of men have their shirts washed and ironed in Mandya. Two of the three adult male Washermen in the village work as farm labourers on the factory cane plantation. Neither wants to act as Washerman; they hope one day to be able to acquire more land and become farmers. They have struck up close friendship with the young Peasants of Wangala and other surrounding villages who also work on the factory plantation. Among these plantation workers caste differentiation plays little part: they walk together to work, sit together at night and chat, and walk or cycle together to Mandya. At the same time, even here Peasants will not take food from the kitchen of the Washermen. Similarly, the Peasant factory plantation workers all sided with the *panchayat* in the case of a young Washerman, a plantation labourer, having an illicit affair with the widowed sister of one of the Peasants. She had returned home from her husband's village after his death and got a job at the factory plantation. When the affair between her and the Washerman became known, a group of Peasants decided to trap the lovers and catch them in *flagrante delicto*. Thus the case eventually came before the village *panchayat* where the Washerman was fined Rs. 100 and his Peasant mistress outcast. For a Peasant woman to demean herself by having illicit relations with a low caste man is regarded by Peasants as an unpardonable offence.

Peasants regard themselves as superior to all other castes in Wangala except for the Aradya, the Lingayat Priestly caste. Thurston describes Aradyas as a 'sect of Brahmins, although they differ in almost every important respect from other Brahmins. Aradyas are worshippers of Siva, they wear both the Brahminical sacred thread and the linga suspended from another thread.'[1]

Wangala's three Lingayat Priestly families constitute 1·7% of the village households and own 1·4% of the village lands. In terms of economic status they are middle-farmers. One elder of the Lingayat Priests is *Guru* to the headman's lineage in Wangala; he is consulted by members of this lineage whenever a marriage is being arranged, or a ritual or ceremony has to be planned. In return he receives annual paddy gifts from the headman's lineage as well as gifts of raw food at ceremonies. From accounts of the past, it appears that the Lingayat Priests used to be more important in Wangala than they are today. Nowadays Peasants turn more to a Brahmin Priest for advice on horoscopes and auspicious dates than to their Lingayat Priestly *Guru*. The *Gurus* complain about the way their flock has turned away from them. *Gurus* of other Wangala lineages, who do not themselves live in the village, have to come on tour through the villages under their influence in order to collect their customary share of the harvest. The transfer of allegiance from Lingayat *Gurus* to Brahmin Priests is a sign of the Peasants' greater integration into All-India Hinduism.

Though the Lingayat Priests occupy the highest position in Wangala's caste structure, Peasants are the dominant caste in village rituals. Village rituals illustrate the total dominance of Peasants in all spheres of social life. The priests who officiate at

[1] E. Thurston, op. cit., Vol. I, p. 53.

the two temples of the All-India deities come from the neighbouring village; they belong to the Lingayat Priestly caste. But at the village deity temple, Wangala's Peasants officiate in ceremonies. None of the other castes are sufficiently successful in the economic sphere to challenge the dominance of the Peasants in Wangala's caste structure.

Intra-Caste Relations

Members of one caste are in Wangala linked together through the operation of a number of different principles: they are linked by kinship and marriage, by age groups, or by friendships between individuals, by creditor-debtor relations, and they form groups who exchange labour. In the political and ritual sphere, kinship is the dominant principle in intra-caste relations. Kinship and marriage ties also link men and women in Wangala with a wider circle of members of their own caste living in surrounding villages; these ties therefore also provide the avenues for inter-village political and economic relations. They also stress the principle of caste loyalty as opposed to village loyalty. In village ceremonies the co-operation of all castes and Untouchables symbolises the village as a unit composed of interdependent castes, whereas lineage ceremonies symbolise the unity of members of the same caste living in different villages.

The network of recognised kinship and marriage ties of each of Wangala's Peasant lineages stretches over a radius of about 20 miles, and links Wangala Peasants with many different villages. Of 142 existing marriages, i.e. marriages where both parties were alive at the time of the census, 54% were between men from Wangala and women from other villages, 37% intra-village, 4% uxorilocal, and the remainder involved immigrant families. Uxorilocal marriages were rare and occurred only when there were no sons to carry on the estate and a son-in-law was 'adopted' to inherit the ancestral property. The children of such uxorilocal marriages were regarded as belonging to their maternal, rather than their paternal, lineage and they worshipped the deity of their mother's agnatic kin. According to the generally accepted principle of agnatic descent they should, of course, fall into the category of 'outsiders'. This does not happen: instead the husband who is brought in from another village is grafted on to the lineage of his wife. However, grafting of this kind does not take place when a man holding hereditary political or ritual office has no male heir. In such cases, straight adoption is practised. In fact, adoption is very frequent among Wangala's Peasants. Adoption and uxorilocal marriage are the devices which uphold the principle of agnatic descent where its rigid application would involve the dying out of a family branch when there is no male heir.

A comparison between the marriages of Wangala Peasants, which I recorded in genealogies traced over four generations, and the existing marriages, shows that 54% of the existing marriages were contracted between native Peasants from Wangala and women from other villages, whereas as much as 85% of the recorded marriages (excluding existent marriages) were inter-village unions. This trend towards a greater concentration of marriage ties within the village may be explained by two factors: first, newcomers to the village and second generation immigrants of the miscellaneous lineages have increased the circle of potential spouses for the exogamous group of indigenous lineages; secondly, since irrigation, the cultivation of cane absorbs so much of the time of Wangala farmers, that they have now little opportunity for touring neighbouring villages to arrange marriages for their sons. At the same time, the trend in the marriage pattern reflects the greater concentration of interest of Wangala farmers on their own land and on their own village economy. Nowadays initiators of inter-village marriages are usually Peasants from neighbouring villages who are keen to strengthen their economic links with Wangala by kinship ties.

At a time when the growing of a cash crop has integrated Wangala's economy, at least to a certain extent, into the regional economy and polity, intra-village marriages have strengthened the network of intra-village relations. These two contradictory processes are going on simultaneously, and they are responsible for a curious blend of traditional practice and innovation in Peasant ceremonies in Wangala. Traditional wedding practice, for instance, is represented by Peasant ritual and the officiation of a Brahmin priest, innovation in the procession of the bridal couple by jeep through the village, and the Western-style dress of the bridegroom. Such innovations involve expenditure of cash, whereas the traditional services are paid for in kind according to custom laid down among Peasants.

The practice of cross-cousin marriage, and marriages to other near kin, was never very general and, like inter-village marriage, is becoming even rarer. Of existing marriages 1% are between a man and his sister's daughter, 1% between a man and his father's sister's daughter, and another 2% are between a man and his mother's brother's daughter, whereas the respective percentages of recorded marriages (excluding existent marriages) are 9%, 7% and 14%. It is likely that the actual percentage of cross-cousin links among recorded marriages may be even higher than I managed to trace, because informants forget cross-cousin links among their ancestors. Most of the recorded and existing cross-cousin marriages are inter-village unions. Therefore it is logical that fewer cross-cousin marriages should take place nowadays, since fewer inter-village unions are formed.

From the details of cross-cousin marriages, it also appears that Peasants in Wangala do not differentiate between matrilateral and patrilateral cross-cousin marriages; either may take place in the course of a reaffirmation of a kinship bond between two lineages of the same or different villages. If we remember at this stage in the argument that Peasants pay bride-price, it becomes clear that we cannot generalise in any way about the relationship between bride-price and cross-cousin marriage. However, there are certain facts which point to a preference for patrilateral cross-cousin marriage in the past. For instance, Peasants themselves explain that the bride's mother's brother gives the bride away under the marriage canopy in order to show that he has declined to marry her himself or to marry her to his own son. But, they say, this act is only a relic of the past, when the village was smaller and cross-cousin marriage more frequent. The practice of marrying a sister's daughter or one's father's sister's daughter is referred to as 'a cow begets a calf', for the bride-price received for the mother is returned when the daughter marries: it is as if a man buys a cow and sells its calf. The disappearance of patrilateral cross-cousin marriage among Peasants in Wangala may be due to the fact that the amount of the bride-price actually paid in cash at the wedding ceremony has remained unchanged and therefore its importance has declined with the increased use of cash in the village economy. The important part played by the bride's mother's brother in the wedding ritual on the other hand still symbolises the importance of matrilateral kin in what is, according to Wangala ideology, a patrilineal society.

The radius of inter-village Peasant marriage ties reflects the narrow range of Wangala's inter-village economic, political and general social ties: 50% of the existing marriages between a native Peasant of Wangala and a woman from another village are restricted to villages within a radius of 4 miles; 82% are within a radius of 10 miles and only 9% are outside a radius of 20 miles. The marriages contracted between Wangala Peasants and women from villages outside a radius of 20 miles stem from the migration of Wangala Peasants. Prior to irrigation a number of Peasants had migrated to Mysore to work in the textile mill, or even as far as the *Malnad*, the hilly part of Mysore, to work on tea or coffee plantations. The contacts these emigrants made with Peasants of the same sub-caste at the places to which they migrated led to a number of marriages between Wangala men and women from more distant villages. Since irrigation, all except one Peasant migrant from Wangala have returned to the village; their womenfolk still keep in touch with their distant relatives and have arranged a number of marriages to strengthen the bond between Wangala and their own native places.

Wangala's Peasant caste is composed of two exogamous clans, called '*palu*' in the vernacular, and a number of miscellaneous or '*childre*' lineages for which the lineage is the exogamous group. Each clan or '*palu*' consists of a number of maximal lineages, called '*votaras*' or '*tendes*'. The two clans are called in the vernacular '*ganhalli palu*' and '*henhalli palu*', which mean literally the man's village party and the woman's village party; the same words are used in the vernacular to denote respectively the group of people accompanying the groom and his bride at a wedding. In my discussion of the clans, I shall refer to them as 'Male' and 'Female'. The two clans intermarry: brides pass from the Male to the Female clan and vice versa. The two clans also intermarry with some lineages of the miscellaneous group, which do not belong to either clan, but most of the intra-village marriages are inter-clan unions. One lineage of the male clan claims to be the founder lineage of the village and justifies its claim by relating the mythical origin of the village.

Many centuries ago a Peasant called Mallegowda (the name of the founder lineage) came to the site of what is now Wangala. There were no people living there then so he settled with his wife to cultivate the land. One day when he was ploughing a field he struck what he thought was a stone, but it turned out to be a *lingam*, the symbol of the All-India deity Siva. The *lingam* grew to the full size of Siva, and Siva spoke to Mallegowda and demanded that a temple should be erected to the worship of Siva within one night at the very spot where Mallegowda had struck the idol. Mallegowda set about building the temple immediately and Siva gave them such strength that he and his wife actually managed to complete the temple structure overnight and the idol, which had shrunk again to its former size, was placed in it. The temple still stands on the same spot, well outside the village, and the elder of Mallegowda's lineage walks daily to worship Siva at the temple.

The first Mallegowda had two sons and one daughter. His sons married girls from neighbouring settlements, but Mallegowda did not want his daughter to move to another place to settle with a husband. One day a young Peasant from Melcote, a place of pilgrimage about 30 miles from Wangala, passed by Mallegowda's house where he was offered hospitality. Mallegowda asked him to stay and eventually suggested that if he married his daughter, he would be given the right to cultivate the last fields within reach of cultivation from Mallegowda's settlement. The young Peasant agreed to this and the offspring of his union with Mallegowda's daughter form what is still called the '*Kadeholade*' or 'last-field' lineage. Mallegowda's lineage forms the core of the Male clan in Wangala and Kadeholade lineage the core of the Female clan. The relationship between the two is ultimately traced through the daughter of the founder of the village.

Clan differentiation is symbolised in the procession of two carts, each representing one clan, on the occasion of the *Marihabba*, the ceremony dedicated to the worship of *Maramma*, the village deity. In each cart sit the elders and other important members of the clan it represents, the rest following their respective cart. The Male clan is accorded higher prestige than the Female. One magnate belongs to the Female clan and he boarded the cart with the elders of the Female clan lineages. He was careful to explain that the story of the origin of the village, related by the Male clan, was a gross distortion; the founder of his own lineage had settled at some distance from the first Mallegowda's house and cultivated fields there. When he finally decided to move nearer to Mallegowda, his fields seemed to be the last fields from the settlement now shared with Mallegowda. This, he explained, accounted for the name of the lineage and not the affinal relationship with Mallegowda. He claims that the right of his lineage to land in Wangala is based on first cultivation, as does the Male clan, and so, of course, objects to the higher prestige accorded to the Male clan.

It is still regarded as preferable to belong to the Female clan than to belong to the miscellaneous lineages which have no part in the village ritual organisation. These miscellaneous lineages make attempts to graft themselves on to a clan, preferably the Male clan, since this has higher status. In my discussion of factions I described the case of the magnate who has managed to become accepted as a member of the traditional *panchayat* and in the process to have his lineage accepted as one of the 'major' lineages in the village. His lineage claims that it belongs to the Male clan and during the procession, which forms part of the ritual at the *Marihabba* ceremony, his lineage follows the cart of the Male clan. In the past his lineage merely watched the proceedings without attaching itself to any clan, as the other miscellaneous lineages still do; but for the past ten years his lineage has taken an active part in the procession as a member of the Male clan. Although his lineage forms the hard core of the 'progressive' faction, nevertheless it has sought attachment to the Male clan of which Mallegowda's lineage, which forms the hard core of the 'conservative' faction, is the dominant member. Thus we can see that this magnate, having achieved high economic status, sought high political and ritual status along traditional lines: he exerted pressure to get his lineage accepted as a 'major' lineage in order that he might become a *panchayat* member; he also claimed that he belonged to the Male clan to get prestige in the ritual sphere. He tried to substantiate his claim to membership of the Male clan by pointing to the fact that marriages by his lineage members were according to the rules of exogamy exercised by the Male clan: his lineage had not married into any of the Male clan lineages, but had married into one of the Female clan lineages. However, his opponents point out that the one lineage with which this magnate's lineage had intermarried within Wangala had only recently been adopted into the Female clan, and is still regarded as a miscellaneous lineage by many a villager. To support their argument, they relate examples of marriages between this 'new' Female clan lineage and other lineages of the Female clan in the last generation. Thus, so they say, this magnate's lineage has not really intermarried with either the Male or the Female clan, but only with one of the miscellaneous lineages. There are still men who argue that this new lineage has no right to be regarded as a 'major' lineage, nor to claim membership of the Male clan. But at the *Marihabba* ceremony none disputed its right to join in the procession with the other members of the Male clan. Possibly the next generation will take it for granted that the lineage belongs to the Male clan, for the children enjoy the whole procession, unaware of the change that this represents.

The myth of Wangala's origin illustrates the point that Peasants make ritual office a function of cultivation rights and economic status. Mallegowda's lineage explains its ritual prerogative on the grounds that it is the founder lineage of the village and had prior cultivation rights. The founder of the village came upon the idol of Siva while he was cultivating the land. The implication is that if he had not ploughed the land he would never have found the idol and he would not have been given supernatural aid to build a temple in one night. The principle of hereditary ritual status is introduced after the initial functional relation between cultivation and ritual privileges. The association in myth between economic and ritual activities provides an element of flexibility in the otherwise rigid hereditary system of ritual status; it enables men who have achieved economic status to claim ritual status.

The myth also shows the extent of Wangala Peasant Society's integration into the larger Hindu culture. The founder of the village was contacted by Siva, an All-India deity, not by a deity of the local or regional pantheon. There is unfortunately no historical evidence available to show when the Siva temple was actually built; but one thing is certain, that, whereas every village in the region contains a shrine to Maramma, the village goddess, very few have Siva temples. It is, therefore, more likely that the first settlers worshipped the local deities to which shrines are dedicated around the village square, than that they built a Siva temple about half a mile from the village. That Wangala's founder should be associated with Siva illustrates the emphasis Peasants place on their integration into All-India Hinduism. Peasants in the region worship Vishnu and Siva but in recent years the worship of Rama, a re-incarnation of Vishnu, has become more popular in the South than the worship of Siva. Many villages in the Mandya region now collect funds for the erection of Rama temples in their villages.

Clan, lineage and faction alignment is reflected in the residential pattern of Peasants in Wangala. (See map 2.) The centre street of the village, in which stands the house of the headman and in which there are the only well and the only drains in the village, is occupied by Mallegowda's lineage and the headman's lineage. In the Muslim street live mostly the structurally younger lineages, a few Functionary households, and the younger of the two lineages belonging to the Female clan in Wangala. The Muslim street is still called by that name although it no longer contains a single Muslim household. The two lineages constituting the hard core of the 'progressive' faction live in a cluster of houses at the Eastern end of the Muslim street. The third street, which is called Shepherd Street, though there is not a single Shepherd household left in the whole of Wangala, contains at the Western end the houses of one of the Male clan lineages and at the Eastern end the homes of the *Kadeholade* lineage of the Female clan. The fourth street contains only relatively few houses, most of which belong to the group of 'no-lineage' households. During the course of my stay, in the whole of Wangala only one house was shared by families of different lineages and even this was only a temporary arrangement.

The residential pattern, in which lineages live in clusters, intensifies social relations within the lineage and consequently increases the possibility of friction among members of the same maximal lineage. Therefore, it also requires a political mechanism to arbitrate and settle intra-lineage disputes. Each cluster of lineage households recognises a dominant member as arbitrator and the various arbitrators within the lineage recognise the hereditary lineage elder as the ultimate authority in intra-lineage disputes. The residential pattern therefore strengthens the political aspect of relations within one lineage.

Relations between Untouchables, like relations between Peasants, are based on kinship, marriage and age association. Their kinship structure is based on the principle of agnatic descent and marriages are virilocal. Exceptions to these general rules are part of the social reality, but they do not overthrow the rules and in fact tend to confirm them. In discussing the political organisation of the Untouchables I have already described the case of Lingaya, who brought up his wife's brother's son, married him to his daughter and settled the couple in Wangala. Though in this case both bridegroom and bride were brought up in the same house, the Untouchable *panchayat* insisted that two feasts must be given on the occasion of the marriage to re-emphasise the distinction between the two kin groups involved in the union. As far as the Untouchable community was concerned, the girl married a man from another lineage, and his actual residence in her home was not allowed to alter marriage practices. Thus the agnatic principle was upheld, though through uxorilocal marriage an outsider may be grafted on to one of the indigenous Untouchable lineages.

Most of the existing marriages of Untouchables in Wangala are between men of Wangala and girls from other villages: 69% of the existing Untouchable marriages are inter-village; 19% are intra-village; and 12% are uxorilocal. There are no recent immigrant A.K. Untouchables living in Wangala at all. The spread of Untouchable inter-village marriage ties is similar to that of Peasants: 55% of Untouchable inter-village marriages are between natives of Wangala and spouses from villages within a radius of 6 miles; 95% have spouses originating from villages within a radius of 10 miles. Untouchable inter-village marriage and kinship ties have less economic and social content than the same ties among Peasants, for the politico-economic relations of Wangala Untouchables are largely concentrated between themselves and Wangala's Peasant farmers, and their intra-Untouchable politico-economic relations may be interfered with by their respective Peasant masters. The dominance of one large exogamous lineage in an agnatic kinship system with virilocal marriage necessitates the spread of kinship ties over a number of villages. In recent years these kinship and marriage ties have been manipulated as political links in the interest of the wider unity of Untouchables as opposed to castes, but the case I shall discuss in a subsequent section illustrates that inter-village Untouchable ties are still fundamentally merely kinship ties, because they have little economic basis, and therefore little political importance. The same applies to the Functionaries; the small number of households per Functionary caste and their economic dependence on Wangala Peasant farmers is responsible for the spread of their marriage ties over different villages and also for the primarily kinship content of these inter-village ties. Even in disputes between members of one Functionary caste, the Peasant village *panchayat* is regarded as the effective judicial authority, rather than the appropriate caste *panchayat*. Because Peasants dominate the economic system in Wangala, and most Functionaries and Untouchables are directly or indirectly dependent on Peasant farmers, Peasants also control political relations between Functionaries and between Untouchables.

Family Structure

Most households in Wangala are composed only of elementary families: only 10% of the total 192 households contain more than the members of the elementary family and an occasional grandparent. Elders complain of the break-up of joint-family living and attribute it to the selfishness of the young. In the course of collecting genealogies, I found ample evidence of the predominance of the joint family among Peasants and Functionaries, but none among Untouchables. The difference in family structure between Peasants and Untouchables in Wangala's past can be explained in terms of difference in economic organisation: joint families can exist only on the basis of jointly owned estates; Peasants had such estates, whereas Untouchables had only small land grants from the Government. On the other hand, ownership of estates does not necessarily involve joint families; in fact, Peasants in Wangala still have estates, and these are even more remunerative than in the past, yet they do not live in joint families any longer. I have already shown the part the sugar factory has played in the break-up of the joint family in so far as it is now in the economic interest of joint families to partition their holding in order to secure cane contracts for a larger acreage. But the sugar factory's policy cannot be taken as the sole or even the most important factor responsible for the disappearance of the joint family system in Wangala. Peasants complain that their womenfolk can no longer live together in peace in a joint family and blame them for the partitioning of joint households. There is, however, no reason to believe that women have become more quarrelsome. In fact women have always been blamed for the partitioning of joint households, even at times when new joint families emerged out of partitioned households. The fact is that the joint family among Wangala Peasants never had more than a three-generation spread. Therefore each joint family partitioned in alternate generations and usually the women were blamed for its break-up. A cyclical process of the periodic break-up of joint families and the emergence of new ones, has given way to a process of change in which joint families break-up under the impact of economic change and no new ones emerge.

The basic cause of the break-up of the joint family system among Wangala Peasants must be sought in the economic changes that have taken place in the village during the past two decades: new economic opportunities and more remunerative cultivation have given rise to the display of individual abilities; at the same time the impact of the nearby town has increased the wants of Wangala Peasants. These two factors have stimulated individual initiative and competitive attitudes, the development of which was impeded by the egalitarian principle operating within the joint family. There is not much room for initiative and economic competition in a subsistence economy where there is little specialisation or trade, but competition is found in every sphere of a market economy. The cause of the change in the form of Peasant family structure may thus be found in the change from a subsistence to a cash economy. The new opportunities to earn cash induce young men to seek independence from the parental productive unit; they want to be able to work and save money for new equipment or such items as watches and bicycles, or to buy jewellery and costly saris for their wives. The desire to raise one's family's social status feeds upon the opportunity to do so. This desire cannot become effective in impoverished villages where every farmer lives at subsistence level and where a wide range of relatives have a claim on his subsistence income. The restriction in the size of the family unit from joint to elementary, facilitates economic mobility, though the custom of inheritance, whereby each son has an equal right to a share in the ancestral estate, may lead to productive units falling more and more below an economic size when population is growing.

On the basis of these data on elementary and joint families in Wangala I suggest two interlinked hypotheses:

(1) In a subsistence economy the joint family is associated with joint estates; correspondingly, if a family in this type of

economy does not own an estate, it cannot expand beyond the elementary size;

(2) if a cash crop is introduced into a society of subsistence farmers holding estates on the basis of joint families, the conversion of the subsistence into a cash economy will necessarily produce competition between the component families and lead to the breaking of wider kinship ties.

These are hypotheses about the relations between economic organisation and kinship structure, and much more data from different societies at different levels of economic organisation would be required to validate them. Bailey, in his study of an Oriya village, also discusses the break-up of the joint family, which he attributes to the diversification of economic interests and activities.[1] However, such diversification is not a necessary concomitant of the growth of a cash economy and therefore the more general hypothesis might be more useful in analysing the evolution of the elementary family unit from the joint family system.

The break-up of the joint family system among Wangala Peasants has an important impact on the distribution of land and income; the partitioning of joint holdings leads to a periodic redistribution of land and consequently to a change in relative economic status of individual households, depending on the size of the ancestral estate and the number of heirs. The purely economic effects of irrigation tended towards greater concentration of wealth in the hands of fewer families, for irrigation offered greater opportunities to the more enterprising men; those who risked cultivation of cane immediately after irrigation, when cane was a new and unknown crop to Wangala farmers, stood to gain most. This economic effect is reflected in the economic differentiation among middle farmers. To cultivate a larger acreage of cane a farmer needed a considerable amount of labour and therefore wanted sons to help him. If he had no natural heir, he adopted as a son the child of one of his cognates or even friends. Adoption is a very frequent practice among Peasants in Wangala. This makes it difficult to disentangle actual physiological, from socially

[1] F. G. Bailey, op. cit., p. 92.

accepted, kinship relationships. Adopted sons or daughters are accorded the status of natural sons and daughters. Only in certain situations are adopted and natural sons or daughters distinguished. For instance, genealogies showed a few intermarriages between men and women of the same clan and on further enquiry it appeared that these were cases of adoption and therefore the rules of exogamy applicable to natural heirs of the families did not apply. However, the distinction between adopted and natural sons disappears after two or three generations and the heirs of such an adopted son are regarded as full members of the lineage into which their ancestor was adopted; the rules of exogamy apply to them as well as to all the natural descendants of the lineage, or clan.

If a Peasant has no son by his first wife, he may marry a second or even third wife to secure a male heir. Polygyny is permitted among Peasants but polygynous marriages are nowadays very rare in Wangala: of the 142 existing Peasant marriages in Wangala only two were to second wives. Adoption is far more frequently resorted to in Wangala than polygyny: 10% of the total male Peasants in Wangala at the time of my census were adopted. Since the distinction between adopted and own sons disappears after two generations it is impossible to say whether the number of adoptions has increased or decreased: the falling infant mortality rate would tend to reduce the number of adoptions, whereas the increased labour requirements would tend to increase them; and it is difficult to weigh up the relative importance of these two factors. It is, however, a fact that if young farmers do not have a male offspring after three or four years of marriage, they begin to think about adopting a small boy from another lineage, often even from another village, for adoption rarely takes place from within the lineage.

The practice of adoption has introduced an element of stability into the relative numerical strength of lineage and families; it counteracts the accidents of birth and death and strengthens the principle of agnatic descent and hereditary political and ritual status; for even if there is no natural heir, appropriate succession is secured through adoption. Thus if a man has no son he upholds the principle of agnatic descent by adopting a son to succeed to his political or ritual status, as well as to inherit his estate and other property.

Adoption and equal inheritance by all male heirs, acting together, militate against concentration of wealth and indeed secure a periodic redistribution of land, even in a period of rapid economic growth such as has taken place in Wangala since irrigation. It remains to be seen how these practices will be affected if Wangala's population grows rapidly and population pressure on land increases, once the margin of cultivation has been reached on village lands.

Relations between Castes and Untouchables

A.K. Untouchables in Wangala are basically agricultural labourers: independent farming is their subsidiary rather than their main occupation. The *per capita* holding of land of Untouchables in Wangala amounts to no more than 0·34 acre, whereas that of Peasants amounts to 0·84 acre. Most of the land Untouchables cultivate is held by them under grant from the Government. The factory's policy to enter into contracts only with owner-occupiers limits their chances of getting contracts for growing cane. Moreover, the extreme meagreness of their resources prevents them from acquiring sufficient initial working capital to embark on cane cultivation. As they are debarred from mortgaging Government-grant land, it is also impossible for them to use their land as security in order to raise funds. Only two of the 28 Untouchable households have managed to cultivate cane and they are the most prosperous of the Untouchable community. They are the ones who occupy the only two houses in the Untouchable section; all others live in small mud huts with thatched roofs.

The yield of 0·34 acre, of which only 0·15 acre is wet land, suffices to feed only a child for a whole year. Land, therefore, does not yield even a bare subsistence living to Wangala's Untouchables. They derive the major part of their income from working as agricultural labourers. This role has been formalised in the pattern of hereditary relations between Peasant farmers and

Untouchables. Each of the households of the male and female clan has a hereditary relationship with one Untouchable household whom they call their '*Halemakkalu*' (old children). The term 'old children' implies an analogy between father-children and Peasant-Untouchable relations. I shall refer to these Peasant-Untouchable relations as Master-Client relations. Each Untouchable household has more than one Peasant master, because of the disproportionate size of the Peasant and Untouchable communities. Peasant masters are responsible for looking after their 'old children' even if only to the extent of keeping the latter from starvation. In fact their duties are much more positive: Peasant masters make annual gifts of paddy and/or ragi and hay to their Untouchable clients at harvest time; they lend money to their clients to finance weddings or funeral rites; they always have to help their clients in case of emergency. Thus the hereditary relationship provides Untouchables with at least a minimum of social security. In return, Untouchables have certain obligations towards their Peasant masters: they must provide labour whenever called upon to do so, although they get paid for it in cash; they have to help in the wedding preparations in their Peasant master's household—whitewash walls, build a canopy in front of the house, chop firewood required in great quantities for the wedding feast, and do other odd jobs; they must also accompany the young bridegroom when he goes to his in-laws' house; at funerals they must carry the torch ahead of the funeral procession; if an ox or buffalo dies in the Peasant master's household the Untouchable client must remove it and may skin it, and in previous years may also have eaten it. The Untouchable client performs a number of ritual functions for his Peasant master as part of the hereditary relationship between them. Apart from the annual gifts, Untouchables also receive gifts from their Peasant masters whenever there is a wedding or other ceremony in the house of the Peasant, and the Untouchable client helps in its preparation or its conduct. Peasant masters are also frequently called to arbitrate in a dispute between Untouchable households.

Thus the hereditary relations between Untouchables and Peasants have economic, political and ritual aspects. The economic aspect has been strengthened through the increased labour requirements of wet lands. The hereditary nature of the relationship between Peasant farmers and their Untouchable agricultural labourers prevents the development of competition between Untouchables for employment as labourers in the village. Except for one Untouchable widow who works on a factory plantation in the next village, none of Wangala's Untouchables has taken up employment on the factory plantation nearby or anywhere in Mandya, or in neighbouring villages. Their economic relations have remained restricted within the boundaries of their own village, apart from one or two exceptions. Thus Untouchables neither compete for employment within or outside their own village. Lack of economic competition among Untouchables has strengthened the unity of the Untouchable community.

That Wangala's Untouchables remained within the boundaries of the traditional village economy may be the result of a number of factors. First, the unilinear development of Wangala's economy and the economies of surrounding villages offered no alternative employment opportunities within easy reach of their houses. The only work they could find in neighbouring villages would be the same agricultural work as they have in Wangala. Secondly, the dominance of Peasants in the regional economy discriminates in favour of Peasants and against Untouchables, and therefore Untouchables find it extremely difficult to secure employment in Mandya's sugar factory or on the factory plantations. For in a situation where economic opportunities are still scarce, economic success remains the prerogative of the dominant Peasant caste. Thirdly, though the holding of land per Untouchable household is very small, it yet offers a strong inducement to stay in the village rather than to try one's luck elsewhere. And fourthly, the social security involved in the Peasant-Untouchable relationship adds a further inducement to Untouchables to remain within the traditional village economy. The combination of these four factors may be taken to account for the immobility of Wangala's Untouchable community; but it is impossible to gauge their importance in relation to one another. Presumably they vary in strength between different Untouchable families.

Economic changes since irrigation have strengthened the ties between Peasant farmers and their Untouchable clients. Peasant farmers have now greater need for the services of their Untouchable clients. At the same time, external political forces of change tended to undermine the very traditional Peasant-Untouchable relationship that had been strengthened through recent economic changes: legislation made provision for the reservation of seats for Scheduled Castes in the village *panchayat*. I have described how ineffective this legislation has turned out to be in Wangala's political system. Party political agitation among Wangala's Untouchables proved to be equally ineffective.

Political agitation by a Mandya Untouchable Congress party supporter, who is an absentee landlord in Wangala, encouraged Wangala Untouchables to rebel against Untouchability. He advocated that they should draw their water from the village well or pond, though this seemed completely absurd to Wangala Untouchables. He explained to them that the Government was prepared to support their right to draw water together with caste members and to enter all the village temples. In reply they pointed out to him that first of all they saw no reason why they should break with traditional practices, for what they wanted was a well and a temple of their own, rather than the right to share these with the caste men; they seemed as eager as the caste men to keep the overt expressions of their caste identity and differentiation from other castes. They went on to sneer at the idea that the Government would give them active support against the village caste households. They pointed out how the Government restricted their right to mortgage land, and how the Government did not help them to buy bullocks or finance their wedding expenditure. If they received help from anywhere, it was always from the Peasants of Wangala and not from the Government. Thus for a long time the Congress politician was able to make little headway.

At last, however, he was able to gain a success. The Untouchables had always been accustomed to perform a drama in the village once a year. In these dramas Untouchables take the parts of other castes; they act as Brahmin priests or kings. This is generally accepted and no caste man objects to an Untouchable impersonating a caste man. Yet the caste audience insists that while the Untouchable acts the part of a caste man he must not violate the rules of his social relationship with caste men. Untouchables are always expected to show respect to caste men and no Untouchable is allowed to sit on a chair while a caste man squats on the floor, for this means that the head of the Untouchable is higher than that of the caste man. Hence, even in dramas, an Untouchable acting the part of a king may not sit on a throne while his caste audience squats on the floor. Whenever an Untouchable played the part of a king, he sat on the ground and not on a throne, so as not to offend the laws which govern the relationship between castes and Untouchables.

Wangala Untouchables rehearsed a drama during my stay in the village. The Mandya Untouchable politician incited them to have their actor-king sit on a throne. Peasant elders heard of these 'outrageous' intentions and called the Untouchable headman, warning him that the caste villagers would not allow the drama to be performed outside the village deity temple unless Untouchables abided by the customary rule. The headman of the Untouchables called a meeting of all the heads of households in their quarter at which the Congressman was also present. The Untouchable elders were undecided whether to risk the anger of the Peasants over the performance of a drama. The Mandya Untouchable politician, skilled in political speech, managed to arouse Wangala's Untouchables into open rebellion against the Peasants of the village: he advised them to perform the drama in their own quarter and promised to secure the support not only of Untouchables from surrounding villages, but also from the District Administration in Mandya.

It may be difficult to understand why Wangala Untouchables were prepared to rebel against caste rules in the case of the drama, rather than against caste rules regarding their use of caste wells and temples. The explanation offered by Untouchables themselves for this apparent inconsistency in their behaviour lies in the different social spheres involved in the two types of rebellion. To rebel against caste rules affecting the use of caste wells and temples by Untouchables would involve a change in everyday activities and relations between themselves and caste households, which they did not want to bring about. Untouchable women fetching water from the caste well might get involved in quarrels with the women from their Peasant master's household, which would raise difficult problems of arbitration. Whereas to rebel against caste rules in the case of the drama meant a symbolic, once and for all, display of their right to equality with castes. In other words, Wangala Untouchables did not want to change the relationship between individual Untouchable and Peasant households, but rather they wanted to change the group relationship between their own community and Peasants, as well as other castes.

The Wangala Untouchables went ahead with the preparation for the drama performance in their own settlement. This involved considerable expense, for they had to hire costumes and a stage to be put up in the open air. In previous years, when the drama was performed for the entertainment of all villagers, each household contributed towards the expense of the performance. This time the Untouchables could not approach the caste households for financial support. The Mandya politician got them a temporary loan which they were to repay out of admission fees. He also got the promise of support from the Mandya Administration, and Wangala's Untouchables busily printed and distributed invitations on which a number of senior administrators appeared as sponsors. On this occasion Untouchables used inter-village kinship ties to secure political support from Untouchables from other villages. While these preparations were going ahead, Peasant elders called a formal *panchayat* meeting to which the heads of all caste households in the village were invited. The meeting was widely attended and a unanimous decision was taken to enforce a lock-out against Untouchable client and daily labour. On this occasion faction differences were subordinated to the Peasants' common interest in preserving the customary relations between themselves and their Untouchable clients. Since the incident occurred during a slack period in the agricultural year the lock-out was not immediately effective. Untouchables therefore continued with the preparation for the drama. Anti-Untouchability legislation put some obligation on local administrators to pledge their support to Wangala Untouchables. However, most of these administrators are themselves caste men, and outside their official duties limit their social relations to members of their own or other castes.

As the day of the performance drew near the village elders held another meeting and decided to ban attendance by caste men at the drama. By way of a counter-attraction, they arranged to have an evening of poetry reading on the same night. They recognised that if they offered no alternative, it would be very difficult to keep Peasants, and particularly their children, away from the drama. The organiser of the Adult Education Authority in Mandya was pleased to learn of the sudden interest of Wangala villagers in poetry and, ignorant of their ulterior motives, happily agreed to provide some cultural entertainment.

On the night of the performance, there was obvious tension in Wangala. Untouchables were busy with final arrangements and anxiously looked at the sky for signs of rain; caste men and women were busy trying to keep their children from running to the ground where the stage was being put up. The poetry reading started earlier than the drama performance, so that caste villagers were gathered with their children in the temple square well before the drama was due to start. Untouchables from surrounding villages turned up to watch the drama, but no caste men from other villages came, for Wangala's *panchayat* had informed the Peasant elders in neighbouring villages of what was going on. Normally, farmers walk for miles to attend a drama in some other village, for drama performances offer rare entertainment. The absence of caste men and women at the drama performance demonstrated caste solidarity in opposition to Untouchables and also demonstrated the strong political importance of inter-village kinship ties, for it was through these ties that inter-village caste solidarity was manipulated. Before the drama actually started, rain began to fall. The Administrators who were caught by the rain on the way to Wangala hastened to return to their homes. The rain did not last long, but the Administrators did not venture forth a second time. So the drama was performed before an audience consisting of Untouchables from Wangala and neighbouring villages.

The small audience made it difficult for Wangala's Untouchables to meet their expenses. At the same time, the lock-out was continued so that none of them earned any daily wages through working for Peasant farmers. Peasants declared the rain to have been the sanction of the village deity against the Untouchable rebellion and Untouchables were not so sure themselves that this was not so. The lock-out continued for a further few weeks. Finally, both Peasant employers and Untouchable labourers found the situation economically untenable. The Untouchable headman approached Peasant elders to lift the ban on Untouchable labour. An *ad hoc panchayat* deliberated the matter and decided to impose a fine on all Untouchable households. The amount of the fine was graded according to the degree of participation in the drama. Untouchables had no choice but to accept the penalty, pay the fine, and hand the money to the *panchayat* treasurer. The Untouchable politician from Mandya had disappeared from the scene and left Wangala's Untouchables in a state of economic dependence on Peasant farmers in the village, just as they had been prior to the dispute over the drama performance. Everyday life had to take its course once more and Untouchable clients continued to work as agricultural labourers for their Peasant masters and to perform the ritual functions in their masters' households.

The balance between Untouchables and Castes had suffered a severe attack, but was once more re-established. External political influence supported by the State's policy and legislation against Untouchability had given the first impetus to the rebellion; external political forces were called in as allies by both the Untouchables and the Castes in Wangala: Untouchables invited the Administrators and printed programmes advertising that they had sponsored the drama; Peasants invited the organiser of the Mandya Adult Education Authority to arrange an evening's entertainment for them. Untouchables found the Administrators unreliable allies. They were left with little support from the wider political system and without any economic support for their political rebellion. Their rebellion was an attack on the social organisation of Wangala without any attempt to re-organise the economic system. It amounted to a political action by economic dependants against their masters and employers. Peasants used economic sanctions against the political rebellion by Untouchables in order to re-assert the traditional social organisation. Economic interdependence of Peasant employers and Untouchable labourers made the resolution of the dispute essential for both parties to the dispute. Economic sanctions against the Untouchables and the feeble support they received from the wider political system forced the Untouchables to accept the *status quo ante*. Wangala Untouchables now continue to perform their customary economic and ritual duties to their Peasant masters, who continue to provide their Untouchable dependants with the comfort of general social security. The failure of the Untouchable rebellion not only demonstrated the dominance of the Peasants over their Untouchable clients, but it also re-emphasised the traditional system. Wangala's Untouchables are now more convinced than ever that their fortunes are tied up with their Peasant masters rather than with the wider system, and the Peasants feel more certain of the power emanating from their economic dominance.

In the course of the dispute between Wangala Untouchables and caste members, Peasant elders took all political decisions and the Functionary caste households followed the line taken by the Peasants: they are economically and numerically of little importance, and thus acted with the Peasants. Functionaries have little occasion for contact with Untouchables in the village. None of the Functionaries offers services to Untouchables. Some Untouchables work as daily labourers for Functionary farmers, but there is no hereditary relationship between them, nor does any ritual in the households of the Functionaries involve the participation of Untouchables. Hereditary relations between Untouchables and Castes in Wangala are limited to Peasants, and then only to those Peasants whose lineages are regarded as major lineages. If a Peasant household does not have a hereditary relationship with any Untouchable household this implies its status of an outsider in the village and it also implies that it cannot call on the economic services of an Untouchable or on the latter's participation in rituals. The magnate who managed to get the status of his lineage raised to that of a 'major' lineage gave annual gifts to one of the Untouchable households whom he called his '*halemakkalu*'. The fact that hereditary relationship between Peasants and Untouchables is taken as an indication of long residence and membership of the 'in-group' continuously revitalises these traditional relations, since new relations are started which in turn become hereditary.

Wangala's social system continues to operate on the basis of the hereditary principle: hereditary obligations govern intra-caste, inter-caste, and Peasant-Untouchable relations; political office is tied to hereditary positions; ritual performance is limited to hereditary office-holders. The traditional social system has survived during a period of economic development. I have argued throughout my discussion of Wangala's economic, political and general social system, that the survival of the traditional system is due to the unilinear nature of Wangala's economic growth, and to the flexibilities which operate within the limits of the traditional social system. At this point I must emphasise the chief reasons for the unilinear growth: firstly, the survival of traditional values, i.e. Peasants prefer being farmers to seeking employment outside agriculture, provided their land yields a 'reasonable' income for themselves and their families; and secondly, the lack of employment opportunities for Untouchables outside Wangala. For if, for instance, commercial activities instead of farming had achieved value among Peasants, quite apart from the comparative economic advantages, the traditional hereditary system would have broken down. Or again, if Untouchables had been given alternative employment opportunities outside their own village, this would have resulted in a break of their hereditary relations with Peasant households. In Part II of this book I shall try to show how the multifarious changes that have taken place in Dalena's economy have struck at the very basis of the traditional system and how the radical economic changes remoulded the social system in a different way and to a different pattern.

PART TWO

DALENA, A DRY VILLAGE

CHAPTER V

ECONOMIC ORGANISATION AND CHANGE

DALENA belongs to the same culture area, to the same ward, and to the same regional economy, as Wangala. Yet there are marked differences between the two villages, noticeable at once even in their appearance. Wangala still looks like the traditional type of village in the area. Though new houses have been built in recent years and some of them are neatly whitewashed, or even elaborately decorated with colourful paintings, their style is unchanged. Habitations are still mud huts or rectangular-shaped mud houses with country-tiled roofs; one half is occupied by the family and the other by the farm animals without any partition whatsoever between the two sections. At night most houses are in complete darkness; the only type of lamp used in Wangala is a tiny oil-lamp which provides scant illumination. By and large, the moon is the only source of light after darkness. If farmers go off to their fields at night to check irrigation flows, they wait until the moon comes up, so that they can see their way. Light is of course an important factor in an area where there are also poisonous snakes. Hence perhaps the fear of new moon nights, which the villagers regard as extremely inauspicious. On such nights the village is in complete darkness; people stay in their homes or, if they venture forth, move about only in groups.

In all these respects Dalena stands in sharp contrast. Dalena has electric lights in the main village streets. These lights are indeed a major landmark along the highway running north-east from Mysore through Mandya to Bangalore, for they are the first to be encountered after Seringapatam, a town 14 miles away, as one travels along the highway to Mandya at night. And they are a source of great pride to the people of the village.

Dalena is situated six miles south-west of Mandya, a few hundred yards off the major highway with which it is linked by a road which motor-cars can use. From the village several footpaths

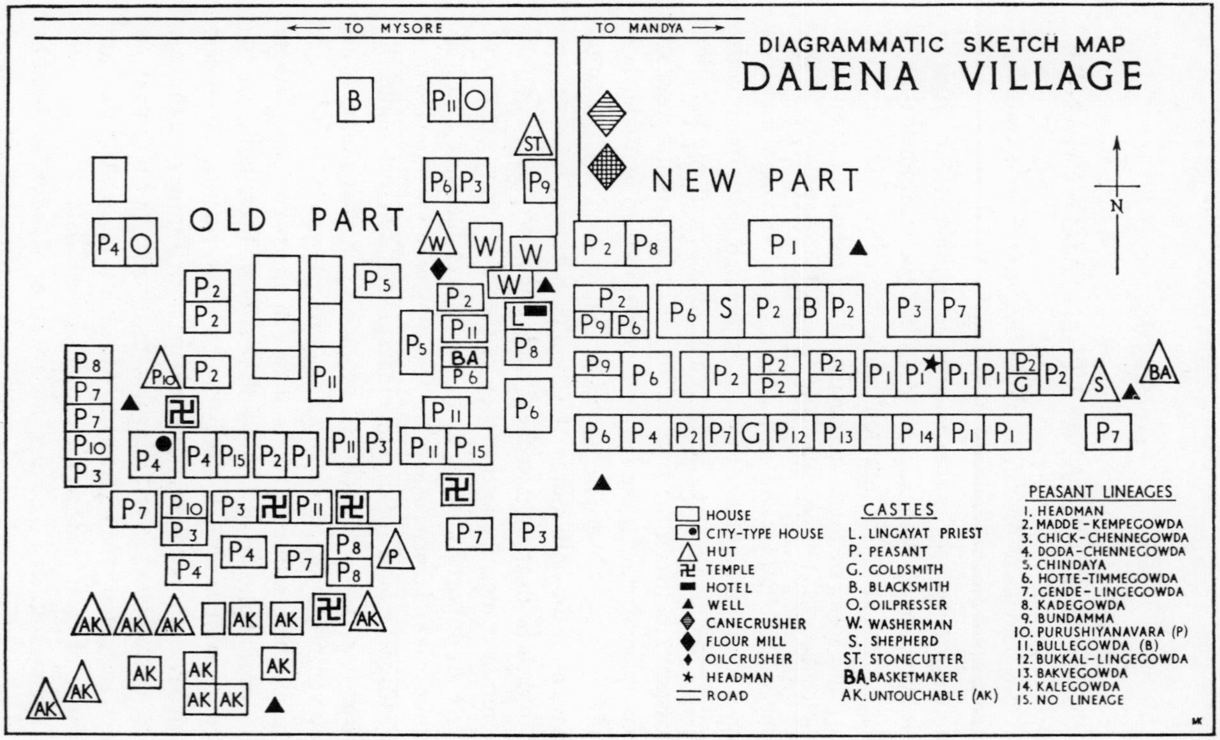

DIAGRAMMATIC SKETCH MAP
DALENA VILLAGE

← TO MYSORE | TO MANDYA →

OLD PART

NEW PART

N

Key

- HOUSE
- CITY-TYPE HOUSE
- HUT
- TEMPLE
- HOTEL
- WELL
- CANECRUSHER
- FLOUR MILL
- OILCRUSHER
- HEADMAN
- ROAD

CASTES

- L. LINGAYAT PRIEST
- P. PEASANT
- G. GOLDSMITH
- B. BLACKSMITH
- O. OILPRESSER
- W. WASHERMAN
- S. SHEPHERD
- ST. STONECUTTER
- BA. BASKETMAKER
- AK. UNTOUCHABLE (AK)

PEASANT LINEAGES

1. HEADMAN
2. MADDE-KEMPEGOWDA
3. CHICK-CHENNEGOWDA
4. DODA-CHENNEGOWDA
5. CHINDAYA
6. HOTTE-TIMMEGOWDA
7. GENDE-LINGEGOWDA
8. KADEGOWDA
9. BUNDAMMA
10. PURUSHIYANAVARA (P)
11. BULLEGOWDA (B)
12. BUKKAL-LINGEGOWDA
13. BAKVEGOWDA
14. KALEGOWDA
15. NO LINEAGE

MAP 3

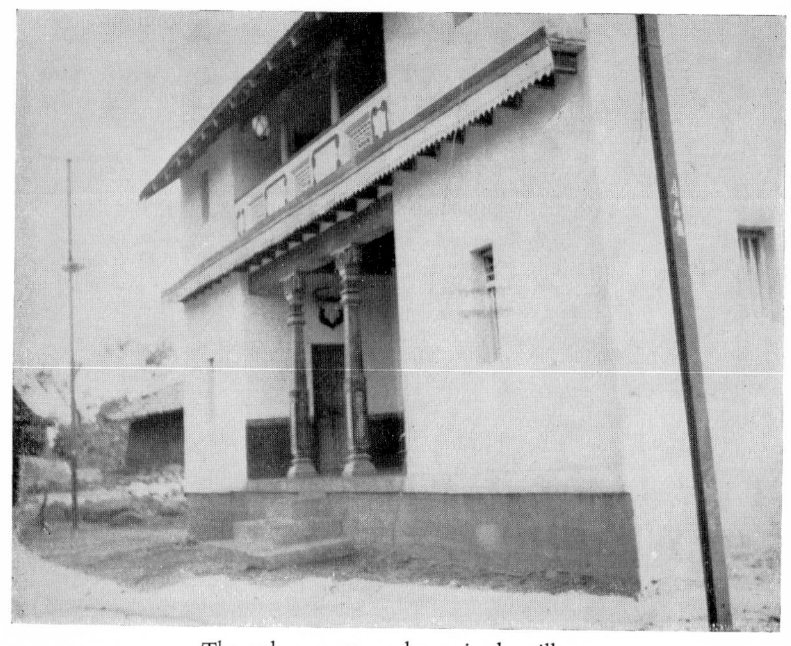

The only two-storey house in the village

PLATE VII. DALENA

and cart-tracks lead to the countryside. As one approaches the village from the main road, the first buildings encountered are the power cane-crusher and rice mill. The presence of electric light and power machinery makes Dalena appear modern and 'industrial' in comparison with Wangala. The approach-road practically divides Dalena into two parts, which I call the 'old' and the 'new', although there are some old dwellings in the new part and some 'modern' ones in the old part. Indeed, the only two-storey city-type house in the village stands at the fringe of the old part. This is the showpiece in the village, and all visitors of standing are taken to it and visiting officials accommodated there. It is an interesting structure: its front resembles the typical middle-class house in Mysore city; it has a porch, and a verandah on the first floor; the entrance is decorated with coloured pictures of Gandhi, Nehru and a few All-India deities, and trophies adorn the walls; it has good wicker furniture which, however, is never used by the occupants, but only by guests. The owners and their families do not actually live in the front, but at the back, which is built in the traditional style, though it incorporates many features of modern houses. The back portion has a separate partition for farm animals, and the customary aperture in the roof, but it has a cemented floor and plastered walls instead of mud floors and walls, and a partition for a bathroom. The more modern kitchen in the front part of the house has never been used; instead, women cook in one of the rooms in the rear portion, where there is no chimney and the walls are blackened by smoke.

Apart from this one outstanding example, there are only a few other recently built houses in the old part of Dalena. Most of the new houses in the village are built in the new part. The old part lies to the right of the approach-road and the new part to the left of it. There are still traces of stones which mark the entrance to the old part of the village. These stones are, no doubt, remnants of what used to be the entrance to Dalena. Villagers themselves use the terms 'upper' and 'lower' to distinguish between the two parts of the caste settlement. Untouchables have a separate but adjoining quarter at the southern end of the old part of the village. (See map 3.)

The approach-road terminates in the village square, at one end of which is the only Government-built caste well in the village and at the other the temple dedicated to Hanuman, the All-India Monkey God. On the right flank of the square stands the Marichoudi, the shrine dedicated to the village deity Maramma, which also serves as the village hall and school. All the temples and shrines of the castes in Dalena are in the 'old' part of the village. Though the house of the headman is situated in the 'new' part, there are no ritual or political centres there. The 'new' part looks comparatively neat and well-organised in three streets, whereas houses in the 'old' part are clustered in a more haphazard fashion along one village street, and are linked at the back by narrow winding passages.

Dalena used to be very short of water; it never had a village tank as Wangala did but only a shallow pond. Women had to fetch water in the dry season from a tank two miles away. About 25 years ago the Government sanctioned the building of a well in the village square. Since then four more caste wells have been built by individual villagers at their own expense—three of them by Peasants and one by a Washerman. The five wells are available to all caste households free of charge; two are situated in the 'old' and three in the 'new' part of the village. Yet another well constructed by the Government is for use solely by Untouchables. Thus Dalena is far better supplied with wells than Wangala. Although Wangala villagers always complain about the acute shortage of drinking water, which really is serious during the hottest months, none of them has ever considered constructing a well out of his own resources. Dalena men regard it as public-spirited to finance the construction of a well, which is then always known by the name of its donor. Thus water and electricity are important items in the life of Dalena villagers. To have constructed a well or to have installed electricity in one's home is not merely to provide an amenity; they are also marks of prestige.

Dalena is a slightly smaller village than Wangala. It has a population of 707 living in 153 households. But the caste composition of the two villages is very similar. In Wangala, Peasants constitute 66% and A.K. Untouchables 14% of the population:

in Dalena, Peasants constitute 80% and A.K. Untouchables 10% (see Table 11). In both villages the remainder of the population is

TABLE 11

Dalena population and landholding by caste

Caste	*Households*		*Landholding (Dalena and elsewhere)*	
	No.	%	*Acres*	%
Lingayat Priest (Saivite)	1	0·66	—	—
Peasant	122	79·75	715·00	97·20
Goldsmith	3	1·96	—	—
Blacksmith	2	1·30	—	—
Oilpresser	2	1·30	—	—
Washerman	4	2·61	3·75	0·60
Shepherd	1	0·66	—	—
Stonecutter	1	0·66	—	—
Basketmaker	2	1·30	—	—
Untouchable (A.K.)	15	9·80	16·50	2·20
Total	153	100·00	735·25	100·00

made up of Functionaries, and some immigrant castes. Peasants are the dominant caste in Dalena as in Wangala; in Dalena they hold all political power, most ritual offices, and 97% of the total lands owned or cultivated by Dalena inhabitants. Dalena has no Muslims and this possibly also explains why it has no flourishing shops.[1] Dalena's only two shops are owned by Peasants and they deal solely in beedies (country cigarettes) and a few essential groceries. There is only one small coffee shop, run by a recently immigrated Lingayat. The coffee shop is a meeting place for caste men, though many prefer to meet in the coffee shops of Mandya's bazaar.

Dalena's village land is still all dry land, in spite of the fact that one of the major canals runs along its northern fringe. The village land lies above the level of the canal and so cannot be irrigated from it. When the canal was originally built the Government had

[1] See above, p. 33.

to acquire land for it from some of Dalena's *ryots*, who were compensated with some of the village grazing land for their own cultivation. Thus while Dalena's land was actually traversed by the canal, it did not become irrigated. The very presence of the canal so near the village site continuously symbolises for Dalena villagers the economic fortune of other villages in the area. Across the canal, and only a mile or two away, lie the irrigated lands belonging to neighbouring villages, where they can see immediately before their eyes the benefits resulting from irrigation and exactly what is involved in growing wet crops. This has spurred them on to efforts leading to their own economic progress, and encouraged them to participate in the economic growth resulting from irrigation in the region.

An analysis of their efforts to share in the regional economy, and of the changes this produced in the economic, political and social organisation of Dalena, provides the theme of the following sections.

Multifarious Economic Opportunities

Dalena is still a wholly dry land village: no more than half an acre of the total village is irrigated. On their village lands Dalena *ryots* can cultivate only dry crops, such as ragi and jowar, and a number of pulses. The uncertainty of rainfall and the poor quality of the soil restrict Dalena *ryots* to subsistence cultivation so far as lands in their own village are concerned. Prior to the advent of irrigation in the Mandya region, Dalena had in fact a largely subsistence economy: small-scale sericulture and sheep-breeding provided the only village sources of cash income. In pre-irrigation days, as we have seen, the economy of Wangala was almost identical with that of Dalena. Both villages had subsistence economies depending on the cultivation of the major dry crops. Irrigation upset the balance of this almost stagnant economy. To Wangala inhabitants irrigation brought one dominant opportunity: their lands became irrigated, and they were enabled to grow cash crops. Their sphere of activities did not change and they remained farmers; only their techniques and the crops they cultivated changed. To Dalena farmers irrigation presented no such single dominant opportunity. Their own land remained dry, although neighbouring villages received irrigation. Within the sphere of their customary farming activities, no new opportunity arose and therefore no chance to derive a greater return from cultivating the familiar dry crops. Thus while they could watch the growing prosperity of their friends and kin in neighbouring villages, their own village economy remained based on dry-crop farming for subsistence.

Yet the event of irrigation in the area near Dalena in 1934 marks the turning-point in the recent history of the village. Dalena villagers, just like Wangala villagers, refer to incidents in the past as having happened before or after irrigation. For although their own land remained dry, the advent of irrigation had its own importance for the village. Since they could not grow cash crops on their own village land, some purchased newly irrigated land in neighbouring villages, where they can now grow crops for sale; only the more prosperous could manage to raise sufficient money to acquire such land. Altogether it was easier for the more prosperous farmers to gain from the new opportunities created by irrigation than for the poorer. Thus one of the magnates was able to open a flour mill in a larger village which already had electricity and was situated at the railway line only two miles from Dalena. He also opened a grocery shop there to cater for the increased requirements of villages in the vicinity.

Those few Dalena *ryots* who could raise funds, and who were sufficiently enterprising, certainly benefited most from irrigation in the area. But even the poorer *ryots* had opportunities which, if successfully exploited, could make them into relatively rich men. For instance, they could become labour contractors for the Public Works Department, though even here it was important for a man to have sufficient money to bribe the appropriate official to secure a contract. And, indeed, a fair number of Dalena *ryots* have come to act regularly as contractors. When the canals were first built some Wangala men also succeeded in obtaining labour contracts from the Public Works Department, but as soon as their lands were irrigated, they returned to being full-time farmers.

Dalena competed with its neighbours for contracts with the Public Works Department, but as the latter's land became irrigated they soon turned to cultivation. Dalena and other dry villages in the neighbourhood thus came to offer a comparatively permanent pool of labour to the Public Works Department. Having established a link with the Public Works Department, they continued to help in the construction of roads and bridges which were built together with the network of canals and channels, so that Dalena contractors and labourers frequently work today many miles away from their own village. Dalena contractors employed in their labour gangs, as they still do, men and women from Dalena itself and from other villages. Membership of the gangs was by no means constant, though each gang had a certain more permanent nucleus of labourers. Since the rate for the contractor w. s fixed, his profit or loss depended on his ability to keep costs down to a minimum. Thus the contractor employed those labourers who worked hardest and cared little whether they were his kin or Untouchable clients. Taking a contract involved a risk and quite a number of Dalena men remember the losses they incurred in the early days. A contractor, they say, must be strict and must not be swayed by kinship or other obligations, otherwise he loses money in the enterprise.

Most of Dalena's poorest farmers and landless have worked at one time or other as labourers for contractors or for the Public Works Department directly. Many prefer to work directly for the Public Works Department because the work is easier and they can take long rests. Contractors demand greater efforts and reward is based on performance. The personal element has therefore largely disappeared in labour relations these days; those who work hardest get most employment.

Since irrigation has not brought economic development directly within the boundaries of their own village, Dalena men had to seek economic advancement elsewhere. Once they came to accept the challenge of the new opportunities, each new effort perpetuated Dalena's economic diversification. Some, for example, sought work in Mandya. Again, when Dalena men approached Public Works Department officials to secure contracts they began to realise the importance of literacy and the status of a white-collar worker. Accordingly, a few sent their sons to secondary school in Mandya and two of these students subsequently managed to secure clerical jobs in Mandya's administration. They work in the Agricultural office there and transmit the latest techniques of farming to *ryots* in Dalena. In this way, one of Dalena's *ryots* came to experiment with the Japanese method of paddy cultivation on wet land he had purchased in a neighbouring village; he succeeded in increasing the yield per acre fourfold, and won the prize for the best paddy cultivation in the region during 1954. Thus their several contacts with Mandya make Dalena men also into more progressive farmers than Wangala *ryots*.

Altogether 26 men (13% of the male working population) go daily from Dalena to work in Mandya: 20 work in the sugar factory; 2 are clerks, 1 is an orderly, and 3 are drivers. Most of them own bicycles and are therefore independent of the bus service. They rarely come back to the village straight after work, but stay on in Mandya, where they sit in coffee shops or go to the pictures with their work-mates, who are from other villages or immigrants to Mandya.

Among these commuters there is only one Untouchable. Three are Washermen, one is an Oilpresser and the remainder are Peasants. Untouchables find it more difficult than others to get jobs in Mandya. They work as labourers for contractors or for the Public Works Department and as agricultural labourers in neighbouring villages. Whereas prior to irrigation their employment was restricted to the village, they now compete for work outside the village, where they are no longer sheltered by the traditional relationship between Peasants and Untouchables. Untouchables work now more days per year than they used to do before irrigation opened new opportunities to them. But they have not been absorbed in more permanent employment and are still largely casual labourers. Some, however, have branched out into market gardening. They grow tomatoes, brinjals (an egg plant), lemons, etc., which they sell at Mandya's weekly fair; they also keep hens and sell eggs.

Most of the men who work as contractors, or labourers, or are employed in Mandya, are also landholders in the village. They cultivate their own lands in their spare time, or else leave them in charge of a male relative who has no alternative occupation to farming. Those who are employed in Mandya all claim that their ultimate aim is to become full-time farmers. Once they have saved sufficient money they intend to buy more wet land near Dalena and settle down to farming. Although aware of the difficulty of purchasing land, even if one has the money, because so little comes on to the market these days, they continue to talk about the future when they will all be rich farmers in the village. The prestige still attached to farming signifies the strength of the traditional element in Dalena's changing economy.

The War brought another set of new opportunities to Dalena men. Development since irrigation had conditioned them to operating in a wider economy and some of them were quick to take to black market dealings when rationing and shortages made these very profitable. A number of the wealthier men are supposed to have made their fortune in this way during the War. Thus one of the Dalena Peasants, who had become a driver before the War, successfully undertook black market transactions by picking up bags of ragi and rice from outlying villages at low prices and selling them in the cities at high prices. He soon accumulated sufficient funds to purchase a lorry and became a lorry contractor. Towards the end of the war he emigrated from Dalena to a town 45 miles away where he works as a lorry contractor. His mother and brothers still live in Dalena with their families and cultivate their estate jointly. The rich migrant brother built them the modern two-storey home to which I have already referred and he periodically comes to visit them in his own private car.

The black market in paddy and ragi also brought big business to the flour mill which the headman of Dalena had established in a neighbouring village. Because of strict rationing laws, black market ragi and paddy could not be processed in the town mills; most 'black' grains had to be taken to mills outside Mandya. As long as no questions were asked the trader was quite prepared to pay a high price for polishing and milling. So the headman made big profits. Kempegowda, the headman's younger brother, saw what was happening at his brother's mill and decided to start a mill in Dalena itself. Jaggery at that time also sold at a higher price than it does to-day, so that it was comparatively profitable for cane growers to process cane into jaggery and sell it as such. Hence Kempegowda thought that if he could install a power cane-crusher at the same time, he could cater for cane growers in the region who grew cane not contracted to the factory. Such power machinery needed electricity. Accordingly, Kempegowda agitated among *panchayat* members for the electrification of Dalena. He volunteered to pay a third of the installation cost and finally got the agreement of the *panchayat*. Fortunately, the main electric lines were within a short distance of the village, so that installation cost was not high. Kempegowda negotiated the purchase of the required machinery for a cane-crusher and flour mill with an agent in Mandya, but before finally settling the transaction, he travelled 275 miles to Madras to visit machinery firms and decide on the type he wished to buy.

By the time Kempegowda got his mill and crusher into operation, the black market was disappearing. For a few weeks he had lorries and carts driving up to Dalena's mill and paying high prices, but then business became slack and was limited to the demand from individual households. Yet Kempegowda continues to be enterprising. He now plans to exchange his motor for a smaller one to cut down the cost of power. The drop in jaggery prices also reduced the demand for his cane-crusher and just before I left the village Kempegowda was seriously considering what other machinery he might install to process cane at prices able to compete with the refinery.

Dalena men have shown enterprise in different spheres and accepted the challenge of the multifarious opportunities that resulted from irrigation in the area. Dalena developed into a kind of servicing centre for neighbouring irrigated villages. Dalena villagers bought carts and bullocks, even if these were not required for the cultivation of their own lands, so that they might carry cane from neighbouring villages to Mandya's refinery at a daily hiring charge. Thus smaller farmers in neighbouring villages did not need to invest in a cart, but simply hired Dalena carts when they were ready to deliver to the refinery. The village has also become a centre for bullock sales. Dalena villagers walk as far as 100 miles to the large cattle fairs now held in Mysore State at the beginning of each year. The fairs are important economic and social events in the life of Dalena villagers. They meet farmers from a wide area; they learn about cattle, prices and bargaining; they enjoy the fun of the fair; and they usually also participate in the religious functions held there. On return to the village the newly acquired bullocks are often utilised for ploughing Dalena's dry lands after the early monsoon showers in March or April and then resold at a profit to farmers in the area for wet crop cultivation. Few of Dalena's *ryots* keep bullocks to cultivate their own dry lands; they use cows and resell the bullocks.

Prior to irrigation in the region Dalena's economy was wholly agricultural and largely subsistence. Irrigation provided the impetus to change; it increased yields and therefore farm incomes; it created new employment opportunities. Under its impact, Dalena's economy diversified. It is no longer wholly agricultural, nor largely subsistence. Many Dalena households derive the major part of their incomes in cash from sources other than agriculture. Yet land is still the basis of the village economy. Dalena villagers did not substitute for their farming activities work in other spheres, but rather supplemented their farming incomes from sources beyond the village boundaries and outside agriculture. Because dry land cultivation requires relatively little attention and because their holdings were small, they were able to branch out into other activities without neglecting their own land. Thus the diversification of Dalena's economy did not grow out of the traditional system; it was superimposed on the traditional economy in response to external changes. However, the basically static traditional system soon came into conflict with the largely dynamic regional economy. The two systems are based on different and conflicting principles: the former is based on the hereditary and personal principle, whilst the latter operates on the impersonal competitive principle. The integration of Dalena into the wider regional economy injected the competitive principle into the village economy, and in turn revolutionised its traditional social organisation.

THE OLD AND THE NEW ECONOMY

The advent of irrigation in the Mandya region has widened the economic horizon of Dalena villagers. Most of them now fulfil economic functions outside their village and often in spheres other than agriculture. Nevertheless, farming remains the dominant activity and the dominant interest. Even if a man's holding is small and not very remunerative, he still regards it as the basis of his existence. Food one must have, and food comes from the soil. Therefore Dalena farmers still pay primary attention to the cultivation of their fields, in spite of their other manifold interests and duties. Factory workers often stay away from their jobs in Mandya when their own fields need attention. Some even give up their jobs if they are needed for farming the ancestral estate, however small it may be. There are two men in Dalena who resigned their jobs at the factory and returned to cultivate their estates, in the one case when the father died, and in the other when the elder brother died.

Most of Dalena's households have estates: only 7% are landless and most of these are immigrants. Land is largely concentrated in the hands of Peasants: they own 96% of all the dry land in the village and all of the wet land owned by Dalena men in neighbouring villages. Washermen own 1% and Untouchables 3% of the village dry land. The other castes are altogether landless; they are recent arrivals in the village. Of the 11 Functionary households, excluding the Washermen, only two are native to Dalena; the remainder immigrated during the last two decades. Two of the four Washermen households are second generation residents and do own some land in Dalena and a neighbouring village whence their ancestors came; the other two are landless. Untouchables in Dalena, as in Wangala, hold some land under grant from the Government. Of the 15 Untouchable households in Dalena, 9 hold land and 6 are landless.

The landholding pattern in Dalena is similar to that in Wangala. Estates are small and no single holding exceeds 15 acres. Dalena's richest man owns only seven acres of wet land in neighbouring villages. Though Dalena's economy is no longer wholly agricultural, landholding, and in particular holding of wet land, is still the major criterion of economic status. All seven magnates in Dalena own wet land in neighbouring villages; but their dominant economic status is not simply a result of their extensive holding of wet land. On the contrary, dominant economic status partly leads to landholding. Immediately after irrigation reached the area, newly irrigated land came on to the market in neighbouring villages and Dalena men who had made money in other spheres were quick to purchase it. Their holding of wet land further increased their wealth.

73% of the total number of Peasant households own and cultivate wet lands in neighbouring villages. The relationship between wet and dry land held by Dalena Peasants is about 1 : 5. The average wet land holding per household in Dalena is 0·80 acre and the average dry land holding 4 acres. Judging by the area of the average estate, Dalena villagers are more fortunate than Wangala villagers, whose average dry land per household is 1·10 acres and whose average wet land holding is 2 acres. But, of course, in terms of yield and profitability of land, Wangala villagers are better off than Dalena villagers. Wet land is at least three times as remunerative as dry land and therefore if we weight the average holding in both villages accordingly, we find that in Dalena it is equivalent to 6·40 acres of dry land and in Wangala to 7·10 acres.

On the basis of this calculation, the difference in the average holding per household does not seem to be sufficiently large to account for the very different development in the two villages since irrigation. But it is important to remember that Dalena farmers' wet land holding is not in their own village, and therefore cultivation is more costly and more exhausting and brings them into contact with people with whom they had previously had only tenuous relations. The cultivation of dry land in the village itself takes up little time in comparison with the time they have to devote to the cultivation of wet crops. During the day Dalena men are mostly away from the village; they are either tending their wet fields in neighbouring villages, working as agricultural labourers in a neighbouring village or at work in Mandya. Dalena is a much quieter place during the day than Wangala. Wangala farmers live sufficiently near their fields to walk to and fro during the day, or ride in their carts. Their womenfolk can easily bring them food to the fields. Dalena men, having much further to travel, have to take their own food along or eat in some house in the village where their land lies. Caste loyalty and forgotten kinship ties become revitalised through these inter-village economic links. If a Dalena Peasant wants to eat in another village, he can only eat from the kitchen of another Peasant, and, to justify his claim to hospitality, he revives long forgotten kin ties or elaborates his affinal links.

Even before irrigation there had of course been some economic ties between different villages. In particular, villages were often linked through the service of Functionaries. For instance, Dalena still has no resident Barber or Potter. The Barber comes twice weekly from the next village and attends to those Peasants who require his services. With all of them he has a hereditary relationship and he receives his annual rewards at harvest time. I moved into Dalena just about the time of the major harvesting season in the year and found the Barber living in the village. Indeed, he was included as a separate household in my first provisional census of the village, because he claimed to be a resident. He bitterly complained that these days Dalena Peasants did not regard it as a matter of course any longer to give him his annual reward and that many quarrels arose over the quantity he claimed as his due. Previously, he did not need to settle in Dalena at harvest time to collect his rewards from the Peasants but, like the Barber who services Wangala, he could simply collect them on his regular visits to the village. The point is that many of the Peasants now prefer to have their hair cut and faces shaved in Mandya's barber shop, and so have dispensed with the economic services of the Barber, but the hereditary relationship is continued, because they still need him on certain ritual occasions.

The Peasants' relationship with the village Washerman has also changed. In fact some Peasants have severed altogether their traditional relations with one of the Washermen families, as a result of a case I shall discuss in a later section. But they have had to transfer the traditional relationship to another Washerman family, for they cannot dispense with the services of the Washerman as easily as with those of the Barber. For while men may have their hair cut in Mandya and dispense with the Barber, women need the Washerman to wash their menstrual clothes. The Washerman remains essential, although from his own point of view the services he renders to caste households are not always the most desirable nor the most remunerative. Washing and ironing clothes for townspeople is much more remunerative and less irksome than working for village caste households. Moreover, Washermen are no longer necessarily confined to their traditional caste occupation. The new opportunities which arose from the irrigation of the area are also open to some extent to members of other castes besides Peasants. For example, three of Dalena's Washermen, all belonging to one family, have become drivers: they never want to wash clothes for other households again, nor do they now perform any of the Washermen's ritual services in Peasant ceremonies. In terms of occupation and ritual integration in village ceremonies they are no longer Washermen, though their caste membership still plays an important part in their relations with other castes within and even outside the village.

The only other three native Functionary households in Dalena are a Goldsmith, a Blacksmith, and an Oilpresser. Of these only the Blacksmith has a hereditary relationship with Peasant households in the village and receives annual payments in kind for the services he renders throughout the year. Most Dalena farmers have a few wooden ploughs. Even those who possess iron ploughs for the cultivation of their wet land in neighbouring villages, employ wooden ploughs on their dry land because iron ploughs are said to dig too deep and so turn up the less fertile sections of the soil. Thus every farmer, whether or not he owns wet land, uses wooden ploughs in the village itself. They are made and repaired by the village Blacksmith. Wooden ploughs indeed

The village Carpenter-Blacksmith repairing a wooden plough

PLATE VIII. DALENA

require more maintenance than iron ploughs, though repairs are effected more quickly and are less complicated than for the latter. Iron ploughs which need repair have to be taken to other villages, where there is a qualified Blacksmith, or else to Mandya.

The Goldsmith makes and repairs jewellery for households from Dalena and other villages. He has no hereditary relationship with Peasant households, and can practise his craft wherever his services are in demand.

The absence of hereditary relations between Functionaries and Peasants, and the lack of landholding by Functionaries, facilitates the geographical mobility of craftsmen and encourages their distribution according to supply and demand. It is much more difficult for a Barber or Washerman to move into another village where, as a result of the death of an indigenous Functionary, there is a demand for their services, because it would involve the establishment of a more permanent relationship between the immigrant Functionary and the resident caste households. By contrast, a Goldsmith, for instance, can shift his residence relatively easily from one village to another. He does not have to sever hereditary ties in the village whence he migrates, nor does he have to be grafted on to the hereditary relations existing in the village to which he moves. This applies also to those castes which immigrated recently into Dalena. The two Basketmaker households are readily mobile. The heads of the two households are brothers. The elder brother was the first to leave their native village in search of a place of work: he lived temporarily in a few other villages before coming to Dalena. Here he settled down as a lodger in one of the Peasant houses and began to make bamboo mats for sale locally and at Mandya's fair. Dalena is suitably situated for the transaction of his trade; he is within easy reach of the irrigated areas and of Mandya. The increased prosperity in the area had increased the demand for mats, so that the immigrant Basketmaker found ample work and consequently sent word to his younger brother to come and join him. The latter came with his family and settled in a small mud hut. Both men continue to produce mats and baskets, and they also built a small shed where they rear pigs. In general, Peasants in the villages do not eat pork because it is associated with low caste status. But in Mandya, where the individual customer is not known, the rule is relaxed, so that the Basketmakers have a profitable market there.

The immigrant Shepherd and Stonecutter are less enterprising. Each emigrated with his family from dry areas in years of drought and came to Dalena where they now derive their income from casual employment with Dalena *ryots*. Probably they will stay in Dalena only temporarily; both families arrived during the last five years and talk of moving on to irrigated villages.

The immigrant Lingayats also arrived during the past five years, but they intend to settle in Dalena. They run the one and only coffee shop in the village. Prior to their arrival in Dalena there was no coffee shop at all. Nowadays, it caters not only for Dalena villagers, but also for men from interior villages who pass through Dalena to reach the main road and the bus services. Besides coffee and tea, Dalena's coffee shop or *hotelu* also sells sweets or curried relishes. In this way the *hotelu* has brought greater variety into village diet and eased its monotony. For only on festive occasions does a housewife prepare these special dishes. Women say that not so many years ago a man would have been happy if his wife could give him two square meals a day. Nowadays, he is not satisfied with this diet any more, and he wants all sorts of fancy dishes, which he purchases for himself at the coffee shop.

The position of women in the community has also been affected since irrigation. For one thing, the burden of their task has been lessened. The establishment of a flour mill in Dalena enables every housewife to have her rice or ragi made into flour in a few minutes as compared with the many hours it took her to perform the same operation by hand pounding. In most cases the labour-saving has resulted in increased leisure, rather than in alternative activities. Their heaviest household task these days is to fetch water from the well, but in comparison with the difficulties Wangala women have in fetching water from the pond during the dry season, this is relatively easy. On the other hand, Dalena women still perform many tasks in the process of cultivation.

Because in Dalena dry crops are still being grown with the same techniques, women perform the same operations as they have always done. Except for ploughing, they are now in fact responsible for the whole cultivation of village dry land. Thus the men are free to tend to their wet land cultivation in neighbouring villages, and to attend to other gainful activities. In this way, the continued co-operation of female labour in the cultivation of village dry land is an important element in the expansion of Dalena's economy.

The attractions of the wider economy have induced a number of Dalena households to emigrate. Within the last 25 years 12 Peasant households have emigrated, of which three have returned and the remainder have taken up non-agricultural work in the bigger towns, where they are 'permanently' settled. Two Untouchable families have emigrated and have become servants to larger Peasant farmers, and one Washerman with his family has moved to Mandya where he works as a lorry driver.

Most of the emigrant Peasants still hold some land in Dalena, which they usually put in trust of a near kinsman. They continue to pay the land tax, so as to maintain their right to the land, but for practical purposes the kinsman who is still living in Dalena has full enjoyment of the land. Among *ryots* land is rarely leased. Emigrants prefer to leave the land in the hands of a near kinsman without deriving any profit from it, rather than lease it to a tenant and earn at least some rent. They argue that a tenant only exploits the soil, whereas a kinsman, who is attached to the ancestral estate, gives it proper care. Furthermore, by giving a kinsman free use of your land, he is put under an obligation to you and this makes it easier to return to the village if you wish to do so. The emigrant forgoes immediate gain from the lease of his land in order to insure himself against an emergency. His choice is similar to that of the man in our society who prefers to pay an accident insurance premium rather than put the money into a bank or invest it. Insurance caters for an emergency, and so does the rent-free letting of one's land. By letting the land rent free the emigrant in fact forgoes the rent he might otherwise have received. This premium ensures that in case he cannot make a living any more in the town, he can return to the village with his family and claim support from his kinsman. Under an arrangement of tenancy, he could not do this. All he could get out of a tenant would be rent, and if he had to return to the village he would find himself without a home and without agricultural equipment. In many cases the landholding of these emigrants is very small indeed, and hardly an inducement for them ever to return to the village. Yet the fact that they regard their holdings in Dalena as an ultimate security reflects both the instability of the wider economy and the great value attached to land.

At this stage I must emphasise that when I refer to the growing prosperity in the area, this is only relative prosperity. In absolute terms there is still extreme poverty and great unemployment in the regional economy. Jobs are scarce, and in many cases remain the prerogative of the dominant castes. Fluctuations in the economic growth of the regional economy, which were largely due to failures in the irrigation scheme, have emphasised for villagers the ultimate value of land as the source of basic necessities. Dalena men have found that in times when the regional economy flourishes, their activities in spheres other than agriculture prove to be more profitable than cultivation; yet when there is even only a slight recession, they are thrown back on their land resources. They well remember the years when the sugar factory actually closed down because no cane had been grown in the area during a whole season owing to the shortage of irrigation water. Factory workers were then suspended, contractors and labourers had no work, cart contractors and bullock traders were idle. They all returned to their original dry land economy. By contrast, Wangala during the same years could still grow paddy and ragi on irrigated fields, for the channels still carried sufficient water for the irrigation of these crops, and thus Wangala farmers were not as severely affected as those in Dalena.

The diversification of Dalena's economy and its greater integration into the regional economy led to greater fluctuations in the development of the village. Previously, variations in rainfall were the only determining factor in the fluctuation of incomes in Dalena. Since the development of the regional economy, Dalena's incomes are dependent on a number of other variables over which the villagers themselves have little control. They are dependent on sufficient water flowing through the canals to facilitate the cultivation of cane; they depend on the villagers' success in a highly competitive situation to secure jobs in Mandya and contracts with the Public Works Department; and they depend on the ability of Dalena men to provide competitive services to neighbouring villages. From a largely stagnant economy, depending primarily on land and on rain, Dalena has changed into a dynamic economy dependent on many links with the external economy. This change has undermined the basis on which the traditional social system had been built and challenged the very principles on which it was organised.

The Importance of Farming

According to village land records, Dalena occupies an area of 665 acres of which 74% is cultivable. These totals differ only slightly from my own very laboriously collected land census which shows that as much as 79% of the village lands is actually under cultivation. 12% of the lands is reserved for grazing and the remainder is taken up by housing sites, roads and footpaths (see Table 12). Since it is essential that each village has some

Table 12

Dalena ownership and use of village lands

Ownership

Land	*Villagers*		*Outsiders*		*Government*		*Total*	
	Acres	%	*Acres*	%	*Acres*	%	*Acres*	%
Dry	493·75	95	31	5	—	—	524·75	100
Irrigated	0·50	100	—	—	—	—	0·50	100
Waste for grazing	—	—	—	—	80	100	80·00	100
House sites, roads and paths	40·00	67	—	—	20	33	60·00	100
Total	534·25	80	31	5	100	15	665·25	100

grazing land, and as the land reserved in Dalena for grazing is probably the least fertile, it seems that Dalena farmers have practically reached the limits of cultivation within the boundaries of their own village.

A considerable proportion of the land owned and cultivated by Dalena farmers lies outside their own village: 19% of the dry land and all of their wet land is situated in neighbouring villages (see Table 13). Only 6% of Dalena's dry land is owned and cultivated by outsiders; these are farmers from neighbouring wet and dry villages who at some time or other have acquired a plot in Dalena through kinship ties. Thus while few outsiders own land in Dalena, 62% of Dalena households possess land in other villages. By contrast, only 4% of the land owned and cultivated by Wangala villagers lies outside the boundary of their own village, and only 9% of Wangala households own this land. At the same time as much as 32% of Wangala's wet land is owned and cultivated by outsiders (see Table 2).

TABLE 13

Dalena type and location of land owned and cultivated by villagers

Type of land

Location of land	*Irrigated*		*Dry*		*Total*	
	Acres	%	*Acres*	%	*Acres*	%
Dalena	0·50	—	493·75	100	494·25	100
Other villages	125·00	52	116·00	48	241·00	32
Total	125·50	17	609·75	83	735·25	100

The landholding patterns of Wangala and Dalena point to a significant difference in the development of the two villages. Firstly, since Wangala still has a large uncultivated area, its agricultural economy may yet expand within its own boundaries. By contrast, Dalena villagers have practically exhausted the extent of cultivable land within the boundaries of their own village and therefore, if population increases and/or if they want to increase their incomes, they are forced to turn to the wider economy, unless they can increase the yield of their village lands. Secondly, the large proportion of Wangala village lands held by outsiders extends the authority of Wangala's indigenous institutions over individuals from other villages, for anyone who owns land in Wangala may be involved in a dispute over irrigation, in which case he becomes subject to the jurisdiction of Wangala's *panchayat*. The reverse picture applies to Dalena villagers. Their landholding in neighbouring villages extends their network of social relations. They have entered into new master-servant relationships in new villages; they compete with a new set of people and they co-operate with a new set of people; they have become subject to new kinds of authority outside their own village. If Wangala's population increases at a much greater rate than Dalena's, Wangala villagers too would have to turn to the wider economy; but at the present rate of increase, it will take a considerable time before Wangala inhabitants will have to follow the course of Dalena people. For the present, while Dalena farmers turn their interests to the wider economy, Wangala farmers concentrate on the development of their own farming economy.

For the purpose of surveying Dalena's economy, I compiled a sample on the same basis as I had done for Wangala.[1] When it came to the allocation of points to households for sorting into economic categories, I had to take two special factors into consideration. Firstly, the price relationship between dry and wet land around Dalena is about 1 : 4, instead of 1 : 3 as it is in Wangala, though sales of land are as rare around Dalena as they are in Wangala. Thus I allocated four points for one acre of dry land and sixteen points for one acre of wet land. Secondly, an important difference between Wangala and Dalena lies in the fact that in Wangala landholding is the sole index of wealth, whereas in Dalena incomes from other sources than land also determine the economic status of householders. However, after my first census of the village, taken at the beginning of my stay in Dalena, I did not know the full extent of incomes derived from sources other than land. The only incomes I knew for certain at

[1] See above, p. 42.

that stage in my study were wages earned by men working in Mandya. I allocated eight points for each wage-earner, because his annual wages equalled about half the annual yield of one acre of wet land under cane. My point allocation thus under-estimates the income of a number of middle-farmers and magnates. Since the poorest in landholding are also those who have only few alternative sources of income, they were hardly affected. When I divided the point allocation per household by the number of consumption units each contained and put all households into economic categories, I found that in Dalena I had seven categories at a point interval of five.[1] Had I allocated points for all sources of income there would most certainly have been even more categories. I subsequently combined the first three categories into one, forming about 76% of the total number of households and constituting the poorest section of the population. Then I combined the next three categories into one, forming 19% of the total number of households and making up the middle-farmers of Dalena. The remaining 5% of the population was made up by the magnates. The fact that I had at first seven categories in Dalena as compared with only five in Wangala, and that in Dalena about 76% of the village households belong to the poorest, whereas in Wangala only about 40% belong to that section, throws into relief the much greater economic differentiation in Dalena than in Wangala.

After I had compiled all Dalena households into three economic categories, I chose one-third of each category at random. Thus my Dalena sample, like my Wangala sample, is a purposive, or stratified, random sample. It consists of 48 households, which amounts to almost a third of the total of 153 households. Data from three households had to be discarded because I found out that these three middle-farmers were telling lies. For instance, one insisted that his household consumed half a pound of coffee per day. Altogether, their consumption was greatly exaggerated and their income greatly under-estimated.

Of the 48 sample households 68% own and cultivate wet lands in neighbouring villages. One-third of these wet land owning

[1] The total number of consumption units in Dalena is 526.

households cultivate both cane and paddy, the remaining two-thirds cultivate only paddy. Thus, though Dalena farmers are aware that cane is far more remunerative than paddy, all farmers owning wet land cultivate paddy and only one-third cultivate some cane. There are a number of reasons for this. The first, and probably the most important, is that cane requires constant irrigation, and this in turn necessitates supervision by the farmer. We have seen that in Wangala many farmers sleep near their fields or walk there at night to make certain their lands get as much irrigation as possible, and we have also seen that many disputes arise over competition for supply of water to individual fields. Dalena farmers find it difficult to devote sufficient time to the supervision of irrigation and they find themselves at a disadvantage whenever they become involved in a water dispute in another village where their wet lands are situated. Therefore they prefer to grow paddy, which requires much less attention to its irrigation than cane. Secondly, cane requires more than double the amount of labour needed for the cultivation of paddy. Paddy is also a more familiar crop to Dalena farmers than sugarcane; it is more like the staple millet crops cultivated on Dalena's dry land. Paddy and millets are half-yearly crops, and apart from transplanting involve very similar operations. Thus Dalena farmers find it easier to perform operations themselves when they cultivate paddy, whereas for the cultivation of sugarcane they have to hire a lot more labour. This fact is reflected in the relationship between cash and subsistence labour input of paddy and cane. The average acre of cane is cultivated by Dalena farmers with a labour input of Rs. 248 paid in cash and Rs. 223 subsistence; the average acre of paddy on the other hand requires only Rs. 67 cash-paid labour and Rs. 130 subsistence labour (see Table 14). Thus while for the cultivation of paddy total labour cost is made up of only one-third cash-paid labour, for the cultivation of cane cash-paid labour constitutes 52% of the total labour input.

There is a further reason why Dalena farmers cultivate paddy rather than cane on their wet lands in neighbouring villages; this is that paddy may be more easily cultivated on smaller and dispersed plots than cane. Often the land Dalena villagers own in

TABLE 14

Dalena cost, output and income per acre

Estimated average

	Cane		*Paddy*		*Ragi*		*Jowar*	
	Rs.	%	*Rs.*	%	*Rs.*	%	*Rs.*	%
Cost:								
a. Subsistence Labour	223	15	130	35	42	29	20	34
b. Hired Labour	248	16	67	18	26	18	7	13
c. Subsistence: Seeds and Fertiliser	356	24	57	16	45	31	4	6
d. Cash: Seeds and Fertiliser	451	31	34	9	1	1	—	—
e. Hired Equipment	73	5	13	4	3	2	—	—
f. Subsistence: Overhead Expenses	72	5	31	8	16	11	16	27
g. Cash: Overhead Expenses	48	3	21	6	10	7	10	17
h. Tax	14	1	14	4	2	1	2	3
i. Total Cost	1,485	100	367	100	145	100	59	100
j. Subsistence Cost $(a + c + f)$	641	44	218	60	103	71	40	68
k. Cash Cost $(b + d + e + g + h)$	844	56	149	40	42	29	19	32
l. Output	1,786	100	362	100	105	100	66	100
k. Cash Cost $(b + d + e + g + h)$	844	47	149	41	42	40	19	29
m. Income: Farm Wages and Profits $(l - k)$	942	53	213	59	63	60	47	71

neighbouring villages is dispersed and each unit may be only a fraction of an acre. The sample farms show that whereas there is a high correlation between the size of the unit cultivated and the output per acre of cane, namely 0·72, there is no such correlation between these two variables in the cultivation of paddy, the coefficient being 0·10. All this is quite obvious when we remember that paddy is cultivated on small terraced plots of about 100 square yards each, whereas cane must be cultivated on levelled land, at least half an acre in size, to make cane-growing an economic proposition. It is practically impossible to trench cane fields successfully on a smaller area than half an acre. Thus, if their plots are smaller, Dalena villagers are virtually forced to grow paddy in preference to cane.

In terms of cash, sugarcane is by far the most remunerative crop Dalena farmers can grow, provided the wet land they hold in neighbouring villages is in sufficiently large plots. Farm wages and profits per average acre of cane amount to Rs. 942 and per average acre of paddy to Rs. 213. Thus farm wages and profits per acre of cane are about four times those per acre of paddy, whereas cane requires a little less than double the subsistence labour spent on paddy. Therefore the difference in the profits accruing from the cultivation of one acre of cane and one acre of paddy is even greater than that indicated above between farm wages and profits of the two crops.

The relationship between total output and cash input is about the same for cane and paddy: in the case of cane, cash costs amount to 47% of total output, while in the case of paddy cash costs constitute 41% of total output. Yet the absolute amounts are of far greater immediate importance to Dalena farmers than the relationship between total output and cash cost, because it is often difficult for them to produce the necessary working capital. It is much easier to find the Rs. 149 cash required for the cultivation of an acre of paddy, than to find Rs. 844 required for the cultivation of an acre of cane. Advances from the factory certainly help to supply some of the necessary money, but not by any means all of it. Shortage of funds thus also deters Dalena farmers from cultivating cane, another reason for their preference for paddy. Only the richest farmers can afford to cultivate cane, and most of them have contracts with the factory. Altogether, Dalena farmers during 1955/6 cultivated 24 acres of cane, of which 22 acres were under contract with the factory, and the yield of the remaining acres was processed into jaggery at Dalena's cane-crusher. To cultivate cane in neighbouring villages is an exhausting operation. Therefore, and this is a fifth reason, cane growing is undertaken only if it does not also involve the risk of falling prices before the cane can be harvested.

Dalena cane growers are much more careful about cultivation of cane than Wangala farmers. For instance, Dalena farmers apply much more fertiliser per acre of cane than Wangala farmers. The total for seeds and fertiliser applied to an average acre amounts to Rs. 485 in Wangala and as much as Rs. 807 in Dalena. However, here it must be noted that in Wangala as much as 77% of the total input in seeds and fertiliser is in cash, whereas in Dalena only 56% is purchased with cash. Thus while the total input of seeds and fertiliser per average acre of cane by Dalena farmers is almost double that of Wangala farmers, the latter's cash expenditure on this item amounts to 82% of that spent by Dalena farmers. Since Dalena cane growers have much greater trouble in getting to their fields, they are more anxious to ensure a good crop. Other factors, of course, may also be responsible for the much greater amount of fertiliser applied by Dalena than by Wangala cane growers. Thus, there may be a difference in the fertility of the soil, though I have little evidence of this; in fact in both villages there is a high correlation between the total amount spent on seeds and fertiliser and the output per acre. Or again the closer contact of Dalena farmers with Mandya and consequently their greater knowledge of scientific methods of cultivation may account for their greater awareness of the effectiveness of fertiliser. Yet since Wangala and Dalena farmers apply for the cultivation of an average acre of paddy about the same amount of fertiliser, I doubt whether Dalena farmers are more aware of the benefits which result from fertilisers than are Wangala farmers. Thus, the most likely reason, and the one always stated by Dalena farmers, for their extensive use of fertiliser for the cultivation of cane, is their desire to ensure a good yield after all the trouble they have to go through before they can finally harvest their cane. The average output per acre of cane grown by Dalena farmers is higher than that shown in the sample of Wangala estates. In Dalena the average output of cane per acre amounts to Rs. 1,786 while in Wangala it amounts only to Rs. 1,597. However, average farm wages and profits per acre of cane are slightly higher in Wangala than in Dalena; i.e. they are Rs. 980 in Wangala and Rs. 942 in Dalena. Thus the greater application of fertiliser by Dalena farmers does not result in higher farm wages and profits per acre. It is of course always difficult for a farmer to know just what is the most economical application of fertiliser, that is to say, what amount of fertiliser supplied to his cane crop will yield the highest wages and profits, and Dalena farmers seem to prefer to be on the safe side.

For a comparison between the labour requirements of wet crops in Wangala and Dalena, we have to note that wage rates for casual agricultural labour are 20% higher in and around Dalena than in Wangala. Daily wages in Wangala consist of Rs. 1·25 plus a meal, and Rs. 1·50 plus a meal in Dalena for adult male labour; female labour is paid Rs. 0·50 plus a meal per day in Wangala and Rs. 0·62 plus a meal in Dalena. Dalena farmers explain this higher rate by pointing to the wage rates paid by the Public Works Department and in Mandya in general. Along the fringe of the irrigation belt, where men constantly work for the Public Works Department or for employers in Mandya, wage rates are tied to the rates paid in the wider economy. The higher wage rates also indicate competition for labour, at least at certain crucial periods in the year, between farmers and non-agricultural employers. In any case, when we compare the average labour input in Wangala and Dalena in terms of cash, this does not directly reflect the difference in effort, but labour input must be weighted by the different wage rates paid in the two villages. However, even then the difference between the labour input in the two villages on the same crops is still marked. For instance, in Wangala the labour cost per average acre of cane amounts to Rs. 242, while in Dalena it amounts to as much as Rs. 471. In terms of cash, the labour cost of one acre of cane cultivated by Dalena farmers is double that cultivated by Wangala farmers. In terms of effort involved, Wangala farmers spend 61% of that expended by Dalena farmers per acre of cane. For paddy the difference in labour input in the two villages is less marked. Average labour cost per acre of paddy in Wangala amounts to Rs. 139, while in Dalena it is Rs. 197. As regards the actual labour input in real terms, Wangala farmers devote to an average acre of paddy only 84% of the labour devoted by Dalena farmers. This comparison of labour costs brings out clearly the greater ease with which Wangala farmers can cultivate their wet lands as compared with Dalena men; it also shows how much less labour Dalena farmers require for the cultivation of paddy than for cane.

Evaluating subsistence input at the market rate of labour, fertiliser and fodder, the average profit per acre of cane grown by Dalena farmers amounts to Rs. 301, while the profit of Wangala farmers amounts to as much as Rs. 658. The marked difference in the profit reflects the greater labour input as well as the higher wage rate paid by Dalena farmers, and also the greater amount of fertiliser they apply.

If we employ the same method of evaluating subsistence input for paddy, we can see that Wangala farmers incur a loss of Rs. 24 and Dalena farmers a loss of Rs. 5 per average acre of paddy. But to the farmer profit is not an important concept. He does not think clearly in terms of evaluating his own labour at the rate paid to casual labourers, nor does he evaluate the manure and fodder produced on his estate. Thus, to the farmer, farm wages and profits, that is to say, the difference between total output and cash input, are the important criteria in his choice of crops cultivated. Nevertheless, farm wages and profits are not the only criteria: I have already pointed out that the availability of working capital is also important. Furthermore, certain crops have higher prestige than others, even if they are less remunerative; for instance, to grow and eat rice is the mark of higher status. Although it might be more remunerative for Dalena farmers to grow ragi on their wet lands in neighbouring villages, they prefer to grow rice, because this attracts prestige and in their own village they cannot possibly grow anything but dry crops.

Ragi is a far easier crop to cultivate than paddy; it requires little labour and fertiliser and only cheap equipment. The total labour requirement per average acre of ragi amounts to Rs. 68 in Dalena as compared with Rs. 197 for paddy and Rs. 471 for cane. Of the average labour input per acre of ragi about 30% is in cash and the remainder subsistence. Altogether the total cash requirement per average acre of ragi cultivated amounts to no more than Rs. 42, which is only about a third of the cash required for paddy and only 5% of the cash required for cane cultivation.

The average yield of dry ragi and jowar is considerably lower in Dalena than it is in Wangala. Possibly the proximity of irrigation affects even the fertility of land tracts that have remained dry. In any case, Wangala farmers apply more fertiliser to their dry crops than Dalena farmers. Average farm wages and profits per acre of dry ragi are Rs. 136 (see Table 4) in Wangala as against Rs. 63 (see Table 14) in Dalena. This big difference is dominantly a result of the greater yield in Wangala, for there is only Rs. 10 difference in the cash input for ragi in the two villages. Though the difference in farm wages and profits between the two villages is not as great with jowar as it is with ragi, jowar too is a more remunerative crop in Wangala than in Dalena. In Wangala average farm wages and profits amount to Rs. 70 per acre of jowar and in Dalena they amount to no more than Rs. 47. With jowar as with ragi, the difference in farm wages and profits between the two villages is due to the difference in yield, rather than to a difference in input; in fact the cash input per average acre of jowar is Rs. 3 less in Dalena than it is in Wangala. The average labour cost per acre of jowar in Dalena is only Rs. 27 of which 75% is subsistence labour. The average cash input per acre of jowar is no more than Rs. 19. Thus in terms of labour input and total cash requirement jowar is the most convenient crop in Dalena. But it is also the least remunerative dry crop. The reason it is still grown to such large extent in Dalena is that farmers practise crop rotation. They may grow two crops of ragi and then one crop of jowar or a crop of pulses. They claim that this rotation helps to strengthen the soil.

The comparatively low cash requirements of the dry land economy in Dalena have enabled Dalena farmers to spend on new wants the cash they earn from wet crop cultivation or other activities. Since irrigation, Wangala farmers have invested in agricultural assets in connection with their wet lands; they have terraced or levelled their lands, and they have acquired costly bullocks and ploughs and applied considerable amounts of fertiliser and manure to their soil. By contrast, Dalena farmers have in the same period made little attempt to increase their agricultural assets within the village. For instance, not a single farmer has even considered irrigating his fields by pumping water from the canal which by-passes the village. The cost of installing a pump to irrigate 10 acres is about Rs. 3,000 to Rs. 5,000, which would no doubt be prohibitive to any one farmer in Dalena. Also the dipsersal of landholding would make it difficult for any farmer to irrigate all his lands from any one pump. Therefore to install such an irrigation pump would require the active co-operation of a number of farmers. But the competitive spirit which is now prevalent among Dalena villagers deters them from such co-operative enterprise. Although villagers readily combine in political factions they are not prepared for such combined action in the economic sphere. The wealthier villagers have invested in flour mills and cane-crushers, enterprises which may be owned and operated by an individual farmer, rather than in the improvement or irrigation of their village lands. Only those farmers who have acquired wet lands in neighbouring villages have increased their agricultural assets. The Dalena sample confirms the high correlation between the wet acreage owned by a household and its agricultural capital, the coefficient being 0·76. Also, as might be expected, in both villages there is a high correlation between total farm output and agricultural capital (the coefficient of correlation is 0·75 for Wangala's sample and 0·79 for Dalena's sample).

Wangala's farming economy is based on four major crops, two of which (cane and paddy) are wet crops and the other two (ragi and jowar) are dry crops. By analysing the costs and output of these four crops we effectively cover Wangala's economic system. In Dalena the position is different; here cane and paddy are the main wet crops, but although ragi and jowar are the major dry crops, they are by no means the only crops grown on Dalena's dry lands. Dalena farmers grow in addition a number of pulses such as dhal, horse gram, cow gram, black gram and green gram; they also grow castor and gingelly as well as a number of spices. Furthermore, they have a number of garden crops, such as coconuts, plantains and mangoes, and vegetables such as brinjals and tomatoes. This greater variety of crops suggests that we cannot analyse Dalena's farming economy on the basis of the four major crops alone. However, from the evidence I have it appears that the area under these various minor crops is relatively small. In addition my enquiries show that in terms of input and output, pulses are almost identical with jowar, so that I am able to treat the acres under these crops as acres under jowar. In the year of my survey only 5% of the total 610 dry acres owned and cultivated by Dalena farmers was in fact under the various subsidiary crops, as against 6% left fallow, and 60% cultivated with ragi and 29% with jowar. Thus, even if Dalena's farming includes a greater variety of dry crops, they are not sufficiently important to upset my analysis, which takes into account only ragi and jowar.

Female labour takes a much greater part in the cultivation of dry crops than of wet crops: women can weed and harvest millets, and they also do the winnowing. Male labour is more predominant in the cultivation of wet crops. The average labour requirement for one acre of ragi is 20 male labour days and 37 female labour days, and for one acre of jowar it is only 10 male labour days and 14 female labour days. The large share of female labour in the cultivation of dry crops has helped Dalena farmers to continue cultivation of their own dry lands even after they had branched out into a number of activities outside their own village. To cultivate Dalena's dry land requires so little male labour that many men could easily be drawn out of the village farming economy without interfering with its total production. In the year of my survey, Dalena farmers cultivated altogether 372 acres of ragi, 177 acres of jowar and 28 acres of various subsidiary crops.[1] The 372 acres of ragi required about 7,440 male labour days and the 205 acres of 'jowar' required 2,050 male labour days. Thus altogether the male labour days required for the cultivation of Dalena's dry crops amounted to no more than 9,490 days, and, assuming a man worked 300 days per year, could be performed by 32 men. Of course actual cultivation does not constitute the only labour requirement in Dalena; men must look after their farm animals, they have to repair their houses and some of their tools; they plait grain containers out of paddy straw, and so on. It must be remembered also that agricultural work is seasonal and

[1] These final 28 acres, as explained above, are treated as jowar to give 205 acres under jowar.

therefore labour is in great demand only at certain periods in the year. Therefore 32 men would not suffice to cultivate all the dry land now being cultivated in Dalena. But if we make a 100% allowance for these various factors, and count a labour force of 64 men, it could certainly cope with present cultivation requirements in Dalena. Actually, when I took a census there were as many as 199 men between the ages of 15 and 55. They formed the bulk of Dalena's male labour force, but not the whole of it. Boys below the age of 15 are well fitted to work on the land and so are men over 55 years of age. Thus probably as much as 68% of the male labour force could be termed under-employed, if Dalena men had not taken to cultivation of wet lands and other economic activities. The high degree of under-employment that might have existed in Dalena, had it retained a wholly dry land farming economy, explains the vulnerability of traditional labour relations in the village.

I have described in detail the types of farm labour existing in Wangala and tried to show how the increased labour requirements resulting from the cultivation of wet crops strengthened traditional labour relations. Here I set out to show how the diversification of Dalena's economy has affected labour relations within its own dry land farming. Prior to the advent of irrigation near their village Dalena farmers made use of the same six types of labour as I described in my account of Wangala's farming economy.[1]

In Dalena, as in Wangala, boys and girls are trained from an early age in farming activities, though these vary for each sex: boys learn to plough and sow, and Dalena girls to weed and harvest, a training which is now lacking among Wangala girls. Apart from actual farming operations, boys learn to look after farm animals, girls to milk and care for buffaloes. Specialisation of labour on the basis of sex starts at an early age. Girls and boys are left to play together until they are about five or six years old and subsequently they are separated and their different training begins. Only a very small percentage of boys and girls go to school regularly, but even those who do, participate in farming

[1] See above, pp. 70–7.

activities, for the school vacations fit in with the rush periods in the agricultural year. Of the boys between the ages of 5 and 15 only 14% are literate; of the girls in the same age group only 6% are literate. Yet this compares favourably with Wangala where not a single girl is literate.

Although the overall literacy rate is very much alike in the two villages—in Wangala and Dalena about 10% of the total population are literate[1]—the levels of education achieved by some Dalena men are far higher than Wangala men have ever aimed for. In Wangala every farmer wants and needs his sons to help him in the cultivation of wet crops, and therefore those few Wangala boys who go to school in Mandya are expected to take up farming as soon as they turn 14. Dalena farmers can more easily spare their sons, because their labour is not needed for dry land farming where women help in the cultivation. Therefore there are now a number of men in Dalena who are literate even in English, and one young man is at present a student of physics at Mysore University. This educational differentiation is part of the process of diversification that has been taking place in Dalena during the past 25 years. To have a son who can speak English not only raises the hope that he will get a white-collar job in the town, but is itself a matter of prestige. Their contact with the wider system encouraged Dalena's enterprising farmers to send their sons for higher education. In Dalena female labour still takes an active part in the cultivation of dry crops. The role of women in Dalena's economy will be discussed in the following section. Here it suffices to say, that while in Wangala subsistence labour consists mainly of men, in Dalena it consists largely of women.

Exchange labour is never practised among women. Men practise exchange labour in Dalena and they use the term '*muyee*' for it, as in Wangala. There are however only very few occasions when a genuine *muyee* group is formed; that is to say, when a group of farmers work their lands jointly, at least for certain operations. The other type of *muyee*, namely where debtors work for their creditors to keep on good terms, is much more frequent

[1] These percentages of literates are based on a study of the total village population and not merely on the samples.

in Dalena. Grudgingly, men do perform such *muyee* services for their creditors.

Untouchable client labour does not exist any more in Dalena. An Untouchable may work for a Peasant farmer because he is the latter's debtor, but this does not necessarily imply any hereditary relationship between them. Such hereditary relationships between Peasants and Untouchables existed as part of the traditional economy, but since Peasants required relatively little labour for their dry land cultivation, the economic content of these hereditary ties was low. The mutual customary obligations continued to operate because the economic aspect of the relationship was supported by political and ritual obligations. As new opportunities arose in the wider economy, outside Dalena's dry land farming, Untouchables took up the challenge of these opportunities. They worked as labourers for contractors and they provided agricultural labour for neighbouring irrigated villages. In this way Untouchables severed their hereditary obligations. Peasant farmers in Dalena were quite pleased to see their economic dependants making an income of their own, and as they were not dependent on Untouchable labour for the cultivation of their dry lands, they also ceased to give to Untouchables the customary annual gift of food grains and hay. With the disappearance of the economic element in the hereditary Peasant-Untouchable relationship, the other elements also seemed to disappear. Peasants are no longer the arbitrators in disputes between Untouchables in Dalena, nor do Untouchables perform the traditional ritual functions in the households of Peasants. Under the impact of the wider competitive system, the relationship between individual Peasants and individual Untouchables has become an impersonal one. There exists still a group relationship between Peasants and Untouchables, which I shall discuss at a later stage, but the individual hereditary relations between Peasants and Untouchables have largely disappeared.

Eight of the 122 Peasant households in Dalena, that is 7%, employ contract servants on an annual basis. Two of these servants are Untouchables from the village, but their service did not grow out of any traditional relationship between the two households. The Peasant farmers wanted servants and therefore employed Untouchables who were always in search of work. Similarly, two of Dalena's poorest Peasants are in service in the village. The remaining four servants are immigrants; two of them work the flour mill and cane-crusher. They are therefore not really agricultural servants. Only the richest households have servants. The Peasant farmers, who have contract servants, claim that they need them either for non-agricultural activities such as looking after the mill, or to help with wet land cultivation in neighbouring villages. None of the farmers who own only dry land could possibly afford to keep a servant. In the past, contract service did not exist in Dalena. Years ago the only type of service—apart from the hereditary bond between Untouchables and Peasants—was '*jeeta*' service, the operation of which in Wangala I have already described. However, in Dalena, *jeeta* service is long extinct. Young men in Dalena did not even understand what I was referring to when I enquired about *jeeta* service in their village and only some older men could explain that it was a custom in force long ago, but no longer practised. In contrast to Wangala, nobody in Dalena remembers the *jeeta* ancestry of any villager. This difference between the two villages may be partly accidental; that is to say, in Dalena the few *jeeta* servants may have been 'freed' so long ago that their descendants have by now been grafted on to the indigenous society. But the difference may also be partly because a greater economic differentiation existed in Wangala before irrigation than in Dalena. Wangala did have some irrigated land even before canal irrigation and therefore even in those days some men must have been considerably richer than the bulk of the population. In Dalena, with its 100% dry lands, economic differentiation was then less marked, and this might partly explain the absence of men rich enough to have *jeeta* servants. Furthermore, a farmer with a few acres of dry land did not really need farm help nor had he sufficient resources to keep a servant. It is also possible that in the past Dalena supplied *jeeta* servants to more prosperous villages in the area.

The low labour requirements of Dalena's dry land economy at the time the regional economy began to expand, largely account for the radical changes that have taken place in intra-village labour relations. Farmers and labourers welcomed the chance to break out of the rut of their subsistence living, and this meant that farmers had to employ, and labourers to work for, men in other villages. In extending their economic relations over a wider area, intra-village labour relations became less intense and lost their customary attributes. Instead, competition has entered into intra-village economic relations. Though the ruling wage rates are generally observed, there are some exceptions; a good worker will demand and get higher pay. Farmers talk about so-and-so being a good worker, well worth an extra few annas[1] per day. Dalena's headman, one of the most enterprising men in the village, pointed out that he prefers to pay a good worker double the rate ruling in the village rather than have two lazy fellows idling their time away on his lands.

The establishment of new economic relations with male and female labour outside their own village has also encouraged Dalena farmers to introduce innovations into agriculture. For instance, Dalena's headman won a prize from the Agricultural Department for the best yield achieved in the area with the Japanese method of paddy cultivation. He, and a number of other Dalena Peasant farmers, were able to experiment with the Japanese method because they did not depend on the customary teams of female labour for transplanting, which we still find in Wangala. Dalena farmers also utilise female labour, but they employ a number of women on an individual basis, pay them a daily rate and make them work according to instructions and under supervision. They draw their labour partly from among Dalena's Untouchable women and partly from Untouchable women in neighbouring villages. As they live on the fringe of the irrigation belt, Dalena farmers can get labour looking for employment even from other dry land villages nearby. The availability of labour coming from other dry land villages constitutes a further factor in the changing labour relations in Dalena, for farmers do not have to rely on men or women from their own village to work their wet lands in neighbouring villages. By con-

[1] One anna is the sixteenth part of a rupee.

trast, Wangala farmers mostly have to depend on labour from their own village for the cultivation of their lands, since they are surrounded by irrigated villages which themselves utilise their own resident labour. I have argued that the rigid labour relations in Wangala are the dominant factor in preventing the introduction of the Japanese method of paddy cultivation. This argument is strengthened by the fact that Dalena farmers, who operate in a new, and not the customary, field of labour relations, have managed to apply the Japanese method. However, we must also bear in mind that paddy is the most important wet crop grown by Dalena farmers. This tends to make them more interested in experimenting with new techniques of paddy cultivation than are Wangala farmers, whose main interest is vested in cane cultivation.

I have shown that paddy requires far less capital investment than sugarcane, since average subsistence and cash overheads per acre of cane amount to Rs. 120 as compared with Rs. 52 per acre of paddy, and that this is one reason why Dalena farmers prefer to grow paddy rather than cane. Since Dalena's own lands have remained dry, farmers have had to spend money on acquiring wet lands and therefore had less to spare for investment in agricultural capital. Furthermore, as Dalena villagers established links with the regional economy their set of values and priorities have changed. Agriculture has lost some of its importance in Dalena, whereas to Wangala villagers it is still the only source of income and therefore the major economic interest. Wangala farmers have increased their productive assets while Dalena farmers have increased their links with the wider economy. This process is reflected in the pattern of agricultural capital among sample households in the two villages. Average agricultural capital in Wangala amounts to as much as Rs. 660 and in Dalena only to Rs. 370. Only 30% of the landholding households in Dalena's sample possess agricultural capital worth more than Rs. 400, whereas 20% of Wangala's sample have agricultural capital worth more than Rs. 1,000 (see Table 28).

In my analysis of agricultural capital I have included all capital items, owned by a household, which may be used for the purpose of cultivation. Thus tools, ploughs, bullocks, carts and so on, all fall into the category of agricultural capital. However, while it is true to say of Wangala farmers that if they own any of these items, their primary purpose is to help in cultivation, this is not so in Dalena. For instance, 64 of the 192 households in Wangala, or just one-third, own carts: all 64 have wet land holdings and utilise their carts primarily to transport cane grown on the family estate to the sugar factory. By contrast, only 20% of Dalena's households own carts and of these 20% own no wet land at all and at least 60% do not grow any cane. These Dalena households own carts primarily to transport cane grown by other farmers in neighbouring villages to Mandya's factory. Thus carts in Dalena are not only used as part of the productive process carried on by farmers themselves, but also form part of the household's commercial assets. Where farmers use their own carts for operations on their own crops as well as to carry cane on hire, it is difficult to classify the value of carts under any one category.

The same difficulty arises in the case of bullocks. I have already mentioned that Dalena farmers trade in bullocks: they purchase at large fairs and sell at a profit to individual customers in the area. Frequently, a farmer purchases a pair of bullocks at a fair, keeps them for a few months, and then sells them at a profit. While he keeps the bullocks he utilises them for the cultivation of his lands. But the main purpose is to resell at a profit. Thus, these bullocks, while they help to cultivate, are at the same time a type of commercial commodity. However, I classified every item of agricultural equipment, which could be used by the farmer in the process of cultivating his lands, as agricultural capital. This means that my figures of agricultural assets among sample households in Dalena are exaggerated. In view of this, it becomes even more significant that the average agricultural assets per household in Dalena amount to less than the average house property per consumption unit. The average Dalena household is composed of 3·8 consumption units: average agricultural assets amount to Rs. 370 per household and average house property to Rs. 378 per consumption unit. Significantly, the distribution of house property is very similar to that of agricultural assets: 30% of the sample households own agricultural assets worth more than Rs. 400 (see Table 28), and 33% own houses worth more than Rs. 400 per consumption unit (see Table 36). Differentiation in terms of agricultural assets coincides with differentiation in terms of house property. In Wangala there is no such coincidence: whereas 20% of the sample households own agricultural assets worth more than Rs. 1,000 (see Table 28), only 3% own house property worth more than Rs. 1,000 per consumption unit (see Table 36). In Dalena every villager tends to regard housing as an expression of economic status, while in Wangala bullocks play this role. To have a good pair of bullocks is the dream of every farmer in Wangala and there is great competition among farmers to own the best cattle. In the same way that Dalena villagers jealously size up one another's houses, Wangala farmers size up one another's cattle. The interest in housing displayed by Dalena villagers reflects their changed values. It costs as much to build a partition for a bathroom as it does to buy a new iron plough. Put to the choice, a Dalena man will be tempted to prefer building a partition for a bathroom. No Wangala villager would even consider such a choice and would certainly purchase the iron plough. In Dalena the influence of the town continuously interacts with the customary set of values and this produces many inconsistencies in the behaviour pattern of villagers. To sum up their conflicting desires we can say that each man wants to live like a townsman and at the same time farm a large estate (by large estate he means no more than 15 acres). I shall at a later stage deal in greater detail with the way this conflict finds expression in social interaction within Dalena. Here I want to emphasise how the participation of Dalena men in the wider economy has affected their pattern of priorities. Housing has become almost as important as investment in agricultural equipment. At the same time there are men in each village who do not fall into this general pattern; in Dalena there are some who are as proud of their cattle as Wangala farmers, while in Wangala there are those who are as houseproud as most Dalena men.

Dalena's economy now differs in many respects from Wangala's but both villages have still essentially rural economies.

Even in Dalena land is still the major criterion of wealth. I was not able to collect the same details about changes in landholding over the last twenty years for Dalena as I did for Wangala. Changes in the landholding of Wangala residents affected only their own village lands and therefore could be verified by an analysis of village records, whereas changes in the estates of Dalena farmers involved mostly land lying outside Dalena, and therefore I should have had to peruse the land records of a number of villages. Data collected on the distribution of land in Wangala enabled me to show the trend of changes whereby farmers sold some of their land to outsiders immediately after irrigation and a few years later began to repurchase it again. By contrast, Dalena farmers competed for land in neighbouring villages as soon as irrigation reached the area. According to information collected from individual landowners, which I was able to cross-check with other informants though not with land records, only about 15% of the wet land now owned by Dalena farmers in neighbouring villages was already in their possession before it was irrigated. The remaining 85% was bought by them mostly in the years immediately after irrigation. I have not found a single Dalena farmer who had sold any of the wet land acquired in neighbouring villages. Dalena's proximity to the irrigated area enables its farmers to cultivate their wet lands themselves, and therefore they do not have to face the same difficulties as absentee landlords in Wangala. Wet land around Dalena is in great demand, but supply has become highly inelastic and very few land sales take place these days. Wet lands at the fringe of the irrigation belt fetch a higher price than wet lands in Wangala at the centre of the region, although in terms of fertility there seems to be little difference in the soils. The pressure from dry land villages has increased the price of wet land at the frontiers of irrigation, but the higher prices offer no greater inducement to sell. There is no regular supply of land: land is sold only as a result of certain extraordinary circumstances, such as having to meet the cash requirements of a particular contingency, or in the case of a family having no male heir. A farmer sells land only in the last resort, for he knows that land is his ultimate security. I heard of a

Dalena farmer who had offered as much as Rs. 3,000 for half an acre of wet land in a neighbouring village, but not even this high price would induce the owner to sell it, although he was deep in debt. By comparison, in Wangala the average price of an acre of wet land is Rs. 1,500.

Apart from its economic importance, landholding brings prestige; furthermore a farmer also usually gets deeply attached to the soil he cultivates. These non-economic considerations strengthen the farmer's resistance to selling his lands. This is as strong among Dalena's dry land holders as it is among farmers of wet land. Even sales of dry land are very rare in Dalena these days. Though far less remunerative than wet land, it is still looked upon by the farmer as the ultimate source of income and security. I have already described how even Dalena's emigrants have retained ownership of their estates in the village. In spite, therefore, of the great changes that have taken place in Dalena, farming still plays an important part in its economy and this lends strength to a partial persistence of the traditional system.

The Role of Women

The organisation of female labour has hardly been affected by the changes that have taken place in Dalena; most women still participate with their menfolk in the cultivation of their dry land estates. Even the wife of the richest man in Dalena goes to weed his fields and he was quite surprised when I mentioned that Wangala farmers prefer their wives to stay away from work on the land. He pointed out that in Dalena they actually needed the continued help of their womenfolk, for it is the man who must be left free to seek his chances elsewhere, while he must be sure that his lands are being tended. Therefore most female labour in Dalena still falls into the category of unpaid labour. There is less demand for female 'coolie' labour in Dalena than in Wangala, because dry land farming does not involve transplanting or the same amount of weeding as wet crops. Dalena's Untouchable women provide the pool of paid female labour and only a few caste women actually work as 'coolies'.

Dalena women are still the pillars of the village dry land economy. The recent economic changes have hardly affected economic activities performed by women. The only major revolutionary change in this connection stems from the erection of the flour mill which frees women from the tedious task of hand pounding and dehusking. When I questioned women about the use they made of the time saved by having their ragi and paddy ground at the mill, a few pointed out that they now had time to keep buffaloes; the milk yield of the buffalo pays for the milling and even leaves some profit. Most women, however, said that they now had more time to look after their children and other household duties.

By and large women in Dalena have less independent income than in Wangala. Income derived from selling buffalo milk enables Wangala women to act as moneylenders: they lend small amounts, usually a few rupees at a time, at high interest rates. They charge interest of one anna per rupee per month, which amounts to a 75% interest rate per year. However, these small loans are usually for short periods of a few weeks or months. On the other hand, it is very rare for a woman in Dalena to lend money. Women in Dalena operate still largely within the limits of the subsistence economy; all cash transactions are done by their menfolk. Dalena men purchase household necessities in Mandya and their womenfolk rarely venture to the weekly fair. By contrast, many Wangala women walk weekly to the fair in Mandya. They carry their baskets of butter to Mandya where they sell it and then make their purchases. When I collected household budgets in Wangala I had to question both husband and wife about their cash purchases, for both would know about the quantities and prices of articles they had bought in Mandya. In Dalena, women knew little about market prices in Mandya. When the Potter from a neighbouring village comes to Dalena, women purchase pots by paying in ragi or chillies or other crops, but only rarely in money. Wangala women usually purchase pots with cash.

The difference in the roles which Dalena and Wangala women occupy in their respective village economies illustrates an interesting inconsistency in the development of the two villages. I have argued that the changes which have taken place in Wangala are in line with the traditional economy, and therefore they have not radically changed economic roles and relations within the village. I have also set out to show how, by contrast, the multifarious changes in Dalena have revolutionised its economic and political system. Yet we find that within the overall pattern of these respective changes, the role of women has been more drastically affected in Wangala than in Dalena. Dalena men have established many links with the regional economy, while their womenfolk continue to function largely within the limits set by the customary subsistence economy. Wangala men, on the other hand, have continued to concentrate all their interests on the cultivation of their land, but their increased income has affected the role of women in the economy. Peasant farmers regard it as a matter of prestige that their womenfolk do not work on their lands any more. Women have learnt to operate in the money economy: they sell milk and butter, they purchase goods in Mandya, and they lend money. All this has made them more independent and has affected the relationship between husband and wife. By purchasing a buffalo, a husband provides his wife with an independent source of income and in turn gives her a certain degree of independence in general. In this context Wangala men are faced with a dilemma. On the one hand prestige is expressed, among other things, in terms of the sort of life they provide for their womenfolk; the more a man frees his wife from work on the land and the more jewellery he gets for her, the higher his prestige, other things being equal. On the other hand, once a man tries to give his wife all those things which bring him prestige, their relationship is affected and he finds her less subordinate. These contradictory interests lead to many quarrels between husband and wife. Dalena women are much more submissive to their husbands and therefore far fewer quarrels arise between husbands and wives.

Economic differentiation has found different modes of expression in Wangala and Dalena. Whereas in Wangala the pattern of life his wife leads is an important element in rating a man's prestige, in Dalena this is not so; here housing, bicycles, watches, dress and speech are more important criteria of prestige. In Wangala it is claimed that a number of elderly women have given substantial help to their husbands in the accumulation of the families' fortunes. I have already referred to the mother of Wangala's richest Peasant farmer, who is said to have been the driving force in the economic success of her husband and son, and there are others like her. In Dalena there is not a single woman of whom a similar claim was made. Dalena women have not branched out into cash transactions, but continue to operate largely within the limits set by their village's subsistence economy. Within the limits of Dalena's dry land subsistence economy women, however, are the dominant force. They provide the major part of the labour required.

Animal Husbandry

Only 15% of Dalena's households have no farm animals at all. Yet it is difficult to analyse the value of farm animals per household, because of their high turnover; farmers sometimes keep a pair of bullocks or cows for no more than a couple of weeks before they resell. The sale value of cattle is more important to a Dalena farmer than its performance on his lands and he is always ready to sell for gain. I gathered my first cattle census at the end of January, just when a number of farmers had returned from cattle fairs with their newly acquired stock. I found then that 57 households, or 37%, owned bullocks. Two months later 25 of them had sold their bullocks. By contrast, Wangala farmers usually keep the same pair of bullocks for at least three or four years. To a Wangala farmer the performance of his bullocks is most important and he sells only when he considers that he needs a pair that will give him better service.

The different economic functions performed by bullocks in Wangala and in Dalena find expression in the different relationship between farmers and their animals in the two villages. Wangala farmers are greatly attached to their bullocks. They hand-feed them with hay or cane leaves, take them drinking to the canals, and when working in the fields often talk to them.

'My bullocks are my best friends' is a frequent expression, and Wangala men cannot conceive how any farmer can live in a house apart from his animals. In Dalena too, farmers care for their animals, but they do not have the same emotional attachment to them. I have never seen a farmer in Dalena hand-feed his bullocks; nor are they so keen to share their living quarters with their animals. True, most of the houses are still designed in the customary style, whereby animals occupy one-half of the floor space in the house. But the newer houses all have partitions which separate the family from its animals. When I left Dalena in July 1956 seven houses were under construction and each incorporated the new idea of separating animals from the household. In Wangala all the new houses are still being built in the traditional style without any provision for separate cattle sheds.

Nowadays, Dalena farmers do not keep their cattle long enough to become attached to them. This makes farmers more amenable to changes in the style of their houses, and supports the influence of the town. Thus they have developed a new style of their own: a combination of the traditional and the urban type of house. Some of the empty derelict houses are now being used as cattle sheds, or sheds for goats and sheep. In Wangala goats and sheep as well as cattle are kept in the same house with the farmer's family. It would thus appear easier to introduce housing innovations in villages where farmers buy and sell cattle frequently, than where farmers keep particular cattle for a number of years and thereby become attached to them. This point is supported by evidence I collected when I toured villages in a Community Project about 30 miles north-east of Wangala. The Project covers a hundred villages and I was able to visit many of these. Wherever I noticed that the Project Administration had been successful in introducing housing innovations, I found that farmers were engaged in other activities in addition to agriculture and tended to trade their farm animals more frequently. In the more strictly traditional rural economies, the Project Administration has made little headway with housing innovations.

The high turnover of animals by Dalena farmers affects the significance of my statistics of Dalena's animal husbandry. As mentioned above, I took the census at a time when farmers were highly stocked. Had I been able to check the census fully about three months later, by which time farmers had sold a lot of their stock, my figures would be very different. Unfortunately, I was not immediately aware of the seasonal variations in Dalena's animal stock. Since I arrived there straight from Wangala, where no such seasonal variations exist, I assumed that conditions would be similar in Dalena. It was only in the course of field-work that I realised there were big differences between the animal husbandry of the two villages. Thus while my figures for Wangala's animal husbandry are representative for the whole year, my statistics of animal stocks in Dalena are biased by the fact that the data were collected at a time when stocks were at a peak. March and April are the months when farmers sell off and accumulate money for the wedding season which starts in May.

Despite these limitations, the figures do help to throw some light on the difference between the pattern of animal ownership in Wangala and Dalena. 37% of Dalena's households (see Table 15) owned bullocks as against 53% in Wangala (see Table 5); by contrast, 54% of Dalena's households owned cows as against 30% of Wangala's households. These figures display the practice of farmers ploughing with cows in Dalena and with bullocks in Wangala. Wangala farmers keep cows solely for the purpose of breeding or dairy farming. In fact, in Wangala only very rarely did I see farmers using cows for ploughing.

The average value of bullocks per bullock-holding household in Wangala is Rs. 382, while it is only Rs. 281 in Dalena.[1] The considerable difference between these two average values can be accounted for by several reasons. Firstly, Wangala farmers have invested in better and more costly animals. Secondly, Dalena farmers mostly purchase at the big fairs where prices are lower. And thirdly, a far greater proportion of Dalena farmers hold cheaper bullocks than Wangala farmers. 21% of Wangala's households own animals worth altogether more than Rs. 600, whereas only 7% of Dalena's households own animals worth more than that amount (see Table 31). To have animal stocks of

[1] For the method of calculating the value of livestock see above, p. 68.

over Rs. 600 implies in general that the farmer owns more than one pair of draught animals—and there are very few of these in Dalena.

Cattle stocks in Dalena do not include a single bull, whereas there are two bulls in Wangala. Bulls are too unruly to be utilised as farm animals and are kept for breeding only. Keeping bulls is hardly an economic proposition. The farmer receives Rs. 2 every time his bull covers a cow, which pays about four days' fodder for the bull. Thus the farmer can hardly pay the maintenance of his bull from the money he receives for its services, and he cannot recover his initial expenditure on purchasing the bull. But to have a fine bull is a matter of prestige. Both Wangala bulls won prizes at a cattle show in Mandya. Their owners took great pains to march them to Mandya and proudly displayed them before men from many other villages. Wangala's bulls are now quite famous in the area and farmers from other villages walk their cows for miles to have them served by Wangala's bulls. Owners are well aware that to keep a bull costs more than it may earn, but the importance and prestige attached to this ownership outweighs economic considerations. In contrast, Dalena farmers take their cows to the veterinary hospital in Mandya for artificial insemination. The veterinary surgeon complained of the backwardness of Wangala villagers who will not take to scientific breeding for improved cattle. When he came to see me in Dalena he pointed out that Dalena farmers seem to be much more progressive about their animals. Dalena farmers are more progressive because they regard cattle as commercial commodities, and because they have more contact with the town and more knowledge of the services available to farmers.

Buffaloes are more common in Wangala than in Dalena: 37% of Wangala's households have buffaloes and only 22% of Dalena's households. Altogether there are 101 buffaloes in Wangala and 44 in Dalena. In both villages buffaloes are kept solely for their milk yield. I have already described (see p. 69) how the rearing of buffaloes is a woman's activity and that the income from milk sold is left to the women. Two reasons may account for the big difference in the number of buffaloes kept by households in the two villages. Firstly, Wangala farmers regard it as a matter of prestige to provide their wives with an independent source of income; secondly, Dalena women still work on the lands of their husbands and therefore have less time to rear buffaloes.

Goats and sheep fall within the sphere of work performed by boys, mostly between 8 to 15 years of age. Sheep and goats are kept for slaughter and trade: 37% of Dalena's households own sheep and 28% own goats (see Table 15). In Wangala farmers

TABLE 15

Dalena value and incidence of livestock ownership

Type of livestock	*Holding households*		*Average value per holding household*	*Non-holding households*		*Average value per household (all households)*	
	No.	%	*Rs.*	*No.*	%	*Rs.*	%
Bullocks (pair)	57	37	281	96	63	105	40
Cows (pair)	83	54	151	70	46	82	31
Buffaloes	33	22	135	120	78	29	11
Sheep	57	37	103	96	63	38	14
Goats	43	28	36	110	72	10	4
Total						264	100

paid less attention to the breeding of goats and sheep: only 15% of the households owned sheep and only 10% owned goats (see Table 5). There most households with sheep or goats keep only two or three of each, and these are kept for eventual slaughter or sacrifice at festivals. The largest flock in Wangala contained only about 20 sheep. In Dalena a number of farmers have herds of sheep or goats. During my stay in the village one farmer negotiated for a loan of Rs. 5,000 under the Rural Industrialisation Scheme to enable him to purchase about 100 sheep for wool production. He intends to bring some shepherds to Dalena, who are skilled in tending and shearing sheep. It is difficult to say whether this venture will materialise, but it shows the enterprising spirit of Dalena men.

In Wangala animal husbandry is subordinated, by and large, to the needs of cultivation. Farmers own bullocks because they need them for the cultivation of their lands; they do not breed or trade in animals. Animal husbandry has a different significance in Dalena's economy. Its primary purpose here is trade. Accordingly, agents (*dalali*) have acquired a different function. In Wangala, cattle agents are intermediaries in every sale of cattle, although such sales are not very frequent because, as I have already pointed out, farmers usually keep the same pair of cattle for a number of years. The high cattle turnover in Dalena has created more work for these agents. It requires considerable skill and diplomacy to be an agent and a number of younger men in Dalena have attached themselves as 'apprentices' to the established agents in the village. Here too, agents operate on the same principle as in Wangala: they receive a small reward independent of the value of the transaction. Nevertheless, the job brings greater economic gain in Dalena than in Wangala. Dalena farmers usually purchase at fairs and sell in neighbouring villages; agents in Dalena are less impartial than Wangala agents, because it is in their own interest to fetch the highest price possible for the vendor from their own village. They do this first of all because they themselves are often also potential vendors and secondly because they subsequently often receive a bonus from the vendor, although officially this is not admitted. Therefore, Dalena's agents have developed from intermediaries into selling agents, and as the cattle trade expands, more and more men enter this field of activity.

Village Entrepreneurs

The emergence of entrepreneurs is probably the most important feature of recent economic changes in Dalena. Lingegowda, the headman, has distinguished himself as the most enterprising of Dalena's villagers. He is an intelligent man, now in his mid-forties, with an impressive stature and a powerful personality. He is not only literate, which is an essential requirement for all head-men in the area, but he also received a few years of secondary education in Mandya. At the time when irrigation reached neigh-bouring villages, Lingegowda was a young man of about 25, still living jointly with his father and three younger brothers. He helped in the cultivation of the relatively extensive joint estate, but was at the same time on the look-out for an independent source of income. As a result of his schooling in Mandya he had friends and contacts there, who finally helped him to secure a contract with the Public Works Department. Lingegowda was the first of Dalena's men to operate in this field. In the village they still discuss how Lingegowda was the first to get a labour gang together. To finance his first ventures he had to borrow from his father. Money was then very scarce in the village and cash wages were low. Villagers say that in the early 1930s a man was happy to work for Rs. 0.15 a day. Official statistics record that daily wages for unskilled labour ranged from Rs. 0.15 to Rs. 1.00 in 1933 and 1934 for the whole of Mysore State.[1] Therefore, at that time, a contractor could manage with very little capital and, it is claimed, could make a handsome profit, even after paying a bribe to the appropriate official. In the last 20 years wages have risen much more than has the rate the Public Works Department pays for a job. At present, a contractor's net profit amounts to about 10% of his gross receipts, whereas twenty years ago a contractor could make as much as 33% net profit. When the canals and roads were being built in the area there was also much more demand for the services of contractors than in these days, when all they are needed for is to clean the canals once a year and to build roads and bridges wherever required.

The profitability of contracting helped Lingegowda to accumulate a few thousand rupees over a span of about ten years. Villagers say that his father was a good man and not grasping like Lingegowda. Lingegowda and his patrilateral cousin, who is the chief moneylender in the village and also an enterprising man, are regarded as the most grasping and meanest men in the village. In fact, they are probably no more grasping, but only more enterprising and more successful, than other villagers. As the first contractor in the village, Lingegowda managed to establish the best contacts and get the best jobs and the most profits. His contacts opened up new avenues of enterprise to him. For instance,

[1] Report of the Agriculturalists' Relief Committee in Mysore, 1935, Table 5.

during the last War he was asked by a friend in Mandya whether he could get hold of ragi or paddy outside the official rationing scheme. Under this scheme the Revenue Inspector, in conjunction with the headman and accountant, placed each household into one of three groups according to whether it produced a surplus of grain, was just self-sufficient, or had to purchase food for consumption. Those households which had a 'surplus' had to surrender it to the authorities at a price fixed by the Government. Each farmer of course tried to understate the yields of his estate. How far he could manage to do this depended very much on his relations with the headman, accountant and Revenue Inspector. As the son of the headman, Lingegowda was in a position to know the actual yield and the forced sales of most estates in the village. Therefore, he also knew where to secure supplies outside the rationing scheme, and so he developed into a keen black market operator. In this way he came frequently to be asked about mills in the villages for, as I have already explained, it was never advisable to have black market grain processed in a mill in the town right under the eyes of the rationing authorities. Lingegowda himself related to me how the idea of starting a flour mill occurred to him when lorries one day stopped just outside Dalena to enquire the whereabouts of the nearest mill. He discussed this matter with friends in Mandya and quickly decided to venture into another new enterprise and open a mill.

Without electricity in Dalena it was impossible to start a power mill. Lingegowda started negotiations in a neighbouring village, which was already electrified and favourably situated along the railway. He purchased machinery for Rs. 4,000 and put up a building worth Rs. 3,000 to house it. In 1945 he had already accumulated Rs. 4,000 ready cash out of profits from his other ventures and he borrowed the remaining Rs. 3,000 from a friend in Mandya by 'pledging' his machinery. Once more Lingegowda's venture proved successful. His mill was the only one within miles, apart from the mills in the town, and lorries and carts with 'off ration' grain are said to have queued up outside it. Within five years he was able to clear off all his debts and accumulate money to purchase wet land in neighbouring villages.

In the meantime, Lingegowda's father had died, he had become headman, and the joint family had been partitioned. Once his father was dead he insisted on partitioning the family property to consolidate his own position and to enable him to pursue his own interests without interference from his younger brothers. His mother remained with him and so did his youngest brother, who is still unmarried. Lingegowda now owns and cultivates four acres of dry land in Dalena and seven acres of wet land in neighbouring villages. Two of his wet acres are under contract to the sugar refinery and on the remaining five acres he grows paddy. I have already described him as a most enterprising cultivator who adopted the Japanese method of paddy cultivation and even won a prize for producing the highest yield of paddy per acre in the area. He is one of the few farmers in the village who have compost pits and who purchase manure from Mandya's municipality. His bullock-driven stone roller for threshing paddy and ragi is the only one of its kind in the village.

In every sphere of activity entered by Lingegowda he has shown himself to be a keen entrepreneur and innovator. He started a grocery shop near his flour mill and just before I left the village he applied for a loan of Rs. 10,000 under the Rural Industrialisation Scheme to build an improved power cane-crusher at a road junction near Dalena. Since rationing and the black market have disappeared, the demand for the services of Lingegowda's mill has declined. Consequently he negotiated to buy a smaller motor so as to cut down running costs. The average daily turnover of his mill amounts to Rs. 5 of which 50% are paid in wages to an operator and in charges for electricity. In comparison with the turnover Lingegowda's mill had in the days of rationing, present profits are negligible. But Lingegowda continues to be optimistic and to display enterprise. His many business and farming interests take him out of the village practically every day. He leaves home early almost every morning and cycles on his own bicycle to Mandya, to his mill, or to his friends; he rarely returns before dusk. At night he sits in his home—one of the few houses with electricity and with modern furniture. Here he reads the newspaper or helps his son, who is now 12 years old and a pupil at Mandya's high school, with his home-work. Lingegowda is well informed on political issues concerning Mysore State and India at large, and he was most keen to learn about life in the West.

In a later chapter I shall discuss the implications of Lingegowda's enterprise and innovations in village political and social relations. At this stage in the argument I am merely concerned with the factors determining new economic ventures. What makes a Dalena man into an entrepreneur? In the case of Lingegowda, enterprise was the result of a combination of favourable factors: firstly, Lingegowda obviously has the necessary ability; secondly, as the eldest son of the headman he received better than average education—he is in fact the only one of his generation who attended secondary school in Mandya; thirdly, his contacts in the town facilitated his first enterprise; fourthly, he was the son of a magnate and yet he had sufficient spare time away from the cultivation of the joint estate to take up other activities; fifthly, his changing environment provided fertile ground for his enterprise and ability. If Dalena men wanted to participate in the expanding regional economy, they were forced to operate outside the limits of their own traditional village economy. They either had to buy newly irrigated land in neighbouring villages, or branch out into non-agricultural activities. By contrast, Wangala men could increase their income by concentrating on the cultivation of their newly irrigated, more productive, wet lands. Not a single man in Wangala has displayed anywhere near so much enterprise as Dalena's headman; on the other hand, there are quite a number of other entrepreneurs in Dalena. This difference between the two villages can hardly be attributed to the accidental superior ability of Dalena villagers, but rather to the more favourable environment in which Dalena's entrepreneurs operate.

The most interesting aspect of Lingegowda's case history is the dynamics of his progress. Each new venture provided the basis for a further enterprise: school contacts led to contracting work; this in turn led to black market transactions and subsequently to the establishment of a mill; with his profits Lingegowda bought wet land, and he developed into an outstanding cultivator; he also opened up a grocery shop and now wants to start another power cane-crusher. By contrast, though irrigation brought a number of changes in Wangala, even the most enterprising man remained a farmer tied to the economic organisation of the customary farming economy. Dalena's headman, on the other hand, operates outside the sphere of his customary village economy. Apart from cultivating his four acres of dry land in Dalena, all his economic interests lie outside his village and largely outside agriculture.

Lingegowda's younger brother Kempegowda owns the flour mill in Dalena which competes with Lingegowda's own mill in the neighbouring village. I have already related how Kempegowda's enterprise resulted from watching his elder brother's success. When Kempegowda first began to agitate for electrification of Dalena, Lingegowda became his strongest opponent. Before the electricity authorities agree to bring electricity to a village they need assurances that the revenue of the village is sufficient to meet the annual charges. This meant that the house tax in Dalena had to be trebled before the authorities would even consider Dalena's application for electricity. Kempegowda was the only one who stood to gain directly from the installation of electricity. The only advantage to the other villagers was that they would have electric light in the streets, for which they were asked to pay a lot more in taxes. Yet the majority of the elders were sufficiently keen on electricity to support Kempegowda's request in opposition to the headman. Competition between Lingegowda and Kempegowda led to a temporary breach in the relationship between the two brothers. However, kinship and ceremonial ties operated to bridge once more the gulf that economic competition had created between them. But their relationship continues to be easily upset because of the conflicting principles it involves: ceremonial and kinship ties operate with the ideal of lineage unity; by contrast, economic competition encourages individual initiative.

A similar conflict exists in the relationship between the headman and Nanjegowda, his patrilateral cousin, and between the latter and Kempegowda. All three men are members of the same lineage and all three men are entrepreneurs—and successful ones

Kempegowda, the headman's younger brother, in front of his cane-crusher

Plate IX. Dalena

too. Nanjegowda is a few years older than the headman; he, too, had acted once as contractor and taken part in black market dealings. Eventually moneylending became his major economic activity apart from agriculture. Therefore he is now no longer a direct competitor of Lingegowda and Kempegowda, who both operate flour mills. Nanjegowda is renowned in the village for his meanness—an attribute often ascribed to moneylenders; and he certainly is the shrewdest moneylender in the village. Usually, loans in the village carry an interest of 12% p.a. and interest is payable annually. I have already explained, with reference to Wangala, that debt relationships are often hereditary and the principal debt is never repaid. In the case of Nanjegowda loans are purely business transactions and they have no personal aspect. He does not regard moneylending as a means to perpetuate a relationship, but purely as a source of income, and he lends in such a way as to have a quick turnover of money. He charges up to 15% interest, depending on the degree of urgency of the loan. To ensure payment of the interest, he deducts the annual interest already in advance from the initial loan. Thus if a man wants to borrow Rs. 100 for one year Nanjegowda deducts Rs. 15 and hands the man Rs. 85 after the latter has signed the appropriate document. Since the borrower has to repay the full loan, he is in fact paying almost 20% interest p.a. Nanjegowda is the only moneylender in the village who conducts his business in this way. Everyone complains about it, but they have all been his debtors at one time or other. It is difficult to assess with any accuracy the extent of Nanjegowda's loanable funds. But judging from details supplied by his debtors in the village, and by answers to enquiries in neighbouring villages, Nanjegowda probably has lent about Rs. 40,000. These loans should yield an annual interest of about Rs. 6,000, but there is always some failure in repayment, amounting perhaps to 10%. This still leaves an annual income in the form of interest of Rs. 5,400 which is roughly equal to a farmer's wages and profits on 6 acres of sugarcane.

It is difficult to compare the profitability of loans with that of land, because land is so rarely sold that it has no market price. However, from those sales which have taken place in recent times it appears that one acre of wet land is priced at Rs. 2,000. Therefore, wet land worth about Rs. 12,000 yields annual farmers' wages and profits of the same amount as Rs. 40,000 loanable funds. Of course we must remember that farmers' wages and profits involve considerable labour by the farmer and his household. Nevertheless, land is certainly the more remunerative investment. Nanjegowda is fully aware of this and tries to acquire land whenever possible. Conditions of the loan usually include a mortgage or a provision whereby a debtor pledges his land in case he cannot repay according to the terms laid down in the agreement. In this way, Nanjegowda uses moneylending as a means of acquiring more land. Moneylending in itself is not a new venture: we have seen that the indebtedness structure forms part of the traditional economic organisation of Wangala. But Nanjegowda transacts his moneylending on the basis of the general principles underlying the modern money economy. Personal considerations and ties are largely of secondary importance and economic gain is the main incentive. Though Nanjegowda is the chief moneylender in the village, he is still primarily a farmer. His ruthless acquisitiveness often comes into conflict with his desire to be a respected member of Dalena's village society. Since Nanjegowda, in his capacity as moneylender, denies the personal aspect of intra-village economic relations, it is difficult for him to secure status within the network of intra-village social relations.

The headman, his younger brother and his patrilateral cousin are the richest magnates in Dalena and the three most enterprising men. They belong to one lineage. This lineage acts as a faction to which most other lineages are in opposition. In my discussion of Dalena's political system I shall show how the enterprise of these three dominant men in the headman's lineage is largely responsible for the present alignment of factions in the village.

The hard core of the faction which opposes the headman's lineage also includes a few entrepreneurs. A number are occasional contractors, while others are moneylenders. But none has been as successful as those I have just been discussing; nor have they been incorporated to the same extent in the regional economy, and the wider competitive system. Hanumegowda, Mollegowda and

Channegowda, the three men in this faction, are primarily farmers, although they also trade paddy and cattle and do contracting jobs. Within the overall changes in Dalena this faction upholds as ideal the traditional system, although its members too fashion their lives on the model of townsmen.

I find it impossible to account for the greater economic success of the headman and his relatives, apart from putting it down to their greater ability and luck. But what is most important to all entrepreneurs in Dalena is the fertile environment, which enabled potential entrepreneurs to develop entrepreneurial skills.

Commuters

So far I have analysed a number of economic activities which have taken Dalena men outside the sphere of their own village economy; I have considered their new roles as industrial and commercial entrepreneurs, and stressed the diversity and dispersal of their recently established economic links in contrast to the concentration and uniformity of customary intra-village economic relations. But many of these ties are fluid and activated only occasionally. In this section I shall discuss the economic life of commuters: men who live in Dalena and work in Mandya; and I shall show how much more constant, rigid and intensive their relations are with the wider economy than are those of entrepreneurs and traders.

Every day 26 men, who represent 13% of Dalena's male population of working age, travel the six miles to work in Mandya. Nineteen of them go on their own bicycles, the others have to get a lift on another's bicycle, walk, or on rare occasions take the bus. In some contexts they stand apart from other Dalena men. Their regular employment takes them out of the everyday life of the village and knits them into town life; their regular cash income distinguishes their pattern of expenditure from those of other villagers. In the eyes of other villagers, the commuters form a group of men who have been lucky enough to find a niche for themselves in the wider money economy.

Yet the commuters are by no means an undivided, uniform

group; among themselves they are differentiated according to certain principles of social organisation, some of which stem from their common residence in the village, others from their participation in the wider economy. For instance age, kinship and caste alignment within the group reflect the principles operative in the traditional social system. On the other hand, differentiation between clerks, factory workers and orderlies results from the wider system in which they work.

These two sets of principles of social organisation often involve the individual in conflicting roles. The case of Timma illustrates the point. He is the eldest son of one of the richer farmers in Dalena. Having completed secondary education he managed to get a job as a clerk in Mandya's Agricultural Department. His father is a lineage elder and a *panchayat* member supporting one faction in the village. As his eldest son, Timma is certainly the heir to the ritual office of lineage elder and possibly to the political office of *panchayat* member as well. He is now 31 years old and has worked as clerk in Mandya for the past seven years. His father and his younger brother, who, like Timma, is already married and has children, look after the estate and they live as a joint family. Among the other commuters there are six other men of Timma's lineage and in the same age group. In the village, lineage ceremonies perpetually reassert the ideal of lineage unity and Timma, as the son of a lineage elder, has an important part in them. Yet on his way to work he never mixes with any of his lineage mates, because they are all factory workers and he is a clerk. The factory workers complain of his arrogance and say that he hardly acknowledges them if they happen to meet in town. Timma obviously makes a point of avoiding them once outside the village.

The only other clerk living in Dalena is Nanja, son of Nanjegowda, the chief moneylender in the village, whom I discussed in the last section. Nanja belongs to the headman's lineage and Timma to a lineage which forms part of the faction in opposition to the headman. Therefore, according to the intra-village alignment, Timma and Nanja belong to two opposing factions; but according to the principles of differentiation based on occupation, they both belong to the same social category, for they are both clerks. Consequently, there are forces at work which tend to unite Nanja and Timma, and others which pull them apart. Timma often used to meet Nanja on his way to town and they would cycle along together; on the other hand, when Nanja's younger brother got married, Timma sided with the other members of his faction in refusing to attend the wedding, although Nanja specially invited him. The social situation largely determines the set of principles upon which a commuter acts. Social pressure within the village made Timma express his allegiance to his lineage as opposed to loyalty to a fellow-clerk. Similarly, in the town, Timma mixed freely with Nanja and kept aloof from his lineage fellows who are factory workers in Mandya. Timma, in this case, acted as a villager when in Dalena and as a member of an occupational group when in town.

However, the principles upon which a man acts as a member of a group are not always so clearly distinguished in the village and the town, but often overlap. For instance, the common interests of factory workers cut across caste differentiation in the village when factory workers of the refinery were all out on strike. The one Oilpresser, who is a factory worker, normally does not mix with his fellow workers in Dalena; Oilpressers are regarded as inferior to the Peasant caste in Dalena. In addition, the Dalena Oilpresser is a recent immigrant to the village and still regarded as an outsider. But when the factory workers were on strike, the Oilpresser was always to be found among one or other of the group of commuters in the village discussing the situation of the strike. On this occasion the common interests stemming from working together cut across caste differentiation within the village. It did not actually involve a breach of caste rules, but it helped to close the ranks of factory workers, irrespective of the different castes to which they belonged.

On the other hand, in certain social situations caste differentiation operates also in the town, and often cuts across occupational differentiation. The general manager of the refinery belongs to the same caste as most of the labourers from Dalena. But these labourers work side by side with men from other castes and even Untouchables. Peasants from Dalena have come to learn that they can use caste loyalty to secure jobs in the town. It can hardly be regarded as accidental that among all the workers from Wangala employed at the factory plantation and all the men from Dalena employed in the factory, there are only four who are not Peasants. Economic success in the town has largely remained the prerogative of the Peasant caste and the town has taken over caste differentiation from the rural areas as a principle of social organisation. However, caste in the town differs from caste in the village; for instance, village rituals periodically affirm the integration of the various castes in the whole village system, whereas in town this integrating mechanism does not operate. I am, however, not in a position to discuss the importance of caste in Mandya town as such, for this falls outside my study, and I can only hazard these remarks on the basis of the data collected from Dalena commuters.

Yeera, the only Untouchable from Dalena who managed to become an orderly in the engineering department at Mandya, is completely isolated from all other commuters. In his case caste and occupational differentiation coincide. On the other hand, Yeera also feels isolated from other Untouchables in Dalena who are envious of his success. His father immigrated from another village, but Yeera himself was born in Dalena. He and the Oilpresser are the only two men among Dalena's commuters who do not own land. Since he has no land and no agnatic kin in Dalena there is little that ties him to the village. His wife and children stay in Dalena, but he himself often spends the whole week in Mandya. The keen competition among Untouchables for the very few jobs open to them makes his life in the village unpleasant, while the competition and the resulting envy undermine their unity as a caste.

All the Peasants who work in Mandya also hold some land in Dalena, and often also in neighbouring villages. In fact, every commuter, while proud of working in the town, wants to become a rich farmer and regards his job as a means of accumulating money to buy land. Halli, a young Peasant, is typical of the group of Dalena factory workers. He is now 24 years old and has been a factory worker for the past five years. He first made his way to Mandya in search of work when he was 15 years old. His father had died when Halli was a young boy and he had stayed with his mother and elder brother in Dalena while his father's brother cultivated their estate. When the latter died without issue he left one acre of wet land and three acres of dry land to Halli and his elder brother Chenna. Chenna was old enough by then to cultivate the estate and encouraged Halli to seek work in the town, for Halli himself was too young at the time to be left in charge of the estate, if Chenna had gone out to work. For a long time Halli walked daily to Mandya in search of work. Finally, he met a Peasant there from another village who was a servant in the staff quarters at the refinery and who found Halli a job as houseboy to a Brahmin engineer working at the refinery. Halli had to stay in Mandya in the household for which he worked, but he regularly took his wages home to his mother in Dalena. After working for four years for about Rs. 20 per month, he managed to get his master to secure him a job in the factory for a monthly wage of Rs. 55. This enabled Halli to return to live in Dalena. In the meantime, his mother had been ill so they had agreed to get a wife for Chenna, for a woman was needed to help in the cultivation of their lands as well as to look after their household. They had to borrow Rs. 500 for Chenna's wedding. When Halli returned to Dalena he came to stay with his mother and Chenna and his wife. By this time, Halli's desire to become a farmer had become more pronounced; he wanted to cultivate together with his brother, but Chenna wanted no interference. In order to participate in the cultivation of the joint estate Halli had to take days off work—for instance, when lands had to be ploughed after a heavy monsoon shower in April. Halli complained that he contributed all his wages to the joint household and got little for it. Chenna likewise complained that Halli was a useless farmer and he had to do all the work himself and share the proceeds with Halli. After many quarrels the brothers agreed to partition. They each took an equal share of the joint estate, but Chenna kept the bullocks, their ploughs and other tools, on the basis that he had cultivated their land alone all those years while Halli had been working in Mandya. Nor did they share the debt incurred for Chenna's wedding. This, so Halli claimed, was a matter for Chenna to settle. Had their father been alive when Chenna married, and had the father incurred the debt for Chenna's wedding, its burden would have had to be shared out equally among the sons. In that case, provision would have had to be made for Halli's wedding expenses also. As it was, Chenna himself had contracted the debt, and although he contracted it in the name of the joint household, it remained solely his responsibility after partition. Halli was left with half an acre of wet land and one and a half acres of dry land, but without any tools or draught animals. His mother joined Halli, who built a partition in their common house to separate his household from that of his brother. His new responsibilities as independent farmer occupy Halli's interests. Until he can afford to buy a pair of bullocks he has to hire or borrow from relatives or friends. To establish himself in the village, he arranged to marry the daughter of one of the rich farmers and political leaders in Dalena. I shall refer again to this marriage; for the present, it is interesting to note that Halli, one of the poorest farmers whose family had little prestige, managed to marry the daughter of one of the village leaders. Halli incurred a lot of debts to celebrate his wedding and three Brahmin members of the refinery staff came to witness Halli's wedding in the village.

Halli's case history sets out the dilemma faced by a poor farmer who lives in a village and works in a town. In the first instance, the small size of the estate induced him to seek an income outside the village, but ultimately he intended to utilise this income to become a farmer of standing in the village. He wanted to translate income earned outside the village into prestige in the village. On the other hand, through working in the town, he adopted some values of the wider society; the attractions of urban life were strong and the village seemed dull in comparison. Thus Halli belongs fully neither to the village nor to the town: in relation to men in the town he often acts as farmer and in relation to men in the village he appears as townsman. His diverse interests have led to the partition of the family estate. Halli now has an uneconomically small holding, but he is forced to take time off from work to look after it. His preoccupation with farming prevents him from looking for advancement in his industrial career. Though a capable young man, Halli is neither a good farmer, because he cannot always tend to his lands when needed, nor a good worker, because he often stays off from work. Halli's case is representative of many small farmers in the area who work in Mandya's refinery. The pull of the land causes a high absentee rate and a high labour turnover rate in the factory. This in turn is responsible for the management's decision to install labour-saving machinery rather than to employ more labour, in spite of the high degree of underemployment existing in the area.

The contradictory pull of village and town on commuters from Dalena accounts for the inconsistency in their behaviour. They are neither good farmers nor good factory workers; they are neither full village members nor have they become townsmen. They want to become full-time farmers and at the same time live like townsmen. This inconsistency in their behaviour both undermines as well as strengthens the traditional village system. They undermine it by subjecting it to the impact of new urban values and they strengthen it by their attempt to translate income earned in the town into social status in the village in terms of traditional values.

Property, Income and Expenditure Pattern

Dalena's appearance reflects the interaction between traditional and modern values, between the old and the new. For instance, most houses in the village are of the traditional style which is still prevalent in Wangala, but quite a number of houses already include a partition for a bathroom, some even have separate cattle sheds—and all new houses are being built in modern style. Similarly, for everyday, most Dalena men simply wear the same type of battered and torn shirt and shorts I have described for Wangala men; but in Dalena there are a number of men who, even on an ordinary work day, always look well and neatly dressed in their fine, clean shirts and dhotis and who proudly display their gold wrist watches. The greater extremes in Dalena are striking by comparison with Wangala. In Dalena we find the luxurious two-storey city-type house of a Peasant overlooking the poorest and smallest mud huts of Untouchables, or we find a smartly rigged out young Peasant cycling past an old Peasant, who wears nothing but a loincloth and a turban.

Economic differentiation in Wangala finds its expression usually only on public occasions, such as weddings and feasts. Normally, all Wangala men are engaged in operations connected with agriculture, for which they all wear roughly the same kind of clothes. The greater uniformity in their dress reflects the greater uniformity in their economic activities. Wangala's prestige structure asserts itself only on social occasions. By contrast, Dalena's prestige structure asserts itself in the everyday life of the village. The greater diversity of economic activities performed by Dalena men is responsible for the greater variety and differentiation in the clothes they wear, even on an ordinary working day. For instance, Nanja and Timma, the two Dalena clerks working in Mandya, always wear suits for work and dhotis when in the village. Their position as clerks in Mandya demands that they wear suits; they could not possibly deviate from the pattern of clerical dress in Mandya and arrive for work in a pair of shorts and a shirt. In Wangala, there is not a single clerk nor a single man who owns a suit of Western style. Who could utilise a suit to work on the land? The only time Wangala farmers adopt items of city dress is at weddings. I have already described how the harassed bridegroom has to sweat in a Western style jacket throughout his three-day ordeal and sometimes is even made to wear shoes. But both jacket and shoes are safely stored, once the wedding is over, and taken out only when required for another social occasion. Dalena men, on the other hand, need their better dress to conform to the pattern of dress conventional in the town. When I asked Molla, a rich young Peasant who is a contractor, and who trades in paddy and grows cane on his land in neighbouring villages, why he is always so well dressed, even on an ordinary working day, he pointed out that he could not possibly keep his contacts in the town, which are essential to his activities, if he were not dressed in this fashion. 'None of the officials in Mandya would even look at me,' he asserted, 'if I appeared dressed like a poor farmer.' He pointed to one of the old and poor Peasant farmers who wore nothing but a loincloth, the customary dress in this area prior to irrigation, and jokingly enquired whether I considered a man dressed like that would stand a chance of getting a contract from the Public Works Department.

Apart from their more elaborate dress some Dalena men also have watches. Altogether there are eight men with wrist watches and three houses with clocks. In Wangala there is not a single watch or clock and the schoolmaster used to send a little boy to my house to find out if it was time for him to finish his class. Wangala farmers in general tell the time by the position of the sun. When the sun begins to climb in the East they know it is time to start work; when the sun is overhead it is hottest and time to break off for a siesta; and when the sun disappears over the hills in the West, it is time to be back in the village, for it will soon be getting dark. Wangala farmers employ labour on a daily or half-daily basis, but never on an hourly basis. An hour or a minute are not important units of time for Wangala farmers and therefore a watch is not a real necessity. By contrast, smaller units of time are more important to Dalena men, particularly to those who work in town. Factory workers have to clock in and out and have to appear punctually for the start of a shift. Similarly, contractors have to keep their appointments at the engineering office, and traders their appointments with wholesalers. But even in town accuracy of time is still not as important as it is in the West; indeed one of the standard jokes of Indians in the city is to refer to a man who is about an hour late as one who acts according to 'Indian Standard Time'. This lack of appreciation of punctuality and clock-time, even in the town, is no doubt largely the result of the predominance of the rural sector in the region. Still, clock-time is more important in the town than it is in villages like Wangala, and Dalena men, since they are directly linked to the town, have adjusted their behaviour to the townspeople's attitude to time. Thus, to have a watch in Dalena is, to some men, a necessity. But the pride they take in wearing gold watches makes it clear that it is also a matter of prestige.

The fact that some items are necessary in the town has made them into important criteria of prestige in Dalena. For example, a watch may be essential for a man who works in the factory, but even those villagers who do not need to tell the time more exactly now also want one, because its possession confers prestige. Similarly, education and literacy have become important factors of prestige in Dalena and the symbols of literacy, namely a pencil or a fountain-pen, are greatly desired in the village. Many an illiterate villager proudly displays a fountain-pen in the breast pocket of his shirt. I am quite sure that the consumption of fountain-pens in the Mandya region far exceeds the requirements of its literate population.

Bicycles are also greatly desired by Dalena villagers. Here again we find that what is essential to some Dalena men becomes a desired object amongst all villagers. Altogether 32 men in Dalena own bicycles, and many more would like to have one at their disposal. Of all luxury items of expenditure, bicycles have the highest priority in the eyes of Dalena villagers. To have a bicycle and a watch is what every villager wants, but they are expensive items: a new bicycle costs at least Rs. 200 and a new watch at least Rs. 40. Expressed in wages, a watch amounts to about one month's wages of a factory worker and a bicycle to as much as four months' wages. None of the bicycles owned by Dalena men were purchased new; they were therefore much cheaper than Rs. 200: some of them were bought second-hand in Mandya's bazaars, others from individuals in Mandya or other villages.

The more elaborate dress, the greater number of luxury items, and the many recent housing innovations, are reflected in a higher average value of non-productive property per consumption unit in Dalena than in Wangala: the Dalena sample shows an average of Rs. 513 (see Table 32) and that of Wangala Rs. 462. The average value of personal property, which includes clothes, jewellery and luxury items such as a bicycle, is only slightly greater for Dalena (Rs. 81) than for Wangala (Rs. 78), but the greater range in Dalena's sample reflects the greater differentiation in Dalena in ownership of personal property. Personal property among the sample in Dalena ranges in value from Rs. 10 to Rs. 320 per consumption unit; among Wangala's sample it ranges from Rs. 10 to only Rs. 220 per consumption unit. On the other

TABLE 16

Dalena average value of non-productive property per consumption unit

Type of property	*Rs.*	%
Personal property	81	16
House	378	74
Household chattels	54	10
Total	513	100

TABLE 17

Dalena sources of average non-productive property per consumption unit

Source of property	*Rs.*	%
Home produced	14	3
Barter	1	—
Gift	259	50
Cash purchase	239	47
Total	513	100

hand, 69% of Dalena's sample have personal property worth less than Rs. 80, i.e. less than the average, whereas only 50% of Wangala's sample have personal property worth less than Rs. 80 (see Table 35). These figures show the extent to which personal property expresses economic differentiation in Dalena.

The average value of house property per consumption unit amounts to Rs. 378 in Dalena and only to Rs. 341 in Wangala (see Table 32). In both villages the range of house property is from nought to Rs. 1,500 in value, but whereas of Dalena's sample 10% have house property worth more than Rs. 1,000 per consumption unit, only 3% of Wangala's sample have that much house property. On the other hand, 6% of Dalena's sample have no housing property at all, as against only 3% in Wangala (see Table 36). This reflects the slightly greater instability in Dalena's population. Temporary immigrants are allocated space on the verandah of some of Dalena's houses where, with the aid of a couple of bamboo mats, they make a living-room for themselves.

The value of household chattels is about 25% higher in Dalena than in Wangala; in the Dalena sample the average amounts to Rs. 54 per consumption unit and in Wangala to Rs. 42 (see Table 32). Household chattels include all kitchen utensils, furniture, idols, pictures and so on. They also include in Dalena the posters which decorate some of the village houses. These include advertisements of American films and often display scantily dressed women engaged in passionate love scenes. Such posters violate the ethical standards of Hinduism, but this escapes the notice of Dalena villagers who see nothing wrong in them and fetch them proudly from Mandya. Though a colourful advertisement of a film with Marilyn Monroe is not exactly what one might expect to find side by side with a photograph of Nehru and Gandhi, villagers do not find this strange at all. Both the pictures of Nehru and Gandhi and the film posters express their interest in the wider economy and body politic; both introduce external values into Dalena's village life.

Dalena villagers have more items of furniture than Wangala villagers and some have more elaborate kitchen utensils. For household chattels, as for personal property, we find that the distribution among the sample indicates a greater differentiation in Dalena: 19% of its sample households have household chattels of more than Rs. 80 per consumption unit whereas only 5% have this amount in Wangala (see Table 37).

The Dalena sample shows a high correlation (0·71) between the economic category, which we must remember is based on landholding, and other income, and the value of a household's non-productive property per consumption unit; in Wangala there is no such correlation (0·10). On the other hand, the average agricultural capital of the sample households in Wangala far exceeds that of Dalena households. By and large, Wangala men have tended to invest more in agricultural capital since irrigation while Dalena men have invested more in non-productive property. However, this picture is not altogether true, for to compare the productive investment in the two villages it would be necessary to compile statistics of industrial and commercial investment in Dalena. But except for the mill and cane-crusher machinery, which involve only two households in Dalena, I was unfortunately not able to collect detailed information of commercial capital. Part of this commercial capital does however appear under the heading of agricultural capital, as I explained in my discussion of animal husbandry.[1] Therefore, some commercial capital appears in the Dalena sample even if my quantitative data do not include a separate category for industrial and commercial capital. Accordingly I think the figures do show the greater productive investment in Wangala, by contrast with Dalena, where more was invested in non-productive property. The greater proportion of cash property to total non-productive property in Dalena (47%) than in Wangala (32%) reflects the more recent acquisition of some items of non-productive property in Dalena. The Wangala sample shows little correlation between cash-acquired non-productive property and the economic category of the household, whereas the Dalena sample shows high correlation between these two variables (0·64). This can be taken as another indication of economic differentiation in terms of non-productive property in Dalena and the comparative absence of this mode of differentiation in Wangala.

I have spoken of weddings and other ceremonies as providing the stage for a struggle for status in Wangala. On these occasions Wangala villagers vie with one another about who wears the finest clothes or the best jewellery and who provides the most elaborate meal. On the other hand, everyday life in Wangala presents a picture of comparative uniformity. By contrast, economic differentiation is striking in Dalena's everyday life, but not as pronounced in the performance of weddings and feasts, though in Dalena too weddings constitute occasions for villagers to strive for status. I witnessed six weddings in Dalena, of which one took place in the household of a magnate, two in the richer section of the middle-farmers, two others in the poorer section of the middle-farmers, and one in a Washerman's household, which belongs to the poorest households in the village. The magnate's household was the only one that celebrated a three-day wedding; all the others lasted one day only.

[1] See above, p. 239.

Nanjegowda, the chief moneylender in Dalena, attempted to use the occasion of his son's wedding to assert his social status in the village. Normally he is regarded as a mean and greedy man, but for the wedding of his son he was prepared to spare no expense. He hired Lingayat cooks to prepare special delicacies for a feast to which he hoped all villagers would throng; he had his house splendidly decorated for the occasion and rose water sprinkled around to give it a nice aroma. Alas, only members of his own lineage, Peasants from other villages and some Functionaries attended the feast, while all other Dalena Peasants boycotted it. Much of the food was left over and eventually given to Untouchables. Nanjegowda bitterly complained of the lack of civility on the part of Peasants in the village and swore that he would never again go to such expense to provide hospitality. Nevertheless, his efforts had not failed to leave their mark, for in spite of their boycott everybody spoke for days about all the things Nanjegowda had prepared.

Yet even the wedding of the richest magnate in Dalena involved less expense than that of the Wangala magnate (see Table 18).

TABLE 18

Dalena wedding expenses for four selected households

Items of Expenditure	*Magnate*		*Middle-farmer (rich)*		*Middle-farmer (poor)*		*Poorest*	
	Rs.	%	*Rs.*	%	*Rs.*	%	*Rs.*	%
Food	612	26	301	33	241	34	76	34
Clothing	454	18	102	12	125	17	75	33
Ornaments	1,100	46	360	40	237	33	41	19
Functionaries	113	4	105	12	75	11	5	2
Miscellaneous	123	6	27	3	34	5	28	12
Total	2,402	100	895	100	712	100	225	100

Compared with other weddings in the village, that of the Dalena magnate was most elaborate, but compared with the weddings I witnessed in Wangala, the Dalena magnate's wedding was not outstanding; apart from specially prepared food, it included no novel item, and there was no car to take the bridal pair in procession round the village, nor a very elaborate band to accompany them. The comparative 'dullness' of the wedding of Dalena's magnate can be easily explained by reference to the weddings of middle-farmers in the village. Even the richer middle-farmers conducted only a one-day wedding and they spent less on it than the poorer middle-farmers in Wangala. In Wangala, I have argued, economic differentiation since irrigation is most intense within the group of middle-farmers. This finds expression in the way a middle-farmer celebrates a wedding in his household and puts pressure on magnates to compete with middle-farmers. All these Wangala middle-farmers derive their income from their estates. By contrast, many of the households within the group of middle-farmers in Dalena derive the major part of their incomes from sources other than agriculture and from outside their own village. Consequently struggle for prestige among middle-farmers in Dalena is differently expressed. To a Dalena middle-farmer it is more important to have a bicycle or a watch than to spend lavishly on a wedding feast. The range within which wedding expenditure operates as a criterion of prestige is largely limited to the village, whereas prestige accorded through ownership of a bicycle and watch operates within a much wider range of relations, including the town and one's fellow workers there. This may help to explain why the total wedding expense of the richer middle-farmer in Dalena is less than half that of a Peasant in the same economic category in Wangala. There the village is the operative unit within which struggle for prestige takes place.

The Washerman's wedding was a very austere affair. It included a feast for a number of the kin of both parties. Peasants attended the ceremony but could not take food. The austerity and cost of the Washerman's wedding in Dalena was very similar to that of the Untouchable wedding I witnessed in Wangala. In certain aspects weddings in Dalena and Wangala are almost identical. For instance, each budget shows that about one-third of the total expenditure is devoted to food; in both villages also the amount given to Functionaries increases with the economic status of the wedding household. Apart from Nanjegowda, the chief money-lender in Dalena, in both villages all the households which celebrated weddings had to borrow money for the occasion; only part of the wedding expenditure came out of accumulated savings.

The average household of Dalena's sample saves 13% of its current income, whereas in Wangala's sample the average household saves 16%. But here it must be remembered that wedding

TABLE 19

Dalena average monthly budget per consumption unit

Income from:	*Rs.*	%	*Expenditure on:*	*Rs.*	%
Subsistence	12	33	Food	16	45
Barter	1·50	4	Clothes	3·50	10
Gifts	0·50	1	Sundries	4	11
Cash:			Ritual expenditure	0·50	1
Manufacturing and trading profits	5	14	Household overheads	3	9
Interest	2	6	Gifts	1	3
Crop sales	5	13	Interest	3	7
Animal products	2	6	Miscellaneous	0·50	1
Crafts	—	—	Savings	4·50	13
Wages (agricultural)	2	5			
Wages (non-agricultural)	3	9			
Miscellaneous	3	9			
Total income	36	100	Total expenditure	36	100

expenditure is after all only delayed consumption, and Wangala villagers spend more on their weddings than Dalena villagers. Thus the greater savings on current consumption in Wangala do not represent a greater thriftiness, but rather a different spending pattern from Dalena households. While Dalena villagers spend more on food and sundries, Wangala men prefer to spend more on weddings. Dalena's average monthly income per consumption unit is Rs. 36, which is about 10% higher than that in Wangala, where it is only Rs. 33 (see Table 39).[1]

[1] Budgets for Dalena were compiled by the same method as for Wangala (see above, p. 99). However, here due to lack of time, I could collect only two monthly budgets per sample household at an interval of four months, as compared

However, the range of savings and deficits in Dalena is greater than in Wangala. 42% of Dalena's sample households and only 38% of Wangala households have a deficit in their current budgets; on the other hand only 6% of Wangala's sample households and as many as 10% of Dalena's sample households have savings of more than Rs. 32 per month per consumption unit (see Table 50). The deficit households represent the poorest section in both villages, but in Wangala most of these households are indebted to creditors within the village, whereas in Dalena many of the deficit households are indebted to men in other villages. This inter-village indebtedness arises from the employment of Dalena men by farmers and contractors in other villages. Similarly, Dalena men have lent more to outsiders than have Wangala men, because of their economic interests in other villages.

In spite of Dalena's greater integration in the regional economy, cash income constitutes only 62% of average income per consumption unit, as compared with Wangala where it makes up 69% (see Table 39). This reflects the development of cash cropping in Wangala as compared with Dalena's agricultural economy which is still wholly subsistence. A comparison of the composition of average cash income per consumption unit in Dalena and Wangala clearly indicates the different natures of the two economies. Manufacturing and trading profits constitute only 4% of Wangala's average cash income, but as much as 23% of Dalena's. On the other hand, crop sales form as much as 65% of Wangala's average cash income and only 21% of that in Dalena. Similarly, agricultural wages form 17% and non-agricultural wages form no part of average cash income in Wangala whereas the respective percentages for Dalena are 9% and 14% (see Table 38). In each case the range among the sample households throws even more light on the differences between Wangala and Dalena: for instance, of the sample households in Wangala 95% had no non-agricultural wages at all and the remaining 5% had less than Rs. 4 per month per consumption unit; by contrast, only 48% among Dalena's sample households had no income from non-

with three monthly budgets taken in Wangala throughout a whole year. Thus the Dalena budgets are likely to be less accurate than those from Wangala.

agricultural wages and 19% had more than Rs. 8 per month per consumption unit (see Table 48). A similar pattern emerges when we compare manufacturing and trading profits among the sample households in the two villages: 89% of Wangala's sample households had no such income at all and the remaining 11% had less than Rs. 20 per month per consumption unit; by contrast, only 67% of Dalena's sample households made no such profits while the remaining third made profits up to Rs. 50 per month per consumption unit (see Table 44).

In both villages the bulk of the household's income is spent on food; the average expenditure in Wangala and Dalena includes 45% spent on food. Altogether the composition of average expenditure per household is almost identical in the two villages. However, the difference between the two villages emerges on examination of the range of expenditure in the two village samples. Total expenditure per month per consumption unit ranges from Rs. 10 to Rs. 45 in Wangala's sample, whereas in Dalena's sample it ranges from Rs. 10 to Rs. 85 (see Table 40). Similarly, expenditure on food per month per consumption unit ranges from Rs. 5 to Rs. 27 in Wangala's sample and from Rs. 5 to Rs. 35 in Dalena's sample, with 10% of Dalena's sample households consuming more than Rs. 25 per month per consumption unit. In both villages 51% of the sample households consume less than Rs. 15 per month per consumption unit (see Table 41). The differentiation in the expenditure on food is largely due to the type of food consumed rather than to variation in quantities of food consumed. I have already explained this point with reference to Wangala (see p. 101).

Although the average expenditure on clothes is practically the same in both villages, here, too, if we compare the ranges in the two samples, we find that Dalena households are more differentiated in terms of clothes. Expenditure per month per consumption unit ranges from nil to Rs. 10 in Wangala and to Rs. 15 in Dalena; 10% of Dalena's sample households spend more than Rs. 10 per month per consumption unit on clothes (see Table 41). Here it must be remembered that the price of a good shirt is about Rs. 8 and the same amount will suffice to buy a cotton sari for a woman.

Thus a difference of Rs. 5 spent per individual per month on clothes represents a considerable difference in the way a man may be dressed. Dalena's sample indicates a considerable correlation between the expenditure on clothes and the economic category of the household (the correlation coefficient is 0·57), whereas there is hardly any correlation (0·37) between these two variables among Wangala's sample. This indicates that current expenditure on clothes varies with income in Dalena much more than in Wangala, a point I have already made in greater detail with reference to personal property.

Similarly, Dalena men spend more on sundries, such as smoking and visits to coffee shops, as their income increases. Expenditure on sundries varies with the economic category of a man's household in Dalena. The cofficient of correlation between these two variables is 0·47 in Dalena and 0·33 in Wangala. Though the average expenditure on sundries per consumption unit is almost the same in the two villages, namely Rs. 3 in Wangala and Rs. 4 in Dalena, here too we find a greater range among the sample in Dalena where expenditure on sundries ranges from nil to Rs. 20 per month per consumption unit, as compared with Wangala where the highest sundries expenditure among the sample amounts to only Rs. 8 per month per consumption unit. 10% of Dalena's sample families spend more than Rs. 8 per month per consumption unit on sundries (see Table 42). This difference in the expenditure on sundries reflects the more frequent visits of Dalena men to the coffee shops and restaurants in Mandya. A number of factory workers regularly eat in restaurants in Mandya, though most of them carry their own food with them in a small container.

The composition of the average budget in Dalena shows income from rent and interest to be almost the same as expenditure on rent and interest. This must not however be taken to indicate that each household earns almost as much in the form of rent and interest as it pays out under this heading. Rather, it indicates the preponderance of poor households which have to pay interest to a considerable extent, whereas there are only a limited number of creditors who earn substantial money in the form of interest and rent. 67% of the Dalena sample households derive no income at all from interest and rent (see Table 44), but only 10% pay no interest or rent (see Table 43). On the other hand 14% of Dalena's sample households derive more than Rs. 10 income per month per consumption unit from rent and interest, while only 6% pay more than Rs. 10 per month per consumption unit in rent and interest. These figures show that there are only a few Dalena men who lend much, while there are a lot of Dalena men who owe a few hundred rupees. Though I have no quantitative evidence on indebtedness in Dalena prior to irrigation in the area, I have ample evidence that in Dalena, as in Wangala, indebtedness has increased since irrigation. This is a function of the availability of cash and the number of creditworthy debtors. For Wangala I have argued that indebtedness runs along traditional social links between Peasants and Untouchables and also between Peasants themselves, and that indebtedness ties have strengthened the other aspects of these links. In Dalena, indebtedness is not necessarily channelled along traditional lines. Moneylending in Dalena is largely a commercial proposition with little consideration for non-monetary obligations between creditor and debtor.

The pattern of non-productive property, income and expenditure, and indebtedness reflects clearly the similarities and differences between the economies of Wangala and Dalena. They are similar in so far as cash constitutes the major source of their income, and expenditure on food amounts to almost half of the total current expenditure per household; on the other hand, they are different in that sale of sugarcane provides almost the single source of cash income in Wangala, whereas manufacturing and trading profits and salaries and wages form the major part of cash income for Dalena villagers. In both villages indebtedness has increased since irrigation, but whereas in Wangala indebtedness relationships coincide with customary relationships which often also have a ritual aspect, in Dalena indebtedness is not confined in the same way, but is more impersonal and reaches out beyond the boundaries of the village.

In both villages incomes have increased since irrigation; in Wangala economic success during the last 25 years depended largely on the size of the landholding, the extent of irrigation and the availability of working capital, and only to a lesser degree on individual initiative and enterprise; by contrast, economic success in Dalena depended to a much greater extent on personal ability and drive. Irrigation in the region presented a different type of economic opportunity to Dalena. In Dalena the emphasis in development since irrigation has been much more on the individual than on the estate. Consequently, economic differentiation in Dalena is expressed more in terms of the individual, in Wangala in terms of the estate. Struggle for status in Dalena takes the form of personal differentiation; a man dresses better, or he builds a more modern house. In Wangala farmers vie with one another over who has the better pair of draught animals or the better plough; it is only on special social occasions such as weddings and feasts that Wangala villagers regard dress as a criterion of prestige.

The greater range of income and expenditure in Dalena than in Wangala reflects the greater extremes of economic differentiation in Dalena. Economic differentiation in Dalena is very much dependent on the development of the regional economy: mill owners, traders, contractors, factory workers and clerks all depend on the regional economy for their income. Provided the regional economy continues to expand, economic differentiation in Dalena may become more formalised; all those who earn cash through contact with the wider economy tend to become more closely associated with the economic class appropriate to their occupation. For instance, factory workers show signs of forming one group distinct from contractors or traders. On the other hand, in Wangala economic differentiation is based on landholding. But since landholding is periodically reshuffled because of partable inheritance, it is less likely to become formalised. Wangala farmers still think that all their sons must necessarily become farmers. But in Dalena most men want their sons to get jobs in town; the headman's eldest son is at present attending high school in Mandya and his father wants him to study further; similarly, Nanjegowda's eldest son is a clerk, his youngest son is studying physics at Mysore University, and only his second son helps in the cultivation of the estate. These cases seem to constitute the germ of a new development whereby only one son may take over the estate from the father while the other sons seek occupation elsewhere. However, as yet, this is certainly no more than a germ of future change, for most of the Dalena men working in town still treasure the hope of becoming full-time farmers.

Though the pull of the land and the attraction of the customary village system is still strong even among Dalena men working in the town, their interests have been turned to the wider economy, as they meet the challenge of the new opportunities stemming from irrigation in the region. By contrast, the economic interests of Wangala villagers have remained centred on the cultivation of their own village lands, since irrigation makes these more productive.

Dalena's Trading Position

In this chapter I have discussed the process of Dalena's economic diversification during the past 25 years and have compared and contrasted it with the recent economic growth in Wangala. As a summary step in the analysis of economic change in the two villages, I have compiled a balance of trade to show the extent and nature of the economic links of each village with the region. I have already explained that while my data on Wangala's cash income have a high degree of accuracy, because most of them came from the factory where I could cross-check my information from the village with the factory records, the data on cash expenditure are probably less accurate because of their dispersal over time and place. In the case of Dalena both village income and expenditure are possibly understated, because both involved manifold transactions throughout the year which informants cannot always remember, even when they are willing to give accurate information. But allowing for this reservation, I consider that a comparison of the trade balance of the two villages reveals some interesting features. For instance, it is interesting to note that exports per consumption unit in Dalena amount to Rs. 323 while in Wangala they amount to only Rs. 308. Similarly it is worth observing that

TABLE 20

Dalena estimated balance of payments for 1956

Cash Receipts	*Rs.*	%	*Cash Expenditure*	*Rs.*	%
1. Manufacturing and trading profits[1]	41,472	22	1. Food[1]	17,280	10
2. Interest[1]	10,368	5	2. Clothes[1]	24,053	13
3. Cane sales[2]	42,864	23	3. Sundries[1]	26,403	14
4. Animal products[1]	13,824	11	4. Household articles[1]	10,368	5
5. Wages (agricultural)[1]	10,368	5	5. Weddings[4]		
			Food	600	
			Clothes	1,800	2
			Ornaments	2,100	
6. Wages (non-agricultural)[1]	20,736	10	6. New houses and repairs[3]	10,000	5
7. Loans[3]	25,000	14	7. Farming:[2]		
8. Miscellaneous[1]	20,736	10	Fertiliser	14,544	
			Labour and Miscellaneous	16,055	9
			8. Tax and water rate[2]	2,431	1
			9. Loans[3]	30,000	17
			10. Balance	29,734	16
Total	185,368	100	Total	185,368	100

[1] Based on sample budgets.
[2] Based on sample input and output details.
[3] Token estimate.
[4] Based on calculation of wedding expenses during 1956.

the excess of exports over current imports amounts to as much as 16% of total exports in Dalena and only to 9% in Wangala. This reflects the greater thriftiness of Dalena men and their attempt to save for investment in different kinds of enterprise as well as in land. In parenthesis it may be noted that while in an industrial community such trade surplus would be regarded as hoarding, because it is not reinvested through the banking system, in an underdeveloped economy it must be seen as savings. In Dalena individuals usually hoard money for future investment. Some store their wealth in the form of jewellery, but farmers find that gold is a less liquid asset than money and nowadays they prefer to hoard cash. For example Kempegowda, the owner of the flour mill, keeps his money in a tin trunk so that later on he will be able to purchase machinery to produce sugar competitive with Mandya's sugar factory.

In Wangala struggle for prestige has led to heavy expenditure on weddings;[1] as much as 5% of village cash income is utilised to purchase food, clothes, and ornaments for weddings (see Table 10). In Dalena prestige rating by wedding expenditure is less important and consequently only 2% of village cash income is devoted to this item. On the other hand, housing accounts for 5% of cash expenditure in Dalena and for only 1% in Wangala (see Table 20).

Dalena villagers receive cash payments from many different sources in the region: factory workers collect their wages in the town; cane is sold to the factory and jaggery to wholesalers; manufacturing and trading profits are made on transactions with villagers from a wide region; interest on loans comes from many villages in the neighbourhood; agricultural wages are earned by Dalena farmhands for work on lands in neighbouring villages. Manufacturing and trading profits constitute 22% of village income, and cane sales constitute 23%. These percentages help to clarify the relative importance of agriculture and other economic activities in Dalena and throw into relief Dalena's integration into the regional economy. The income of town workers constitutes as much as 10% of village cash income and their wages more than cover the cash expenditure on food of all Dalena villagers. This makes it clear that if the regional economy were to decline and Dalena men were to lose their jobs, Dalena's standard of living would be seriously affected.

Dalena's economic growth depends on development in the regional economy. In consequence Dalena villagers display concern in the economic and political activities of the region: they discuss the availability of irrigation and the factory's attitude to overdue credits; they discuss the possibility of getting jobs in the factory or in the Administration; they talk about their trade union, and about political development in Mandya; they also fetch news from the cattle fairs they attend regularly each year. They are

[1] I have ascertained that the number of weddings held in Wangala and Dalena during my survey was representative of a normal year.

fully aware that the present rate of consumption in Dalena can be maintained only as long as more and more Dalena men can derive an income from sources outside agriculture. There are always rumours going around Dalena that some factory or other is going to start up just outside the village which will provide further employment, but I was never able to find any basis for them, save wishful thinking.

It is significant that Dalena men think in terms of factories as a means of improving their lot. Similarly Dalena men, who have electricity in the village, and who are continuously handling machinery in the factory, are much more aware and appreciative of modern technical development. Their attitudes are in sharp contrast to those of men in Wangala who visualise their own economic improvement only in terms of larger estates and more irrigated lands. Only one or two Wangala men have ever considered activities outside the agricultural sphere, although some had been employed in Mysore's textile mill. One man in Wangala requested me to start the manufacture of railway engines in the village to help improve their lot; he argued that the Europeans had got rich because they have been able to manufacture machinery. But he was soon shouted down by others who pointed out that Europeans might have machinery, yet this did not necessarily mean that they were rich, because without rice and ragi, nobody could be rich; they often pitied me because as a European I had to make do without rice or ragi.

The diversification of interests among Dalena men, together with the spread of their economic relations over a wide range beyond the boundaries of their own village, have affected Dalena's indigenous economic organisation. In the following two chapters I shall discuss the repercussions of these internal economic changes on the political and social system in Dalena.

CHAPTER VI

POLITICAL ORGANISATION AND CHANGE

PRIOR to the advent of irrigation in the region, Dalena's political system was almost identical with that of Wangala; both villages had *panchayats* which were composed of the elders of their 'major' Peasant lineages; and the leaders of both villages belonged to a Peasant caste *panchayat* composed of elders from a number of neighbouring villages. The Peasant caste *panchayat* was the governing authority in all matters affecting the Peasant code of behaviour; the village *panchayat* was the authority over all intra-village matters. Since irrigation, both Wangala and Dalena have been subject to the impact of external political and social forces of change, such as democratic legislation, the impact of the town, and Westernisation. But, as I have shown in detail, they have left Wangala's political system almost unimpaired. By contrast, Dalena's political system has radically changed. I shall argue in this chapter that Dalena's political system has changed because of the village's greater economic diversification and its greater integration into the wider economy, as compared with the unilinear economic development that has taken place in Wangala since irrigation.

Dalena's greater economic integration involved greater political integration into the wider body politic. For instance, we have seen that Dalena men working at the factory in Mandya all belong to trade unions which operate within the wider political system. Here they learn to elect their representatives; and for many villagers working in Mandya this is their first encounter with a mode of selecting leaders which conflicts with the customary principle of hereditary authority in intra-village political institutions.

At the time of my study, the reorganisation of Mysore State and the formation of the big Karnataka State formed the topic of heated discussion among townspeople in Mysore State. Dalena men working in Mandya brought daily political news to the village. All the Dalena commuters and another dozen Dalena farmers attended a meeting held in Mandya to protest against the formation of Karnataka State. Dalena men are aware of the problems of the wider political system. By contrast, Wangala men were oblivious to the impending political changes in Mysore State. A number of houses in Dalena display photographs of Gandhi and Nehru, whereas in Wangala not a single photograph of these All-India leaders appears anywhere. Dalena's many different economic links have brought the village strongly under the impact of the town. These urban influences have given a further impetus to radical changes in Dalena's political organisation.

THE 'NEW' VILLAGE *PANCHAYAT*

In Dalena, as in Wangala, Peasants are the dominant caste and all political power in the village is vested in them. Dalena's indigenous Peasant households are organised in 14 lineages. There are also two Peasant households which have recently immigrated into Dalena: they are said 'to belong to no lineage'. In fact, of course, these 'no lineage' households also belong to lineages which are represented in greater numbers, and which are important, in the villages whence they came; but in Dalena they rank as too unimportant (of 'no lineage'). They have no economic, political, or ritual power. That they are referred to as 'no lineage' emphasises, however, that households within a village are important within a lineage system; the lineage controls domestic life and ritual activities, and also unites for political action.

Each of the fourteen lineages has an elder whose position is hereditary. He is the ritual head of his lineage; formerly political power was vested in him and still is in some cases. Dalena, like Wangala, has the concept of the 'major' lineages composing the *panchayat*. That is to say, villagers regard some lineages as more important than others, without giving any specific criteria for this preference. At present, Dalena's *panchayat* is made up of nine members who are drawn from eight lineages; the headman's lineage is represented by two men, namely the headman and his patrilateral cousin whom I have described as the chief money-lender in the village. Five of the *panchayat* members are lineage elders; the remaining four are not elders but important men in their own right. Three of these are magnates, and the fourth is an intelligent and able arbitrator.

Dalena Peasants no longer insist that membership of the *panchayat* and consequently political status must be hereditary. *Panchayat* members are still thought to represent 'major' lineages, but the individual member is no longer necessarily a hereditary lineage elder. However, the ritual status of lineage elder is still regarded as strictly hereditary and the position of lineage elder is still important in intra-lineage relations. But in the organisation of the village, positions of authority are now being separated from the hereditary ritual offices. The system of hereditary political offices is being replaced by an elective system. This change had begun well before the *Mysore Village Panchayats and District Boards Act 1952*, which aimed to introduce universal adult franchise and democracy into local government in Mysore. The election under the provision of the Act, which took place in Dalena at the beginning of 1955, merely confirmed the existing membership of the *panchayat*. To satisfy the provisions of the *Panchayats Act*, one Untouchable had also to be elected. However, his membership of the *panchayat* is as illusory as that of the two Untouchables in Wangala.

The elected *panchayat* in Dalena differs from the traditional hereditary *panchayat* which consisted of the lineage elders of the major lineages, but this change had already begun before the recent legislation. I have described how the conduct of the election in Wangala led to the nomination of candidates who were not the recognised leaders in the community. Legally, these men constituted the new *panchayat*, but in fact it is the traditional *panchayat* which continues to exercise effective authority in the village. To Wangala villagers the idea of elected authority introduced by the new legislation was still completely alien, and the whole election misfired. Dalena men, on the other hand, had already accepted a deviation from the hereditary principle in political authority and therefore at election time the nine dominant men in the village could manipulate people so as to get themselves elected. The four lineage elders, whose lineages are represented by other men of their respective lineages, are too unimportant in the economic sphere to have sufficient political influence in the village to oppose the non-hereditary *panchayat* members. For instance, the elder of Chick-Chenna's lineage is one of the poorest farmers in the village. His place in the *panchayat* has been taken by the eldest brother of the rich emigrant who has built the two-storey house in the village. Even the elder agrees that it is more appropriate for his richer lineage fellow to act as *panchayat* member than for him to contest the latter's leadership.

The three *panchayat* members who are magnates, but not elders, achieved their political status as a result of their economic success. Here diversification of the economy has enabled some households to emerge as magnates, even though they were not magnate households before irrigation. Economic differentiation since irrigation has reshuffled economic, and consequently political, power in Dalena. This process happened at the same time that the commuters became acquainted with the principle of elected representation in trade union matters. The commuters have added strength to the shift from hereditary to elected authority in Dalena. This shift took place only in cases where there was a glaring difference between the economic status of the lineage elder and of a magnate belonging to the same lineage. As in the case of Chick-Chenna's lineage, villagers would regard it as strange if a lineage were to be represented by a poor farmer when it included one of the richest households in the village. Thus we can see that the change from hereditary to elected authority was primarily the result of economic differentiation in Dalena since irrigation, but was further facilitated by the different ties Dalena men now have with the wider body politic. In Wangala, on the other hand, irrigation stressed the already existing economic differentiation between magnates, middle-farmers and poorest.

Dalena's 'new' *panchayat* does not appear to be as active as the traditional *panchayat* was in the days before irrigation. Nowadays, the main activities of Dalena's *panchayat* are the collection of taxes and the payment of the village electricity bill. The *panchayat's* records over the last ten years show that matters such as allocating housing sites, intra-village disputes, and arranging village ceremonies and feasts, were discussed but rarely led to a decision acceptable to all members. As Dalena's economy diversified, so the interests of its people diverged. Manifold economic contacts with Mandya and surrounding villages have integrated Dalena into the wider economy and reduced the number of subjects on which all Dalena villagers have common interests. Accordingly, there are only rare occasions when Dalena *panchayat* members manage to reach a unanimous decision. Furthermore, Dalena villagers are also split into two opposing factions, which makes the operation of the formal *panchayat* even more difficult.

However, in Dalena as in Wangala, *ad hoc panchayats* deal with day-to-day matters and disputes in the village. But factional differences are more rigid than in Wangala and therefore even *ad hoc panchayat* meetings take into account the factional allegiances of the disputing parties. If they belong to different factions, then two or three *panchayat* members whose factional allegiance is not clearly defined are called to arbitrate; if they both belong to the same faction, then a few members of this faction will act as arbitrators. For instance, when Kempegowda, the headman's younger brother, was involved in a quarrel with an Untouchable over the latter's right to sell a tree already pledged to Kempegowda in payment of a long-standing debt, two of the 'neutral' *panchayat* members were called to arbitrate. On the other hand, in a dispute between Kempegowda and another man belonging to his own lineage, the headman and his patrilateral cousin were asked to be arbitrators, since the parties were all of the same faction. The most popular arbitrator is the village chairman, the head of what I call the 'conservative' faction in Dalena.

The chairman has in fact assumed most of the headman's authority in Dalena. He is a magnate, but he gained his wealth more from inheritance than by personal enterprise; his ancestral estate has remained undivided for three generations. He is literate, and has personality and ability to lead and influence others, but is not an outstanding entrepreneur, like the headman. The chairman has a large following; he is usually about the village and his advice is sought on all sorts of problems and disputes and his decision accepted as final. Except for signing petitions, which the headman is obliged to do by law, the headman has little active authority left in the village. The headman in fact spends most of his time outside the village, tending his wet lands, or looking after his mill and shop in the neighbouring village, or in Mandya. Previously it used to be the headman who commanded communal labour in the village; now this power has passed into the hands of the chairman. Again, it is the chairman who compiles the rota of night watchmen, orders Untouchable village servants to sweep the village streets, and helps the accountant in the collection of taxes, although this is still officially the duty of the headman.

The displacement of Dalena's headman at first puzzled me, because he is such a capable man and leader. I had no difficulty in understanding the displacement of Wangala's headman, for he was very ineffective, and I found the temporary acting headman a much more capable man for the job. But this is not the case in Dalena, where the headman is by far the most capable man in the village. When I tried to investigate the matter further, my Peasant informants in Dalena related the following mythical history of the village:

The village site used to be about half a mile from its present site and the settlement was then called Mudapatna. One of the Peasant women offended a *sanyasi* (holy man) living at the time in Mudapatna, and he cursed the village and all the houses were burnt down. Most inhabitants were killed except for the few who were working in their fields at the time of the fire. The two surviving families moved to the present site of Dalena and are the ancestors of two of Dalena's lineages, namely the P. and the K. lineages. The P. lineage held the headmanship in the beginning. But later it was cursed by a woman who had married into the lineage, as a result of which it began to die out and there are now only a few households left of what used to be the basic and strongest lineage in the village.

At the time of Tippu Sultan, Muslim ruler of Mysore at the end of the 18th century [who was defeated by the British in 1799], land was still plentiful and did not belong to the Government. Anyone had the right to cultivate waste land and cultivation gave right to possession. During Tippu Sultan's rule, a soldier came one day to Dalena with a girl he had kidnapped, but not married, and they settled down to farming. The couple had seven sons and seven buffaloes. Each son was reared with the milk of a buffalo and this gave the sons tremendous strength. The father was very anxious that his sons should not be asked to fight and so he kept them hidden until one day he was asked to report to a Government revenue official in another village. When they found out that they had been soldiers together they soon became friends and the official promised the father of the seven sons to grant him a wish. The father desired that his sons should be allowed to remain farmers in Dalena and that their right in the village should be made permanent. The official then granted them the headmanship. From that day the seven sons became real terrors: they stole and killed sheep belonging to other villagers, they confiscated the best land and claimed rights to cultivate it. They appropriated to themselves whatsoever they fancied and no villager was strong enough to oppose them. Finally, one day, a man of B. lineage [now a major lineage in Dalena] managed to kill six of the seven buffaloes belonging to the soldier's sons. This deprived six of the sons of their strength and they too were killed. One brother alone survived with his buffalo and he became headman, the ancestor of the present headman. The headman's lineage is still called buffalo-lineage because its ancestors depended on the strength of buffaloes.

For my informants this myth of Dalena's origin sufficiently explained the extraordinary ability and strength of their present headman. His outstanding success in the economic sphere is associated with his descent from a man reared on buffalo milk and therefore having supernatural powers; his economic drive is explained in terms of the greed displayed by his ancestors. The hereditary position of village headman is questioned in the mythical story by the reference to the illegitimate birth of the seven sons, since no wedding ceremony was held for the immigrant soldier and his kidnapped wife. In fact, some accounts of the myth hinted that while the mother of the seven sons was a Peasant, her husband belonged to a different caste.

The myth clearly indicates the villagers' attitude to outstanding ability and success; they never trust it, but rather attribute it to supernatural causes. The displacement of Dalena's headman by the chairman, who is also a leading personality, but not such an outstanding man as the headman, may be related to the set of beliefs exhibited in the myth. Villagers prefer as their political leader a good arbitrator rather than a strong personality to defend their interests against the outside world. But another factor must also be taken into account in this connection. The headman's many interests take him outside his village and leave him little time to devote to the running of Dalena. Wangala's displaced headman was very different from Dalena's; his case shows that Peasants expect their village leader to have certain abilities above the average. The experience of Dalena's headman suggests that his abilities must not be too much above the average. In both villages the acknowledged leaders are men of superior ability, but not outstandingly successful economically. Outstanding economic success is mistrusted and is attributed to supernatural associations.

Through the myth of origin villagers have established the *raison d'être* for the headmanship and they can explain the abilities and success of the headman, as well as the rise and fall of a number of Dalena lineages. It is significant that the myth relates that a Government official granted the right of headmanship to the ancestor of the present headman, for the external authorities are of great importance to Dalena's intra-village political life. Both factions try to rally external powers to their support in intra-village matters. To Dalena men the ultimate sanction in any intra-village political dispute is the appropriate authority in Mandya: in many instances this is the police. In one instance, the headman's faction applied for support to the Mandya police to ensure the peaceful procession of a Washerman's bridal pair through the village; on another occasion, the chairman's faction applied to the police to withhold permission for the other faction to perform a drama in the village. By contrast Wangala men refer their intra-village disputes to an external authority only rarely.

Wangala's *panchayat* is also still sufficiently effective to counteract even the court's decision in a land dispute, and land disputes, we must remember, are the ones most likely to be taken to Government courts. Dalena's *panchayat*, on the other hand, is not regarded by villagers as having the ultimate power to decide disputes among themselves. Therefore, Dalena men turn to the wider political system where they seek this ultimate sanction. Through their many contacts with Mandya they have come to appreciate the functions of the Administration and they have also learnt to operate the wider political system by appeal to caste loyalty or bribery. Such attitudes towards the wider political system are already contained in the myth of origin. There, the headman derived his political authority from the Government official through their common background as soldiers; similarly, today the headman gains political support from the Administration through his friendship with a number of town officials. An analysis of the myth suggests that its present form may be related to the operation of Dalena's political system.

Thus, though Dalena's *panchayat* is no longer based on the hereditary principle, it is also less active than was the traditional *panchayat* which still operates in Wangala. Dalena has become part of the wider economy and consequently part of the wider political system, whereas Wangala has remained a largely independent economy and therefore also largely an autonomous political unit.

Village Factions

Dalena, like Wangala, is split into two opposing factions, with a floating support oscillating between the two. We have seen that Wangala factions are organised on the basis of lineage. In Dalena, too, lineage is an important principle of faction organisation, for factions become operative on occasions such as weddings when the ritual unity of the lineage is stressed. For instance, when the son of Nanjegowda, who is a leader of the headman's faction, celebrated his wedding, it was boycotted by most villagers, though all members of his own lineage attended the ceremony. A few other villagers also attended and they were immediately referred to as 'strike-breakers'. One of them was the man who by custom had always stored the village vessels used at all Peasant weddings; and as soon as the chairman learnt this he ordered the vessels to be thenceforth kept in the fine two-storey house. Thus the chairman took immediate action against one of the few men who had broken the village boycott. He objected to breach of the boycott not as disloyalty to the lineage, but as disloyalty to the village faction, under his own leadership.

The chairman is a dominant personality in the village and his faction is known by his name. He commands most support in the village and his activities in the village are all aimed to establish his firm leadership. He is literate and a magnate in wealth; in addition he knows about the land and family histories of most villagers. On the other hand, the headman, who is the leader of the other faction, is not at all well acquainted with individual family histories, for he is too much occupied with his economic activities to spend much time in the village and collect all the gossip.

Dalena men cite one dispute to account for the present faction alignment in their village. Timmegowda, a Peasant, had illicit relations with the wife of Karaya, a Washerman. Timmegowda took some meals in Karaya's house. The case was reported to the caste *panchayat* and Timmegowda was fined Rs. 50 for breaking the caste interdining taboos; no mention was made of his illicit relations with Karaya's wife. Timmegowda paid his fine and stopped eating with his mistress, but continued his illicit relations with her. Karaya one day discovered Timmegowda with his wife and a quarrel broke out between the two men. Karaya, the Washerman, hit Timmegowda, the Peasant—and to hit a higher caste man is one of the gravest caste offences. Two Peasant elders rushed to the scene and stopped the fight. The Peasant caste *panchayat* met again to consider this case. Timmegowda's relations with Karaya's wife were still not discussed, and not even Karaya mentioned them in his own defence. Karaya was supported in Dalena only by the members of his own joint family. Other Washermen in Dalena kept clear of the dispute. To them economic expediency outweighed caste loyalty. In the interests of preserving Peasant superiority in Dalena's caste structure, the Peasant elders felt that severe punishment was necessary. The case was then considered by the village *panchayat* and members decided that all Peasants should sever their economic and ritual relations with Karaya and his family. He was also required to pay a fine of

Rs. 100 to the *panchayat* fund. Karaya's family argued that they could not pay the fine if Peasant households broke off economic relations with them. Karaya's appeal was unsuccessful; the fine was maintained and the economic sanctions against his family were put into force. Peasants who used to have a hereditary link with Karaya and his family severed the bond and transferred their custom to the other Washermen households in the village. Karaya's family owned a little land and continued to cultivate it. Two of Karaya's brothers had already secured jobs as drivers working for a lorry contractor in Mandya. Two more brothers managed to get jobs in Mandya as lorry and contractor drivers. Karaya built up a laundry clientele in Mandya. He collects laundry in Mandya once a week, washes it with soap in Dalena, irons it with a newly acquired iron box, and delivers it back to his Mandya customers. Karaya now earns more money by washing and ironing clothes for Mandya customers than he could ever have earned by washing for Dalena Peasants. After the breach with his Dalena clients Karaya's wife left him. He wished to marry again. His father found him a second wife and tried to make preparations for the wedding. The conservative faction under the leadership of the chairman refused to allow the wedding to take place in the village until Karaya had discharged his debt of Rs. 100 to the *panchayat* fund. As Dalena Peasants had already severed all economic and ritual relations with Karaya and his family they had no more effective sanctions to stop the Washerman's wedding. They threatened to break up Karaya's wedding procession by force if he insisted on continuing with his arrangements. Karaya's father approached the headman and successfully appealed to him for support. But when the matter was discussed at a *panchayat* meeting, the headman faced strong opposition from the chairman and the whole 'conservative' faction. At this stage, the dispute between the Peasants of Dalena and a Washerman turned into an intra-Peasant faction dispute. The headman, with the backing of his lineage, re-opened economic and ritual relations with Karaya and his family. The headman's lineage households are nowadays the only customers of Karaya in the village. The headman applied for police protection from Mandya for Karaya's wedding and the day passed without a breach of the peace. Karaya still has not paid the Rs. 100 fine to the *panchayat* fund and this case still forms the core of village factional disagreement.

Although the case started over ten years ago, to Dalena men it is still the most important dispute between the two factions. This is because it symbolises the headman's individual actions in opposition to the whole village. The headman had dared to support the Washerman after a *panchayat* meeting had severed all economic and ritual relations with him. The headman explains his actions by referring to the conservatism of the other villagers. He says that he supported Karaya because he thought it a deserving case, and that there was no reason why Karaya's wedding should not have been held in Dalena, even if he still owed Rs. 100 to the *panchayat* fund. But in fact, the headman probably regarded Karaya's case as a welcome chance to show his disagreement with the whole village administration. He obviously wishes to undermine the strong hold the chairman has over the village, and openly criticises it as backward. He is a most enterprising innovator and would like to see more enterprise too in the village administration. For instance, he would like to have a school built near the approach road leading into Dalena. However, in opposition to the headman's demand, the 'conservative' faction has put in a claim that the school building should be erected in the middle of the village, on a site owned by the headman. Whenever the headman suggests any village improvement, the 'conservative' faction opposes it with some scheme of its own, which in turn is unacceptable to the headman. The only scheme that was passed by the *panchayat* in the last ten years was the electrification of the village—and that was opposed by the headman, because he feared the competition from a mill in Dalena. Thus the enterprising headman's efforts are continuously being frustrated in village affairs; this probably accounts for his open stand in the case of Karaya and also accounts for the importance attached to this case by Dalena villagers.

The headman's lineage includes two other magnates, who are among the most enterprising men in the village. Thus the whole lineage is considered by other villagers to be a lineage of innovators.

They are no doubt envious of the success of these innovators, and they are certainly critical of it. For it is from these innovators that the most radical change in Dalena has resulted; they have broken most with traditional values. In addition they turn most to outside authorities. The headman, for instance, was the first to bring Mandya's police to the village, when he summoned them to protect Karaya's wedding procession. This was a breach in Dalena's traditional autonomy. The 'conservative' faction tries to uphold traditional values, though its following includes most of the commuters, as well as the bulk of the farming population of the village. These commuters support the 'conservative' faction because they wish to raise their social status in the village according to customarily accepted criteria of social ranking. Therefore, although in terms of contact with the town, commuters are more closely allied with the innovators, on other issues they are opposed to the innovators because they want to become full farmers and lead the life of farmers in the village. For them the values of the farming society are more important in the village than their links with the wider economy.

In Dalena, faction differences are more rigid than in Wangala, because while Wangala is still a wholly farming society, Dalena's economic development has diversified the interests and activities of villagers. Wangala's 'progressives' are all full-time farmers just like the 'conservatives'. Whenever there is a drought, or a cattle or crop disease, all villagers are equally affected, whatever their faction, and they all join efforts to avert the disaster by appealing to the appropriate deity or to the appropriate authority in Mandya. But in Dalena there are far fewer occasions now which affect all villagers jointly and so serve to unite them. Consequently, sectional interests now outweigh joint interests. Dalena's 'progressives' are still farmers, but they have ventured into commercial and industrial enterprises. They now have regular dealings with business enterprises in the town, with Government, court and police officials, and with many individuals in other villages. Through their regular contact with the Administration in Mandya, they have learnt to manipulate the wider political system by calling on caste loyalty or by bribery. Thus the innovators are in a much better position to get things done when it comes to getting support from the Administration in Mandya.

However, even the 'conservative' faction managed to get police support when the 'progressive' faction once wished to enact a drama in the village. The 'conservatives' insisted that before starting rehearsals for the drama, the 'progressives' must first promise to take part in a village feast that had not been celebrated for three years because of their opposition. The 'progressives' refused to come to terms on the matter of their participation in the joint village feast, and in spite of the 'conservatives' opposition began dress rehearsals. The chairman at once went to Mandya police and explained that the performance of a drama in the village might under the present circumstances lead to disturbances, whereupon the police wrote a letter to the headman informing him that a police licence must first be obtained before the drama could be enacted. Rehearsals for the drama were suspended. Both the 'conservative' and 'progressive' factions utilise Mandya's police to strengthen their own side in intra-village disputes.

Another important point to notice in this connection is the 'conservatives'' eagerness to have the village feast performed and the refusal by the 'progressives' to participate in it. When I analysed Wangala, I argued that factions are informal pressure groups which act as mechanisms whereby gains in economic status might be realised also in terms of political and social mobility. I have shown how in Wangala feasts are being duplicated in order to create more ritual offices for the economically successful, but structurally younger, lineages. But in Dalena we find that many of the village ceremonies are no longer celebrated at all. For instance, there were long discussions before the New Year's celebration during my stay in the village. Finally, the ceremony was performed, but no one belonging to the headman's lineage had any ritual function to perform in any of the village feasts. Their participation was purely formal and not instrumental to the performance of the ceremonies. The 'progressive' faction in Dalena does not seek ritual status in the village as does the progressive faction of Wangala. But it represents in Dalena a new element in village organisation, the breakaway unit which is undermining the traditional unity of the village. To the headman the village ceremonies are no longer of great importance; he is more interested in the wider political and social system, in which his economic interests are now vested.

The conflict between the 'innovators' and 'conservatives' operates on all major issues and in every major dispute, but hardly affects day-to-day life in the village. Innovators employ labourers from the 'conservative' faction and 'conservatives' employ the poorest of the headman's lineage. Indebtedness also cuts across faction alignment. The headman's patrilateral cousin is the chief moneylender in the village. He is a very shrewd and thrifty businessman, and, much as villagers may dislike him, most of them have been forced at one time or the other to become his debtors. Marriage ties also cut across faction alignment; there are a number of marriages in existence between the chairman's and the headman's lineages.

The many new economic and political ties between Dalena men and the wider economy and the State at large, are responsible for the fundamental cleavage between 'progressives' and 'conservatives' in Dalena. The continued existence of cross-cutting relations within the village ensures the bridging of the cleavage between the two factions in everyday life in Dalena.

Village and Government

In my analysis of Wangala I showed how the village has remained a largely autonomous political unit, linked to the wider State political system only through the person of the Revenue Inspector. His intermediary position, I have argued, helped to reduce the friction between the wider political system and the indigenous political organisation of the village. Dalena's Revenue Inspector had been appointed only shortly before I moved into the village, and he had not yet had time to develop an identification with the villagers' interests. The fact that he is an Untouchable also influences his activities in the village. When he comes to visit the village, he is not received with the courtesy accorded to a man belonging to a caste. For instance, once when he had come to the village and the chairman had talked to him, they both walked past the coffee shop, and the chairman invited the Revenue Inspector to take some coffee with him. The Revenue Inspector declined, and the chairman did not press him. As soon as he had gone, the chairman commented publicly that the Revenue Inspector had not been able to accept coffee because he would have had to take it outside like all other Untouchables, and this would have been an affront to the dignity of his post. The Untouchable Revenue Inspector dresses like all other city officials and tries to carry himself like any other caste official, but the knowledge that he is an Untouchable has already preceded him to the villages for which he is now responsible and influences the villagers' reactions to him. It is difficult to say what the effect would have been on Wangala if an Untouchable Revenue Inspector had been introduced there, but it is likely that their objections to him would have been even more acute and outspoken than those of Dalena villagers. In Dalena the headmaster of the school is also an Untouchable and is held in considerable esteem by most villagers, whereas the Untouchable school-teacher in Wangala enjoys no prestige at all. However, what is plain is that Dalena men attach importance to the Revenue Inspector's Untouchable status and this in turn influences his position in the village.

I have referred to the numerous ties Dalena folk have with the wider political system through trade union membership, contacts with officials in Mandya, and so on. These are reflected in their attitudes towards politics in general. Unlike Wangala, where nobody reads papers and few are politically aware of the wider State system, Dalena men are acutely conscious of, and interested in discussing, wider political issues. The difference between the two villages emerges clearly over the question of the reorganisation of Mysore State. Wangala men discussed desultorily for a couple of days the possibility of the Maharaja's deposition, but were unaware of any other issue, whereas the Peasants of Dalena quickly saw a threat to the dominance of their caste in the area, and took part in political demonstrations to protest against the proposed reorganisation.

Commuters also took part in a strike organised by the trade union for the benefit of the workers employed by the factory on a temporary basis. The trade union held that the factory employed much too high a proportion of temporary labour and thus deprived a large number of temporary labourers of the benefits of permanent employment. It called a strike of all 'permanent' as well as all temporary employees to alleviate the position of the temporary workers. All Dalena factory workers are in permanent employment and they took part in the strike. They also participated in a demonstration through Mandya in aid of the strike. All these and other activities are organised by urban leaders in Mandya; when Dalena men take part they do so in their capacity as factory workers, not as villagers. Thus while they may be expressing their own political awareness, they do not by their behaviour involve the political system of the village in the wider system of the State.

Similar 'progressive' attitudes are expressed by Dalena men towards many innovations sponsored by the Administration. Thus Dalena farmers take their cows to the Veterinary Department to be artificially inseminated, whereas Wangala farmers insist on having them covered by the village bull in spite of departmental pressure.

In their relations with the outer world, Dalena people are thus much more 'progressive' than those of Wangala. At the same time, the point should not be pressed too far. No Dalena man, for example, has become a member of the Congress Party, nor do they know any better than Wangala men who their elected representative is in the Mysore legislature. What they do know is that before the election some townsmen used to come to the village, made them a lot of promises which were never fulfilled, and once the election was over never appeared again. They remember that they voted for a Peasant, but they do not know his name, nor where he lives. Thus with respect to the wider State system Dalena is very similar to Wangala. Both villages are still largely autonomous political units, although Dalena has many more individual ties with the wider political system than Wangala. But both villages continue to work as political sub-systems within the State.

CHAPTER VII

SOCIAL ORGANISATION AND CHANGE

AFTER having discussed in previous chapters the changes in Dalena's economic and political structure as a result of irrigation in the region, in this chapter I shall consider the changes that have occurred in general social relations, such as caste, kinship and ritual relations. In the course of the discussion I have already referred to these general social relations, but here I shall deal with them in greater detail.

Irrigation in the region has been the dominant factor of change affecting Dalena's economy during the past 20 years: it led to the diversification of the village economy, to the conversion of the village economy from subsistence to cash, and to the reaching out of Dalena villagers to income opportunities outside their own village. All these changes have radically changed Dalena's village economy, and its political organisation. Economic roles and relations have changed considerably during the past 20 years: men who used to work for other farmers in the village are now employed outside the village in spheres other than agriculture. Membership of the three economic categories (the magnates, the middle-farmers and the poorest) has changed slightly since irrigation in the area. Three of the magnates raised themselves to that status from being middle-farmers, and some of the poorest have risen to the status of middle-farmers through their jobs in the town. There is much greater economic differentiation among Dalena villagers than among Wangala villagers. But in both villages, economic differentiation coincides with caste differentiation. All the magnates in Dalena are Peasants and so are most of the middle-farmers. On the other hand, all Untouchables belong to the poorest section in Dalena's population. Untouchables have found difficulty in securing jobs in the town, and have remained largely casual labourers to farmers in Dalena or in neighbouring villages, or to contractors. In a situation where jobs are still scarce they have remained the monopoly of the dominant caste. Peasants form 80% of Dalena's population and Untouchables 10% of it. The remaining 10% is taken up by eight different castes, and most of these are recent immigrants to Dalena. Thus irrigation in the region affected mainly intra-Peasant caste relations and relations between Peasants and Untouchables, but hardly affected relations between Peasants and Functionaries.

Caste Composition

Castes in Dalena are organised into a hierarchical structure, yet it is difficult to define the place of all castes in relation to one another in the hierarchy. Here, as in Wangala, different criteria determine a caste's rank in different situations. In both villages Peasants are dominant in terms of economic and political power, but Lingayat priests as a caste are regarded by Peasants as superior in social status. Peasants will take food from Lingayat priests, but do not expect Lingayats to take food from them. In Dalena the head of the Lingayat priestly household is a recent immigrant and runs the village coffee shop, which makes it easy for Peasants to eat there. The Blacksmith and the Goldsmith in Dalena are of the same *Panchala* Left Hand caste grouping as the ones in Wangala; and in Dalena as in Wangala even Untouchables do not eat from them, even though the Blacksmith is a vegetarian, which normally gains merit in Hindu society.

The Oilpresser families rank below the Peasants in caste rank; no Peasant man or woman will eat from an Oilpresser kitchen, while some Oilpresser men but no Oilpresser woman will eat from Peasant kitchens. Other castes such as the Washerman and the Barber regard the Oilpresser as ranking nearly as high as Peasants, for these other castes also eat from an Oilpresser kitchen. There are two Oilpresser families in Dalena. One still performs its caste function while the breadwinner of the other is a factory worker and immigrated to Dalena only because his wife is related to the indigenous Oilpresser, and his wife helps out with the job of oilpressing.

There are four Washermen families in Dalena. Three of them

perform the traditional Washermen's services for Peasants in the village. The fourth is the one which was involved in the dispute which I considered earlier in some detail and who washes clothes on a customary basis for the headman's lineage only.[1] This Washerman is now one of the richest middle-farmers' households. Its income includes the wages of three brothers who are drivers and the laundry earnings from Mandya of the other brother. It is one of the three houses in Dalena where electric light has been installed, and it also has a large gramophone acquired by one of the drivers in Mandya. The family has broken off all relations with the other Washermen in the village and now lives almost isolated from village social life. Since it washes clothes for only the headman's lineage in the village, the family is rarely called upon to perform any ritual services for Peasants. On the occasion of Nanjegowda's son's wedding, the Washerman had to perform his ritual functions again, but this was one of the rare occasions when he is asked to do this now. The other three Washermen's families perform the economic services for the remainder of Dalena's Peasants, and also all the ritual services expected from a Washerman. Those Peasant households which had hereditary relationships with the Washerman's household that was involved in the dispute transferred them to the other Washermen's families in the village. In Dalena, too, as in Wangala, many housewives now wash their own clothes and even those of their menfolk, but they cannot dispense with the services of the Washerman because of his ritual duties in washing menstrual clothes.

The Untouchables in Dalena own some little land and hold some land under Government grant, but none of them owns any wet lands in neighbouring villages. They are the poorest section of Dalena's population. They work as labourers on farms in Dalena or in neighbouring villages or for contractors.

Intra-Caste Relations

Members of one caste are linked together in Dalena by a number of ties: they are linked by kinship and marriage, by age groups,

[1] See above, pp. 285–7.

by friendships between individuals, by common work in Mandya, or by working together for a contractor.

Kinship and marriage ties link individuals of one village with men and women in other villages. These ties emphasise inter-village as opposed to intra-village links. Most of the marriages link

TABLE 21

Radius of Peasant men's inter-village marriage links (extant marriages)

	Wangala		*Dalena*	
Miles	*Nos.*	%	*Nos.*	%
0–2	11	14	23	22
2–4	27	36	52	50
4–6	14	19	8	7
6–8	5	6	5	5
8–10	6	8	2	2
10 and over	13	17	15	14
Total	76	100	105	100

Dalena Peasants with spouses from other villages: of the 124 existing marriages, i.e. marriages in which both husband and wife were alive at the time of my census, 68·5% are between men from Dalena and women from other villages, 0·8% are uxorilocal marriages, and 30·7% are between Dalena men and Dalena women. A comparison between the recorded marriages of Peasants (i.e. those marriages occurring in agnatic genealogies of four generation depth) and the existing marriages shows that whereas among existing marriages 68·5% were contracted between a man from Dalena and a woman from another village, of the recorded marriages (excluding existent marriages) only 44% were such inter-village marriages. This shows a trend towards a greater proportion of inter-village marriages, which can plausibly be explained by the marriage pattern following the pattern of landholdings in neighbouring villages. As Dalena farmers bought wet lands in neighbouring villages they wanted to strengthen their foothold in these villages by marriage ties. Of the existing Peasant marriages between Dalena men and women from other villages, 22% are with women within a radius of 2 miles, and another 50% are with women from villages between 2 to 4 miles distant from Dalena (see Table 21). Thus 72% of all existing inter-village marriages in Dalena were between men from the village and women coming from villages within a radius of 4 miles, which is the area in which Dalena men have their wet land holdings in neighbouring villages. 14% of all the existing inter-village marriages are between men from Dalena and women from villages outside a radius of 10 miles. These wider spread marriage ties developed when Dalena men migrated to towns farther away, and then married there or arranged marriages there. If we compare these figures with the marriage spread of Wangala marriages, we find that while only 50% of all existing marriages between a native Peasant from Wangala and a woman from another village were with women of villages within a radius of four miles, this figure is as much as 72% for Dalena marriages. This difference displays the importance of nearby villages to Dalena men. Affinal ties have become much more important since irrigation in the area; a man visits his affines much more frequently if they happen to be in a village in which he holds wet lands. He may even take his meals in his affine's home, while he is working on his wet lands in their village. Thus his relationship is much closer than it is with affines in other villages in which he has no personal economic interest.

The practices of cross-cousin marriage and marriages to near kin are very rare among Dalena Peasants and are becoming rarer still. Among the existing marriages only 2% are between a man and his sister's daughter, 1% between a son and his father's sister's daughter, and 2% are between a son and his mother's brother's daughter, whereas among the recorded marriages (excluding existent marriages) the respective figures are 4%, 4% and 7%. The higher figures for recorded marriages may still hide an understatement of such cross-cousin marriages in the past, for cross-cousin ties are often forgotten and a number of cross-cousin marriages are contracted between girls from Dalena and men from other villages and these marriages do not fall within the range of existing marriages, nor do they appear very accurately among the recorded marriages. For if a woman marries out of the village, she has lost her social importance there, and becomes a member of the lineage of her husband and of his village.

Kinship relations among Dalena Peasants are organised around lineage cores. Although there is a clear distinction between the 'Male' and 'Female' clans in Wangala, the distinction made in Dalena is far from clear. In Dalena there is the concept of the two clans and lineages are assigned to one or other category, yet Peasants do not celebrate any feast at which the distinct nature of the two clans is symbolised. Dalena's fourteen lineages are much smaller and more dispersed than Wangala's lineages. Lineage alignment is reflected in the residential pattern of Peasants in Dalena; each lineage occupies a cluster of houses, although in the 'new' part of Dalena most lineages are represented by one or two households. But most of the headman's lineage is settled in the 'new' part, whereas the other lineages have still the bulk of their members living in clusters in the 'old' part of the village. The attraction of building new houses in the 'new' part disperses lineage households. Almost all new houses are being built in the 'new' part, though the city-type house itself was still built in the 'old' part. But the man who had this house built is not actually resident in the village, which probably explains why he built it there instead of in the 'new' part. He had this house built for his relatives and built it where their previous house had been. As an outsider to the village, the position of the new house had not been as important to him as it is to residents; he was interested only in erecting a city-type house in his native village. But residents in the village all wish to build their new houses in the 'new' part of the village, nearer to the main road. This tendency has increased the demand for housing sites in this area and has led to a land dispute. According to a Government rule, application for the acquisition of new housing sites must be made to the Revenue Authority. In 1955 twelve Dalena men applied for a total of $1\frac{3}{4}$ acres of land for new housing sites. A few of the applicants started negotiations with the three owners of the land in question while their application to the Revenue Authority was pending and they came to an agreement over purchase. However, the agreement was challenged by the other applicants. Finally, after many quarrels, eight of the twelve applicants reached agreement with the owners of the land and their claim to purchase this land for housing sites was passed by the *panchayat* and sanctioned by the Revenue Authority. These eight men belong to six different lineages. Thus when they build their new houses side by side this will result in a further mixing in the settlement of lineage households.

But wherever there are still clusters of lineage households, there is a recognised arbitrator for each cluster. These arbitrators in turn recognise the lineage elder as their ritual and political head. Thus the traditional residential pattern strengthened political leadership within a lineage, and created the possibility of new leaders emerging in any one of the clusters of households. For instance, some commuters have thus emerged as political leaders. The commuters are always eager to strengthen the traditional political and social organisation in their own village and therefore are keen to accept political positions within it by becoming arbitrators for their cluster of lineage households.

One Dalena commuter managed to marry higher in the social scale in the village merely because he was a commuter. I have already mentioned Halli's wedding to the daughter of the village chairman. In accordance with the rules of marriage, a marriage between the two lineages was possible but it was not probable, because the chairman's lineage had a higher social status than Halli's. The chairman had eight daughters and no sons. He married his eldest daughter to her maternal uncle in a neighbouring village. At the beginning of 1954 Halli sought the agreement of the *panchayat* chairman to marry his second daughter, who was then about 9 years old. The negotiations were conducted through the lineage elders of their respective lineages.

Halli regarded a marriage to the chairman's daughter as highly desirable: he expected the union to increase his prestige in the village, and since the chairman had no sons, Halli also hoped that he could become a full-time farmer by cultivating part of the chairman's holding. The chairman provisionally agreed to the marriage because he regarded it as a desirable thing to have a factory worker as a son-in-law; Halli would bring a regular cash income into the house and would also be a good husband according to the urban pattern. Both sides expected to gain from the union and the wedding was provisionally fixed for Spring 1956. However, a few months before the agreed date the chairman began to have second thoughts; he let it be known in the village that he was about to set out for Mysore where, with the aid of the rich emigrant contractor from Dalena, he hoped to find a suitable husband for the daughter he had already pledged to Halli. To marry his daughter to a city man seemed to the chairman even more desirable than to marry her to a factory worker living in the village. When Halli learned of the chairman's intentions, he had one of his literate friends in Mandya write a long letter pointing out what a grave mistake the chairman would make if he broke the agreement. It would be inauspicious for the future life of his daughter; and it would also undermine the chairman's influence in the village and lose him the support of the commuters. The chairman reconsidered the matter, cancelled his trip to Mysore, and the wedding between Halli and his daughter took place.

The threat of loss of influence refers to the chairman's leadership of the 'conservative' faction in the village. For most of Dalena's commuters support this faction and are opposed to the 'progressive' faction headed by the innovators, the headman in particular. Halli's threat implied a strong sense of unity among the commuters which does not in fact exist, for they are divided among themselves according to their occupations in the town, and according to caste and lineage affiliation within the Peasant caste. It does suggest, however, that the commuters feel themselves to be a group apart from the rest of the village, at least in certain situations.

But the real importance of the case is that it indicates the high value Dalena people place on working in town. Here the chairman had allowed his daughter to marry a man of a lineage inferior to his own, and from a very poor household within the lineage at that, because Halli was a factory worker. Halli was probably not so suitable a match as the chairman had hoped to find in Mysore. Nevertheless, through his years of work in Mandya, Halli had acquired many of the modern ways of the town which the chairman regarded as desirable in a husband for his daughter. Despite the fact that the chairman was generally known in the village as a traditionalist, he sought for his daughter not an ordinary villager, but a man who would look after her in the modern urban style. But this is not the only paradox. Halli managed to marry higher in the social scale because he was a factory worker, and he used his work in the factory to achieve higher prestige within the traditional social system of the village.

Chennu, another factory worker, sought to raise his prestige in the village in a different way by becoming a medium, a *devaru gudda*, which means literally 'god's hillock'. Mediums act at certain village festivals or whenever there is a particular emergency and Peasants wish to consult certain deities. Each medium impersonates a particular deity and each village has more than one medium. Sometimes more than one medium represents one deity in a village. Whenever the deities are to be consulted, Untouchable village drummers come to beat the drums, while the idols of the particular deities are worshipped. The ritual and the beating of the drums sends the medium into a trance. When the drums suddenly stop and silence reigns, Peasants question him. Most of the questions I recorded on such occasions referred to the chance of survival of a sick member of a family, or to the chance of the wife bearing a son in families without male offspring. Most answers given by the mediums were favourable, but the grant was conditional on the suppliant performing regular offerings to the deity. If the prediction conveyed by the medium turned out to be false, the suppliant never blamed the deity or the medium, but always blamed himself for having failed to perform the offerings. God and mediums are regarded as infallible, while men are fallible.

In theory, the qualifications for mediumship should be inherited within a family. In fact, neither of the two Dalena mediums inherited his qualification. On the death of a medium, Dalena Peasants make a pilgrimage to the nearby Cauvery River where the son or nearest agnatic kinsman of the deceased erects a temporary shrine to the deity he had impersonated and Peasants bring their offerings of rice, jaggery, plantains, coconuts, betel leaves and areca nuts. Untouchable village servants come along to beat the drums until one of the Peasants present goes into a trance and the deity reveals himself through the new medium. In theory, the new medium is the nearest kinsman of the expired medium, but in fact this happens rarely, and men of different lineages become mediums, though the agnatic principal of succession is usually respected.

Six years ago the last Hanuman—Monkey god—mediu¡m died; the deceased had belonged to one of the 'male' clan l neages. Chennu, the factory worker, also belongs to one of the 'male' clan lineages, though not to the same one. Chennu's family is among the poorest in the village, but he himself had raised his economic status by becoming a factory worker. He is a young man eager to establish a position in the village. He had bought himself a bicycle and a gold watch and always wore a shirt and a dhoti. Prior to the death of the Hanuman medium, Chennu had gone into a trance several times at village ceremonies, but the villagers had denied his claim to mediumship. However, during the 'transference of medium' ceremony, his behaviour during his trance convinced Dalena Peasants that Chennu really was the new Hanuman medium. As the final test for a new medium, a Peasant acolyte splits a coconut on the head of the medium. Although a few other young Peasants had also made feeble attempts to go into a trance, Chennu was the only one who survived the final test uninjured.

To be a medium yields certain prestige in the village. As a medium, Chennu now receives offerings at each Peasant ceremony held in the village, and he is garlanded by the temple priests at certain festivals in the year. How far Chennu's desire and success in becoming a medium was a conscious attempt to raise his social status in the village, and how far he was a genuine obsessive, is difficult to say. The fact remains that Chennu had tried in several different ways to raise his social status in the village and becoming a medium certainly helped him the most. Chennu has Sanskritised his behaviour since becoming a medium. He could not however imitate the other Dalena medium, who has become a vegetarian, because he claims as a factory worker he has to take food in restaurants in Mandya and it is difficult to be a vegetarian there;

but Chennu has vowed to remain a bachelor, and the villagers respect his abstinence and celibacy.

Chennu, a factory worker, who in so many ways imitates the urban way of life, yet raised his social status by becoming a medium in the village. In turn he revitalised a customary belief. The belief in mediumship is tied up with a closely integrated society, for only in such a society can the person of a medium be associated with a certain deity. Thus while opening his society to the impact of the town on the one hand, Chennu also helped to perpetuate the traditional closed society. He personifies a fusion of the new and the old in the process of social change in Dalena.

The other medium in Dalena is already an elderly man, who impersonates the deity Muttrapa. Yet there is already a young man named Timma of another lineage who goes into a trance at festive occasions in the village and also acts as medium for the deity Muttrapa. So far he is not recognised as a Muttrapa medium, and in fact is usually laughed at and held back when he enters into a trance. But no doubt in future years this young man will also become the acknowledged Muttrapa medium, for he is acting as if he were the medium already. Timma is also eager to become a factory worker and would probably develop along the same lines as Chennu has done if he could get a job in the factory.

In Wangala there were four mediums but, in contrast to Dalena, no social prestige attached to them in their everyday life except for one who is the Wangala 'chairman'. The other three mediums were just ordinary men and were never given any special offerings because they were mediums. The chairman is the only medium who has social recognition, and in fact he acts as medium only when the matter involves the whole village. Thus he went into a trance when a buffalo disease had killed 35 buffaloes in a couple of days. He pronounced on behalf of the deity that the village must reunite and hold a joint feast. But he was also expressing his own feelings, for he is the one man in Wangala who always tries to reunite the village in celebrating traditional feasts. Nevertheless, the death of the buffaloes was so threatening that the village supported him.

One may speculate whether the different attitudes expressed by

Dalena and Wangala villagers towards their mediums are due to the different economies in which the medium beliefs operate. It is possible that Dalena men attach prestige to the person of a medium, because their economy has diversified and put emphasis on the individual, whereas Wangala's economy is still traditionally rural with little weight attached to the individual, and no importance therefore attached to the person of a medium. However, this is purely speculative, for I have no evidence to show that Dalena's attitude towards its mediums has changed at all since the diversification of the village economy.

We have seen that the commuters in Dalena try to raise their prestige in the customary pattern of behaviour; they marry higher in the social scale, they try to become mediums, and so on. The commuters are involved in two distinct sets of social relations which originate in their work in the town and their residence in the village. They occupy different roles as factory workers or townsmen and as villagers, the dominant role at any time being determined by the social situation. If they are in town together with fellow workers their behaviour will be subject to the social pressure arising out of their set of relations with other workers; if they are together with other Dalena men they will come under the impact of social pressure operating within the village social system. Being involved in two different sets of social relations leads to inconsistencies in their behaviour; on the one hand through their daily contact with the town they introduce urban values into the village, and on the other hand, through their desire to become full-time farmers and acquire prestige in the village they support the traditional system. The strong pull of farming makes it difficult for them to adjust themselves to the urban environment. It leads them to act as villagers even when in the town and it also tones down their introduction of urban values to the village.

Dalena is thus still an independent social system, and has not become merely a dormitory for commuters, like other villages near bigger towns. It is the desire of all commuters to become full-time farmers which is largely responsible for the persistence of Dalena as an independent social system. If these commuters were to accept employment in the town as the source of their future income, Dalena's unity would no doubt be undermined.

I have discussed how intra-Peasant caste relations are based on kinship, marriage, friendship, and employment in the town. Relationships between Untouchables in Dalena are based on the same principles, but there is only one Untouchable who has got a job in the town. Most of the Untouchables work as labourers on farms in Dalena or surrounding villages, or they work for contractors,

Marriage ties among Untouchables are mostly inter-village. As much as 77% of all Untouchable existing marriages are between Untouchable men from Dalena and women from other villages; only 7% are between an Untouchable and a woman from the same village; and 16% are between men and women who have immigrated into Dalena. Most of the Untouchable households in Dalena belong to one lineage, although there are three different Untouchable lineages in Dalena. Each lineage has its own lineage deity and there is a temple in Dalena's Untouchable quarter to the deity Manchamma, the lineage deity of the dominant Untouchable lineage in Dalena. Among all existing Untouchable marriages there is only one between a man and woman both from Dalena. About 48% of all inter-village marriages of Untouchables are between men from Dalena and women from villages within a radius of 4 miles, whereas 40% are between men from Dalena and women from villages outside a radius of 10 miles. Thus the marriage ties are about equally distributed between near and far villages; and this reflects the spread of economic interests of Dalena Untouchables. On the one hand, they are labourers in nearby villages; on the other hand, some of them have been labour migrants to far away places whence they bring their wives.

Polygyny is permitted among caste Hindus and Untouchables but there is not a single household in Dalena with two wives. It would be far too heavy an economic burden for an Untouchable to have to support two wives. Even for a Peasant it is a heavy financial burden and no Peasant household in Dalena is polygynous.

Family Structure

In my discussion of Wangala's family structure I have already dealt with the break-up of the joint family among Peasants. The same development has occurred in Dalena, and the elementary family has emerged as the dominant family unit in domestic life. Only about 8% of all Dalena households still live as joint families, while the remainder are all nuclear families. My data show that in the past Dalena Peasants used to live in joint families, but there is no evidence that this was so among Untouchables. As I have argued in the section on family structure of Wangala, joint families only exist on the basis of joint estates, and since Untouchables did not own joint estates, they never lived as joint families. Peasants on the other hand used to have joint estates and had joint families. But these joint families broke up as the economy of the village diversified and changed from subsistence to cash. Elders in Dalena complain that the young people of to-day are so selfish that they do not want to share things, and thus account for the break-up of joint families. Young men are no more selfish to-day than they used to be in the past, but nowadays the range of goods that they possess is much wider; they have more items of clothing and other personal property, which they may not wish to share with their brothers. With the conversion from a subsistence to a cash economy, new goods came within the reach of Dalena men and as they entered the competitive system of the market economy they tended to throw off the burden of the joint family with its emphasis on sharing.

In Dalena the joint family broke up with the diversification of the economy, in a process similar to that described by Bailey for an Oriya village.[1] Yet in view of the changes in Wangala's family structure it is probably the conversion from a subsistence to a cash economy rather than the diversification of the economy that is responsible for the break-up of the joint family system.

In Dalena adoption is much less frequent than in Wangala; only about 2% of all the men in Dalena are adopted, whereas the percentage is as high as 10% for Wangala men. The practice of

[1] F. G. Bailey, op. cit., p. 92.

adoption is tied up with the cultivation of estates. A man wants to adopt a son only if he has an estate that he wishes to pass on to a son and for whose cultivation he wants a son's help. This explains the much higher rate of adoption in Wangala than in Dalena, for in Dalena less emphasis is placed on the cultivation of a man's estate. His estate is only of secondary importance, particularly his estate in the village itself. Dry land farming requires so little labour that no man would even consider it worth his while to adopt a son to help him in its cultivation. In Wangala we have seen that adoption tends to rule out the effects of variations in births and deaths among different families. But in Dalena men are less inclined to adopt sons than they are in Wangala and therefore in Dalena adoption does not counteract the accidents of births and deaths. Even the chairman, with eight daughters, did not adopt a single son. Thus his estate will ultimately have to go to a son-in-law, a prospect which prompted Halli to seek the chairman's daughter in marriage.

I have argued in this section that family structure in Dalena has changed from the joint to the nuclear family, just as it has done in Wangala, because in both cases the village economies changed from subsistence to cash. I have also shown that adoption is much more frequent in Wangala than it is in Dalena, because farmers in Dalena do not regard their dry land holding as sufficient incentive to adopt a son, whereas Wangala farmers consider their wet land holdings too important to be left without a male heir. Some adoption still takes place in Dalena primarily to perpetuate the lineage and to have someone who will take care of old people.

Relations between Peasants and Untouchables

Untouchables in Dalena own and cultivate an average of 1·10 acres of dry land per household, whereas Peasants cultivate about 5·9 acres per household. None of the Untouchables own any wet land in neighbouring villages. Thus while about one-third of the average holding per Peasant household is wet land, all land held by the Untouchables in Dalena is dry. One acre of dry land is not sufficient to yield even enough food for one individual per year, let alone food for a whole household. Thus Dalena Untouchables depend for the major part of their income on wages from agricultural labour or from casual labour for contractors.

Dalena Untouchables no longer have any hereditary relationship with Peasants in their own village. They used to have the same hereditary relationship with their Peasant masters that still exists in Wangala, but since irrigation in the area these hereditary relations have disappeared. Dalena Peasants no longer give their Untouchable clients any annual rewards, nor do they employ them exclusively on their land, nor do the Untouchable clients perform any ritual services for their Peasant masters. In fact, the word *Halemakkalu*, by which a Peasant master referred to his Untouchable clients, has fallen into disuse in Dalena. Thus the disappearance of the economic aspect of the hereditary relationship between Peasants and Untouchables has led to the disappearance of the ritual aspect. We have seen how the Peasants continue their economic relationship with the Washermen because, for instance, they need the continued ritual services of the Washerman. If Peasants really needed the continued ritual services of their Untouchable clients they would have to continue their economic relationship with them. But it seems that the Untouchable's ritual services to his Peasant master are not sufficiently important for the master to keep on paying the customary annual rewards. Thus previously the Untouchable client would have carried the torch ahead of the funeral procession of his master's household, or would have helped in cleaning and whitewashing the house, or in the erection of a leaf canopy outside the house on the occasion of a wedding in his master's house. If there is a death in a Peasant household they still send for the Untouchable to come and carry the torch at the funeral procession, but he no longer pays any attention. I once saw a Peasant send for an Untouchable to come to the funeral procession of his wife. The Peasant who delivered the message could not enter the house of the Untouchable, and he was told that the Untouchable was not at home, which was not true. When I entered the house and asked the Untouchable about his refusal to go to the funeral procession, he pointed out that the Peasants did not do anything for him, so he saw no reason why he should go and do something for them. This is now the general attitude of the Untouchables in Dalena towards their old masters. The masters no longer give their Untouchable clients annual rewards, so the Untouchable clients do not perform any of the ritual functions.

The hereditary relationship between Peasants and Untouchables in Dalena broke off after irrigation entered the area and brought a number of new employment opportunities for Dalena men. Untouchables then sought work wheresoever they could, and they did not always look to their own Peasant master to give them work to do. Previously, each Peasant regarded his Untouchable client as one of his liabilities; now he does not have any responsibility for him. If an Untouchable could get work elsewhere, his Peasant master was only too happy to be relieved of his responsibility.

As a group, however, there are still relations between Untouchables and Peasants in Dalena. Untouchable women sing songs at certain Peasant rituals; Untouchable men ares till the village town-criers and the village drummers. While the individual relationship between any particular Peasant and any particular Untouchable household has disappeared, the relationship between Untouchables and Peasants still continues. For instance, every night there are two Peasant watchmen and one Untouchable watchman on duty in the village. This job used to be very important prior to the introduction of electricity, but nowadays it means that the three watchmen sleep the whole night; the two Peasant watchmen sleep in the *marichoudi*, the village shrine, and the Untouchable sleeps at some nearby house. But the job of watchmen is still continued and performed by Peasants and Untouchables jointly. The continued services by Untouchables to the Peasant community, rather than to individual Peasant households, are ensured by the conditions under which they hold their Government-granted land.

It may seem surprising that Dalena Untouchables, although they have broken off their hereditary relationship with Peasants, have not made any efforts to rebel against Untouchability, such as Wangala Untouchables did in the drama incident. However, if we remember that Dalena Untouchables are all the time competing with each other for the scarce jobs in the area, it will become obvious why they have not displayed the same unity as Wangala Untouchables. For Wangala Untouchables the labour market is organised on the basis of hereditary relationships with their Peasant masters and they therefore do not have to compete with each other for work. This enabled them to develop a greater uniformity in behaviour than among Dalena Untouchables. Competition for scarce jobs prevented Dalena Untouchables acting as a united group against Peasants in their village.

Dalena's social system does not operate any longer on the basis of the hereditary principle; *panchayat* membership is not based on hereditary elders, nor are relations between Peasants and Untouchables based on hereditary links. Greater individualism has entered Dalena's social system since the diversification of its economy. The multifarious economic changes that have taken place in Dalena since irrigation reached the area are responsible for the changes in the political and social system. The diversification of Dalena's economy widened the economic horizon of Dalena villagers and consequently also their political horizon. They now have so many different economic links with the regional economy that their political attitudes and social relations have changed. By contrast with Wangala, Dalena has changed in most aspects of its social life, while Wangala has remained very much the same as it was before irrigation. The relative stability of Wangala's social system since irrigation I attribute to the unilinear change that irrigation has brought about, whereas the many changes that have taken place in Dalena since irrigation reached the area I attribute to the multifarious changes that have taken place. It is thus the different nature of the economic changes that is responsible for the different lines of development we have traced in Dalena and Wangala. Yet, we must remember that both villages are still independent social fields, which can be usefully studied in isolation from the environment of which they form a part. Neither Wangala nor Dalena are so much involved in the wider regional system that it has swallowed up their identity.

CHAPTER VIII

CONCLUSION: ECONOMIC DEVELOPMENT AND SOCIAL CHANGE

A GREAT deal has been heard about 'changeless India' and about the 'timeless and changeless Indian village'. If this book does nothing else it should at least dispel this naïve notion. In my review of events which occurred in Wangala and Dalena during the past 25 years I have demonstrated that villagers were not slow to react to new economic opportunities. In fact they were no slower than farmers the whole world over. 'Most of the farmers of the world are not motivated by abstract ends or speculative results. . . . For them "seeing is believing". . . . The distrust of new and untried ways is an obverse of the faith in the known, that which with all its ups and downs, has supported the society since time immemorial.'[1] Both Wangala and Dalena villagers accommodated themselves relatively quickly to the new economic environment created by irrigation in the area. I have shown how irrigation integrated villages into a regional economy and how the different roles Wangala and Dalena occupied within the wider economy set each village on a different path of development.

The decision to irrigate the Mandya region did not originate in any source indigenous to the villages. Rather it was the Government of Mysore which planned the irrigation of a certain area in order to increase the productivity of the land. Similarly, it was Government initiative which underlay the further efforts required to bring about the economic expansion of the region by setting up a sugar factory at Mandya and by making the town the headquarters of a separate District Administration. In this respect then the changes I have described for Wangala and Dalena are not unique or of local interest only; they are representative of the increasing modern tendency whereby new economic potentials created by Government result in the incorporation of subsistence

[1] M. Mead, *Cultural Patterns and Technological Change*, UNESCO, 1953, p. 198.

economies in the wider cash economy. In this final chapter therefore I shall discuss the general principles underlying the social changes that occurred in Wangala and Dalena.

In the preceding chapters I discussed *how* Wangala and Dalena changed since irrigation reached the area. Here I shall analyse *why* certain changes occurred in Dalena and not in Wangala, and beyond this *why* the two villages changed as they did.

In much of anthropological literature, social change is analysed as it has arisen in situations of culture contact which involved the diffusion of an alien more advanced culture among 'primitive' peoples.[1] Such diffusion may be in terms of technology, religion or political institutions. In all such work there is a distinction drawn, explicitly or implicitly, between change in which basic elements of the society alter, and change in which social action, while not repetitive, does not alter the basic social forms.[2]

In my own study, which is one of the effects of economic engineering rather than of culture contact or diffusion, I found that some aspects of social structure changed while others remained the same, and that some aspects of culture changed while others persisted. To explain this uneven change I find I must further distinguish between different types of structural relations and different aspects of culture. Arising out of the discussion in the preceding chapters I have categorised structural change into economic, political, ritual, familial and organisational change according to the functional relations involved. Cultural change I shall discuss in terms of change in economic and prestige values. I have chosen these aspects of culture out of a great variety, firstly, because I regard them as major determinants of social behaviour, and secondly, because these were the aspects of culture which changed or were responsible for some structural change in the two villages under discussion.

Since unrestricted social mobility is usually regarded as essential

[1] See e.g. B. Malinowski, *The Dynamics of Culture Change*, Yale University Press, 1945, M. Gluckman, *Analysis of a Social Situation in Modern Zululand*, Rhodes-Livingstone Paper No. 28, 1958, M. Mead, *New Lives for Old*, William Morrow & Co., N.Y., 1956.

[2] R. Firth, 'Social Organisation and Social Change', *Journal of the Royal Anthropological Institute*, 1954, p. 17.

to an expanding economy, it would be very interesting to know how far caste values are tied to economic relations and will change with the latter, and how far they are independently perpetuated through the educational pattern. In order to give a clearer picture of caste values we would require a close study of the education children receive in their homes and at school, and of how far differentiation of castes is inculcated into the mind of the young through listening to religious stories or watching religious dramas. Thus a study of villagers' caste values would have to include an analysis of personality formation. Unfortunately, lack of time prevented me from carrying out such analysis of caste values.

All peoples, civilised as well as primitive, are obliged to make a selection and rank certain objects and certain modes of conduct as more desirable, more agreeable or more worthy than others. Each society has such set orders or preferences usually referred to as its system of values. (Values formally defined are preferences regarding objects and actions in their social context.) The value scales are imposed upon members of the group by the ordinary process of social conditioning, and what attracts or repels one person tends also to attract or repel his fellows.[1]

Values then are responsible for the direction of social behaviour; if values change, social behaviour will also change. However, since a change in social behaviour usually involves a change in different aspects of culture as well as a change in several types of structural relations, it is difficult to allocate it to any one of our categories. For instance, if we observe that sons cease to work for their father's estates and rather work as casual labourers for other farmers, this would involve, according to our categories, a change in prestige and economic values as well as a change in economic and familial relations. Therefore although the categories of structural and cultural changes are interconnected, for analytical purposes I propose to discuss each category separately. I do not claim to cover all types of structural relations, nor all aspects of culture. For instance, I shall not discuss change in religious beliefs because this was not an important variable in the culture change which

[1] I. Hogbin, *Social Change*, Watts, 1958, p. 58.

occurred in the two villages under discussion. Except for the few Muslim families in Wangala, inhabitants of both villages were Hindus before irrigation reached Mandya area and they are still adhering to the same religious faith. They did not change their religious beliefs, only their religious practices changed, and these I shall discuss under the heading of 'ritual change'.

Thus I am aware of the limits to the application of our categories of social change to other such studies. But since social behaviour has so many different aspects I find it impossible to deal with all of them and restrict my discussion to those which are relevant to an understanding of social change in Wangala and Dalena.

Structural Change

(*a*) *Economic Change*

By economic change I mean a change in economic roles and relations. Both Wangala and Dalena have undergone considerable economic development during the past 25 years, that is to say in both villages the output of goods and services has increased considerably with the same or greater labour input. Both villages have changed from subsistence to cash economies, but the resultant economic changes were quite different in Dalena and Wangala. Wangala's economy has remained wholly agricultural, while Dalena's has diversified. At this point I am not dealing with the reasons for this different kind of economic development, only with the actual facts of it. The reasons will become apparent when I deal with cultural changes. For the present it suffices that while Wangala remained a discrete agricultural economy, Dalena's diversification led to its closer integration into the regional economy. Some Dalena men took up employment in the town, some became contractors for the Public Works Department, bought carts for hiring out, or bullocks for trading, while yet others bought land or worked as agricultural labourers in neighbouring villages. Dalena's agricultural village system was thus hinged on to the wider industrial and commercial system. The Wilsons have observed that as the range of relations increases, the degree of dependence upon neighbours and contemporaries diminishes.[1] Thus as Dalena men increased the range of their economic relations, the interdependence between farmers and their agricultural labourers decreased and consequently the hereditary economic relations between Peasant masters and Untouchable clients disappeared.

Individuals act in their self-interest as they perceive it and are usually unconscious of the social relations which affect and help to determine their behaviour, or of the effect their behaviour has in turn on social relations. When Dalena Peasant farmers ceased to give to their Untouchable clients the customary annual reward they thought they were doing this merely to save what they had come to regard as uneconomic expenditure. They were not aware that they were terminating an economic relationship, nor did they realise that they had been prompted to do this by the increased range of their economic relations.

The major part of Dalena's economic structure was incompatible with the new economic environment in which Dalena men now operate and therefore most economic relations changed. It would have been uneconomic for Dalena farmers to employ their Untouchable clients on wet lands in neighbouring villages, because of the time wasted in walking to and from the lands. At the same time it would have been impossible for Untouchables to work for farmers outside their own village whilst remaining committed to labour for their Peasant masters whenever the latter required their services. The employment of men outside their own village was thus incompatible with the indigenous employment structure and therefore hereditary employment relations gave way to impersonal ones.

Yet some aspects of the customary economic structure still persist unchanged. For instance, when Dalena Peasants broke off their hereditary economic relations with one of the Washermen because he had offended a man of their own caste, they did not dispense with these hereditary relations but merely transferred them to another Washerman. In this case economic relations remained unchanged, and only the personnel involved changed.

[1] Godfrey and Monica Wilson, *An Analysis of Social Change*, Cambridge University Press, 1954, p. 86.

The extension of economic ties by Dalena men outside their own village did not affect the customary relations between Peasants and Washermen. Peasants still require the services of a Washerman and the Washerman still wants to get his food by washing clothes for Peasants. Thus the tithe relationship between Peasants and Washermen is not incompatible with the new economic situation in Dalena and so far it persists.

Similarly, the economic role of women is unaltered in the new system. They continue to operate in the customary subsistence farming economy. Their continued work on the land is not merely compatible with the new economic system, it is in fact essential to sustain it. If wives ceased to work the village dry lands, their menfolk would have less spare time to seek employment outside their village, or to cultivate their wet lands. Even if farmers employed more Untouchable women, rather than use their own wives for the agricultural work, they would still have to devote more time to the cultivation of their village dry lands, for they would have to supervise their paid labourers. It is, in short, the continued agricultural labour of their wives that enables Dalena men to participate in the wider cash economy. Dalena women still continue to pay for goods and services in kind rather than in cash; they pay the Potter, who comes from a neighbouring village, in quantities of ragi or paddy. Very rarely does a Dalena woman venture to purchase goods at Mandya fair; she leaves the cash purchases to her husband. This division of labour between husband and wife is quite compatible with the participation of Dalena men in the wider cash economy and therefore traditional economic relations between them have persisted in the changed economic environment.

Thus we see that incompatibility provides a clue to change. Incompatibility causes friction and leads to change. Conversely, compatibility may ensure the continued functioning of customary relations. In my analysis of economic development in Wangala I have shown how irrigation raised the whole economy to a higher level at one stroke. In spite of the change from subsistence to cash, Wangala remained a wholly agricultural economy. Therefore, its employment structure remained unaltered. Peasant farmers now require more labour, so they employ their Untouchable clients and their Peasant debtors for more days per year. The greater labour requirements for cash cropping can be quite easily met under the traditional system of hereditary economic relations. The unilinear economic development in Wangala set up no incompatibility, no friction between new wants and old ways, in the indigenous employment structure, which therefore persists. But not only do they require the same type of agricultural labour; Wangala Peasants still need the same services from their Functionaries. Therefore, when the indigenous Blacksmith desired to sever his hereditary bonds with Peasant households, he was made to provide a substitute before the *panchayat* agreed to release him from his obligations. As in the case of the Dalena Washerman, Wangala Peasants retained the economic relationship, while allowing the personnel to change.

The persistence of a rural economy in itself, however, does not ensure the absence of economic change.

> The potato and the pig, for instance, when introduced among the Maori of New Zealand radically altered the economic structure. They reduced the amount of labour put in on other crops, and on fowling; they altered the production balance between men and women, they gave commoners a chance of earning relatively higher incomes and elevating themselves in the social scale; they even helped to change the scheme of ritual by reducing the amount of economic magic demanded. Together with other factors, such as the musket, they were the basis for important structural changes in Maori society.[1]

Thus we see that although the Maori remained a wholly rural society the introduction of new crops radically changed the economic structure. Probably the most important factor in this change was the redistribution of wealth. If irrigation of Wangala lands had brought about a reallocation of economic resources, this would have undoubtedly caused friction in the traditional economic organisation and led to its change. But far from upsetting it, irrigation in fact emphasised the existing economic differentiation and economic relations could continue unaltered.

The economic role of wives is the only part of Wangala's

[1] R. Firth, *Elements of Social Organisation*, Watts & Co., 1951, p. 85.

economic structure which has changed since the advent of irrigation. Wangala husbands can devote all their time to the cultivation of their village lands. It became a matter of prestige for a husband to relieve his wife of the duties of helping him cultivate his lands. The continued agricultural labour of wives was incompatible with the new status criteria and therefore economic relations between husband and wife changed.

Though the change from subsistence to cash economy has integrated Wangala into the wider cash economy, the resulting economic relations are so tenuous that they hardly affected the indigenous economic structure. As producers Wangala's economic relations are almost confined to Mandya's sugar factory which, since it occupies a monopsonistic position *vis-à-vis* the farmers, is able to dictate the conditions of the contract for the cultivation of cane. On the other hand, as consumers, Wangala villagers purchase goods from so many different sources that no formalised economic relations result. Such formalised economic relations remain confined to the village and as we have seen these have hardly changed.

The point of theoretical interest emerging at this stage of the discussion is that economic development may occur without any change in economic roles and relations, provided it does not result in a reallocation of resources or in an increased range of economic relations. Far from undermining the economic structure of any society such economic development may even strengthen the existing pattern of economic relations.

(*b*) *Political Change*

By political change I mean change in political roles and relations. In Dalena there have been radical political changes. *Panchayat* members are no more necessarily lineage elders; Peasants are no more the arbitrators in intra-Untouchable disputes. Dalena villagers working in the Mandya sugar factory participated in a strike and quite a number of villagers attended a meeting held in Mandya to protest against the reorganisation of Mysore State. Their many links with the wider economy have brought about an awareness of wider political issues.

The increased economic mobility created by economic diversification led to a redistribution of wealth, which became incompatible with political leadership based on the hereditary principle. The new magnates sought political expression for their newly acquired economic status and the poorer hereditary lineage elders had no power to oppose this quest. This development preceded the first *panchayat* election under the new democratic legislation. Dalena villagers had already begun to accept the idea that political office need not be hereditary and therefore the elections legalised the already established departure from a strictly hereditary political system. Dalena's elected *panchayat* is a far less effective council than its traditional *panchayat* used to be. Cases formerly settled by the *panchayat* are nowadays taken to the courts in Mandya.

In short, in Dalena economic diversification led to a close integration into the wider economy and subsequently also into the wider body politic. The increased range of economic relations increased the range of political relations.

By contrast, Wangala displays no such change in formalised political relations. The village *panchayat* still consists of hereditary lineage elders and continues to settle most disputes between villagers. Peasant masters are still arbitrators for their Untouchable clients. The new democratic legislation did not affect the functioning of the indigenous hereditary *panchayat*, because it was introduced into a system of unchanged economic roles and relations. The reserved seats for Untouchables remain a fiction as long as Untouchables continue in a dependent economic relationship on their Peasant masters. If the new democratic legislation had been accompanied by a redistribution of land in favour of Untouchables, it would probably have been effective in bringing about Untouchable representation in the *panchayat*. As it was, political legislation did not aim at any economic change and was therefore ineffective.

The only change in Wangala's political relations occurred in the sphere of factions. Two of the structurally younger but economically powerful lineages have combined against two of the politically and ritually dominant, but economically declining lineages.

Factions in Wangala provide a mechanism whereby economic status may be translated into political influence. But since irrigation emphasised the existing economic differentiation rather than increased economic mobility and since it also strengthened the villagers' uniform interest in farming, Wangala's factions are not rigidly opposed. In this they differ from Dalena where factions display the basic cleavage between innovators and conservatives and where economic diversification has increased economic mobility. Economic change in Dalena was followed by political change, whereas the persistence of Wangala's economic structure was responsible for the persistence of its political structure.

(*c*) *Ritual Change*

By ritual change I mean a change in traditional religious ritual roles and relations. In Dalena the break in the traditional economic relations between Peasant masters and their Untouchable clients led to a severance of ritual relations between the individual households involved. Since the Peasant master refused to give his Untouchable client the customary annual reward, the latter refused to perform his customary ritual services for the former. In a society such as Dalena where every service demands a reward, it would have been unreasonable to expect Untouchables to continue their ritual services to their Peasant masters after the latter had broken off economic relations with them. Thus nowadays an Untouchable no longer carries the torch ahead of a Peasant funeral or helps to build a canopy for the wedding in his master's household. Yet the ritual relationship between Peasants and Untouchables as groups is still effective. Untouchables continue to act as drummers at village festivals. The continued group relationship between Peasants and Untouchables is in accordance with the holding of Government-granted land by Untouchables as a reward for services to the village as a whole. Furthermore, Untouchables perform their duties as a group because they are scared of Peasant violence. In the Mandya area clashes have occurred between Peasants and Untouchables. However, as fewer and fewer village ceremonies are being performed in Dalena, the significance of this group relationship is declining.

Dalena Peasants still have their customary ritual relations with their Functionaries. The Barber and Washerman continue to perform important ritual services in Peasant life-cycle rituals. These ritual relations are in line with the continued hereditary economic relations between Peasants and Functionaries. Though ritual still plays an important part in the life-cycle of individual Peasants its importance in economic life is declining. While most farming activities are highly ritualised, non-farming activities are not ritualised at all. After every harvest each lineage performs a thanksgiving ritual to the lineage deity on the land of the lineage elder. By contrast, no ritual is performed when a factory worker receives his wages or a contractor his pay. As more non-farming activities assume importance in Dalena, the prominence of traditional ritual in economic activities is declining. Altogether the prominence of ritual in village life is decreasing. The rigid faction opposition between innovators and conservatives prevents the celebration of joint village festivals. During the whole of my stay in Dalena I did not see a single ceremony performed by all villagers jointly. The discussion over joint village ceremonies always broke down over the refusal of innovators to participate. For these innovators, economic success rather than ritual roles is the ultimate criterion of social status. They are therefore not interested in participating in village ceremonies.

In Wangala, where the economy is still wholly rural, ritual occupies a dominant role in economic activities. Here ritual status is still the ultimate determinant of social status. Since ritual status is always hereditary, at least in theory, while economic status may be acquired, there is always a tendency for men to try and translate their newly gained economic status into ritual status through exerting political influence. I have described how factions lead to the duplication of ceremonies in the village and thus to the creation of new ritual offices.[1] Thus in Wangala we find an increase in the number of intra-Peasant ritual relations, while ritual relations between Peasants and their Untouchable clients and their Functionaries continue unaltered. Peasants still pay their annual reward to their Untouchable clients and their Functionaries and

[1] See above, pp.. 132–4.

these two dependent groups continue to perform their ritual services in Peasant ceremonies.

There has therefore been some ritual change in both villages, but while the change in Wangala was intra-caste and resulted in an increased number and intensity of ritual relations among Peasants, in Dalena the change was inter-caste, resulting in a disappearance of ritual relations between Peasant masters and their Untouchable clients.

(*d*) *Familial Change*

By familial change I mean change in relations within the family. I have argued for both Wangala and Dalena that the conversion from a subsistence to a cash economy led to the breakdown of the joint family unit among Peasant farmers. 'It can be stated as a theorem valid in a high percentage of cases, that the greater the opportunity for profit in any social cultural situation, the weaker the ties of extended kinship will become.' [1]

Thus economic development, whether or not it brings about economic changes, will almost invariably result in the breaking up of joint family ties. The partitioning of joint families affects the relationship between father and sons. Under the joint family system in Wangala and Dalena sons showed extreme respect to their father; now that the custom of partitioning has been adopted many more quarrels arise between father and sons. The sons assume an attitude of greater independence once they realise that they have a right to become independent farmers as soon as they are married and able to set up their own *ménage*. At the same time the relationship between brothers has also changed. Younger brothers showed greater respect to their elder brother as long as he was, or was expected to be, the manager of the joint estate. Tupa, the young Wangala Peasant who quarrelled with his father over his share of the family estate and joined the faction in opposition to his own lineage, is an extreme example of the disrespect shown by a man to his father and brother.[2] The

[1] R. Linton, 'Cultural and Personality Factors Affecting Economic Growth', *The Progress of Underdeveloped Areas* (ed. by B. F. Hoselitz), University of Chicago, 1952, p. 84.

[2] See above, p. 129.

public condemnation of his action, on the other hand, illustrates the value Wangala villagers still attach to lineage unity.

Greater economic independence affected the respect shown by men towards their father and brothers. It also affected the relationship between husband and wife in Wangala. Buffaloes and moneylending give Wangala wives an independent source of income, which makes them less subservient to their husbands. Wangala husbands are faced with a dilemma: on the one hand the life they provide for their wives is a major determinant of their own social status; on the other, if they release their wives from agricultural labour and provide them with buffaloes as an independent source of income, wives become less obedient to their husbands. Wangala women have learned to operate in a cash economy; they go to the weekly fair at Mandya where they purchase the household requirements and where some of them sell the butter they have made out of buffalo milk. The money earned from such sales they keep for extras for themselves or their children, whereas the household requirements are purchased with money provided by the husband. Dalena women are far less independent than their Wangala sisters. They still function in the customary subsistence economy and continue to work the lands of their husbands. Status criteria in Dalena are unaffected by the sort of life a husband provides for his wife. Women are in fact the pillars of the traditional village farming economy. Even the richest man's wife works on his fields. Because economic relations between husband and wife are unchanged, familial relations between them are also unaltered; the wife shows her husband the customary respect. By contrast, in Wangala where the wife occupies a new economic role familial relations are also changed and the wife is much less subservient to her husband.

(e) *Organisational Change*

By organisational change I mean a change in the principles of social organisation. In Wangala the hereditary principle is still basic to the social organisation. Office as a lineage elder or *panchayat* member is still hereditary; likewise, relations between Peasant masters and Untouchable clients are also hereditary, as are those between Peasants and Functionaries and between creditors and debtors. The hereditary principle is quite compatible with Wangala's economic system in which economic status is largely inherited. A man's economic status is determined by the size of the ancestral estate and the number of heirs that have to share it; personal initiative can hardly help to raise his economic status. Although the relative economic status of successive generations of households may be quite different, this has nothing to do with the personal ability and efforts of the particular householder, but rather is a result of the accidents of birth and death. The five present magnates in Wangala were all fortunate in being sole heirs to their ancestral estate. Since heredity continues to determine the economic status of households in Wangala, it also continues to be the general principle of social organisation.

Another aspect of the hereditary principle is the personal element in the relationship between the members of different social groups. This personal element creates emotional attachments between the parties to such a hereditary relationship. For instance, the hereditary relations between Peasant masters and their Untouchable clients bridge the gulf between castes and Untouchables by giving each Peasant master a personal interest in the well-being of his Untouchable client. Conversely, the Untouchable client develops an emotional attachment to his Peasant master and takes a personal interest in the cultivation of his master's lands or in the performance of rituals in his master's household, quite apart from his obligations.

However, the hereditary principle of social organisation is only compatible with a closely integrated society, in which economic, political and ritual relations are concentrated within the boundaries of the village. Once the range of these relations is extended beyond the limits of the particular society, the dependence on fellow-villagers will diminish and the personal element in the indigenous relationship will give way to an impersonal one. This is what happened in Dalena, where participation in the regional economy has increased economic mobility. Personal ability and drive rather than the size of the ancestral estate or the number of heirs with whom it must be shared became the effective determinant of economic status. The growth of the competitive spirit is seen in the elimination of the hereditary relations between Peasant masters and Untouchable clients. Though in the traditional system too, labourers were distinguished into good and bad, the personal performance of the labourer is now the chief criterion: the better the worker, the more he is sought after. In turn competition amongst the Untouchables themselves has undermined their unity and prevented any combined protest against the system of untouchability itself.

The greater economic mobility created by Dalena's economic diversification has similarly undermined the traditional principles of political organisation. Some of the *panchayat* members are no longer elders of lineages. Hereditary claims to political office now yield before the power exerted by newly established magnates. Furthermore, the principle of group mobility in the political sphere has disappeared in favour of mobility of the individual household. In Wangala, the magnate who sought political office had to get his lineage raised to the status of 'major' lineage before his membership of the *panchayat* was generally recognised. By contrast, in Dalena a magnate's economic power has become generally accepted as sufficient qualification for political office.

Yet agnation remains an important principle of political organisation in both villages. In Wangala and Dalena factions are organised on the basis of lineage, and so is membership of the *panchayat*. The introduction of the new competitive principle and the persistence of the agnatic principle cause an inconsistency in Dalena's present social organisation. This gives rise to friction on the one hand and allows for political manipulations by individuals adhering to opposing principles of social organisation, on the other.

Dalena's radical economic change, its integration into the regional economy, undermined the very principles on which its society had been organised; the absence of such economic change allowed the hereditary principle to continue unchallenged in Wangala.

Cultural Change

(a) *Change in Economic Values*

Wangala villagers give farming the dominant place in their system of economic values. To be a farmer used to be, and still is, the ultimate aim of every Wangala villager. Land yields food and food is essential to life. However, farming is not merely an economic activity, or a means of making a living, it is rather a way of life. Each farmer develops an emotional attachment to his soil, and so long as he can make a 'reasonable' living by working his lands, he will continue to be a farmer. Irrigation increased the income a farmer can derive from his lands and therefore strengthened the value he attaches to farming. This largely explains why Wangala survived as a wholly rural economy, in spite of the opportunities offered in the regional economy. The ownership of even a small fraction of an acre keeps a Wangala man from moving out of his village, as we saw even in the case of a craftsman such as the Goldsmith.[1] And even the landless seem to prefer agricultural labour to any other type of work. They have grown up in the rural environment with its personal relations between farmer and labourer and prefer the relative security these offer to the hazards of life in the town. On the other hand, it must be noted here that a concerted policy on the part of the sugar factory and the Administration in Mandya to employ landless Untouchables from surrounding villages would no doubt have attracted Wangala's Untouchables to employment in the town. However, the discrimination against Untouchables in Mandya reduced their employment possibilities in the town and they have therefore remained in their villages. Wangala Untouchables are very disgruntled with their poverty, but they all cherish the secret hope that one day they too will become farmers of standing. None of them complains about his inability to get a job in the town. The only employment they seek is work on the factory plantation. Thus the value attached to farming has percolated through even to the poorest Untouchables. As long as population pressure does not force some of Wangala's villagers off the land, they will

[1] See above, p. 82.

continue their agricultural activities, and will continue to give farming highest preference in their system of economic values.

In Dalena, too, villagers used to attach highest value to farming. But as they saw irrigation making their neighbours richer, while their own lands remained dry, they decided that they too would participate in the economic expansion of the region in whatever way they could. Thus they began to attach higher value to increasing their income than to farming. Yet farming is still the ultimate aim of every Dalena man, even if at present he is a factory worker. All hope to accumulate sufficient money to buy land and become full-time farmers. Even though they are aware of the shortage of land, each hopes that he at least will be fortunate enough to acquire land, once he has saved sufficient money to purchase it. The persistence of the value attached to farming reflects both the instability of the wider economy and the resistance to changes in value. Villagers realise that income from non-agricultural sources depends on the continued expansion of the wider economy, whereas land will always yield food. They well remember the years when the sugar factory in Mandya closed down and they were all thrown back on dependence for their livelihood on their lands. Thus in terms of the wider economy the value Dalena villagers attach to farming is quite consistent with their experience; only in terms of the village economy, with its shortage of land, is it inconsistent. However, the system of economic values held by many generations in Dalena's past, and inculcated into villagers during their childhood, is not so easily eradicated or changed. The resistance to a change in economic values appears to be a general social phenomenon. The value attached to landholding in Britain led the new industrialists of the Industrial Revolution to invest in large estates. It took many years before the old economic values were displaced by new ones. There appears to be a time lag between a change in the economic environment and in the economic values held by individuals in a society. Thus we may expect that the value Dalena villagers still attach to farming will give way in the future to a preference for employment in the town. In the meantime the contradictory pull of the value attached to earning money and the preference given to farming causes some curious inconsistencies in their behaviour pattern. For instance, factory workers are all envied for their jobs by their fellow-villagers, while they themselves all want to become full-time farmers. These factory workers introduce new prestige criteria into the village on the one hand; on the other, their desire to become farmers prompts them to perpetuate the traditional village system. Chennu, the factory worker who had bought himself a gold watch and a bicycle, thereby showing the urban influence on his behaviour, yet desired to become a medium in the traditional religious system of the village, whereby he perpetuated customary beliefs.[1] Indeed, all the factory workers in Dalena support the conservative faction. It is this persistence of the value attached to farming that is largely responsible for the fact that Dalena has not been swallowed up in the wider system but continues to have a social identity of its own. Once villagers give higher preference to working in the town than to being farmers, Dalena will probably become a dormitory for men working in Mandya, provided the regional economy continues to expand.

Thus we can see that, given the difference between wet and dry lands, the system of economic values determined the type of economic development which took place in Wangala and Dalena. The persistence in the preference given to farming by Wangala villagers led to the development of a wholly rural economy, while the greater value attached to earning money by Dalena villagers led to the diversification of their economy. Yet the high priority Dalena men still give to farming indicates that there is a time lag between a change in the economic environment and in economic values, which slows down the rate of social change. The value attached to farming strengthened Wangala's traditional economic system and delayed the breaking up of Dalena's social system.

(b) *Change in Prestige Values*

Economic development has considerably increased the strife for prestige in Wangala and even more so in Dalena. Both

[1] See above, p. 302.

societies are used to a rank-conscious caste system. It is not surprising therefore that when increased economic mobility led to a challenge of those with ascribed status by those with achieved status, the struggle for prestige became intensified. The different criteria of prestige employed in the two villages reflect the different type of economic development they have undergone. Dalena's economic diversification led to greater economic differentiation and thus to the development of more and more refined criteria of prestige, arising out of the contact with the town. Dress has become an important criterion of prestige. The richest Dalena men wear fine, clean shirts over a dhoti even on ordinary working days, while the poorest still wear only a loincloth. The richest Dalena men have to dress better in order to impress officials in the administration in Mandya whom they approach for contracts, or farmers from other villages where they hold land. The two Dalena men who are employed as clerks in Mandya wear western-style suits when they go to work. Thus the prestige accorded by dress arises out of the different economic activities performed by Dalena men. In Wangala rich and poor alike work on the land and use tattered cotton shirts and shorts for everyday wear. Here uniform occupation has prevented dress from becoming an important criterion of prestige except on special occasions such as village festivals or weddings.

Expenditure on sundries in Dalena displays similar differentiation to clothing. The richest Dalena men smoke cigarettes and pay frequent visits to Mandya coffee shops where they drink coffee or tea and take sweet or curried relish. The poorest still only chew betel leaves and nuts. The prestige accorded by dress and expenditure on sundries clearly reflects the impact of the town on Dalena villagers. The urban influence is also noticeable in the number of English words used by Dalena men. By using English words those who have contact with the town want to distinguish themselves from mere country yokels. Thus men with urban contacts always refer to the last house in a street as '*coneh lasht maneh*', *coneh* being the vernacular word for last and *maneh* for house. In this expression they use the English as well as their own vernacular word to denote the term 'last'. In other instances, such as '*clean illa*', meaning 'it is not clean', they simply substitute an English word for their own vernacular one. All Dalena villagers have adopted English words for foreign innovations, such as *rodu* for road, *bassu* for bus, *hotelu* for coffee shop, *party* for faction, and *chairman* for the village political leader. Wangala villagers use the same English terms to denote foreign concepts, but indigenous ones like 'last' and 'clean' they express in their own vernacular. English is the language spoken by officials in the town through contact with whom many English words find their way into Dalena's vocabulary. Wangala villagers have fewer contacts of this kind and therefore less occasion to pick up as many English words as Dalena villagers. Thus the use of English words has become a prestige criterion in Dalena because of its many links with the town, whereas this is not true of Wangala with its concentration on peasant values and activities.

Yet Wangala's prestige system too shows signs of urban influence. The hiring of a jeep for the bridal procession through the village, or the provision of a Western-style jacket and shoes for the bridegroom's outfit, are examples of the cultural impact of the town on the village. That the urban influence is mostly displayed at weddings, which otherwise are celebrated in the traditional manner, indicates an assimilation of new to customary types of behaviour, rather than a displacement of old by new patterns of behaviour.

Increased expenditure on weddings in Wangala expresses a concern for prestige in a closely-knit community. By contrast Dalena villagers have so many different links with surrounding villages and Mandya that the struggle for status within the traditional, closely integrated, village system has lost some of its importance to them. In their eyes, items which are readily transportable, and which can easily be shown off outside their own village, award prestige. These items, such as dress, pens, pencils, gold watches, or bicycles, will yield prestige to their owner in a wider sphere of social contacts and not just in his own village. Accordingly, rather than introduce novel items into the traditional wedding procedure, which after all would yield prestige only among a very limited number of people, Dalena villagers prefer to spend money on purchases of items which they can display easily on visits to neighbouring villages and to Mandya.

Similarly, the prestige value Wangala villagers attach to men relieving their wives of agricultural labour on their own lands expresses a preoccupation with prestige in an integrated society. For the sort of life a man provides for his wife can be regarded as a matter of prestige only by those people who can actually observe it. By contrast, Dalena men's manifold links with the regional economy have increased the range of people among whom they seek to establish their status. Therefore, quite apart from the economic necessity of Dalena wives still working their husband's land, it would yield them prestige only among their fellow-villagers if they were to relieve their wives from agricultural labour. To impress Mandya officials and farmers from neighbouring villages they have to wear fine clothes, smoke cigarettes, own a gold watch and a bicycle.

The type of home a man owns is a matter of prestige in both villages. The poorest villagers, who live in mud huts with thatched roofs, look up to those who live in mud houses with tiled roofs, and these in turn look up to those who have built new houses. In Wangala, however, all new houses are still built in the customary style; the family shares the living space inside the house with its farm animals. Although villagers always admire the city-type house none has ventured yet to imitate it. The farmer's emotional attachment to his farm animals makes it inconceivable that he live separated from them. This attachment seems to be a common occurrence in rural communities. In the Chinese village described by Martin Yang, cattle are classified as members of the household and have a day set aside for the celebration of their birthdays.[1]

However, once farmers begin to trade in cattle, the attachment lessens, and they are more ready to accept housing innovations. For instance, Dalena villagers all build their new houses in a new style with separate cattle sheds and partition for bathrooms. But they do not copy the city-type house; instead they have developed a compromise between the traditional village type and the new

[1] M. Yang, *Chinese Village*, New York, Columbia University Press, 1945, p. 47.

city-style house. 'Any innovation, no matter how far-reaching the implications and how great the pressures for its acceptance, will be projected against existing cultural patterns and will consequently undergo a reinterpretation to bring the new cultural elements into consonance with the total way of life of the group.'[1]

The persistence of the traditional type of house in Wangala and the introduction of a new compromise style in Dalena demonstrate two important principles of cultural change. Firstly, the principle of cultural inertia by which customary forms of behaviour will continue unless acted upon by a strong external force; and secondly, the reinterpretation of new cultural elements to bring them into line with the total behaviour pattern of the group.

Wangala villagers continue building their new houses in the traditional style because the impact of urban values was not strong enough to eradicate the villagers' attachment to their farm animals. By contrast, Dalena villagers all build their new houses in a new style, because firstly they do not keep their farm animals long enough to become attached to them, and secondly they have been so much exposed to urban influences that the imitation of urban living has itself become a prestige criterion. Yet a straightforward copying of the city-style house would have contravened the whole pattern of behaviour of Dalena villagers; they are still farmers and have to have cattle sheds, and they still like to collect rainwater through a central square opening in the middle of the roof. Furthermore women, being more conservative than men because they are less subject to external influences, still prefer to cook in the old type of kitchen. I have mentioned earlier the one two-storey city-type house in Dalena built by an emigrant son for his mother and brothers.[2] It is used mainly for storage, while the family itself lives in the back portion. The persistence of these traditional ways is reflected in the style of the house itself which embodies features of the traditional as well as of the urban type of house.

[1] M. J. Herskovits, 'African Economic Development in Cross-Cultural Perspective', *American Economic Review*, 1956, Vol. 46, p. 454.

[2] See above, p. 195.

Dalena men adopt habits and manners which confer prestige beyond the boundaries of the village, but they also compete for prestige among themselves. Traditional values still remain significant in this contest as we saw in the case of Chennu who sought to become a medium. But what is important here is that mediumship, for example, yields prestige only among the conservative faction. The progressive faction does not regard ritual status within its own Peasant caste as a criterion of prestige. It considers economic assets as according the highest prestige; the headman is looked up to by followers of his faction because he is one of the richest men in the village and has installed electricity in his house and bought some furniture such as a table, chairs and a wooden cot. Since economic differentiation in Dalena coincides with caste differentiation there is no challenge to the prestige ranking of castes, and the struggle for prestige goes on within the Peasant caste itself.

In Wangala ritual status is still the ultimate criterion of prestige between castes and within the Peasant caste. The two Untouchable households who live in mud houses are looked up to by their fellow-Untouchables who live in mud huts, but not by Peasants who live in mud huts. In this case ritual differentiation outweighs economic differentiation.

Ritual status within the Peasant caste is, at least in theory, strictly hereditary. Thus the prestige structure is influenced by the hereditary principle operating in Wangala society. The fact that the leaders of the progressive faction try to create new hereditary ritual offices speaks for the high prestige attaching to ritual status. Yet, in Wangala too, the standard of living is a prestige criterion; the rice-eater has more prestige than the ragi-eater; the man who smokes cigarettes has higher prestige than the one who only smokes country cigarettes. This co-existence of a ritual and economic aspect to prestige introduces an element of flexibility into the prestige structure and makes it impossible to talk of clear-cut prestige classes. The hereditary executant of a ritual office will be accorded prestige by virtue of his ritual performances; he need not be a wealthy man with a new house or celebrate his son's wedding with great expenditure. On the other hand, the Peasant who has no ritual office but who spends lavishly on the wedding of his son will also be regarded as a man of prestige. The newly introduced economic criteria of prestige undermine the rigid ritual prestige structure of the past.

Economic development has effected a change in prestige values in both Wangala and Dalena, because the higher incomes allow for greater refinement in prestige criteria. But whereas in Wangala the ritual aspect is still the ultimate criterion of prestige, in Dalena the economic aspect has become dominant in prestige rating. We have seen that Dalena's greater economic differentiation and integration into the wider economy have led to the displacement of the ritual by the economic aspect of prestige. Conversely, Wangala's greater isolation and economic uniformity is responsible for the persisting dominance of ritual criteria in prestige rating.

Conclusion

In the preceding analysis of the elements of structural change in Wangala and Dalena I have argued that economic development need not necessarily produce economic change. Only where the new economic system was incompatible with features of traditional economic organisation did we find a change in economic roles and relations. But wherever there was such economic change we also found corresponding changes in political and ritual roles and relations as well as in the principles of social organisation. Thus we have established a positive correlation between economic, political, ritual and organisational change, with economic change being the determining variable.

Economic development led to the disappearance of the joint family unit in both Wangala and Dalena. Familial change may thus occur quite independently of any other structural change, whereas we have seen a consistency in economic, political, ritual and organisational change.

Finally, in my analysis of cultural change I have tried to show how the persistence of economic values delayed social change. I have also argued that economic development results in some change in prestige values and the latter are influenced by the principles on which the society is organised, as well as by its economic structure. Thus I have drawn certain functional relations between economic development and the different aspects of structural and cultural change. These functional relations can be traced out in the social events which occurred in Dalena and Wangala during the past 25 years. The possible general validity of these functional relations has to be tested by many more studies of economic development and social change.

APPENDIX I

TABLE 22

Population, by age and sex

Age	Wangala				Dalena			
	Male	%	*Female*	%	*Male*	%	*Female*	%
0–4	93	18·50	73	15·10	58	15·90	54	15·90
5–14	111	22·10	118	26·90	88	24·00	60	17·60
15–24	104	20·70	112	24·60	65	17·90	80	23·60
25–34	80	15·90	65	14·30	70	19·10	54	15·90
35–44	57	11·40	42	9·30	36	9·80	31	9·00
45–54	35	6·90	32	7·00	28	7·60	35	10·10
55 and over	23	4·50	13	2·80	21	5·70	27	7·90
Total	503	100·00	455	100·00	366	100·00	341	100·00

TABLES 23–26

Householders' farm wages and profits

23. *Per acre of paddy*

Rs.	*Wangala* *No.*	%	*Dalena* *No.*	%
(Loss)–0	2	4	1	3
0–40	6	12	2	6
40–80	8	15	—	—
80–120	9	17	7	22
120–160	13	25	4	12
160–200	7	13	5	15
200–400	4	8	7	21
400 and over	3	6	7	21
Total	52	100	33	100

Tables 23–26 (*contd.*)

24. *Per acre of sugarcane*

Rs.	*Wangala* *No.*	*Wangala* %	*Dalena* *No.*	*Dalena* %
200–400	4	9	1	9
400–600	8	18	2	18
600–800	4	9	1	9
800–1,000	7	16	3	28
1,000–1,200	13	30	1	9
1,200 and over	8	18	3	27
Total	44	100	11	100

25. *Per acre of jowar*

Rs.	*Wangala* *No.*	*Wangala* %	*Dalena* *No.*	*Dalena* %
(Loss)–0	1	6	5	12
0–20	2	13	14	33
20–40	2	12	5	12
40–60	4	25	13	31
60–80	6	38	1	2
80 and over	1	6	4	10
Total	16	100	42	100

26. *Per acre of dry and wet ragi*

	Wangala				*Dalena*	
	Dry ragi		*Wet ragi*		*Dry ragi*	
Rs.	*No.*	%	*No.*	%	*No.*	%
(Loss)–0	—	—	—	—	7	17
0–40	2	8	—	—	8	19
40–80	3	12	—	—	18	43
80–120	6	24	—	—	8	19
120–160	8	32	—	—	1	2
160–200	6	24	—	—	—	—
200–240	—	—	2	22	—	—
240–280	—	—	1	12	—	—
280–320	—	—	2	22	—	—
320–360	—	—	2	22	—	—
360 and over	—	—	2	22	—	—
Total	25	100	9	100	42	100

TABLE 27

Average agricultural capital and annual indirect cost per estate

	Wangala Rs.	*Dalena* Rs.
(1) Agricultural capital	660	370
(2) Interest p.a.	79	44
(3) Depreciation p.a.	47	28
(4) Maintenance p.a.		
(*a*) subsistence	144	80
(*b*) cash	24	18
(5) Indirect cost (2 + 3 + 4) p.a.	294	170

NOTE: Agricultural capital includes the value of draught animals as well as all farming tools and equipment, but excludes land.

TABLE 28

Distribution of agricultural capital per estate

Rs.	*Wangala* %	*Dalena* %
0–200	19	33
200–400	17	37
400–600	9	7
600–800	11	9
800–1,000	24	9
1,000–2,000	9	5
1,200 and over	11	—
Total	100	100

NOTE: Agricultural capital includes the value of draught animals as well as all farming tools and equipment, but excludes land.

TABLE 29

Average value of livestock of various kinds per household

	Wangala		*Dalena*	
	Rs.	%	*Rs.*	%
Bullocks (pair)	203	59	105	40
Cows (pair)	43	12	82	31
Buffaloes	77	22	29	11
Sheep	20	6	38	14
Goats	3	1	10	4
Total	346	100	264	100

TABLE 30

Incidence of animal ownership of various kinds and average value per household

Kind of livestock	*Wangala*		*Dalena*	
	No. of holding HH.	*Average value per holding HH.*	*No. of holding HH.*	*Average value per holding HH.*
		Rs.		*Rs.*
Bullocks	102	382	57	281
Cows	58	144	83	151
Buffaloes	72	265	33	135
Sheep	29	143	57	103
Goats	19	26	43	36

TABLE 31

Distribution of the value of domestic livestock in all village households

Value of domestic livestock	*Households*			
	Wangala		*Dalena*	
Rs.	*No.*	%	*No.*	%
Nil	52	27	24	16
0–300	56	29	71	46
300–600	44	23	47	31
600–900	25	13	7	4
900–1,200	10	5	1	1
1,200 and over	5	3	3	2
Total	192	100	153	100

TABLE 32

Average value of non-productive property per consumption unit

	Wangala		*Dalena*	
	Rs.	%	*Rs.*	%
Personal property	79	17	81	16
House	341	74	378	74
Household chattels	42	9	54	10
Total	462	100	513	100

TABLE 33

Sources of average non-productive property per consumption unit

	Wangala		*Dalena*	
	Rs.	%	*Rs.*	%
Home-produced	20	4	14	3
Barter	2	—	1	—
Gift	295	64	259	50
Cash purchase	145	32	239	47
Total	462	100	513	100

TABLES 34–37

Distribution of value of property per consumption unit in sample households

34. *Non-productive*

Value	*Households*			
	Wangala		*Dalena*	
Rs.	*No.*	%	*No.*	%
0–200	16	25	9	19
200–400	17	27	20	42
400–600	7	11	7	14
600–800	14	21	2	4
800–1,000	5	8	2	4
1,000 and over	5	8	8	17
Total	64	100	48	100

35. *Personal*

Value	*Households*			
	Wangala		*Dalena*	
Rs.	*No.*	%	*No.*	%
0–40	20	31	10	21
40–80	12	19	23	48
80–120	20	31	7	15
120–160	7	11	1	2
160–200	3	5	4	8
200 and over	2	3	3	6
Total	64	100	48	100

Tables 34–37 (*contd.*)

36. *House property*

Value Rs.	*Households* *Wangala* No.	%	*Dalena* No.	%
0–200	30	47	25	52
200–400	11	16	7	15
400–600	12	19	5	11
600–800	7	11	2	4
800–1,000	2	4	4	8
1,000 and over	2	3	5	10
Total	64	100	48	100

37. *Household chattels*

Value Rs.	*Households* *Wangala* No.	%	*Dalena* No.	%
0–20	11	17	7	15
20–40	25	39	16	33
40–60	20	30	12	25
60–80	5	9	4	8
80–100	1	2	2	4
100 and over	2	3	7	15
Total	64	100	48	100

Tables 38 and 39

Sources of average monthly income per consumption unit

38. *Cash*

	Wangala Rs.	%	*Dalena* Rs.	%
(1) Manufacturing and trading profits	1·00	4	5·00	23
(2) Rents and interest	1·00	4	2·00	10
(3) Crop sales	14·50	65	5·00	21
(4) Animal products	1·00	4	2·00	10
(5) Crafts	0·50	2	—	—
(6) Wages (agricultural)	4·00	17	2·00	9
(7) Wages (non-agricultural)	—	—	3·00	14
(8) Miscellaneous	1·00	4	3·00	13
Total	23·00	100	22·00	100

TABLES 38–39 (*contd.*)

39. *All sources*

	Wangala		*Dalena*	
	Rs.	%	*Rs.*	%
Subsistence	9·00	28	12·00	33
Barter	0·50	2	1·50	4
Gifts	0·50	1	0·50	1
Cash	23·00	69	22·00	62
Total	33·00	100	36·00	100

TABLE 40

Distribution of total monthly expenditure

Monthly expenditure per consumption unit	*Sample households*							
	Cash expenditure				*Overall expenditure*			
	Wangala		*Dalena*		*Wangala*		*Dalena*	
Rs.	*No.*	%	*No.*	%	*No.*	%	*No.*	%
0–5	1	2	2	4	—	—	—	—
5–10	7	11	7	15	—	—	—	—
10–15	18	28	16	33	5	8	1	2
15–20	19	30	11	23	10	16	9	19
20–25	9	14	5	10	12	19	8	16
25–30	9	14	2	4	12	18	11	23
30–35	1	1	2	4	14	22	8	17
35–40	—	—	—	—	4	6	3	6
40 and over	—	—	3	7	7	11	8	17
Total	64	100	48	100	64	100	48	100

TABLES 41–43

Distribution of monthly expenditure per consumption unit in sample households

41. *Food and clothes*

Monthly expenditure per consumption unit	Households							
	Food				Clothes			
	Wangala		Dalena		Wangala		Dalena	
Rs.	No.	%	No.	%	No.	%	No.	%
0–5	—	—	—	—	52	80	34	71
5–10	13	22	4	8	12	20	9	19
10–15	20	31	21	44	—	—	5	10
15–20	20	31	15	32	—	—	—	—
20–25	10	14	3	6	—	—	—	—
25–30	1	2	3	6	—	—	—	—
30 and over	—	—	2	4	—	—	—	—
Total	64	100	48	100	64	100	48	100

42. *Sundries and household overheads*

Monthly expenditure per consumption unit	Households							
	Sundries				Household overheads			
	Wangala		Dalena		Wangala		Dalena	
Rs.	No.	%	No.	%	No.	%	No.	%
0–2	17	27	14	29	5	8	2	4
2–4	29	45	21	44	46	75	38	79
4–6	15	23	6	13	12	16	8	17
6–8	3	5	2	4	1	1	—	—
8–10	—	—	2	4	—	—	—	—
10 and over	—	—	3	6	—	—	—	—
Total	64	100	48	100	64	100	48	100

TABLES 41–43 (*contd.*)

43. *Interest*

	Households			
	Wangala		*Dalena*	
Rs.	*No.*	%	*No.*	%
Nil	3	6	5	10
0–2	41	63	27	57
2–4	18	28	9	19
4–6	1	2	3	6
6–8	—	—	1	2
8 and over	1	1	3	6
Total	64	100	48	100

TABLES 44–48

Distribution of monthly income per consumption unit in sample households

44. *From manufacturing and trading profits*

	Households			
	Wangala		*Dalena*	
Rs.	*No.*	%	*No.*	%
Nil	57	89	32	67
0–5	3	5	5	11
5–10	1	2	4	8
10–15	2	3	1	2
15–20	1	1	2	4
20 and over	—	—	4	8
Total	64	100	48	100

45. *From crop sales*

	Households			
	Wangala		*Dalena*	
Rs.	*No.*	%	*No.*	%
Nil	17	27	30	63
0–5	2	3	10	21
5–10	6	9	5	10
10–15	12	19	1	2
15–20	8	12	1	2
20–25	7	11	—	—
25 and over	12	19	1	2
Total	64	100	48	100

Tables 44–48 (*contd.*)

46. *From animal products and miscellaneous sources*

Households

	Animal products				*Miscellaneous sources*			
	Wangala		*Dalena*		*Wangala*		*Dalena*	
Rs.	*No.*	%	*No.*	%	*No.*	%	*No.*	%
Nil	44	69	25	52	37	58	25	52
0–2	8	12	7	15	18	28	4	8
2–4	9	14	4	8	5	8	6	13
4–6	2	3	4	8	3	5	5	11
6–8	1	2	6	13	—	—	3	6
8 and over	—	—	2	4	1	1	5	10
Total	64	100	48	100	64	100	48	100

47. *From interest*

Households

	Wangala		*Dalena*	
Rs.	*No.*	%	*No.*	%
Nil	43	67	30	63
0–5	16	25	10	21
5–10	4	6	5	10
10–15	1	2	1	2
15 and over	—	—	2	4
Total	64	100	48	100

48. *From agricultural and non-agricultural wages*

Households

	Agricultural wages				*Non-agricultural wages*			
	Wangala		*Dalena*		*Wangala*		*Dalena*	
Rs.	*No.*	%	*No.*	%	*No.*	%	*No.*	%
Nil	29	46	21	44	61	95	23	48
0–2	5	9	11	23	2	3	6	13
2–4	10	14	9	19	1	2	6	12
4–6	6	9	3	6	—	—	3	6
6–8	4	6	—	—	—	—	1	2
8–10	2	3	2	4	—	—	3	6
10 and over	8	13	2	4	—	—	6	13
Total	64	100	48	100	64	100	48	100

TABLE 49

Distribution of monthly deficit per consumption unit in sample households

	Households			
	Wangala		*Dalena*	
Rs.	*No.*	%	*No.*	%
Nil	42	63	28	58
0–2	8	13	6	13
2–4	8	12	10	21
4–6	3	6	4	8
6 and over	3	6	—	—
Total	64	100	48	100

TABLE 50

Distribution of monthly savings per consumption unit in sample households

	Households			
	Wangala		*Dalena*	
Rs.	*No.*	%	*No.*	%
Nil	25	39	20	42
0– 4	13	20	12	25
4– 8	9	14	6	13
8–12	6	9	4	8
12–16	3	5	1	2
16–20	1	2	—	—
20–32	3	5	—	—
32 and over	4	6	5	10
Total	64	100	48	100

APPENDIX II

GLOSSARY

English to Kannada

(*The Kannada terms are written in Roman script and spelled phonetically*)

Barber	Ajambru
Basketmaker	Koramasetty
Blacksmith	Veerachari, Matachari
bought land	konda jemeenu
caste	jati
dry land	kushki jemeenu
Female clan	henhalli palu
Fisherman	Besta
Goldsmith	Achari
household	kula
inherited land	pitrar-ge-ta jemeenu
jaggery	bella
jowar	jola
lineage	vothara, tende, paike
Lingayat Priest	Aradya
Madras Peasant I	Modaliar
Madras Peasant II	Vennegowda
Male clan	ganhalli palu
Oilpresser	Ganega
paddy	batta
Peasant	Vokkaliga
Potter	Kumbara
ragi	ragi
rent (cropsharing)	vara
rent (fixed)	guttige
Revenue Inspector	Shekdar
rice (raw)	akki
rice (boiled)	anna
Shepherd	Kuruba
Stonecutter	Golla
sugarcane	kabbu
temple	devastana
Untouchable A.K.	Adikarnataka, Holeya
Untouchable (Vodda)	Vodda

Village accountant	Shanbogue
Village council	Panchayat
Village headman	Patel
wet land	thari jemeenu

REFERENCES

BAILEY, F. G., 1957. *Caste and the Economic Frontier.* Manchester University Press.

BUCHANAN, F., 1807. *A Journey from Madras through the countries of Mysore, Canara and Malabar.* W. Bulmer and Co., Cleveland Row, St. James's.

DUBOIS, ABBÉ J. A., 1906. *Hindu Manners, Customs and Ceremonies* (translated by Henry K. Beauchamp, C.I.E.). Oxford. Clarendon Press.

FIRTH, R., 1939. *Primitive Polynesian Economy.* London. George Routledge & Sons Ltd.

1951. *Elements of Social Organisation.* London. Watts & Co.

1954. 'Social Organisation and Social Change', in *Journal of the Royal Anthropological Institute,* Vol. 84.

GLUCKMAN, M., 1958. *Analysis of a Social Situation in Modern Zululand.* Rhodes-Livingstone Papers No. 28. Manchester University Press for the Rhodes-Livingstone Institute, Northern Rhodesia.

HAYAVADANA RAO, C., 1927. *Mysore Gazetteer.* Bangalore Government Press.

HERSKOVITS, M. J., 1956. 'African Economic Development in Cross-Cultural Perspective', *American Economic Review,* Vol. 46, p. 454.

HOGBIN, I., 1958. *Social Change.* Watts, Forty Drury Lane, London W.C.2.

HUTTON, J. H., 1946. *Caste in India.* Cambridge. Cambridge University Press.

LEWIS, O., 1954. *Group Dynamics in a North Indian Village.* New Delhi. Government of India Press.

LEWIS, W. A., 1955. *The Theory of Economic Growth.* London. George Allen and Unwin Ltd.

LINTON, R., 1952. 'Cultural and Personality Factors affecting Economic Growth', in *The Progress of Underdeveloped Areas* (ed. by B. F. Hoselitz). University of Chicago.

MALINOWSKI, B., 1945. *The Dynamics of Culture Change.* Yale University Press.

MCDONALD, H. C., 1862. *Descriptive Sketch of Various Castes in the Province of Mysore.* Bangalore.

MEAD, M., 1953. *Cultural Patterns and Technological Change.* UNESCO.

1956. *New Lives for Old.* William Morrow & Co. N.Y.

RICE, L., 1878. *Mysore and Coorg Gazetteer.* Bangalore.

SASTRI, V. K. N., 1932. *The Administration of Mysore under Sir Mark Cubbon (1834–1861).* London. George Allen and Unwin Ltd.

SENART, E., 1930. *Caste in India* (translation by Denison Ross). London. Methuen & Co.

SRINIVAS, M. N., 1952. *Religion and Society among the Coorgs of South India.* Oxford. Clarendon Press.

1954. 'A Caste Dispute among Washermen of Mysore', in *Eastern Anthropologist,* Vol. VII, Nos. 3 & 4.

1955. 'The Social Structure of a Mysore Village', in *India's Villages.* West Bengal Government Press.

SRINIVAS, M. N., 1955. 'The Social System of a Mysore Village', in '*Village India*', *American Anthropologist*, Vol. 157, Memoir 83.

THURSTON, E., 1909. *Castes and Tribes of Southern India*. Government Press. Madras.

WILKS, M., 1805. *Report on the Interior Administration, Resources and Expenditure of the Government of Mysore*. Bangalore.

WILSON, GODFREY and MONICA, 1954. *An Analysis of Social Change*. Cambridge University Press.

YANG, M., 1945. *Chinese Village*. New York. Columbia University Press.

Census of India. 1891, 1901, 1941, 1951.

The Constitution of India. 1955. Law Publishers. Allahabad 2.

Ministry of Labour. *Report on an Enquiry into the Conditions of Agricultural Workers in the Village Archikarahalli, Mysore State*. 1951. Govt. of India Press. New Delhi.

P.E.O. Publication No. 9. 1955. *Leadership and Groups in a South Indian Village*. Government of India.

Report of the Agriculturalists' Relief Committee in Mysore. 1935. Government Press, Bangalore.

INDEX